Nancy, Lady Astor

SUNSHINE OF PLYMOUTH

Vicky Norman

VICKY NORMAN

The Author with a copy of her last book
Scattered Homes Broken Hearts

SALUTATION

The Author tenders sincere thanks to everyone, too numerous to mention, who gave useful information. I am indebted to Pamela Trudie Hodge who has helped with the presentation of this book and whose unfailing support has been invaluable.

First published in 2009 by Joseph Louei, The Astor Hotel. 14-22 Elliott Street, Plymouth, Devon, PL1 2PS United Kingdom
Tel: +44 (0) 1752 225511 Fax: +44 (0) 1752 251994 enquiries@astorhotel.co.uk

ISBN Pb: 978-0-9562436-0-7
    Hb: 978-0-9562436-1-4

Information and photographs compiled and edited by Vicky Norman
Design and artwork - TKD - Tony Knowles Design, Plymouth Tel: +44 (0) 1752 707007 tkdesign@blueyonder.co.uk
Printed and bound by Latimer Trend & Co Ltd., Plymouth +44 (0) 1752 201930 sales@trends.co.uk

A stunning profile of Lady Astor in one of her Hon. Degree cap and gowns

Photo by kind permission of Mutley Conservative Club
Digital copy by Trevor Burrows Photography

A striking portrait of Lady Astor which hangs on the wall in the Astor Room

JOSEPH LOUEI

Joseph Louei was born in Malayer, Persia. Plymouth in Devon has been his chosen home for the past thirty-two years. He really loves the city and its people. He started work at the Holiday Inn, worked his way through all departments learning all aspects of catering. An astute businessman he became successful in his profession and succeeded in purchasing the Astor Hotel. He is committed to promoting tourism and he is a great supporter of fellow-entrepreneurs.

Having been introduced to the legend of Lady Astor by his mother, he stated that one day he would have a book written in her memory. He has a sincere affection for Lady Astor and greatly admires her achievements. His dream can now be realised by the presentation of this book.

Photo courtesy of Joseph Louei, Astor Hotel, Plymouth

A wedding at the Astor Hotel, Plymouth, Devon, April 2004.

INTRODUCTION

In passing, also, I would like to say that the first time Adam had a chance, he laid the blame on a woman.
Lady Astor 1879-1964.

This book is not for the purist or the perfectionist, neither is it an attempt to present it as a biography, for there have been many books written about Nancy, Lady Astor, by authors far more knowledgeable and they were privileged to have access to private photographs and records. This book is for one purpose, written by an ordinary person, to show the humanitarian links and to give a background history of Lady Astor and the effect she had on the every day ordinary folk as well as the aristocracy. For the working class citizen her passing lingers still with sadness, for they have seared into their memories and stored in their hearts the kindnesses and the gifts that she shared with them. Nancy was a remarkable Lady, although an enigma, who endeared herself to every level of class as she enriched so many people's lives. This book is another reminder to the world of the need to keep English social history alive and to inform the next generation of citizens what this lady achieved that was so precious to all who knew her and which, through her efforts, enhanced the quality of life for so many people. The Author extends an apology to anyone inadvertently offended and to inform all readers that every effort has been made to obtain copyright from the correct sources. Should any reader question copyright please accept this as a genuine mistake.

CONTENTS

FOREWORD

The Author extends grateful thanks for this foreword contributed by the 4th Viscount Astor.

William Waldorf Astor.
The Right Honourable Viscount Astor.

I am very pleased to have been asked by Vicky Norman to write the foreword to this memoir of my grandmother, Nancy, Viscountess Astor, and of her long association with the people and city of Plymouth.

In 1990, I attended the service held at St Andrew's Church to commemorate the fiftieth anniversary of the German Blitz on Plymouth. After the service I talked to many of those who had lived through those appalling times in the city. It was very moving: despite the long years that had since elapsed I found that so many people still remembered clearly, as if it were yesterday, Lady Astor's untiring work for the city as it reeled before the German onslaught, and her presence in their bombed-out streets and homes. They echoed what all who met her, from every walk of life, used to say: with Nancy it was once met and never forgotten.

Her energy and vitality, and her affection for the people of Plymouth were visible to all. Although her family was from Virginia, where she was brought up and which she loved until her dying day, Plymouth became her adopted home. All her life she believed that the world could only benefit from the deep and enduring link between the British and American peoples, and that it was symbolised by Plymouth, where the Pilgrim Fathers had so long ago made history.

At an early age Nancy acquired the strong Christian faith that was later to furnish her with her deep commitment to public service, and with the determination to work for her adopted country. It was my grandfather who first gave her that opportunity, when his own father's death compelled him to withdraw from representing the city in the House of Commons. His wife, Nancy, agreed to stand in her place, anxious but undaunted by the thought of entering a Parliament of more than six hundred members none of whom wanted for one moment to accept the fact of the first woman M.P.

From that time onwards my grandfather was her rock and support, through seven Parliamentary elections and the arduous years between, while Nancy took the forefront with her unflinching and flamboyant character. Although she is now often remembered for her lightning wit it was her political victories, both for women and for children, and for her work for the provision of education and health for those whose need was great, that endure to this day.

Her dedication to Plymouth saw its finest hour during the war, when the naval docks and harbours exposed the city as a prime target for the Luftwaffe. Night after night the people endured the bombs and flames of the enemy's fury, but through all that time, although she also had vital duties in the House of Commons, Nancy's top priority was to give what help she could to Plymouth. With my grandfather at her side - they were by then Lord Mayor and Lady Mayoress – she never flinched from going among the devastated streets and homes, each inspiring as best they could the wounded, the bereaved, the tired and the frightened inhabitants, and providing material help and ideas for reconstruction.

I remember her as a wonderful grandmother. She radiated enjoyment, and life became exciting whenever she came to stay. This may have been partly because her idea of fun was to allow us to do all the things my father would not allow. There was of course a price to pay for that: in return we had each morning to join her in her bedroom, for Bible readings and for her to implant in us the religion which she herself had always found so valuable.

Throughout her life she carried within her a remarkable combination of gaiety and Christianity, while offering to all whom she met, and knew, and worked among, the mix of duty and pleasure which has to this day remained in the memory of so many. In that respect at least, Vicky Norman's memoir is aptly entitled: *The Sunshine of Plymouth.*

CHAPTER ONE
THE SUNSHINE OF SUTTON

'THE SUNSHINE OF SUTTON' *Quote in the New York Times December 1923.*

Love, an if there be one,
Come my love to be,
My love is for the one
Loving unto me. (First verse of an ancient song)

Suffice it to say that much has been written about Viscountess Nancy (Nannie) Witcher Langhorne Astor (1879-1964) who was made a Companion of Honour in the summer of 1937. This book attempts to reveal the human touch that this grand lady had with children, royalty, ambassadors, citizens and the poor people. There are incidents still etched into the memories of people in the city of Plymouth, Devon, England, who remember her glorious years. It also tells how in her lifetime she touched the lives of people from all parts of the world with her constant wit and energy proving that status was not always necessary to achieve success in communication with the ordinary citizen. Passionate in her debates and reforms of child welfare she once said, "When you go into the slums of a big town and see the swarms of children playing in the streets; when you smell the odours and see the dirt and hear the everlasting racket which goes on, you wonder what sort of lives the people who live there can lead, what sort of pleasure they can find, and what sort of happiness or satisfaction is possible to them. But when you go into the insides of the houses and tenements, and get to know the people, you find that human nature is the same everywhere and that the finest virtues often flourish in these terrible surroundings." Every morning in her early days Nancy would leave Cliveden in a horse drawn carriage looking like a Dickensian figure of cherubic countenance, her energy was extraordinary. After a long day in London and in the House of Commons she would return to Cliveden about seven, change into tennis clothes and play two or even three sets of singles with one of her nieces, then down to the river (before the war) in her cream-coloured car, driven at speed, she would swim across the Thames, talking all the time about God, or advising someone on the bank about the way to live, she would touch the bottom of the far bank, tell the swans to go away, and swim back again still talking. A real fire brand.

Nancy Langhorne first came to England in December 1903 with her mother and a friend. She loved the English ways and soon made friends. Nancy came again in December 1904 to participate in the Leicestershire Foxhunt at Market Harborough that was reputed to have the finest hunting in the world. Her first suitor in England was John Baring, later 2nd Baron Revelstoke (1863-1929) he was chairman of his family's bank the Baring Brothers. He was however sixteen years older than Nancy and if she had married him she would have been a widow by 1929. He was very fond of Nancy and gave her many presents but the relationship had cooled by June 1905. Another suitor was Phillip Kerr, later Lord Lothian. Nancy had mixed feelings and decided that she would return home to Virginia in July 1905. Waldorf Astor's closest friend was the beautiful Princess Marie of Rumania, granddaughter of Queen Victoria, however romance was not in the air as it was Nancy Langhorne who later married Waldorf Astor. Nancy, the extrovert, and Waldorf, quiet and reserved with high ideals, they were to be the perfect match.

Nancy Langhorne 1898 at Mirador, Virginia, taken on her 19th birthday.

Photo by Tomas Jaski Limited Strand London by kind permission of Charles Prynne
Digital copy Trevor Burrows Plymouth Photographer

Nancy in earlier years had been a brilliant horsewoman and a sure shot with a gun; later golf was to be her favourite game and she would often be seen with a sprig of lemon-scented verbena pinned to her brooch, and almost always holding a golf club. She played well and distinguished herself in parliamentary matches. Her presence was to lead to many a controversial issue with various politicians but was never boring. She was known as a very volatile lady, provocative when challenged by crass politicians during her reign in Parliament, and was a mistress in delivering many famous quotes. In the minds of ordinary citizens there is one Latin quote that could almost have been written for her 'Nemo me impune lacessit' (no one hurts me with impunity.) One Member of Parliament described her as 'the cheekiest little sparrow that ever sat on a door-step.' William Douglas Home's opinion of Lady Astor, the former Southern Belle, who had become the first woman to sit in Parliament and who became an English Lady, had led him to say,

'My love has amethysts for eyes
Twin fairy tails for feet
A tongue that seldom peaceful lies
A figure trim and neat
Two ankles of the smallest size
And Plymouth for a Seat!'

SINCERITY AND FRIENDSHIPS

Nancy was sincere in the challenging of sensitive political issues and her ability to communicate at all levels was to win her admiration and respect and she radiated excitement and protection. Champion of the underdog, a good samaritan, a soap-box orator, ruthless, generous, stern yet gentle, she was all these things. Nancy had a magnetic charm but did at times have a brutal candour, which upset some of those people close to her. She stirred into action all whom she met and was to bring together great literary figures, leaders of political persuasions, and at the same time mingle with the common folk. Nancy had confidence in her own abilities and courage for courage was needed if she was to succeed. She had long and loyal friendships accepting their influence on her life, strong friendships with people such as Arthur Balfour the last of the great aristocratic Tory Prime ministers, Rachel Macmillan responsible for setting up the Macmillan Nurseries for children, 'Red Ellen' Wilkinson another socialist campaigner. George Bernard Shaw the Irish born writer and playwright, was a great friend who was also a member of the Bloomsbury Set and a dedicated Fabian Socialist.

The Fabian Society was founded in 1884; it was considered an intellectual movement concerned with the research, discussion and publication of socialist ideas, the Society was named after the Roman General Fabius Cunctator. All Labour Prime Ministers have been members of the Fabian Society and it has played a central role for more than a century.

Another of Nancy's friends was Philip Kerr who was a Roman Catholic but later converted to Christian Science as Nancy had said prayers for his healing during a deadly illness. Philip Kerr later became Lord Lothian. Another friend was Henry Jones the Professor of Moral Philosophy and she also corresponded for forty years with Sean O'Casey, the Irish Communist playwright. Another friend of Nancy's was Harry Vincent Hodson (1906-1999) who was elected to a Prize Fellowship at All Souls in 1928, he was the first ever Prize Fellow in economics. He became a writer, a journalist and an editor. His editorial conquests were the Round Table, a quarterly journal. (1934-1939) The Sunday Times (1950-1961) and he became the first Director of the Ditchley Foundation the world famous Anglo-American Conference Centre.

HAPPY HOSTESS

Lady Astor was many things. Just over five feet tall, with blue twinkling eyes, attractive, neat, outspoken, sharp, witty, clever and charming, some would say she was a loving caring person with a wonderful sense of humour; others disliked her outspoken personality; she was a fighter and her feistiness brought results, but most

Photo number 519 courtesy of the Virginia House Trust, Plymouth

Nancy, Lady Astor receiving a parcel from the postman in 1923

of all she was extremely kind, many women shared her aesthetic nature. She was a woman of great heart and character, and without doubt one of the greatest hostesses of her day. Nancy was gifted with the attributes of an anarchic, radical comedian, lack of caution, deadly mimicry, comic timing, and an uncanny intuition for hitting the weak nerve and she would slip into imitations and mockeries with a row of celluloid teeth worn crookedly or even make them out of orange peel, and lift the atmosphere with laughter particularly if the conversation at the dinner table had suddenly become strained. She was always inventing wild games. For fun, wearing her false teeth and her hair in a frizz on top, she would mimic characters and have everyone in fits of laughter; her mimicry and impersonations of politicians and members of the aristocracy and theatre personalities amazed her guests. Nancy's funny facial expressions entertained those who came to lunch or dinner so brilliantly that even the person with the stiffest observation of protocol would break into fits of laughter, however, visiting guests and ladies did not always take it in good part and it did on occasion offend some people. Then Nancy would look at them and smile the same insouciant smile kept for guests who were reluctant to join in the fun.

In 1936 Waldorf and Nancy, always encouraging good relations with the League of Nations, organised a big party at 4, St James's Square. Nancy, the perfect hostess, had entertained the Ambassadors from many countries. She loved dancing and one of her favourite dances was the Paul Jones. Another game she enforced on the Ambassadors was a sight to behold; here was a Viscountess with some of the world's important politicians playing musical chairs into the early hours of the morning. Nancy however, always finished the parties a 4am and then a hot meal would be served, usually bacon and eggs. As a hostess Nancy always made the running, led the conversation, dominated the party, commanded the staff and teased the guests, other husbands as gifted and distinguished as Waldorf might well have been embarrassed, not Waldorf, he just sat back and laughed at her jokes, and quietly enjoyed her behaviour, even though sometimes it was outrageous.

Waldorf loved Nancy and his quiet sense of humour sometimes came out. In 1944 a song sung by Frank Sinatra, that had been dedicated to his daughter Nancy born in 1940, became quite popular in England as well as the United States, it was called, Nancy with the Laughing Face, the melody was composed by Jimmy Van Heusen (1913-1990) and the words were written by Phil Silvers (1911-1985) who later became famous for his television role (1955-1959) as Sergeant Ernest Bilko. Although not a singer Waldorf, in private of course, if in a good mood, would sing this song to Nancy and it pleased her. Lady Astor had a sharp sense of the ridiculous and she could have made a fortune on the variety stage; it was a talent shared with her clever niece Joyce Grenfell, the entertainer. For six years Joyce Grenfell and her husband lived at Parr Cottage, in Cliveden, that Nancy had given her as she had no home of her own then. This meant Joyce would often be invited for lunch; with two talented mimickers at the table there were moments of extreme hilarity. Nancy would on occasion torment Joyce and theirs was a love hate relationship yet both were extremely fond of one another. Joyce would say little to antagonise Nancy, however, she felt some of the remarks levied at her as harsh; in later years Joyce said, "I have learned a lot about letting the past slip off and I am growing daily more grateful to God for the little I know and understand." Joyce worked hard at looking after the wounded servicemen during the Second World War at the Hospital at Cliveden spending many hours speaking to them, writing their letters, running errands and shopping for those unable to use all their limbs, and often spending six hours washing the dishes. Joyce left Cliveden in 1943 to look for a small flat and to begin her radio and stage career full-time; a member of the ENSA group she had a full and busy life. Nancy frequently arranged parties for the hospital staff and would spend hours making sure everyone had a good time and every serviceman, member of staff, and the Red Cross nurses would be given a gift by Nancy Astor and Joyce Grenfell. Nancy liked to mix her guests with her distinctive notions of hospitality. She entertained royalty and the rich and famous. But most importantly she entertained the ordinary folk who would never otherwise have found themselves in such company. Lady Astor had lunch with the first twenty families to leave for Western Australia in January 1924 under a new emigration scheme; those families would have been pleased to be the guests of such a well-known Member of Parliament. In March 1926 the Astors organised a dinner and dance at St James Square and attending the dance were high ranking aristocrats; the Earl of Krona (or Crona) Sir Owen Semen, Lady Standing, Mr Stanley Baldwin and Lady Dorothy MacMillan. One wonders what was discussed at that magnificent dinner party. The dinner was followed by a dance in honour of the Rhodes Scholars from Oxford for which the Prince of Wales was present. In 1931 old friends Bessie Braddock and Charlie Chaplin visited Elliot Terrace and her Ladyship had a great time entertaining them.

NANCY'S BIRTHPLACE

Nancy, the seventh child of eleven, was born in Danville, an Independent City in Virginia, also called the City of Churches because it has more churches per square mile than any other city in the state of Virginia. It is bounded by Pittsylvania County, Virginia, and Caswell County, North Carolina, in the United States of America. Nancy was born on the 19th May 1879 (although there are those historians who say she was born on the 17th of May) into a poor family. Named Nancy (Nannie) Witcher Langhorne, little did the world know what an impression she was to make in American and British History, and that she was to be, in the eyes of many of Plymouth citizens, albeit not all, the recognised first Lady. Her father, affectionately known as 'Shilly Langan' had been a Confederate officer, a small time slave owner damaged by the Civil War and had to rebuild his business. The family wealth had been regained or even surpassed through her father's skills as a tobacco auctioneer and in railway development. She was the apple of her father's eye and was very much a tomboy in her younger years; as she became an adolescent her father's success brought the family wealth. Her father refused to send her to college, a fact that Nancy deeply resented; however on reflection that decision was to create a new chapter in English history.

The four-bedroomed home in which she was born was Langhorne House, at 117, Broad Street, and in 1988 the Danville Historical Society introduced a fund raising programme to prevent the demolition of the home which was the birthplace of Nancy; they finally succeeded and renamed the former home as Lady Astor House. When Nancy was eleven years old her father, having eventually come into the realm of the wealthy, moved his family to a colonnaded house called Mirador, built between 1825 and 1830, a colonial red-bricked house with a farm, near Charlottesville, at the foot of the Blue Ridge Mountains. As a child she attended Saint Paul's Episcopal Church in Richmond and throughout her life had the courage of her religious convictions.

RELIGIOUS BELIEFS

As a young lady she had had serious thoughts to be a missionary but having been introduced to several young men and with a secret desire to visit England she put the idea out of her mind. A confirmed Christian Scientist she practiced her belief in life and every day would read the bible; she was very religious and once remarked that the bible was a wonderful book. "I read little else except The Times newspaper, I read the bible for two hours every morning, read the old testament and see how God comes out in flashes here and there, then read the new testament about Christ, the spirit, that is what man has and what man must be!" Nancy had been given the book written by Mary Baker Eddy called Science and Health with a key to the Scriptures by her sister Phyllis and read it with interest and it was from that book that her beliefs changed. For the rest of her life Nancy never wavered in her newfound religion. Nancy's deep religious sense found its formal setting in the Christian Science Church and she was a diligent student of the Scriptures, with a strong horror of sin and a crusading spirit which spurred her to pursue reforms regardless of party divisions. Her children would, in the morning, go to her bedroom to be given her version of a Christian Science lesson. Bibles were strewn about the bed, the text for the day marked and ready. It would be a rapid, repetitive delivery, with her face covered in cold cream she would say, "Man is made in the image and likeness of God." "Hold up your shoulders!" that was a frequent order from Nancy, or in a form of a greeting she would forcefully say, "Hold on to the Truth." "Hold the Right Thought" was another of her parting cautions. Lady Astor who frequently went to the Wednesday meetings at the Christian Science Church in Ford Park, Mutley, Plymouth, would, during the service, regularly bob up and down to issue a testimony. Christian Science was recognised among many well-known Americans, the very popular teetotal singer and dancer Ginger Rogers (1911-1995) was a confirmed believer, as is the present day American singer, actress, and animal welfare advocate Doris Day.

AN ENIGMA

There were times when Nancy could be petulant and it was well known that she disliked Communists with one exception, that of Sean O'Casey the writer. She disliked also the French and Catholics and was cautious about the Quakers, but in later years she mellowed and became more tolerant toward all of them. The Americans had followed Nancy's career with pride for having a Virginian girl standing for the British Parliament was unique. On her first election as Coalition Unionist Candidate (later to be amalgamated with the Conservatives) she had 14,495 votes; her opponents Mr Gay the Labour Candidate had 9,922 votes and Issac Foot the Liberal Candidate had 4,139, such was her popularity. She made the City of Plymouth her home and it's people her pride, her whole life was to be joined with the people and etched also in her heart was the place of her birth, native Virginia and her adopted City of Plymouth. She had become very fond of Plymouth and her private charity had also been unstinting. We honour her still and today generations of citizens still benefit from her achievements. Lady Astor was an enigma, you either loved her or hated her - there was no in between, her love of life was a tangible awareness of her own worth, she embodied the best traits from the human touch. She warmed the hearts of all those she met who liked her; she was not too proud to speak to anyone and was judged by many as a warm, vibrant and wonderful person.

Talking to people in seeking memories revealed feelings of admiration. At the mere mention of Lady Astor their eyes would light up and behind the twinkling eyes was fire, passion and mutual respect. Their faces would change as the memories surfaced and they would tell of the remarks or conversations they still remembered, vivid and clear, as if it could have been said yesterday. It was as though the number of years since her death never existed, such was the impression this lady had on the ordinary folk. Lady Astor was strong willed and usually outspoken and her verbal battles with Winston Churchill during their time in Parliament were legends in their own right. Nancy did not care personally for Winston Churchill although she always accepted that he had been the saviour of his country when his leadership in World War Two united the nation. Whatever anyone said of her Nancy always stood for compromise, common sense, friendly co-operation and sensible negotiation. Nancy knew a good deal more about political affairs than most of her critics; her one stumbling block was her inability to be tactful and diplomatic in the right places.

She was well known for a variety of quotes but one stood out above the rest because women of her generation revelled in her saying, "My vigour, vitality, and cheek repel me, I am the kind of woman I would run from." Many did, but only those who did not have the strength to challenge and share the views of this formidable lady. She also said, "No one sex can govern alone, I believe that one of the reasons why civilization has failed so lamentably is that it has a one-sided government." There were some citizens who thought that Lady Astor was a bigot. Admittedly she could on occasion be extremely rude, and her two well-used words were "Shut Up!" She was stubborn in her refusal to admit she was wrong when perhaps an emollient word would have done. As the biblical line says, 'A soft answer turneth away wrath.' Often comments she made would be distorted as she did have the propensity to aggravate. She did not tolerate fools gladly and is there any living person who is not of the same ilk? Many harsh remarks were made about her brashness but she also had a myriad of good points. This great lady was a paragon in the eyes of many. Nancy's public action and her militancy were controversial, but her love of people gave her the irresistible human touch.

FREEDOM TO VOTE

On the 14th December 1918, the first year women had been allowed to vote in Britain, Constance, Countess Markiewicz (nee Gore-Booth) (1868-1927) by her marriage to Count Casimir Markiewicz from Poland was elected as a Sinn Fein Member of Parliament representing St Patrick's Division of Dublin. She had fought in the 1916 Easter rising in Ireland when she led one hundred and twenty Republican soldiers, an act for which she was subsequently imprisoned and sentenced to death. However, after the amnesty in 1918, she was elected to Westminster. This came about because of a Bill that became law in February 1918. The Bill granted votes to women over thirty years of age who were householders or wives of householders. That same year a resolution moved by Lord Robert Cecil (1830-1903) to permit women to sit in the House of Commons was carried. However, in protest, Constance Markiewicz did not take her seat. As a member of the Sinn Fein party she was disqualified from taking the seat in the British Parliament for refusing to take the parliamentary oath. Instead she helped establish the first independent Irish Parliament of the modern period, Dáil Éireann, in Dublin. These new rights opened the door for Coalition Unionist Nancy to stand for Parliament if the Plymouth Conservative Party so desired. Already popular in Plymouth her application was accepted. Nancy's elevation to Parliament had also been enhanced by her marriage to Waldorf Astor after the failure of her first marriage to the handsome rich Bostonian Robert Gould Shaw with her divorce in 1903.

WALDORF'S INFLUENCE

It was on a transatlantic crossing with her father in December 1905 that Nancy met and fell in love with Waldorf; they became engaged in March 1906 and married at All

Souls Church, Langham Place, in the parish of Saint Mary-Le-Bone on the third of May 1906. For this occasion the Church of England's ban on the marriage of divorced persons was waived and they honeymooned in Italy and Switzerland. Nancy said when asked why she banked her allowance from her father "You don't marry an Astor and spend your own money." Waldorf came to Plymouth in 1908 and from 1909 until 1919 he was Member of Parliament for Plymouth. With the death of his father he reluctantly became Viscount Astor in the House of Lords, which gave Nancy Astor the opportunity to run for the seat left vacant by him, which she duly won ousting Isaac Foot the Liberal Party candidate. Issac Foot was a Solicitor in partnership with Edgar Bowden in a well-established law practice. He took great interest in his application for the constituency, as he served on many committees notably for free Library and Education. He also served on Plymouth's Town Council and founded the Young Liberals in Plymouth. Issac Foot was a strong and devoted member of the Wesleyan Church. Nancy was not keen on standing for the constituency that Waldorf had vacated when he was elevated to the House of Lords, he could have had a brilliant career in politics but his love for Nancy was so strong he became instead her political manager. Being the first woman elected to take the seat in Parliament in England she proved to be a staunch Unionist Conservative; she could inspire and motivate. It must be pointed out that Waldorf wrote many of Nancy's speeches and he would on occasion give her an audible prompt. It is said of her that she spent all her time in the House of Commons getting into trouble, while Lord Astor spent his time in the House of Lords getting her out of it. One wonders if members of the male population who resented Nancy's articulate speeches made this comment. Waldorf became the first Lord Mayor and Nancy the first Lady Mayoress of Plymouth.

CAMPAIGNING DAYS

Nancy, although extremely rich and influential, championed women's rights and was indeed a wonderful friend to the children and people of the poor. Plymouth in the year 1919 was the third most deprived area in the country. During her campaigning days she would, on occasion, upset the women, as she was quite discourteous which did not go down well with some people. Nancy had been touring Coxside and she unfortunately failed to knock on the door of a lady's home in Clare Buildings and just walked in! The occupant of the flat was a labour stalwart and was furious at the discourtesy and ordered Lady Astor out of her home saying, "Excuse me, Lady Astor, but I would never go into your house without knocking, so perhaps you would treat me the same way!" Lady Astor took the point in good grace and went out outside, knocked and asked if she might see her. Although the labour contingent marched in unison through the Barbican there were many who put their crosses against Lady Astor's box. Oswold Moseley helped Nancy Astor in her campaign to be elected to the House of Commons in 1919, as at that time he was a friend, however, with Moseley becoming a black shirt in the 1930s she disassociated her political link with

Lady Astor campaigning for votes in 1919.
Seen with Albert Charlie Symons a former coal heaver by trade

him. He later wrote about Nancy saying, "She had, of course, unlimited effrontery, but also enormous charm." Nancy would address the audience and then she would go across to some old woman scowling in a neighbouring doorway, who simply hated her, take both her hands and kiss her on the cheek. Nancy would give out bread or coal to the poor during her political campaign; sometimes it was resented and often turnips or potatoes were thrown into her carriage whilst touring the Sutton constituency.

Nancy campaigned vigorously at the Barbican and the fishermen, or their wives, would challenge her and Nancy had to win them over. One person shouted out "You've got enough brass to fill a kettle," Nancy's reply? "Well you have enough water in the brain to fill it!" Nancy would stop and talk to mothers with children, and one could listen to her banter and her fun as she passed the time of day with the shopkeepers and everybody in the street. During her campaign in her early years, she met some extremely hostile hecklers in the areas of Laira, Coxside and the Barbican, which she had to overcome if she was to succeed in achieving the status of Member of Parliament. Heckling was allowed under the English Public Meeting Act of 1908. With hard work and her ability to mix with all walks of life they, too, came to respect her.

Eventually Nancy won the working class over and when they saw that she was sincere about their welfare and doing good in her own way, they relented. The Barbican and city workmen appreciated the fact that she had helped to form the first working men's union in Plymouth. Albert Charley Symons who was a coal heaver living on the Barbican would often throw crass remarks at Nancy when she was campaigning for votes and he was continually criticising the class distinction, but when he saw the good that Nancy was doing he changed his mind and from then on supported her cause. The meeting of the newly formed working men's union was held in a gas lit room off Sutton Road where children were begging for food nearby. Robert Dick, born and bred on the Barbican, was thrilled when he had his photograph taken with Lady Astor in an Astor Home for retired people; she constantly supported the old folk on the Barbican. When Nancy spoke in the House of Commons she had one thing on her mind, looking after the working class of Plymouth.

When electioneering on her peripatetic journey Nancy would often be on the receiving end of barracking, not only from the common folk but also from political colleagues. Nancy would tour in her carriage drawn by beautiful sorrel horses wearing red, white and blue ribbons and the inciters would shout remarks at her but she was not put off and carried out her intended tour. In Plymouth her first set speech was at a meeting at the Masonic Hall on the 4th November 1919. One citizen remembers vividly an occasion when Nancy, on one of her forays into politics canvassing for her first seat in Plymouth had been, on account of her position, allotted a senior naval officer as a minder to accompany her on her doorstep campaigning. Nancy knocked on many doors and upon knocking on one particular door, a small girl answered. Lady Astor asked if her mother was at home, the little girl replied, "No, but she said if a lady comes with a sailor, they are to use the upstairs room and leave ten bob!" (Old English ten shillings).

Another time when being heckled someone shouted out that she was too rich to be appointed by the poor. She made a quick repost," It won't be the millionaires living on the Hoe who will elect me!" Her verbal quips brought a lot of humour and lifted the spirits of all women. In reminiscing, many remember the taunting that the family of Isaac Foot of the Liberal party, once her political enemy, bestowed on her. Isaac Foot was quite eccentric at times. At political meetings he would sing such songs as Out Came Mother and Me and When Father papered the Parlour, he was a known pacifist and some had regarded him as pro-German because during the First World War he represented conscientious objectors in court. However, he wore the Liberal colours with pride. The Foot brothers campaigning for their Father's cause would torment the Astors and their supporters by chanting this jingle.

Who's that knocking at the door?
Who's that knocking on the door?
If it's Astor and his wife,
We will stab them with a knife.
And they won't be Tories any more!

Of course, with today's political climate and political correctness, this would not be allowed as it would be deemed as a threat to their safety, but in the nineteen twenties and thirties politicians were considered fair game for torment and sedition. The Astors took it all in their stride and oddly enough in later years the Foot family became the closest of friends and both families had a firm mutual respect for their political views.

DRESS SENSE

For her Parliamentary attire Nancy wore a long black skirt, a white blouse, open at the collar with white cuffs on the sleeves, and a long black velvet jacket, she also wore a very long string of pearls, 'Babies' Chain' she used to call it, as she would allow babies to play with her expensive pearls. Every one waited to see what hat she would wear, as it was the custom for Members of Parliament to wear hats when in attendance. A hush came over the entire assembly in the House of Commons as Lady Astor stepped into the sacred Chamber, accompanied by Arthur Balfour and David Lloyd George, wearing a black velvet costume and her chosen hat and at last the great hat debate had been settled. She chose a crown-fitting toque made of black velvet. In sixteenth century France ladies wore a plumed velvet cap with a full crown and with a small rolled brim. She had, however, her hat modernised and shaped as a tricorn, the modern toque hat is a small brimless close fitting hat usually cream coloured. When in Plymouth Nancy loved to shop and bought her best clothes in Plymouth, not London. Her favourite shop was Pophams, Torrington House, even in the height of the blitz she dressed immaculately.

One of her outfits was a neat mauve suit and her underwear was kept in sets in silk pouches and they were decorated in Lord Astor's racing colours, blue and pink. Nancy would, on some days, get through five sets of clothes. She also wore pink satin dressing gowns, which was one of Waldorf's colours. In December 1941 Pophams were advertising the delivery of their new style shoes and Nancy was always buying shoes; it is likely she bought some of the Raynes shoes, smart and in colours of black or blue. Gloves were also available; for two coupons one could buy a pair of fur-backed gloves for prices between twenty-one and sixty-five shillings, depending on the quality of the item. She loved her hats and in the 1930's new fashions were on the market like the canon hat and the Breton hat usually Reslaw models; popular too were the Condor model hats. Nancy also loved her jewels but she would never wear emeralds; she liked sapphires, pearls and diamonds. When she bought diamonds her favourite supplier was Tiffany's in the United Kingdom, their reputation for diamonds was second to none.

MEMBER OF PARLIAMENT

Wherever, or whenever, Lady Astor entered a room an air of expectancy broke out. In London and in Plymouth she was the mistress of the double entendre, questioning and answering in one voice and knowing that the audience mostly agreed; her understanding of the nature of the Barbican folk was one to be admired because she could talk on any level to peer or pauper. As seen in the New York Times in December 1923 she was popularly called 'The Sunshine of Sutton.' Her election victory in retaining her seat, having beaten the Labour candidate Captain G.W. Brennan was cheered by a huge crowd and that initiated a great demonstration. It was achieved with eighty per cent of the population voting. Nancy declared, "I can promise you I will work for you in the future in the best way I can, and I shall try to teach you to sing God save the King and not the Red Flag." When interviewed by the New York Times she told them, "I attribute my victory to the hard work that I have done for Plymouth and my personal connection with the people. I am a social reformer, and Plymouth prefers people interested in social reform to those interested in socialism and communism."

Her speeches in 1922 are recorded in her book published in 1923 called My Two Countries. On her tour of the United States and Canada at the Women's Pan American Conference in 1922 Nancy had to deal with the stigma left by Margot Asquith who, on her previous lecture tours in America, had caused quite an upset in her criticisms of the Americans for not joining the League of Nations. However Nancy had a very warm welcome and conducted herself admirably and made it clear that the League of Nations and friendship between England and America was paramount and in her final speech in New York emphasised the need for America to be a part of the League of Nations, but it was said in such a manner as not to offend. After seven weeks the Astor entourage left for England sailing on the RMS Cunard Line's ocean liner the Aquitania. In January 1930 the Liner George Washington brought American delegates of the Five Power Conference including the Secretary of State, Henry Lewis Stimson (1867-1950) to Plymouth. It is possible that Lady Astor entertained them in view of her strong views toward Anglo-American relationships. Germany pulled out of the League of Nations in October 1933 and there was a cooling of relationships. In 1946 the League of Nations formally dissolved its assets passing them to the United Nations.

She was to represent the people of Plymouth for twenty-five years, an extraordinary length of tenure; she represented the city through some of its darker days during the Second World War. A fearsome campaigner, her commitment was to the moral transformation she believed women could effect in government. Two years after Lady Astor's election to Parliament, Mrs Margaret Wintringham, (1879-1955) Liberal Party, also a woman's suffrage member, entered the House of Commons and Nancy at last had a companion to share those male dominated times. An advocate of the non-drinking fraternity and a staunch supporter of the Temperance Society Nancy would often say, "One reason I don't drink is because I wish to know when I'm having a good time." The Western Independent newspaper reported in their article on the 4th June 1922 this statement, "Lady Astor has herself opened several Milk Bars in the country and considers that their growing popularity in this country will help forward the cause of temperance." Lady Astor spent many precious days, trying to obtain voluntary subscriptions for the Coal, Soup, and Blanket Societies under the committee of the Devonport Charities. The annual meeting for the charity would meet in the Devonport Guildhall, Plymouth, and Mayor Clifford Tozer (1930-1931) would preside. Many older citizens will remember the soup kitchen in Green Street, Plymouth, all those years ago.

One of Plymouth's most distinguished sons, Michael Foot, who nearly became Labour's top man although his family members were all Liberal, is now in his nineties, and what wonderful memories he must have. Nancy proved her worth, as she was to have a long and distinguished career as Sutton MP serving from 1919 to her retirement in 1945. One wonders what she could have achieved if she had been offered a Ministerial Post in Parliament. In London and Plymouth she had a total of five secretaries and involved herself in every challenge that would improve the quality of life for the poor. It was a shame that the all-male domain prevented the first lady MP from perhaps turning many outdated acts. Nancy would have excelled in Social Reform as she spent most of her life in this field and it was her most passionate desire. She once remarked, "My abiding interest is in people, especially the needy, the helpless and the young. My husband and I are absolutely at one in our interest in social problems. He approaches them from the point of view of the son; I from the view point of the mother." Lord & Lady Astor with their five children sailed on the S.S. Samara in 1926 for a holiday in Boston, United States, and when they arrived writers and photographers were waiting to greet her. Lady Astor suddenly surrounded by questioning reporters, said with good humour, "Well here I am, what can I do for you?" She spent some time answering their questions and proved to be an Ambassador for Great Britain and a friend of the United States.

SOROPTIMISTS, GUILDS, ASSOCIATIONS

In 1930 Doctor Mabel Ramsay pioneered the formation of the Plymouth Soroptimist Club; after originally starting out as a Venture Club, there were thirty-four members, which included Nancy Astor. The club prospered with members predominately from the profession, and they were, and are now, a world wide voluntary organisation of women. They promote the welfare of the communities and women's participation in international, national and local levels, with emphasis on social and economics issues. They are a friendly group and their objects of achievement are the advancement of women, high ethical standards, human rights for all, equality development and peace (Nancy's passion) through international good will, understanding and friendship. They have helped women and children all over the world, particularly those who suffer as a result of war and armed conflict. What a superb legacy this group of very special ladies inherited for they have continued to help many charitable organisations worldwide and Nancy would have been proud of the wonderful record they now hold.

Nancy was a very generous Lady and proved to be a wonderful benefactor to the people as she gave huge gifts to Plymouth in perpetuity. Nancy belonged to so many groups and organisations in Plymouth that one wonders if she ever had any time to herself; she gave her all in helping wherever she could and if she were living today she would be there supporting all the people. Nancy was the first honorary member of the Plymouth and District Association of University Women in Marlborough House, Buckwell Street. Another group, of which Nancy was an honorary member, was the National Federation of Old Age Pensioners Association since its formation in 1957. The Guild of Social Service celebrated their Golden Jubilee in 1957 and Lady Astor was still serving on the committee. The foundation stone for the Buckwell Street site was laid in 1959 and among the crowd watching the event was Nancy. In 1960 the new premises christened Marlborough House opened, today the building is known as Ernest English House.

Lady Astor's love for people led her to pursue a public life to the full to embrace the citizens of Plymouth in showing that she cared even though she no longer represented them in Parliament. The Dowager Viscountess had spent the month of November 1957 in Plymouth where she was engaged in many activities and meetings; she attended the Scott Lecture Theatre where she paid tribute to the great courage of the Plymouth people during the blitz. The City Librarian, Mr Best Harris, was presenting a series of colour and black and white filmstrips of the damage to the City; twenty-five thousand people had already seen the filmstrips but the theatre was still full to capacity. Nancy expressed the hope that the filmstrips would be seen by other cities and cities in America. Lady Astor commented that Coventry had had much publicity about its war damage whilst Plymouth hardly got a mention despite it being the worst bombed provincial city. Whilst in Plymouth Lady Astor, with her son Mr John Jacob Astor, opened the annual bazaar organised by the Sutton Division Conservative Association in the Royal Assembly Hall, Plymouth, and spoke to an audience of four hundred people; she also greeted Lieut-General Sir John Glubb who had given a lecture under the auspices of the Plymouth Lecture Society.

TRAGEDIES

In 1931 a tragic accident took place in Plymouth on the 4th February of eight officers and aircraftmen killed as a result of their Blackburn Iris 111 number N238 Flying Boat from squadron 209 Mountbatten, crashing into Plymouth Sound. They had been returning from an air defence training exercise in conjunction with fighter aircraft from Roborough. On coming in to land at Batten Bay in a glide and not under engine power, with Wing Commander Charles Tucker at the controls the aircraft, instead of following a gently declining angle of descent, nose-dived straight into the water at an estimated speed of seventy miles per hour, its angle of descent unchanged. The mystery surrounding the crash was that the weather was so fine and the sea was calm and no mechanical fault was attributed to the crash; the final assumption was that it was pilot error. Barbican fishermen were first on the scene in an attempt to rescue the crew, and they pulled two of the airmen out of the water, an RAF launch with personnel from Mount Batten were quickly on the scene to rescue further crew. Sadly eight of the twelve were killed. Lady Astor was deeply distressed and attended the funeral with thousands of citizens and servicemen lining the streets. When their funeral cortege, carrying the three bodies recovered from the sea, made its way to Ford Park Cemetery, Lady Astor was there giving her moral support and as representative of her political ward as were the Mayor, Town Clerk and other dignitaries.

On the 19th May 1935 at the Wool Military Hospital, Bovington Camp, Dorset, following a road accident, at the age of forty-six, Aircraftman Shaw, known as Lawrence of Arabia, (1888-1935) died shortly after eight o' clock in the morning. Lady Astor cried at his funeral in Moreton on 21st May 1935 and was overcome with grief as she had been very fond of Lawrence, they had been great friends. Many famous people attended his funeral, including Winston Churchill, General Wavell and the author Henry Williamson.

On the 17th September 1939 the fleet aircraft carrier HMS Courageous was sunk by German U-boat U29 in the Atlantic at the Southwest Approaches; she was the first British war ship to be sunk by submarine in the Second World War. The ship sank in twenty minutes and 518 were killed; she had had 1,200 crewmen. At that tragic event many children were orphaned, as the crew were mostly Plymouth and Devonport men and Dr Barnado's 'Ever Open Door' orphanage at Welby in Tavistock Road, Peverell, suddenly had a very large intake of children. It was Lady Astor who rallied to help the stricken families. In peace and war and even after the war she was constantly attending various functions that would involve the welfare of children.

NURSING AND HOSPITAL SUPPORT

Nancy was a great admirer of the nursing fraternity and she fought to get better conditions and pay for hard working nurses. At the Hospital Fair in 1931 the Nurses lined the paths to meet royalty and members of the aristocracy. Helpers and supporters wore charming costumes to promote the effort being made for the cause of the suffering. His Royal Highness, Edward, Prince of Wales, attended along with prominent members of Plymouth, which included Lady Clinton and the Earl of

Mount Edgcumbe, high-ranking serving officers including Admiral Sir Lionel Halsey, Major Leslie Hore-Belisha MP, Sir Henry Lopes, Lord Astor and Viscountess Astor MP, Lord Radnor, Hon Alice Brand, Lady Mary St Aubyn with prominent Aldermen, Councillors and Mr R.J Fittall Town Clerk and loyal citizens.

Lord and Lady Astor gave financial help and were supportive in their visits to the hospitals and clinics where they were helpful and kind to the blind citizens, and were responsible for ensuring that cleaner milk was supplied to the local population. In 1918 children were suffering from typhoid fever caused by drinking contaminated milk and in the 1920's/1930's it was still happening. Nancy fought hard to have the milk treated and made safe to drink. They were deeply involved with support for the Local Government Reform Bill, which stopped empty beds in hospitals when very ill patients were waiting for a bed.

Photo courtesy Phillippa Stonier – Joyce's youngest daughter

Lady Astor with Plymouth Nurses circa 1932.
Lady top left of Nancy's hat (behind nurse with glasses) is Joyce Stonier (nee Jeffery)
1914-2007. The eighteen year old was training to be a nurse.

POLAR EXPLORER'S SUBMARINE VISIT

In June 1931 the Polar Explorer Sir Hubert Wilkins's Submarine Nautilus had received permission from the Admiralty to bring the submarine to the Dockyard at Devonport, Plymouth, for emergency storm damage repair. The vessel arrived at the Breakwater, dropped anchor and later was towed to the Dockyard for inspection. Whilst he was in Plymouth Sir Hubert invited special guests to come aboard to view the vessel and two of his guests were Lady Astor and her friend Thomas Edward Lawrence, Lawrence of Arabia.

SPORT SUPPORT

Nancy supported sport wherever she could and her loyalty to young people ensured that their needs were met where she could have an influence. The Western Evening Herald reported on a meeting at the YMCA in 1931 where Lord Astor was presenting sport trophies, Lady Astor, with the Hon Phyllis Astor, had accompanied him for part of the evening (they had another engagement elsewhere and had to leave early) Nancy was given a rousing ovation by the members and she spoke to some of the members, saying,

"Go on with your games and get the right spirit, the team spirit. What is so difficult in public life and in private life too, is petty jealousies, which make things so ugly, we have to guard against the littleness of the people who want to shine, and the funny thing is that nobody wants to watch the people who want to shine. What we are up against is that old sinner, the mortal mind, and the carnal mind. St Paul knew it well. It is full of vanity, pride and greed and we are so busy watching it in our neighbour that we forget to watch it in ourselves. As I tell my children, if you watch your thinking for ten minutes you will be astonished how much self comes in. Even in good deeds we see ourselves doing them. We always get ourselves into the picture, and I am convinced from what I see in life that the only people who have a good time are the people who forget about themselves."

GENEROUS GIFTS

Her generosity knew no bounds. Not many people know that Lady Astor also paid for Christmas dinners to be sent out from a shop to the poor in Plymouth, it is thought that even her staff did not know. A worker who had fallen ill was invited to Cliveden to convalesce for a month and was treated as almost one of the family. On his recovery when he left, Nancy gave him a watch and he treasured it all his life. Lady Astor had a great affection for the Barbican children and if a child visited Elliot House on the Hoe the child would be taken into a room that had a large trunk and

Lady Astor's maid would sort out a dress or a warm blanket for the child. Lady Astor had ensured there was always a supply of goods sent by her friends in America. Barbican Folk would say, "She buys her votes with blankets" but nothing could be further from the truth, Nancy was giving not buying. The children loved Nancy Astor and they would sing every time they saw her, "Vote, Vote, Vote, for Lady Astor" at the top of their voices.

The Astors generosity never waned, as year after year they would put their personal money into buying land and gifts for the Plymouth citizens. They gave a playing field in South Devon Place for organised games for elementary school children and contributed to scholarship grants. The Astor Park Playing Fields, Cattedown, bought in 1917 by Lord and Lady Astor is still used today and the citizens of East End in the Cattedown district brought it to life in the summer of 2004 by holding a Carnival coupled with artistic displays. Fun and games, sandpits and paddling pools, street theatre, displays of World War Two vehicles, arts and crafts, alternative medicine, acupuncture and holistic massage; if Nancy had lived she would have been there having a go and being involved. As reported by The Herald, a local newspaper, in September 2007 the Cattedown residents had formed a people's power committee to oppose an application for a store in their neighbourhood to be allowed to sell alcohol twenty-four hours a day. The residents were outspoken in their opposition saying it would fuel alcohol-related anti-social behaviour. The East End had gone through seven years of regeneration and the local residents were proud of their area and the small children who used the park had to be considered. Nancy would have approved of their action as Astor Playing Fields were for sporting and festive activities. Nancy, Lord Astor and their children visited the Playing Fields on occasion. Lord Astor opened the Green Waves Football Club in October 1929 and generations of boys and young men played football there.

The Astors bought the Bennetts Flour premises and had it converted into a club, named the Victory Club in Peacock Lane near Howe Street. The boys and girls could participate in dress making, cookery, dramatics, choirs, gymnastics, boxing and Sea Cadets. A Ways and Means committee was formed to raise funds for poor children to have holidays at Maker Camp, Cornwall. Her involvement with young mothers did not go unnoticed as the Astors arranged a social centre for mothers and children at the East End Assembly Rooms. Her constant visits to the various orphanages were a delight to the children. When they heard of her impending visit, due to their own method of communication, the event would be welcomed. Every time Lady Astor visited an orphanage some rigid rule would be altered and gifts and sweets would be given.

COMMUNITY VILLAGE

In 2008 a wonderful project, which has transformed a neglected neighbourhood into a 'community village,' received a national prize, the £14 million East End scheme, which has revitalised a run-down area with new buildings and facilities and was chosen as the country's best regeneration scheme at the Local Government Chronicle awards. Nancy's beloved East End where she sought to help the citizens of Cattedown, Coxside and Prince Rock all those years ago has been reborn and praise must go to the Local Government, City Council and the community groups who worked so hard to achieve the end result. Astor Park has been given a 'funky' play area, a basketball court, a youth shelter and events space which improvements will allow the Astor Park to live on for the youth to develop their characters.

FILM STAR

Fun loving Nancy also appeared in a film called Royal Cavalcade in 1935 where she played herself; the film was directed by Thomas Bentley and Herbert Brenon. Many famous stars, dancers and musicians appeared in the film. The ballerina Anna Pavlova, actress Hermione Baddeley, singer Florrie Forde, actor Jimmy Hanley and the very young John Mills, comedian George Robey and well-known actor Ronald Shiner. It was a feature length documentary covering a twenty-five year period; the film was an encapsulation of the comings and goings of the British Empire since the 1910 coronation of King George V. The highlights, drawn from the newsreel files of several English and European archives, included Captain Scott's arrival at the South Pole (and the tragic aftermath), the First World War, the Roaring Twenties, and the 1930's Depression. Of special interest to show business buffs was the footage of the first Royal Command Performance at the Palace in 1911.

A FEMINIST VIEW

In an interview with Constance Waller in London on February 23rd 1936, Lady Astor said, "These are the things in which I believe. I am a feminist," she said, "an absolute feminist! And I am growing more so. I think women are wonderful, the amount that we have achieved in the time since we had the vote is almost unbelievable, and look at what has been done for children, for women, for housing in those years. Do you realise that not many years ago a man had absolute control of his children think of that, look at the open-air nursery schools that have been started. Helping to keep children healthy, giving poor children from slum homes beauty and cleanliness, so that as they grow up they will demand beauty and cleanliness that is how we will get rid of our slums. We have had the age of consent raised, we have forced the government to raise the school leaving age, children, children, children, and they are never out of our thoughts." Known to the public principally for her teetotal fanaticism, her sharp tongue and the regularity with which she inspired laughter, Nancy remarked, "I have always been passionately interested in children when I was a girl I wanted to know about any child I saw. I have always felt like that about children."

When asked about her torture as a Member of Parliament she said, "They tried to make my life hell." There was control but a slight bitterness in her voice. "Then I went to the House of Commons where I had more friends in it, I should think, than anyone. I knew so many of them and had known them for so many years intimately. I am a Christian Scientist I am very religious, when I was young I had a long serious illness, I was weak and delicate. I had the best doctors and they told me I should never be well, I found Christian Science and practised its beliefs and was completely cured, you only have to look at me now. Life is what is inside you, what you make it, the world is a staging place but God is here, God is Love, you must let in the spirit. The bible is the most wonderful book; I read little else except The Times, which I have to read, I was reading the bible for two hours this morning. The Old Testament to see how God comes out in flashes here and there and the New Testament about Christ, the spirit, that is what man has and what man must be, religion is a private thing isn't it? Before I do anything I think what is my real motive is it quite outside myself – good! If it is, I will go ahead."

ANCIENT FISHING FEAST

The annual Fishing Feast at Burrator Reservoir with its Devon name Ye Olde Fyshynge Feaste is an annual act of homage to Sir Francis Drake for his building of the Leat in the sixteenth century. The ceremony dates back to the early 1700s; it is a local custom which survives to the present day, and for the last one hundred years the event of the Fyshynge Feaste has been linked to the Mayor of Plymouth's Annual Survey of Waterworks. The Lord Mayor, Councillors and Dignitaries usually dress in ceremonial costume of wigs, tricorn hats and robes when attending the ceremony. It is one of the few remaining survivals of ancient usage connected with the Corporation that is still observed. It is believed that it originated in Elizabethan times. The historic ceremony recognised the leat that Sir Francis Drake had built in 1591 to bring clean water to the city. Usually the pure river water taken from the weir was tasted in a goblet, and then followed by a toast with Madeira wine in another communal silver goblet, known as the Loving Cup. The toast would be, "May the descendants of him who brought us water never want wine." Originally the ceremony was called the Survey of the Waterworks and Fyshynge Feaste and was a men-only day outing for Plymouth's Mayor and his council. They would catch trout while they waited for lunch to be served and after lunch would inspect the leat until they ended up at an inn, where the innkeeper would cook their trout.

In modern times the Operations Director for South West Water Services takes a goblet filled with pure water from Burrator Reservoir and presents the same to the Lord Mayor and requests him to drink from the goblet saying, "To the pious memory of Sir Francis Drake." Passing the cup from one to the other, each drinks and repeats the words. Another goblet, being filled with wine, is then presented by the Head of Finance to the Lord Mayor who drinks the toast, "May the Descendents of him who brought us water never want wine." Once again it is passed to everyone to make the same toast. The goblets had a significant history in the performance of the ceremony. One silver gilt goblet is engraved with the arms of Plymouth and those of the donor. Its inscription reads, The gift (spelt guift, old English on the cup) of Sir John Gayer, Alderman of London, Ano Domini 1648 with a Hound Sejant as a maker's mark. A silver gilt replica of the Gayer cup (1648) used for toasts at the Fishing Feast had been given to the Mayor of Plymouth in 1925 to mark the Burrator Reservoir extension and is used in the present day to mark the occasion. It too has a coat of arms on the front and is inscribed around the inside of the rim (unfortunately illegible) and on the outside of the rim there is also an inscription. The other goblet reads, "The Gyft of John Wyht of London. Haberdasher to the Mayor of Plymouth and his Brethren forever to drink crosse one to ye other at their feastes or meetings" John Wyht died on the 5th June 1585. The maker's mark is WC conjoined, date 1584 London, and the silver gilt baluster stem is chased with fruit. A silver replica of the 1585 Union Cup, used at the annual Fishing Feast ceremonies, had been given to the Chairman of the Plymouth Water Committee in 1917. Because of her dislike of alcohol, when Lady Astor attended the yearly celebration of Plymouth's most ancient ceremonies, amendments were made to ensure that she was not offered wine or alcohol at the event. As a teetotaller, Nancy would not entertain drinking wine, so during her reign as Lady Mayoress the ancient toast was truncated for her sake, removing reference to wine and Nancy would then say, "May the descendants of him who brought us water never want." After conclusion of the ancient ceremony everyone retires to the nearest venue for a delicious lunch.

In the Doidges Annual, a yearly local diary featuring important historical events pertinent to Plymouth, is a photograph of Lady Astor proudly holding aloft the Drake Cup. It is made of silver gilt with cover and is in the form of a globe divided by the equator. It is believed Francis Drake had given the cup to his friend Sir Anthony Rouse (Rous/Rowse) of Halton, Cornwall. The cup sits in a base (which may have been made earlier) that bears the mark of the maker, Abraham Gessner of Zurich. The cup is engraved with a map based on one made by Rumold Mercator (1545-1599) in 1587. He was the son of the Belgium cartographer Gerardus Mercator. The map on the cup, however, must have been inscribed later because it shows details of the coast of South America, China and the Solomon Islands, which were undiscovered before 1595. The cup probably passed by marriage to the Thomas Peter family from whom it was bought in 1947. The National Art Collection Fund, which bought the cup in 1947 later that year, presented it to the city of Plymouth in recognition of the city's war effort during World War Two. The cup is now on display at the National Trust Buckland Abbey Manor and is on loan from the Plymouth Museum and Art Gallery.

ENGLISH HERITAGE

Plymouth owes much to Lady Astor who was passionate about English history; she served on many committees and contributed financial aid wherever she could to preserve precious historic buildings. She had been very keen to see Buckland Abbey, the former Cistercian Abbey of St Mary and St Benedict's founded in 1278, preserved (it had once been the home of Sir Richard Grenville and of Sir Francis Drake) Buckland has an old English derivation 'book land' (it is recorded in the Domesday Book) it had once belonged to Amicia de Redvers, Countess of Devon, the widow of Baldwin de Redvers, 6th Earl of Devon. Nancy had a strong influence in ensuring that the National Trust acquired the Abbey, nestling on the edge of Dartmoor hidden deep in the valley of the River Tavy, in 1947. The Abbey had been severely damaged by fire in 1938 and the premises had been unoccupied for some years and the building steadily deteriorating before its rescue. In 1941 the Admiralty had requisitioned the Great Barn as a granary and stored wheat in the barn for future supplies to the fleet. Nancy had talked to Captain Arthur Rodd a Yelverton landowner and explained to him the idea of presenting the Abbey to the National Trust and in 1946 Captain Rodd presented the Abbey, its garden, the drive and lodge to the National Trust. It involved a lot of hard work and finance by the National Trust and Plymouth City Council to restore it to its former glory. Mediation between the National Trust and the Plymouth City Council in 1951 resulted in the Council accepting a full repairing lease of the property from the National Trust and the converted Abbey became a branch of the City Museum and Art Gallery. It was financed largely with grant aid from the Pilgrim Trust supplemented by the fund raising efforts of the Friends of Plymouth City Art Gallery and Buckland Abbey, and is still financed to this day.

Lord and Lady Astor continued to be generous to the South West and to Buckland Abbey when they commissioned four expensive murals to be installed in the Abbey in 1951 in celebration of the Festival of Britain. The artist was Roland Pym (1910-2006) illustrator, theatrical designer and a mural specialist; his work was similar to the work of Rex Whistler and Osbert Lancaster. Two of the murals represent the battle with the Armada in July 1588, a third shows the course of Drake's voyage around the world between 1577 and 1580 and the last portrays his ship, The Golden Hind. It was to be the last largest financial gift given by Lord and Lady Astor together as Waldorf, Viscount Astor died in 1952.

LADY ASTOR PULLS A PINT

When Lady Astor opened the Aggie Weston establishment for sailors she was asked to pull the first pint and she remarked that it ought to be a pint of milk. Nancy fought against drink and felt very strongly on how it affected poor families. Alcohol was an anathema to Nancy. Today one cannot help but note that irony has strange bedfellows, as Nancy was such a strong opponent of drink and fought fiercely against alcohol, had she been alive today she would indeed be very amused to learn that her portrait hangs in the premises of a local gin distillery. Odd that it should take pride of place in these surroundings, when the portrait should enhance the walls of the Astor room in the Guildhall, where all traces of her have been removed except, on the wall, the framed text of her Freedom of the City award. It would have been prudent if the portrait had been hung in the enclosed Armada Shopping Centre for all generations to see or in 3, Elliot Terrace her former home. Perhaps the gin trade was remembering when in June 1923, as reported by the New York Times, Lady Astor auctioned three bottles of gin in the House of Commons for sixty pounds each. She had consented to serve as auctioneer as the proceeds were going to a memorial for an old colleague and pioneer woman trade unionist, Margaret McMillan. In a lecture given to the bidders before she performed the auction she said, "I would not give tuppence (old English money) for them."

HONORARY DEGREES

The Statute, recognising full academic status for women at University, came into force in 1920. Lady Astor had had conferred on her four Honorary Degrees by leading Universities. Notably that of Hon Doctor of Law LL.D; College of William & Mary, Williamsburg, Virginia, USA, 1928; Hon Doctor of Law LL.D. University of Birmingham, Warwickshire, England, 1930; Hon Doctor of Literature, Reading University, Reading, Berkshire, England, 1937. Hon Doctor of Law, LL.D. Exeter University, Exeter, Devon, England 1959. She became the first female Freeman of Plymouth in July 1959, although she had to wait until she was eighty years old before the honour was bestowed upon her. Maybe it was because Nancy had had a secondary school education where as Waldorf had a university degree. In May 1959 she had celebrated her eightieth birthday at Cliveden with a birthday party given by her family and friends. When the honour of the Freedom of the City in Plymouth was granted, because of her age she was less physically nimble. Why did she have to wait so long? Many citizens felt that Plymouth City Council in those years had been quite tardy in not granting her the honour when she was younger; after all she had retired from politics in 1945. Nancy already had the Freedom of the City in Danville, Virginia, USA where she was born which had been conferred on her in 1922 and the City renamed the street in which she was born as Lady Astor Street. She was intensely proud to have that honour bestowed on her.

On her 80th birthday Nancy Astor said "Years ago I thought old age would be dreadful because I should not be able to do the things I want to do. Now I find that there is nothing I want to do after all." For her 80th birthday present she asked her family for a diamond ring and they were quite surprised that she still wanted diamonds at her age, but Nancy loved her diamonds. The Astor family too were conscious of the cost and had to ensure that the Astor millions did not run out. Nancy got her wish and had her beautiful diamond ring, whether is was bought from her favourite jewellery shop is unknown. Nancy was also a keen buyer of china, read classical books, and adored antiques.

ROYAL CONNECTIONS

There are some people who would say that Lady Astor had an obligation to live up to the advantages that her wealth had given her and that the title she held was to be used to the highest standard of public communication. Nancy did not need to use that obligation in her approach to life, as to her it came naturally, and her deep-felt love for everything in life where her influence could make a difference on ordinary people has never been equalled by any person living or dead. She had to discuss commerce, exercise political persuasion, meet and entertain royalty; the Bowes-Lyons were very fond of Lady Astor and so too were the Royal Family. The nation was indeed grateful that King George V1 and Queen Elizabeth had restored the reputation of the monarchy to a population that had been shattered when King Edward abdicated. We were graced with a King and Queen who duties to the public exceeded all that was expected of them and they won the respect and the admiration of the whole country for their undying loyalty. Our present Queen Elizabeth always called Lady Astor 'Aunt Nancy' (in private of course) when she was a very young girl.

In her retirement years, when living in London, Lady Astor would invite guests for lunch or dinner and in her eightieth year she was still presiding over luncheon parties, but usually kept it to a number of eight persons. Nancy's Austrian chef served some delightful meals. On one occasion the Queen Mother, having lost her beloved husband, as had Nancy in 1952, came to lunch at Nancy's invitation. The Queen said, "You know Aunt Nancy, you made history by being elected to the House of Commons and taking your seat." Lady Astor replied, "Ah! But remember Ma'am, you made a King!" In future years Nancy would frequently tell this tale and it was repeated many times at lunch parties. Nancy was afraid of only three things in her life, cats, spiders and Queen Mary. The late Queen Mary was herself a formidable lady and had been well respected. Although at times she looked severe, underneath the rigid exterior was a heart that had England stamped on it. There was an occasion during the war in December 1941 when Queen Mary, doing her bit for the war effort, simply dressed and wearing an apron, had been helping in a West of England Canteen. Many of the

Lady Astor with his Royal Highness Prince Phillip attending a lunch function

men were quite unaware that royalty was serving them a snack. Two Tommies (British soldiers) had entered the canteen and seeing the Queen behind the counter hailed her, "Hi Missus, two cups of tea please." They were duly served. A helper in the canteen later told a reporter "Queen Mary was delighted, she said it was the first time in her life she had ever been addressed as missus!"

DUTY CALLS

Nancy, in fulfilling her public duties, continued to entertain film stars, attend public functions, and challenge the causes of the poor and needy of the working citizens of the city, meanwhile living the role of wife, mother and homemaker. Nancy's warmth in her response to other human beings, particularly to those in need, was sincere. The fact that she would shake hands with high ranking statesmen yet still shake the hand of her Great Western Railway driver when she arrived at North Road station in Plymouth indicates the ease with which she dealt with protocol. Lady Astor's politics in the Houses of Parliament caused very many hilarious scenes. In the Daily Sketch newspaper March 21st 1936 there was one scene that before Mr Eden spoke made the whole house laugh. Lady Astor was responsible for the most hilarious scene witnessed in Parliament for many years, she entered with a big bunch of flaming red carnations on her black coat, and as she sat down the Socialists cheered because red was their colour. Lady Astor blushed and covered the flowers with her paper; the Socialists cheered even louder than ever. Lady Astor took it in good spirit, and a friend reminded her that the Conservative colour was blue. This was the year that her grandson was born so it certainly was a year to remember. In 1936 Nancy after a very bad cold lost her voice, which meant engagements in Parliament and Plymouth had to be cancelled, hard to imagine - Nancy voiceless?

POLITICAL END

By the time the Second World War had ended in 1945, there had been no General Election for nearly ten years; Nancy's last election was in 1935. After the war Nancy's political style was becoming outmoded and the wind of change was evident; the new social revolution was underway. The Conservative Party of Plymouth were eager to adopt Lady Astor again. Nancy, undefeated seven times, had for a quarter of a century fought and expressed her ideas in Parliament. Her announcement to retire from politics was a disappointment among her constituents. However, it was not really her own decision for she had been strongly advised by her husband to retire. Was Waldorf right in advising her to stand down? It was his love for Nancy that won the day. She wanted to continue but both Waldorf and Nancy knew that the political scene had changed dramatically. Waldorf sensed this and persuaded her to make the momentous decision. Unhappy at the thought of ending her career she still took his advice and stood down with good grace and retired from the world of politics. There is no doubt his influence was the key factor in reaching this decision, Nancy's constituents were tolerant toward her but there were also feelings of antagonism. Nancy had a human fault in that, on occasion, she could be cruel, but that was offset by the generosity, which she showed to people.

It was already evident before the war, when her performance in Parliament had become open to ridicule. It would not have been prudent to continue as she had reached the age of sixty-six and could she have fought the battles with the fire she had had in previous years? No one will ever know if she would have succeeded in being re-elected one can only stipulate that momentous step which ended her political career as she stepped out of the political arena in the House of Commons. In retrospect it may have been better to have let her stand and then, if she failed, she could have put it in perspective; as it was Nancy never quite forgave Waldorf for ending her political career, however, one fact did emerge from that decision, Plymouth citizens had lost, forever, a fighting firebrand. Waldorf, who had always acted as her main stay in organising her election campaigns, no longer felt able to deal with the heavy exertions involved as his health was failing and, serving Plymouth as Lord Mayor for most of the war years until 1944, had taken its toll, he was both physically and mentally exhausted. Waldorf could see, what Nancy could not, that he and Nancy had been out of touch with the political arena; during the war all political views were put aside as Coalition Government controlled the country. His views had changed, too, as he became more liberal minded. He had helped to plan the re-building of Plymouth and was longing to further improve his farm and his wish was to lead a more normal life. A brilliant man, yet so gentle in his manner, somehow sensed that a Labour victory was possible.

GOODNIGHT SWEETHEART

When the Plymouth citizens learned of Nancy's impending retirement in 1945 they began to make their way to Plymouth Hoe and congregate outside 3, Elliot Terrace. Many came from the Barbican area and some camped on the parterre outside and when a large crowd had arrived they all sang in unison 'Goodnight Sweetheart - Goodnight' Nancy was overcome and to hide her tears she admonished the crowd by saying, "Thank you from the bottom of my heart, what are you doing here? If you all don't go home and get some rest and get those voters out tomorrow your sweetheart will be no-body's baby when the votes are counted" They cheered her with gusto and sang once more, 'Goodnight Sweetheart - Goodnight' and dispersed. Plymothians had said their goodbyes to a champion of their cause in their own unique way. That year 1945 the Conservatives lost and the Labour party won a landslide victory. Winston Churchill was once more put out to pasture. In Plymouth, Lucy Middleton won the seat for Plymouth Sutton, with a labour majority of 4,679 votes and was Member of Parliament until 1951. In part of her farewell speech at the House of Commons on the 15th June 1945 Lady Astor said; "I leave with the deepest regret and the profoundest respect for the House of Commons, I am heartbroken at going, I shall miss the House."

THE RETIREMENT YEARS

So began her retirement years and the Plymouth citizens had lost a champion of their causes. In 1946 Lord and Lady Astor decided to travel to the United States of America to visit old friends and for Nancy to see her aged aunt, whom she had not seen since before the war. Nancy was then sixty-six years old but she was still world famous and while she was in New York was bombarded by reporters. To one of the reporters she remarked; "I am an extinct volcano!" this was duly reported in the New York Times. Wherever she went they hinged on every word she said, so she took the opportunity to use the publicity to further enhance the Anglo-American friendship, attending several Legislatures and Universities to promote unity between Great Britain and America. We owe a great deal to Lady Astor for bringing American and British Subjects together in friendship. From the very beginning of her early political service until her health failed in 1964 she continued to promote friendship between the two countries.

Photo courtesy Charles Prynne. Digital copy Trevor Burrows Plymouth Photographer
Original photo by Jane Bown, London

Lady Astor at 80 years old taken at 100, Eaton Square, London

It is believed that Lady Astor had intended to stay on in Plymouth in her retirement years because she had bought a plot of land on the Barbican close to Lambhay Hill, near the old Plymouth Castle, to have a bungalow built there and to be near her beloved Barbican folk, however, with the death of Waldorf she gave the land to the people and it was turned into a small garden to be enjoyed by all pensioners and retired fishermen. Lady Astor's beloved husband Waldorf died in 1952 and she was utterly devastated and her lifestyle was to change as she endeavoured to adjust to life without him, it was a considerable blow. She did not attend the memorial service in London but chose to come to Plymouth to attend a service at Saint Andrew's Church, which, still roofless, was laid out as a Garden Church. Nancy moved out of Cliveden leaving the home in the care of William the next Viscount and spent her time between Hill Street, London and Rest Harrow in Sandwich. In the late 1950s, she moved into a flat in Eaton Square, London. Nancy, in her seventies continued to annoy many politicians, perhaps her quote about the welfare state in 1950 annoyed many authorities when she said, "The Welfare State will end up as the 'Farewell' state." In 1958 under the Premiership of Harold Macmillan the Life Peerage Act came into force whereby women could sit in the House of Lords. It would have been a golden opportunity for Nancy to be recognised by the nation for all that she had done in her twenty-five years of service and for the public service she continued to give throughout her life, cruelly she was not offered a peerage by Harold Macmillan and it must have been a terrible disappointment for her. Once more she had been rebuked.

In 1959 Lady Astor came to Plymouth and performed the launching ceremony for H.M.S. Plymouth, the first ship for 250 years to bear the name. It was clear the speed and timing had gone in the delivery of her speeches, although she was still very witty, however, she was getting increasingly forgetful and her memory was beginning to fail leaving a blunter weapon in its place. She was warring with her children, having alienated them with her overweening possessiveness. Nancy had held literary lunches in the past and she was always looking to improve her knowledge and had always moved among those who were well educated. She made personal attempts to better herself and would entertain high profile writers like George Bernard Shaw, James Barrie, Henry James, and Rudyard Kipling. She continued to meet people and regularly invited friends and guests to lunch. One of her favourite guests was the writer Peter Fleming. Later Nancy left Cliveden, in Buckinghamshire, and moved to Hill Street, Berkeley Square, London; meanwhile the former London home at 4, St James's Square had been sold. She would spend the weekends in Cliveden to be with her son William, the third Viscount, and many high profiled people would dine with them. One very important person who dined with the Astor family in 1953 was King Gustav of Sweden. In 1958 Nancy moved to 100 Eaton Square London where she would still entertain and usually have six to eight guests at lunch.

On occasion she would travel to Rest Harrow in Sandwich, Kent, which belonged to the Astors and had originally been a golfing cottage near the seaside and was quite near the Sandwich Golf Course. Nancy's brother-in-law, Mr Spender Clay, who was an architect designed the new house in 1912 to replace the old cottage. One of Nancy's passions was golf and whenever or wherever she could play, out would come her golf clubs. George Sayers was one of the best golf instructors in the world and had taught Lady Astor in her early years how to play. They stayed life-long friends and often met to socialize. On one occasion Lady Astor invited George Sayers and his family to New York City. Lady Astor lived at the Waldorf-Astoria Hotel then, which was opulent and luxurious. Her suite occupied two floors and there was a winding staircase with very tall French doors which opened onto a balcony. The doors were open because the day was warm and sunny and she talked mostly about golf. The family presented to her a full set of George's custom made golf clubs, which was a lovely gift, and she was most pleased.

Nancy deeply felt the loss of her favourite sister Phyllis who had been eighteen months younger than herself and who had wonderful gifts. She was a brilliant horsewoman and also possessed talent as a musician; whereas on the musical side Nancy was tone deaf. Both sisters had been involved in high jinks when courting their beaux in Virginia. Nancy had written to friends in her later years stating that Virginia, in her teenage years, had been the best years of her life, she said in her letter, "Nothing could be quite as lovely as my life in Virginia." Her lifetime had been spent with divided loyalties between Virginia and Plymouth. When Plymouth failed to accept Waldorf Astor on the council in 1944, the Astors political links with Plymouth were broken and the citizens had lost the opportunity of a brilliant negotiator to fight other political needs for the devastated city, yet Nancy remained passionate about Plymouth and still did her best to remain loyal to the city and continued her interest in the city she had represented for so long and made regular visits while her health permitted.

Nancy never quite gave in and the fire was still smouldering when, in 1950, she was at a conservative meeting in Paddington Town Hall, London. The hall was packed and hundreds of would be patrons were shut out, such was her popularity. She faced a hostile crowd and a woman shouted and challenged her by saying, "Aren't you from a very wealthy family?" Nancy replied, "The Astors are very rich, don't you wish you were?" Nancy stated that she would give the last drop of her blood to save the Old Country from socialism. A section of the crowd began by singing the Red Flag immediately Lady Astor began singing God save the King at the top of her voice. Nancy bought property in Southern Rhodesia during the political crises and even began to participate in local politics there, but it was short lived and on her death the property was sold at a huge financial loss. Nancy moved into her niece's home near Oxford in the early 1960s, as she needed more personal care. She was making unpleasant remarks due to her illness and would often say cruel things, thankfully her niece Nancy Lancaster adored her and Lady Astor received loving care from her and Nancy's maid, Rose Harrison, who was with her until the end of her life.

NANCY ASTOR AND MARY STOCKS

Barbara Hooper in her 1996 book 'Mary Stocks (1891-1975) An Uncommon Place Life recalled that in 1964 Mary Stocks (nee Mary Danvers Brinton, later Baroness Stocks) was called upon to write and broadcast tributes about Lady Astor. Mary Stocks and Nancy Astor were as unlike, one may think, as any two women could be. Nancy an American Southern Belle married to an aristocrat and Mary an academic, a feminist, and a radical. Over forty-five years their friendship had deepened and endured into a kind of mutual devotion as her friend Mary visited Lady Astor regularly at her London home in the later years and at Rest Harrow. Baroness Stocks, Life Peer of Kensington and Chelsea, had in her early years been a great champion of the women's suffrage movement. A University Lecturer, Pioneer Social Reformer, College Principal, a broadcaster and a member of the House of Lords. Nancy and Mary were both philanthropists in a changing world. Like Nancy she was at times perceived as a tiresome eccentric, also like Nancy she fought for victims of poverty and prejudice. One of her famous quotes went like this,

"Today we enjoy a social structure, which offers equal opportunity in education. It is indeed regrettably true that there is no equal opportunity to take advantage of the equal opportunity." *Baroness Mary Stocks.*

In October 1956 Mary Stocks was asked by the BBC Women's Hour programme to interview her old friend and political opponent Nancy Astor. Mary had been a women's rights campaigner; she was appointed Principal of Westfield College in 1939 and was a leading figure in the 1950's era participating as a regular broadcaster and leading panellist on the well-known programme Any Questions. The interview was held at Lady Astor's home in London and the programme duly recorded and Mary paid the princely sum of eight guineas. Mary said to Nancy in her interview, "You know, the thing that struck us almost immediately when you came on the scene was your courage. You say you felt nervous, but we got the impression that you were not afraid of anything, not even of your party whips." Nancy replied, "I was not afraid of my party whips because the women had voted me in and I felt it was my duty to vote the way I felt right, I was interested in women, children and social reform. I wanted the world to get better and I knew it could not get better if it was going to be ruled by men." When Nancy was asked if she was embarrassed by criticisms or taunts about her wealth she merely said, "Oh, not the slightest, I adored being rich."

SOCIAL ACTIVITIES

Even in her retirement years Nancy continued to be active in any organisation of which she was patron or president, she would go to the meetings and join in from the platform, still feisty and determined not to be a passive observer. In fact, so active was

Nancy that even at the age of seventy-five, if the fancy took her, she would still cartwheel to prove how fit she was. In those years of retirement Nancy would often return to Cliveden when her son, by then Viscount Astor, handed the house and its amenities over to his mother for a week-end to act as hostess to any old or new friends she might care to invite. Nancy's social selection of guests included many interesting people such as, Mary Cavendish, Duchess of Devonshire (1895-1988) who lived to the grand age of 93, and her sister Beatrice Edith Mildred Ormsby-Gore (nèe Gascoyne-Cecil) the Dowager Lady Harlech (1891-1980) the widow of 4th Baron Harlech; daughter of the 4th Marquess of Salisbury. Lady Harlech had been Lady of the Bedchamber to Queen Elizabeth, the Queen Mother. Another visitor was Sir Edward Coke, a former Secretary to Queen Mary. Nancy's holiday weeks at Rest Harrow were enjoyable and relaxing as the two women who were to have an influence in her last years stayed with her at the peaceful home. The two women were the Marchesa Casa Maury (1894-1983) (formerly Freda Dudley Ward) reputedly to have been a former mistress of Edward, Duke of Windsor, and Joan, Lady Altrincham (1897-1987) formerly Joan, Lady Grigg (nèe Joan Dickson-Poynder) who was the organiser of maternity and nursing services in Africa. The Marchesa Casa Maury had a calming affect over Lady Astor and the younger members of the Astor family were pleased and quietly grateful. Nancy's last years were spent alone without influence and she was deeply upset at the loss of old friends and her beloved husband. But her generosity never wavered. Once when out walking along the seafront at Sandwich, she saw an elderly person who obviously was pretty hard up, so Lady Astor went over and slipped him a £5 note, and said, "Happy Christmas."

On the 3rd July 1957 Saltram House and its estate passed into the care of the National Trust. Saltram was an 18th Century Mansion with rooms designed by Robert Adams in the George 11 era and was home to the Parker family and Earls of Morley. In 1937 a second National Trust Act was passed enabling the trust to hold land and investments to provide for the upkeep of its properties. The new legislation made possible the Country House Scheme whereby a house owner could transfer their home to the Trust while continuing to live in it. Six years later the Chancellor of the Exchequer announced his intention of taking advantage of the Government's power to accept houses and land in payment of death duties and of bequeathing such properties to the Trust. Once the houses and land were given to the National Trust the donors were no longer responsible for tax. Plymouth has Lady Astor to thank for Saltram House, as it was she who advised the last of the Parker family, as they too were faced with very high death duties, to consider bequeathing the House and estate to the National Trust. They heeded her suggestion and in 1957 the National Trust became its owners. The Parker family lived there for the rest of their lives and when the last member died the National Trust became the sole owners.

Nancy's retirement years were fraught with regret at not being involved in the political scene and her last years with Waldorf were strained as she blamed him for the end of her political career. She was constantly in conflict with her family, her inability to control her crass remarks were beginning to embarrass her family and close friends, yet she was still bright and sharp. Her mind was beginning to drift back to the past and she would constantly repeat the same conversation particularly when important guests were visiting. Her family understood and bore the atmosphere of indiscretions, yet even in her twilight years her thoughts were still of other people. Nancy had a very generous nature and she would promise cheques to various people for causes she considered worthwhile. Unfortunately the cheques would be for quite large sums of money for although still in control of her cheque books, she did not seem to be aware of the sums involved, or that the expenditure of her finance had to be carefully monitored. Thankfully Lady Astor was graced with loving, caring staff and her very efficient Secretary would have the task of writing to the promised recipient to say. "Lady Astor is very sorry, she does not have enough money in her account to cover it."

THE FINAL GOODBYE

Nancy spent her last years at her daughter's home at Grimsthorpe and she was well looked after. When the end came for the Dowager Viscountess Astor, this dynamic woman spoke her last words which was proof of her love as she slipped away saying "Waldorf, Waldorf." Her loyal servant Rose Harrison took care of Nancy for over thirty years and was with her until the end. Nancy was to grace this earth for eighty-five years and what a mark she made. With an indomitable spirit, beauty and wit, her death at the age of eighty-five on the 2nd May 1964 was a great loss not only to her family and friends but also to all Plymothians. She was original in every thing she did. May had been a milestone in her life, born in May, married in May and died in May. Her most highly rated achievement was as the People's Friend. The Astor family spanned fifty-six years linked with Plymouth City, and when Lady Astor died a very special part of history died with her. Friends across the sea and many politicians were to mourn her loss; more so, because it was the end of an era and it is doubtful we will ever see her like again as she had that most precious gift, the human touch. To true Plymothians she will always be, 'Our Nancy.'

Nancy Astor continued to break new ground in Parliament even after her death. She was the first woman commemorated in the precincts of the House of Commons when a bronze relief portrait of her was unveiled. The sculpture was by Michael Rizzello; it was indeed a wonderful tribute to a woman who had made an enormous contribution to the life of the Palace of Westminster.

Photo courtesy Charles Prynne. Copy by Trevor Burrows Plymouth Photographer

Nancy, Lady Astor, in 1919

Photo by kind permission of South West Image Bank – Plymouth Barbican Association Reference PD/15/1

Lady Astor Primrose League ladies outside 3 Elliott Terrace, Plymouth 1923 election campaign.

LADY ASTOR ON THE SEX FILM

Commercialisation and Its Evils

NEW CONTROL NEEDED

ECONOMY AND SOCIAL SERVICES

LADY ASTOR hit out last night at the commercialisation of "sex-appeal" in the cinemas.

She called it "degrading and disgusting."

"I love a good cinema, but there are certain forms of cinema which are not good for young people," she said in a speech at the annual meeting of the Beaconsfield Habitation of the Primrose League, when Lord Astor presided. "We in the House of Commons are not at all satisfied about some of the films which are being shown in this country. I have always said that for the film trade to appoint a Censor themselves is perfectly ridiculous. The Government ought to have some control over it as they have over the B.B.C. I am not a prude or anything like that, but I am appalled at some of the things young people see.

THE INTERESTS OF CHILDREN

"I know that there are American films shown in this country that cannot be shown in America. Just look at some of the posters and think whether they are very inspiring or good for the children. Why, they do not have that in Russia! They may have too much propaganda, but at least the cinemas do not degrade the people.

Lady Astor confessed that she personally hated watching "those vamps," but had a weakness for cowboys. "It's all that unattractive sex appeal I am complaining about," she said. "I am not attacking cinemas as a whole. I think they are going to be wonderfully useful. Grown-ups can see what they like. What I am concerned with is the children."

Photo courtesy Western Independent and
The Plymouth Reference Library

Lady Astor's views on the sex appeal films being shown in the Cinemas.
She was speaking at the Primrose League meeting in Plymouth July 1932.

Photo courtesy of Miss Jean Tozer (JP Retired)

The Prince of Wales with Lord & Lady Astor at the civic luncheon held at the Guildhall July 1931

First left Rear Admiral Reinold. Second left Admiral Sir Lionel Halsey Third left Mayoress Mrs J Tozer; standing behind her Lord Astor; beside the Mayoress the Prince of Wales, gentleman standing behind Major McCormick the Bishop of Plymouth, to the right of Prince of Wales is Mayor Clifford Tozer; next Lady Astor with the picture hat, gentleman alongside Brigadier Liddell, gentleman end right the Earl of Mount Edgcumbe.

45

Scene on Nomination Day in the Plymouth Council Chambers October 1931
First left Clifford Tozer: Second left unknown. Third left Nancy, Lady Astor: Fourth left Mr Fittall Town Clerk.
Second from right Mr L Hore-Belisha. End right unknown.

Photo by kind permission Charles Prynne Original photograph by Time Magazine (no longer existing)
Digital copy Trevor Burrows Plymouth photographer

Lady Astor takes a stroll in the snow-covered garden during a visit to Mirador House,
near Charlottesville at the foot of the Blue Ridge Mountains USA in 1946.
Her father Chiswell Dabney Langhorne purchased 'Mirador' in 1890.

Photo: Copyright News Review March 1939
Digital copy Trevor Burrows Plymouth photographer

Lady Astor in one of her honourary degree outfits

Lady Astor outside the Houses of Parliament

Portrait by Dorothy Wilding with Nancy's signature bottom right

The Astor family at Cliveden in the 1920s.

Left to right back row: William (Bill) Waldorf Astor (later 3rd Viscount) (1907-1966)
Viscount Waldorf Astor (2nd Viscount) (1879-1952)
Left to right front row: Francis David Langhorne Astor (1912-2001) Michael Langhorne Astor (1916-1980)
Nancy, Lady Astor (1879-1964) John Jacob (Jackie) Astor (1919-2000)
Nancy Phyllis (Wissie) Louise Astor (later Countess of Ancaster) (1909-1975)

Photograph. Left Nora Langhorne Grenfell, Nancy's sister and mother to Joyce Grenfell. Right Nancy Langhorne Astor on an electioneering campaign in the 1920's.

CHAPTER TWO
NANCY'S PUBLIC WORK

"Life is what is inside you, what you make it, the world is a cruel place, but God is spirit, God is love, you must live in the spirit."
(Nancy Astor from an interview 1936)

Nancy's record of public service was to know no bounds as she fought for justice and quality of life for the poor and was supportive of endless Bills in the House of Commons. Her work rate was prolific as, when elected, Nancy received hundreds of letters from women with a grievance. Women and children were her first concern but Nancy was also a supporter of world peace, she championed a better understanding between England and the United States of America. She was bitterly disappointed when in 1920 the United States Senate again refused to ratify the Treaty of Versailles and prevented the United States joining the League of Nations. Nancy favoured and supported the Plumage Bill that was first introduced in 1908 by the Royal Society for the Protection of Birds. In 1912 a committee met to consider the best means to protect, maintain and encourage the increase of all useful species including those used in the feather trade. The bill was brought in to prevent bird and feather being used for hats and to control the millinery trade and stop birds being killed for fashion. The bill was finally passed in 1921. In addition, Nancy challenged for the more humane slaughtering of animals.

In her manifesto of 1923 she clearly earmarked her desire to undertake and challenge for the rights of her citizens. Her promise was to get a better standard of life for the people, to fight for a higher moral and social standard and seek peace in Europe through the League of Nations. She thought highly of the Royal Navy and advocated more foreign buyers for English goods. Helping to instigate measures for the Safeguard of Industries, she expressed her desire to develop new communities in the Dominions and Colonies being helped by preferences such as lower duties on tea, raisins, coffee, sugar, tobacco and other goods grown in the colonies. Nancy was totally against food taxes, she maintained that meat, bacon, bread, cheese, eggs etc., must be kept free of taxes, and she tried hard to stimulate agriculture by getting more men employed on food production here in Britain. She was passionate in her efforts to sweep away slums and build more houses and showed total commitment when she and Lord Astor had the Mount Gould Housing Estate built in 1925 for the poor families from the Barbican, a poor area of Plymouth. Her pursuance of work to be achieved sooner rather than later was tackling needed public work such as bridges, electrification of railways and bringing cruisers to the Dockyard to keep the men in work.

Photo from a private collection
Copyright Western Morning News
Digital copy Trevor Burrows Photography Plymouth

Lady Astor wearing her Parliamentary
outfit 1919

Her achievement in introducing a bill into Parliament in her early years surprised even her most critical opponents. She was the first woman to have a Private Members' Bill become law 'The Intoxicating Liquor Bill' (Sale to Persons Under 18) which prevented the sale of liquor to the under 18s and Guardianship of the children's bill was passed in July 1923. In Plymouth that same year Nancy was extremely busy devoting herself to the citizens of Plymouth. She attended so many functions it has to be assumed that her private life was very limited. She officially opened the Devon and Cornwall Training School and Home for Nurses in Durnford Street Stonehouse. It had been formerly known as the Three Towns Nursing Association Maternity Home, later it suffered severe damage in the bombing of Plymouth May 1941; although it was rebuilt after the war it was never again used as a maternity home but as a District Nursing Home. Now the joined up houses have been converted into flats for residents and a residential home for adults with learning disabilities. In Parliament in December 1941 Lady Astor had challenged Mr Ernest Bevin (1881-1951) then Minister of Labour in Winston Churchill's Coalition Government, as to how many Service men had complained about the conscription of married women. Representations from the Navy and Air Force were the strongest to protest. Lady Astor was unhappy at the treatment of the women conscripted into the services as they were, in her opinion, being treated as chattels. The services were concerned at the difficulties of having married women in the front line or of being attached to serving personnel in war zone areas, the problem of women on board ships and their conditions would not allow females to integrate. The House of Commons had passed the new National Service Bill through all its stages in December 1941 and was sent to the House of Lords where it received the first reading. During the Committee stage of the bill Members of Parliament Lady Astor and Mrs Mavis Constance Tate, Conservative MP and British Women's Rights campaigner, were among those who wished to have amendments to the Bill.

Mr Bevin promised not to compel women to serve intoxicating liquor in canteens if they objected, and another amendment was made that included a clause, and accepted by the Government, to prevent women being compelled to use lethal weapons. The effect of one of the amendments would have been to prevent the exemption of childless married women of suitable age from service in the women's armed forces. Lady Astor said it was unfair to conscript women unless equal compensation was given in case of women being injured. Lady Astor's concern was how they were to be treated as she had already pointed out in the House of Commons the treatment of the Auxiliary Territorial Service (ATS) women who were being used for nugatory work, despite the fact that the ATS was formed on the 9th September 1938. However, conscription became law in 1941, which put the women on a par with the men, and were to be given equal opportunities. With the collapse of France in 1940 and the worry of a German invasion all women had to serve either in the services or industry. ATS women became anti aircraft gunners and served with Heavy Artillery Batteries, and as Radio and Signal operators, Sperry Predictors, Language translators, Map-readers, Plotters, Drivers, Despatch riders, Morse intercept operators, and some joined the Special Operations Executive (SOE).

Nancy worked hard in Plymouth giving her time and money; she set up the very first Hospital League of Friends and was the founder of Mount Gould's League of Friends and sat on the first committee for voluntary service. Their aims were to raise money to help hospital and patient needs. Nancy had to share her time between her duties in the House of Commons and attending public meetings and functions in her beloved city of Plymouth. Through both World Wars she had been passionate about the care of servicemen. During the First World War (1914-1918) she opened the Veteran's Auxiliary Home Hospital at Mount Priory House, Plympton, Plymouth; the War Committee of the British Red Cross Society and the Order of St John supported the hospital. Other generous supporters were by private means (The Astors contributed) individuals and public bodies. The house has since been demolished and today the Old Priory School stands in the grounds and twelve detached houses are built at the site of the house. In the summer of 1919 Lady Astor, along with local dignitaries, unveiled the War Memorial on Plymouth Hoe.

Waldorf Astor and Nancy piloted through the House of Commons the very first National Service Act, which was the foundation of the National Health Service today. One should note that Nancy, being the first woman to take a seat in Parliament, was surrounded by six hundred and forty nine male Members and no facilities were available for ladies in Parliament at that time. She was given a private room, which could also be used by future women elected members. She had to withstand the battery of male resentment that greeted her in Parliament for many years after she took her seat. Early political friends were Lionel George Curtis (1872-1955) writer, public servant and a fellow of All Souls College Oxford and Geoffery Dawson (formerly Geoffery Robinson) (1874-1944) later Lord Dawson former journalist and Editor of the Times newspaper. One could imagine the fight Nancy had on her hands to be acknowledged as a serious contender. When one contentious opponent said; "Here we have entry into one of the most famous male places in the world," Nancy replied; "Well it is not any more!" A former Labour Prime Minister for Great Britain (1945-1951) Clement Atlee (1883-1967) said, "Nancy Astor could be as bold as brass but she was in fact a kind and compassionate woman with, especially where women were concerned, a great sense of justice."

The tactics used by members of Parliament toward Nancy when she was elected were in some cases hostile. They did all they could to make her feel unwanted, once even setting up a special debate on venereal disease in the hope she would not be able to sit through it, to prove a woman was not fitted to be a Member of Parliament. Nancy was made of sterner stuff, she said that the only intelligent thing to do was to call together women who were politically active (all Labour supporters) and told them, "All I can offer is to tell them for you, if you can make use of me I am at your service." This was how Nancy met Mary Stocks (1891-1975) and the two women who were to become her Parliamentary aides, Hilda Matheson (1888-1940) her Secretary (later a BBC talks director) and Rachel (Ray) Strachey (1887-1940) political advisor (1929-1934) to Lady Astor on women's questions, she was also a member of the Bloomsbury Group and cousin to Mary Stocks and had read mathematics at Newham College, Cambridge. These women were to have a very significant part in Nancy Astor's life. Nancy could not have managed to fight the case for women without these friends; nearly all her friends were Labour. The Tories refused to speak to her and just froze her out. This was the environment Nancy had to deal with when representing her Plymouth constituents. What women owe to Nancy Astor for what she did in her first two lonely years as Member of Parliament will never be fully recognised.

Left to right: Amy Johnson, Charles Chaplin, Lady Astor and George Bernard Shaw
Photo taken at 4, St James Square London circa 1930s

Nancy fought (but lost) against the socialist and communist policies of the Capital Levy and of handing over our shops, mines, factories, business and trade to be run by Government Officials. Her argument was sound as the Capital Levy was aimed at the idle rich, but it hit the workers and lessened trade. She continued to improve her already successful achievements in supporting children, women, pensioners, allotment holders, education and business. Although she did not wish to impose prohibition in Britain she did support the policy of the churches to reduce the effect of excessive drinking and reduce the amount of alcohol being consumed, which affected the poor families most when waiting for their husbands to hand over the wage package to support the family. Nancy stated that she did not represent any single class, yet often her policies were attacked by some in every class, her motto was: A better world can only come if we have better men and women in all walks of life. Written on her paper to the Electors in 1923 were these words: I do not promise to cure all your troubles at once, but I will strive to change the world into a much better place for your children. Nancy helped to achieve the settlement of war debts, the London reparations settlement of 1924 recognised as the Dawes Settlement with Germany. In Plymouth, she was instrumental in installing the Local Government Bill of 1924, which gave Plymouth a centralised Local Authority. Nancy voted against the issue of a revised prayer book in 1927. All of England was in turmoil over the debate, which threw churchmen into a quandary; the revised prayer book bill caused quite a stir. The venerable Archbishop of Canterbury had hoped to reconcile within the church two fiercely divergent groups of the clergy. It was a blow to the Episcopate as the votes were 238 against and 205 for. The shock of the defeat put workers into redundancy as three well-known printing houses who had made preparations for printing the new revised prayer book had to sack staff, who were employed for the task of supplying millions of copies, when the contracts were cancelled. Bitter arguments ensued and quarrels within the church ended with several Bishops resigning.

Nancy was involved with the 1925 Treaty of Locarno, which established arbitration between France and Germany and guaranteed both countries against unprovoked attack. The political situation in Germany was shaky in the 1920's with the Weimar democracy which arose from defeat in the First World War and which replaced a semi-authoritarian imperialist regime, but it never had wide support. However, it struggled along until the late 1920's when it is thought that the final crises arose for the Weimar Republic as being linked to the Wall Street crash of October 1929, marking the world wide slump, which ruined many businesses, and many people lost all their money. In 1933 Adolf Hitler (1889-1945) who had been born in the small Austrian town of Braunau was appointed as Chancellor of Germany and in 1938 Austria and Germany formed the Union 'Anschluß' It was not particularly popular with the Austrians, however the union was formed, history was made, and its consequences for the future were to dramatically change the world.

Nancy achieved some measure of success with the Kellogg Peace Pact to outlaw war; the Kellogg-Briand Pact had its genesis in the international anti-war and disarmament conferences held in the 1920s in the aftermath of World War One. In 1927 the Kellogg-Briand Pact, also called the Pact of Paris and, more formally, the Treaty for the Renunciation of War, was a multilateral treaty signed by fifteen nations in Paris on 27th August 1928, and later almost universally ratified; Nancy also travelled widely and was known to have visited Palestine and Russia. She also shouldered the responsibility for keeping Juvenile Unemployment Centres open during the winter to keep young, out of work juveniles, off the street and advocated raising the school age to sixteen. She campaigned for preventing boys under sixteen from working in underground mines and advocated better welfare for infants, and milk for children. She backed the De-Rating proposals intended to increase work by stimulating mining, engineering, agriculture, ship-building and railways and fully supported the measures for safeguarding the conditions of employment of British workers in certain industries and worked to ensure the Factory Bill was amended to protect the workers from exploitation. In May 1928 the voting age for women was brought down from 30 to 21 years. Her dedicated work for the Y.M.C.A. did not go unnoticed as she attended most meetings in Plymouth and Sundays was not a day of rest for Lord and Lady Astor as in May 1928 they had many engagements connected to Mothering Sunday and the Y.M.C.A. A breakfast meeting at the Central Young Women's Christian Association, Old Town Street, Plymouth, where Lady Astor spoke was then followed by a service at Saint Andrew's Church. Lord Astor presided at another meeting in the afternoon, and attended the evening service at Virginia House, meanwhile in the afternoon Lady Astor was the speaker at the Y.M.C.A. service in Union Street. Most of her spare time was spent in serving the public although she did manage to get a breather on the moors between Cadover Bridge and Sheepstor where she visited the Church and admired the finely-carved screen. When she could Nancy loved to visit the moors, but her visits were limited.

Her success in obtaining a grant for training unemployed women was a victory highly praised by the out of work women who, until the grant, had no voice, and she supported the bill for granting pensions for women. Nancy was appointed a member of the Home Office Committee on Women Police and was one hundred per cent behind the bill. In 1925 she introduced the Public Places (Order) Bill to amend the laws relating to street solicitation. As a result of this bill, a Committee was set up to recommend various changes; this was a private bill to protect prostitutes from being convicted for soliciting. Lady Astor supported the Government's proposals under which cheaper electricity should be provided and she was the only Conservative who voted consistently against the betting tax. Further debates covered more bills, equal votes and pay for women. She advocated early closing of the public houses and was disturbed by the effect drink had on family life. One must remember the kind of social life of the 1920's/1930's when many men on receiving their wage packet would head for the pub whilst the wife and children were waiting at home for the income to support the family. Because of the life style in the 1920's, drinking was one of the pleasures a workingman could still have, unfortunately some did not go home until all their money had gone. However, the wind of change was on the horizon as in April 1930 the Housing Act paved the way for slum clearance in cities, new houses would be built and new communities would be developed.

Her quote about the rights of women "We are not asking for superiority for we have always had that; all we ask is equality" still rings today with passion for it was a strong statement challenging the male members of Parliament. Civil servants past and present who were, in some instances, shamefully treated with contempt until her strong support changed the minds of the rigid bureaucrats, have never forgotten her campaign for equal rights and for equal pay in the 1920's in the Civil Service and the bill to reduce shop hours for women. In 1921 Lady Margaret Rhondda founded the Six Point Group with six very specific aims, the satisfactory legislation on child assault, the widowed mother, the unmarried mother and her child, equal rights of guardianship for married parents, equal pay for teachers and equal opportunities for men and women in the Civil Service and Nancy gave her support. Nancy seconded The Equal Guardianship Bill where mothers and fathers would have equal rights of custody of their children and furthered the cause in the Children (Provision of Footwear) Bill. Lady Astor, Margaret Bondfield and other women members introduced a Bill to provide boots for children in distressed areas. The Bill was unique in that it was the first all women's Bill to be brought to the House of Commons. Nancy was prominent in the Child Adoption Act 1926 which legalised and provided safeguards for child adoption.

Nancy drew attention in Parliament for the need for town planning and the removal of slums and to build better houses, the poor law was so outdated she harried to have it amended and also fought for pensions for widows with young children. The welfare of the Navy was always in her heart and she did much to get the Jerram Committee set up to deal with serious hardships then existing in the Navy. She constantly raised questions on lower deck matters in Parliament and persistently pressed for marriage allowances for Naval Officers, cost of living allowances on Foreign Service, and for the requests put forward by the various Service Organisations. She worked tirelessly to get the construction of cruisers at Devonport, the lengthening of the slip, and many improvements in the conditions in the Dockyard as well as in the three services. For all her working life and in retirement she gave the services her full support. She took a very strong line to support a progressive education policy for more secondary schools and more nursery schools and fought for better conditions of employment for teachers. Nancy was a great admirer of Lilian Parker the Social worker who later became well known in the sphere of prison reform and Nancy herself supported a reform of the penal system, working in close touch with the Howard League for Penal Reform and the National Society for Lunacy Reform. Nancy took a personal interest and visited the Borstal Institution for Girls in Aylesbury, Buckinghamshire, and was a member of the Holloway Discharged Prisoners Aid Society, which helped women prisoners.

Her loyalty to Plymouth and the deep affection she held for its population revealed itself in the practical gifts she and Lord Astor gave to the city. The playing field in South Devon Place (Astor Park) for organised games for elementary school children, by scholarship grants some still in existence, Virginia House (now closed) Astor Institute (now demolished) and the Mount Gould Housing Estate (sold in 1952). In London and Plymouth she spoke frequently about public health and urged authorities to set up maternity and child welfare clinics, improve hospitals and give additional help to the blind. Nancy took a great part in co-operation with the voluntary societies in considering amendments to safeguard the health services of maternity, tuberculosis, blind, mental deficiency and venereal diseases in the new Local Government Reform Bill. In Plymouth there was a development where one Health Authority was established whereas before there had been four separate practices. Lady Astor constantly challenged 'sweated conditions' in industry and she gave her support to Trade Boards because they protected the worker from exploitation, and urged an eight-hour working day. She worked hard toward the Factory Bill. Her practical interest in housing where she fought for slum clearance and decent homes for families resulted in the birth of the Mount Gould Housing Estate in Plymouth.

Being a Member of Parliament meant long hours and intense public relations; Nancy had hundreds of letters from her constituents containing questions on pension rights, coupled with letters of complaints and requests for help, which highlighted various concerns. She helped to pass the Act under which widows and children got pensions and support; the Equal Franchise where women got the vote on the same terms as men, Equal Pay for Equal Work. For many years women worked hard and had less pay than the men, the new act gave some measure of equality. The Guardianship of children to allow parents to have equal rights of custody, better provision for women who apply for maintenance was passed in 1925. The first all women's bill to be brought into the House of Commons was the bill to provide boots and shoes for children in poor areas. The Child Adoption Act in 1926 legalised and provided safeguards for child adoption. The unique 'At Home' informal meetings at her home to meet the ordinary people, setting up informal conferences and making her home a centre of hospitality for a large number of politicians, business people, literary guests and public men and women breached the gap between rigid rules in Parliament and comfortable liaison with ordinary citizens.

Since women have had political power, four times as many Bills were passed to better the conditions of women and children. This remember was in the 1920's. What could Nancy have achieved if she had had a Ministerial Post? Public morals were often debated and Nancy was the only woman Member on the Joint Committee of Lords and Commons to hear evidence about moral and sexual offences, and to decide on a Bill to deal with them. During all the months of this debate she was in constant touch with the women's societies and those with expert knowledge, thus armed with facts and figures were able effectively to cross-examine witnesses, and when the Committee finally drew up its Bill, apart from two of the clauses which Nancy opposed and were left out, was passed. Nancy was appointed a member of the Home Office Committee on Women Police and she introduced the Public Places (Order) Bill to amend the laws relating to street solicitation. Lady Astor supported the Government proposals under which cheaper electricity was provided; she was the only Conservative who voted against the Betting Tax. She took up the mantle to support the fishermen and advocated an insurance scheme whereby fishermen would get compensation for loss of gear and damaged nets caused by many ships sunk in the channel during World War One. As Member of Parliament she was consistently both in England and America promoting peace and friendship. She took an interest in the history of Plymouth and the influence that Lord and Lady Astor had in bringing interesting people to Plymouth was to put the City in the forefront of world news. In an interview with Constance Waller in London on 23rd February 1936 Lady Astor said: "These are the things in which I believe, I am a feminist, an absolute feminist, and I am growing more so. I think women are wonderful. The amount we have achieved in the fifteen years we have had the vote is almost unbelievable. Look at what has been done for children, for women, for housing in those years, do you realise that not many years ago a man had absolute control of his children, think of that. Look at the open air Nursery Schools we are starting, we are making children healthy, giving poor children from slum homes beauty and cleanliness, so that as they grow up they will demand beauty and cleanliness, that is how we will get rid of our

Photo courtesy of Westcountry Publications

Campaigning for votes, Lady Astor with residents from the Barbican Plymouth
They had a deep affection for her having won their respect

slums. We have had the age of consent raised, we have forced the Government to raise the school leaving age, children, children, children, and they are never out of our thoughts. I have always been passionately interested in children. When I was a girl I wanted to know about any child I saw, I have always felt like that way about children."

In July 1936 Nancy spoke strongly to the press about the League of Nation's future, she was disappointed at the temporary failure of some of the principles involved and shocked at the withdrawal of the United States. The League was formed on four principles that were; that it should be a league of great nations; that the world should be free for democracy; and that the world should be a disarmed and a Free Trade world. With the withdrawal of the United States it would be practically impossible to

Courtesy Sunday Independent and Westcountry Publications. Digital copy Trevor Burrows Plymouth Photographer

Lady Astor campaigning for votes in Plymouth 1923

impose sanctions. Instead of being a world free for democracies, Europe has become far more autocratic than it was before the First World War. Nancy insisted that the ideal is right, and sooner or later it is bound to prevail. The League of Nations appeared to be on the brink of failure and there was controversy between France and Italy, the two great powers then were England and France. England was accused of letting down the League but Nancy passionately denied this by saying, "I am disgusted with the form of people who are saying that England has let down the League. She has done nothing of the kind. Other nations which were supposed to have acted with us have not done so." Lady Astor said that this country ought to have some understanding with France that it would be no party to 'encircling Germany and have her caged like a wild animal in Europe' "if you do that, it means war." The Foreign Office and the Government's policy was flawed and Lady Astor said' "I think we have made some blundering mistakes, but nothing to what our opponents would have done had they been in office." Would that Plymouth had such passionate representation today for many ordinary people never see or speak to their Member of Parliament, and usually the only contact is an advertising leaflet put in the letterboxes of our homes just before elections are due. There are instances where members of the public have written to officials and MP's and have not had the courtesy of a reply. Nancy never failed anyone and she would not have approved the discourtesy to the people of Plymouth whom she adored, nourished their needs, and gave thousands of pounds to where it was needed. Effective campaigning required intelligent, consistent and committed action from well-informed individuals as well as wise stewardship of time and resources. Nancy used all these attributes to further her political manifesto, although not without her enemies she was, nevertheless, fearless in pursuit of her principles. When Nancy toured on her election campaigns people broke through the police cordon to shake her hand and threw flowers from windows as she passed in her carriage. She was indeed a most remarkable lady.

Photo by Dorothy Wilding London Photographer. Digital copy by Trevor Burrows Plymouth Photographer

A beautiful portrait of the Viscountess Astor in her Coronation regalia
Worn on Coronation day 12th May 1937 at the Coronation
Of King George V1 and Queen Elizabeth at Westminster Abbey

Lady Astor electioneering in her beloved city of Plymouth circa 1930s
A reporter takes notes for a press report

CHAPTER THREE
WALDORF VISCOUNT ASTOR (1879-1952)

"Much of what I have been able to do here in Plymouth is due to the stimulus and to the suggestion of my wife. Freedom is the greatest heritage of man!"
(Quote by Waldorf Astor from his speech when awarded the Freedom of the City July 1936)

The Astors were originally Spaniards and their name then was Astorga but early in the eighteenth century they emigrated to Germany, where they dropped the final 'ga' and became Astor. John Jacob Astor (born Johann Jakob or Johann Jacob Astor) (1763-1848) was the first prominent member of the Astor family and the first multi-millionaire in the United States. He was the creator of the first trust in America. The Astor fortune began when Johann Jakob Astor with two of his brothers emigrated to America from the little German town Walldorf near Heidelburg in 1783. The Astors founded a settlement called Astoria on the Pacific coast and they became successful fur traders. Jakob Astor expanded his business to owning a fleet of a dozen merchant vessels to transport his furs to the Far East and Europe. He wisely invested in real estate, and died as the richest man in America in 1848 and the Astor family were to become multi-millionaires. They owned part of 5th Avenue, New York, and huge hotels like the Waldorf-Astoria and the Ritz-Carlton. The New York hotel Astor House that was opened in 1836 was for a time the finest hotel in New York City. John Jacob Astor built the luxurious Greek Revival style hotel designed by Isaiah Rogers. 'Meet me at the Astor' was to become the by-word of the well to do New Yorkers when they visited the luxury hotel. It was originally called the Park hotel with 309 rooms in six stories with gaslight, bathing and toilet facilities on each floor. The American public hailed the 'Astor House' hotel in Manhatten Island as a 'Marvel of the age,' it was to last for eighty years until it closed in 1913. The succeeding generations of the Astor family carried on investing in real estate and enhanced their fortune. John Jacob Astor's great grandson William Waldorf Astor left America disillusioned with his failure to succeed in Politics and came to England bringing his fortune of £34 million pounds with him.

One of the striking features of American mass popular culture is the widespread fascination with the British royal family. A foretaste of this phenomenon occurred in the winter of 1860, when the first member of the British royal family ever to visit the United States, Albert Edward, Prince of Wales (later King Edward VII, 1841-1910), created a sensation in New York City. About 300,000 people, one half of the city's population at that time turned out to see the prince ride through town; so many members of the city's high society gate crashed a ball given in his honour on October 12, 1860, that the dance floor collapsed.

The Astor wealth did not protect them from family tragedy as proven in the loss of a son John Jacob Astor 1V born in Rhinebeck, New York (1864-1912), coheir and first cousin to William Waldorf Astor. John Jacob Astor was the only son of William Backhouse Astor (Junior) (1830-1892) and Caroline Webster Schermerhorn (1830-1908). She was from a Dutch Aristocratic family and was known as America's 'The Mrs Astor' because of her expensive social parties. In the year 2007 the Newport Rhode Island USA mansion that was the 20th century summer house of the Astor family was being put up for sale for £8million. The estate agents claim that Cole Porter wrote one of his most famous songs, Night and Day, while staying there in the 1930's. The thirty-nine roomed Beechwood mansion lies in five acres of land and has spectacular ocean views. Situated on Newport's famous Bellevue Avenue it was the former home of the then newly weds in 1851 of Caroline Webster Schermerhorn and William Backhouse Astor who went on to entertain four hundred socially prominent people of their day. The summer home was one of many from Manhattan USA to Paris, France. The home continues today as the only living museum operated by the Beechwood Theatre Company which portrays members of the Astor Family.

John Jacob Astor 1V (1864-1912) known as 'The Colonel' a title obtained from America's war with Spain in 1898-1899, was commissioned as a Lieutenant Colonel in the United States Volunteers. He was forty-seven years old when he died and one of the richest men in New York. He perished in the sinking of the Titanic on the 14th & 15th April 1912 in the North Atlantic. He had been travelling first class, after boarding the vessel at Cherbourg and presented with ticket number 17757 after paying £247.10s. 6d for the fare, and was placed in State Room A56 on board the ship with his nineteen-year-old second wife who was then five months pregnant; he had made sure she had been put into a lifeboat. His badly crushed body (number 124) was recovered from the sea a week later on the 22nd April 1912 by the passing cable ship steamer the Mackay Bennett, his body was still floating erect in his life belt and in his jacket was his gold watch and nearly 2,500 dollars. His body was taken to Halifax and then on to the Astor Estate at Ferncliff, located in the Hudson Valley of Rhinebeck, New York. On the 1st May 1912 a funeral service was held at the Episcopal Church of the Messiah where he had been a serving warden for sixteen years. He was buried at Trinity Cemetery, New York. His cousin William Waldorf Astor made no remark about his death; and he did not attend the funeral. The cousins had inherited the family feud from their former relations. The loss of human life on the Titanic was dreadful and many heart broken families were to lose loved ones, many pets were also lost in the sinking and the Astor family pet, their precious Airedale terrier dog Kitty also perished. When it became evident that the ship was sinking some men released the dogs from their kennels to give them a chance to survive, however many perished and only five were rescued, some small dogs made it to the lifeboats. One dog however had a remarkable survival experience and was responsible for some survivors being picked up by the Carpathia who had sailed to the aid of the Titanic and that was a black Newfoundland dog called Rigel who had belonged to the first officer who perished in the sinking. Rigel had been swimming in the icy sea for three hours when the rescue ship arrived; thankfully he was still strong enough to bark. The Carpathia, anxious to rescue as many people as possible, did not see the lifeboat nearest to them. The boat was in danger of being run down by the oncoming ship, the survivors were too weak to shout, but Rigel barked furiously and Captain Rostron of the Carpathia ordered the ship to stop. Swimming in front of the lifeboat Rigel led the survivors to the gangway. The dog was brought aboard the ship and a sailor Jonas Briggs from the crew adopted the dog for the rest of its natural life. The ship's cat Jenny did not sail on the doomed Titanic and escaped drowning when the ship sank as she had had a litter of kittens and had been landed at the port of Southampton before Titanic sailed into the North Atlantic, which saved her life.

The two Astor cousins had been in business together when in 1897; John Jacob Astor built the Astoria hotel New York, adjoining the Waldorf hotel, which had been built by his first cousin William Waldorf Astor. The new complex became known as the Waldorf Astoria hotel on the west side of Fifth Avenue, New York. William Waldorf Astor inherited his father's assets in 1892 estimated at $300 million thus becoming the richest man in America. He chose to enter politics and public life. He was fluent in languages, particularly German, Italian and French; he was a financier and journalist, and he became owner of the Pall Mall Gazette and the Pall Mall Magazine. It was acknowledged that he was an intelligent man and he had a passion for art and history. The great-grandson of John Jacob Astor III (1822-1890) and Charlotte Augusta Gibbes (1825-1887) was born in New York and was educated privately in Europe. He married Mary Dahlgren Paul in 1878 and had five children, of which two died in childhood. He had stood for election to the New York State Legislature as a

Republican; he became a state Senator and served from 1878-1881 and as United States minister to Italy (1882-1885). He was unsuccessful in reaching the House of Representatives. In 1890 he emigrated to England, becoming a British subject in 1899.

Photo from a private collection. Copy taken by Trevor Burrows photographer Plymouth

Lord and Lady Astor with two of their children (circa 1920s)

When he arrived in England his first priority was finding a home. At first William rented Lansdowne House in London, later he rented the country estate of Cliveden before finally purchasing Cliveden-on-Thames in Taplow, Buckinghamshire (because of boundary changes now known as Upper Thames Valley, Berkshire) from Hugh Lupus Grosvenor, 1st Duke of Westminster at a cost of one and a quarter million dollars in 1893. The original Cliveden House had been built in 1666 by the Duke of Buckingham. Waldorf senior gave the house and the estate to his eldest son Waldorf in 1905 with several millions of pounds to maintain their lifestyle and enhance the building on his impending marriage to Nancy Langhorne as a wedding present. Cliveden, overlooking the Thames above Windsor and Maidenhead, was designed by Charles Barry and built in 1850 in the Italianate style; the original owner was the Duke of Sutherland. William was named a peer of the Realm in King George's V honours list New Years Day in 1916, two weeks later in his robes, as Baron Astor of Hever Castle, he made a twenty-minute appearance in the House of Lords, and William was created a Viscount in 1917. Being a member of the peerage meant that he was entitled to a Heraldic peerage flag and motto. He chose the motto 'Ad Astra' and had the emblem of a falcon surmounted by an eagle, with three stars and flanked by two standing figures, an American Indian and a Fur Trapper. He became part of Edward, Prince of Wales circle of friends. William's grandson Gavin Astor faced with crippling death duties sold Hever Castle in 1982. It was divided into separate lots and sold by auction. Waldorf William Astor the first Viscount has given his name (it is thought) to a now known salad concoction called the Waldorf Salad comprising celery, nuts and sliced apples with a mayonnaise coating. Waldorf wanted nuts with his salad. However, there is a conflict of opinion as to who did invent the famous salad concoction. History also points to Oscar Tschirky the Maître D'hôtel of the New York Waldorf Astoria hotel in 1893 as being responsible for its creation.

The first Viscount bought the Sancy (also known as Sanci) diamond in 1892. It was a fiery stone of Indian origin that is shaped like a peach pit and weighed 55 carats. Fourteen years later he gave it to Nancy his future daughter-in-law as a personal wedding gift. The beautiful Sanci diamond is steeped in myth. Diamond derives its name from the Greek word 'Adamas' which means 'invincible' also it is the derivation from middle English 'diamaunt' and from old French 'diamant.' The precious stone is considered as the anniversary gemstone for the thirtieth and sixtieth year of marriage, some say it has a mystical power offering faith, joy, repentance, life, purity and innocence. The history of the Astor diamond formerly owned by Waldorf Astor first Viscount is reputed to be from the fourteenth century when it belonged to Charles the Bold of Burgundy who lost it in battle in 1477. Its history from then on is thought to have been from Constantinople (now Istanbul) when it was purchased by Nicholas Harlay De Sancy (Baron de Sanci) about 1570 from whom it took its name; he was the French Ambassador to Turkey in the late 16th Century, other historians say that the stone was named after a former owner Seigneur de Sancy. In 1596 he sold the stone to King James 1 of England and in 1635 it was in the hands of

Charles 1, later the stone was the prized possession of Cardinal Jules Mazirin who bequeathed the Sancy to the French Crown. It re-appeared many years later among the French Crown Jewels. It was lent to the French Kings Henry 111 and Henry 1V, later it was purchased by Queen Elizabeth of England and in turn it descended to the Stuarts. The stone disappeared in the Crown Jewel Robbery during the French Revolution in 1782, five years after the Revolution the stone found its way to a Spanish Nobleman and eventually in 1828 to Prince Nickolas Demidoff, whose family owned industries and silver mines in Russia. In 1978 the fourth Viscount Astor sold the Sancy diamond to the Bank of France for $1 million and today it is displayed alongside the Regent Diamond in the Louvre in Paris.

Waldorf Astor, son and handsome young heir to one of the world's richest men was born on the 19th May 1879. In 1890 Waldorf came to England at the age of eleven with his family, as a young man he attended Eton College, Berkshire, and then New College at Oxford University where he obtained a degree in history and was made a Master of Arts. The young Waldorf married Nancy Langhorne in 1906 and there is no doubt that his immense wealth was a factor she took into consideration. Tall and good-looking, at evening parties wearing an old-fashioned white tie tucked under his collar and a square-cut, high white waistcoat, he seemed to belong to a long departed Edwardian world. Yet he was a very intelligent man. Waldorf was madly in love with Nancy and she loved him enough to make a go of the marriage. Waldorf was the eldest son of the first Viscount Astor and Mary Dahlgren Paul. Waldorf and Nancy had five children between 1906 and 1919. William (Bill) Waldorf Astor (1907-1966) who later became the 3rd Viscount, Nancy Phyllis Louise Astor (nick-named Wiss or Wissie) In 1933 she married James, Lord Willoughby de Eresby, who succeeded his father the 2nd Earl of Ancaster in 1951, Phyllis became Countess of Ancaster (1909-1975) The Hon, Francis David Langhorne Astor, newspaper publisher (1912-2001) (he was a great friend of George Orwell) Michael Langhorne Astor (1916-1980) became Member of Parliament for Surrey (Eastern 1945-1951) and John Jacob Astor (Jakie) (1919-2000) Major the Hon Jakie Astor, was Commander of the Phantom 'J' squadron during the Second World War and his brother Michael Astor was also an officer in this squadron. John Jacob Astor joined the Life Guards during the war but transferred to the Phantom Regiment and later to the SAS. He had a supporting role in the 1942 commando raid on Dieppe and ended the war with the rank of Major and was awarded the MBE, a Legion d' Honneur and the Croix de Guerre. He received a Knighthood in 1978 for contributions to agriculture. Sir John died at the age of 82 years in the year 2000 after suffering from Parkinson Disease.

Nancy's oldest son was Robert Gould Shaw (1898-1970) from her first marriage. The present 4th Viscount had this to say: "Bobby (his nickname) was always very close to Nancy and was often better able to deal with her than any other of her children. He was a great character with a wit similar to Nancy's, and we, as children all loved him.

It was extraordinary that Nancy, daughter of a confederate Colonel, should marry first Gould Shaw son of the Union Colonel who commanded the first black regiment in what Nancy always called 'The war between the States.' After her marriage to Waldorf, he and Nancy provided for Bobbie throughout his life. William Waldorf senior's younger son John Jacob V (born 1886) succeeded to the ownership of Hever Castle, Kent, in 1918, having completed a distinguished service in the Life Guards during the First World War in which he was badly wounded. In 1956 he was granted a peerage as first Baron Astor of Hever and the two titles remain in the family today. Hever is classified as a Grade 1 listed building and it is treasured as part of Britain's Heritage.

The Astors in their own home 3, Elliot Terrace Plymouth certainly lived near to some famous people, as in the 1900s next door to them was Joe Kennedy, President Kennedy's father, and at number five Elliot Terrace Captain Anderton of the famed Anderton and Rowlands Funfairs, he too was a very wealthy man and the family owned countless yachts and Rolls-Royces. Well educated and with a friendly social commitment they threw fabulous parties which suited the Astors. So began the love affair between the Astors and Plymouth, and they quickly settled and soon became friends with Mr Shirley Benn (later Sir Arthur Shirley Benn) (1858-1937) (created 1st Baron Glenravel 1936) Conservative Member of Parliament for Plymouth Drake. He and Waldorf together formed a political partnership. It was quite unique for representatives of the House of Commons and the House of Lords to live in the same area as their constituents. The United Kingdom Parliament constituency was created for the 1918 General Election; Waldorf had come to Plymouth as a Unionist Parliamentary Candidate and had been successful in the second of the General Elections of 1910. Nancy Astor in her political canvassing in 1910 to help her husband Waldorf obtain the Plymouth seat for Parliament, knocked on nearly thirty thousand doors. Ill health did not allow Waldorf to enter the services in the First World War although he was a member of Queen Victoria's Household Calvary. He became an Inspector of Ordnance Factories and in 1917 he held the post as Parliamentary Secretary to Liberal Welsh speaking David Lloyd George (1963-1945) Lloyd George was a firm nonconformist and Prime Minister of Britain from 1916-1922. Waldorf, Viscount Astor, also became a member of the Cabinet Intelligence Branch, Chairman of the Unionist Committee for Social Reform, and had been one of the munificent founders of the Royal Institute of International Affairs in the 1920s and was also a founder member of the Round Table. Waldorf was a quiet, brilliant man overshadowed by the peerage and Nancy, however, he was a firm man with a mind of his own, aside from his money his capabilities in writing Nancy's speeches and his love of the Plymouth people kept him fully employed. He cared so much for the people and always put them first, whilst Nancy was the star of the show Waldorf was the splendid background scenery, yet neither would have been so successful without the other.

Nancy Astor became one of the leading hostesses of England, making devoted friends and she gained a practical knowledge of English politics and learnt how to speak in public. The Astors could command respect from many notable people but the politicians kept them out of the seats of power. Waldorf Astor (Conservative) was again successful in regaining his seat in 1918 but following the death of his father Viscount Astor he was forced to surrender his seat in the Commons. In the resulting by-election, his wife Nancy agreed to stand and in 1919 became Member of Parliament for Plymouth Sutton Division. Waldorf challenged the rules hoping to have them changed to allow him to stay in the Commons, he did not want the title of Viscount and his desire was to be involved with political issues. His loss was Plymouth's gain because we were blessed with a great man who helped to change the lives of so many people. It was not until 1963 that renunciation of Peerages became

Photo from a private collection. Digital copy Trevor Burrows Plymouth Photographer

Waldorf Astor circa 1906

possible far too late for Waldforf who died in 1952. With elevation to the House of Lords Waldorf lost the possibility of a brilliant political career. He was an astute Member of Parliament, unassuming but totally committed to his political beliefs, as it was; his Public service to the people throughout the years took a dreadful toll on his health. In March 2007 the Members of Parliament in the House of Commons carried a vote by 337 votes for, to 224 votes against, recommending that every member of the House of Lords should be elected to qualify to sit in chambers; this unique development had taken ninety-eight years to attain.

One must contemplate what happens next in the long promised reform of the second chamber. How ironic that Lord Astor was already an elected Member yet had to give up his political representation and take his seat in the House of Lords. Waldorf succeeded his father William Waldorf Astor as the second Viscount Astor and entered the House of Lords in 1919. Nancy was indeed fortunate that she had married a selfless husband who sacrificed his own political career to be her guiding light. Plymouth Parliamentary boundaries in the 1920's were named West, Central, and East. Waldorf and Mr Shirley Benn campaigned for them to be changed to Devonport, Drake and Sutton; Sutton division was made up of the working class population. By 1947 the Drake Constituency was eliminated by Parliament. Plymouth in the year 2003 due to its expansion involved amalgamation of various additional neighbourhoods, which meant boundary lines becoming outdated. The Boundary Commission for England announced in 2004 in its review of the Parliamentary constituencies for Devon, Plymouth and Torbay and recommended the creation of two new (revised) seats for the City, whereby Plymouth South is now to be known as 'Plymouth Sutton and Devonport' and Plymouth North will henceforth be known as 'Plymouth Moor View.' The Plymouth Sutton and Devonport constituency covers the Compton, Peverell, Efford and Lipson, Sutton and Mount Gould, St Peter and the Waterfront, Drake, Stoke and Devonport Wards.

Waldorf had excelled at Oxford and it was whilst rowing at Oxford that he strained his heart and this was to affect his health for the rest of his life. His venture into journalism resulted in becoming owner of the newspaper The Observer in 1919; he also had interests in the Pall Mall Gazette newspaper, and by 1921 he owned the Sunday Western Independent. Waldorf continued serving in the government. His posts were, as parliamentary secretary to the Local Government Board from January 1919 to June 1919, and parliamentary secretary to the Ministry of Health June 1919 to April 1921, he had been very active in its creation in 1919. Waldorf had been a staunch supporter of the Coalition Government established by David Lloyd George in the first World War, in January 1917 he was appointed as the Prime Minister's parliamentary secretary, in July 1918 Waldorf became parliamentary secretary to the Ministry of Food. In 1921 Waldorf's health was again a worry as he was diagnosed with sciatica, which nearly crippled him and on advice from his doctors toured North

Africa where the dry weather perhaps would help him to recover. As it was not as successful as was hoped he returned to England and turned to Christian Science with the help of Nancy who was devoted to the Christian Science belief.

At the age of 26 Waldorf was diagnosed with tuberculosis and his health was becoming a real concern to his family and friends. Waldorf had the makings of a brilliant political career and it must have been frustrating for him as his health hampered his ambitions. In New York, America, April 1922, Lord Astor in a speech introduced himself as "The Husband of Lady Astor" proving that he had quite a sense of humour. In the 1920's Waldorf bought the Island of Jura in the Hebrides, Scotland, as a holiday retreat where his family and friends could stay; he had a sporting lodge on the Island. On the 24th August 1941 Nancy and Waldorf, tired and exhausted from their heavy workload and lack of rest from the bombing, decided to take a well-earned rest and went to the Island for a ten-day quiet holiday. Waldorf had become concerned as Nancy's dominating personality had upset a few critics who advocated that she gave up politics and concentrated on social service activities, in retrospect this was really her forte as her brash talk sometimes lacked sensitive feelings and her family thought that perhaps she had too much power. Gentle diplomacy was not one of Nancy's attributes; a holiday break would ease the wall of aggression. One famous writer later stayed at the Island of Jura as a guest of David Astor. He was George Orwell the Socialist writer, known as Eric Blair to the local people and he and David Astor became firm friends and whilst on the Island George wrote the book titled 1984 which was published in 1949.

Waldorf became an honorary Colonel in 1929 in the service of the Devon Heavy Brigade. Another post held by Waldorf was Chairman of the Royal Institute of International Affairs (1935-1949) He served as a Governor of Guys Hospital and was involved with the Peabody Trust; he was also the longest serving Lord Mayor of Plymouth from 1939-1944. A week before Christmas in 1937 Waldorf was again taken ill with a chest complaint; he and Nancy sailed to Florida, USA, where it was hoped the sun would be good for him. Nancy did not want to go because it would mean missing all the Christmas parties at Cliveden, the family party, the children's party and the staff party. The parties at Cliveden were very special as everyone dressed up as well-known characters and the staff party given every year would not be the same, the Astors took great care of their staff and most were looked after like family. After recuperation Waldorf and Nancy returned to England in February 1938. Ill health was to blight his life throughout the years yet he worked hard devoting himself to public service; he was taken ill again in 1938 and in extreme pain with gallstones. In June 1943 Waldorf, again unwell, spent time at his summer home at Jura while Nancy stayed in Plymouth, and after a few weeks rest Waldorf was able to continue again with his heavy workload.

King George V in October 1928 decreed the raising of Plymouth town to the status of City and in May 1935 His Majesty granted the Lord Mayor status to Plymouth as a Jubilee Gift with the active help of the Prince of Wales who was Lord High Steward of Plymouth. Lord and Lady Astor and the Plymouth Fathers were grateful, as without the Prince of Wales's help, Plymouth may have failed to achieve the honour. In 1935 the Astor family were to prove staunch political members in Parliament as six of the Astor family represented their constituents in the House of Commons and the House of Lords under the Stanley Baldwin premiership. Waldorf in the House of Lords and in the Commons Lady Astor, also her son William Waldorf Astor (known as Bill) Conservative member for East Fulham, later to be 3rd Viscount Astor, Nancy's brother-in-law Major Hon John Jacob Astor (promoted to Lieutenant Colonel) Conservative member for Dover, later became 1st Baron of Hever, and her son-in-law Gilbert Heathcote-Drummond-Willoughby (1907-1983) 3rd Earl of Ancaster known as Lord Willoughby de Eresby Conservative member for Rutland and Stamford, and her nephew Arthur Ronald Lambert Field Tree Conservative member for the Borough of Harborough. There is no question that the Astor family had a large influence on politics of the day. Lady Astor's representation of the Sutton Division had continued in spite of challenges at seven general elections, Lord and Lady Astor had held together a remarkable record of twenty-five years of unbroken parliamentary services. During sixteen years (from 1919) Plymouth had been in the fortunate position of having representatives in both the House of Lords and the House of Commons. Vote for Astor and you got two Members of Parliament.

On 18th May 1935 a banquet was held at the Plymouth Guildhall to celebrate the bestowal of Lord Mayoralty upon the City. The Right Honourable, The Viscount Astor was officially awarded the Freedom of the City by Plymouth on the 3rd July 1936, the highest honour which Plymouth Corporation can confer upon an individual, it is jealously guarded and is given only when the Council and the people generally are satisfied that the recipient has, in the words of resolutions, rendered distinguished services to the state and to our city. This indeed was a wonderful tribute to a man so well respected. For this very special ceremony Lady Astor and her daughter Lady Willoughby de Eresby attended with other members of the Astor family, they flew from London to attend; all three political parties were in attendance. It was wonderful to note that also in attendance was the doyenne of Clovelly Court Christine Hamlyn even though she was in her eightieth year. When Lord Astor signed the Roll he declared, "that during the thirty years I have been associated with Plymouth I have had three lines of contact, to help in civic life, National Political Work and Private Social Work. Those of you who know us will not be surprised when I tell you that much of what I have been able to do here in Plymouth is due to the stimulus and to the suggestion of my wife. Freedom is the greatest heritage of man!"

When Lord Astor was elected as Lord Mayor on 9th November 1939 at the Guildhall he appointed Alderman W.J.Waldron Modley and his wife as Deputy Lord Mayor and Lady Mayoress. With the declaration of war all politics as far as Municipal Government was concerned was relegated to the background and all three parties,

Conservative, Labour and Liberal agreed and for the first time unity between all members allowed for a cohesive and successful period of stability. Lord Astor's leadership during the Second World War was at its most efficient and one of the many things he did for Plymouth was the giving of the former house called Manor House as it was known as in the 1860s later to be called Manor Lodge and eventually renamed the Astor Hall. Lord Astor gave the University Hall of Residence before a University was practical politics; the Hall of Residence was established in Astor Hall, Devonport Road, Stoke. After the war Astor Hall became the home for the Scattered Homes Children who had returned from Clovelly, later when children's homes were finally closed and children were being fostered or adopted under new legislation it became a home for the disabled people but due to financial expediency in the year 2007 it is shortly to be closed and another property given by the Astors will disappear into oblivion.

Lord Astor's quiet manner and gentleness was lined with steel and he studied in detail whatever he did in the field of public life. When he was made to step down as Lord Mayor of Plymouth in 1944 a man with important international contacts and influence at Whitehall was lost to the City, many City Aldermen tried to retain him on the Council, one or two even offered to step down themselves to allow him to continue, his term of office had been very unique in that normally each political party nominated members to take turn as Lord Mayor, it has to be recognised that Lord Astor (and Nancy Astor) were not elected members of the Council. With his removal from the post Waldorf's expertise was lost to the City Fathers and it also meant that many Astor family links with Plymouth were lost forever, with the exception of Astor relations who serve as trust or committee members, or on occasion visit the city, they meet representatives of local government and perhaps the serving Lord Mayor and a close circle of friends, but spend little time with the ordinary every day working folk and are reluctant to respond to letters from members of the public. Lord and Lady Astor always honoured these everyday courtesies and they would be disappointed at the lack of friendly communication with the ordinary Plymouth citizens because Nancy and Waldorf acknowledged every letter and every request made to them.

The Lord Mayor's Services Welfare Fund and the Air Raid Relief Fund inaugurated by Lord Astor when he first became Lord Mayor in November 1939 and the wonderful Women's Voluntary Services ensured that all Colonial and Dominion servicemen and women and all bombed out citizens were well cared for while they were in Plymouth during the war years. The first Secretary given the formidable task of taking care of the funds was the Manager of the Midland Bank Mr Arthur Brunyee. The Fund was well organised and publicized and the response of the public was such that there was throughout the war a steady stream of money flowing into the Fund. Lord Astor had appealed for an assured income, firms and staff paid weekly or monthly subscriptions; staff would have agreed amounts deducted from their wage packets, perhaps sixpence a week from the worker seemed a small deduction but with all workers subscribing the Fund swelled. With hospitals being damaged, material and equipment being lost the normal voluntary funds could not cover the cost of replacement and repair. Extra efforts were made to enhance the much needed funds by collection boxes set up in churches, public houses, Sunday school collections. Children responded by collecting silver paper, tinfoil, waste paper and the guides and scouts collected from all areas. Every one helped out where they could even turning out to clear up the broken glass, the rubble and the dirt after every air raid. The American people were generous in helping where they could, one gentleman named Mr A Samuels living in Michigan Avenue, Chicago, sent the sum of twenty-five pounds to help those in distress. Plymouth firms and every day citizens organised raffles, card games, and jumble sales to support the much-needed fund. One can but admire the unity of the Plymouth citizens and the City Fathers who struggled to maintain a devastated war torn city population in those highly dangerous years. The Welfare Fund was used in many ways; one large donation was given to the British Red Cross in order to ensure that parcels would be sent regularly to Plymouth Prisoners of War. Canteens, Hostels, and Clubs were financed by the fund for the benefit of service men and women. A separate fund was allocated for the Air Raid Relief Fund; the money came from many sources and from all parts of the world. The forty daughter towns of Plymouth throughout the world gave practical sympathy gifts in money or kind to mother Plymouth. The gifts were used to help bombed out families and to relieve distress and to ensure people were clothed and fed. Waldorf's scheme had come as a blessing to the war torn citizens and one has to admire his forethought in setting up the Welfare Fund. The wonderful support given to those in need of help by the Guild of Social Service must not be forgotten; they worked in close liaison with the Lord Mayor's welfare fund. Waldorf himself was generous and every year up until his death in 1952 he gave an annual subscription of fifty pounds to the Guild of Social Service. Waldorf was personally a very generous man, when he found out that Nancy's Party Agent Mr Jim Mallett was bombed out from his undertaker business, he was determined to help him. Mr Mallett was most distressed, as the only thing he was able to save from his home was his black cat and from his garage his bowler hat. Waldorf had been thinking of changing his Daimler car but responded at once to a suggestion by Nancy that it be given to Mr Mallett so that he could restart his business, a grateful Mr Mallett never forgot that kind act. Nancy ensured that he had food by ordering a chicken from Churchill's the Fishmonger, and it was duly delivered.

Waldorf Astor founded the Cliveden Stud he had started with hunters in 1900 but turned to runners in 1905, he loved his horses and the first three he purchased were thoroughbred quality mares, Maid of the Mist, Popinjay and Conjure, which became the foundation of his superb stud and which he purchased from Lord Rosebery in 1905. It became one of the most famous studs in England. From these horses came the future winners, Conjure bred five winners, horses with names linked with Plymouth as well as family chosen names such as, Winkipop, Concertina and her offsprings, Short Story and Pennycomequick, other horses were Mannamead, High Stakes, Court Martial and Ambiguity, Saucy Sue, Pay Up and Crag An Eran. Lord Astor's colours were light blue, with pink sash and pink cap. His magnificent animals won four hundred and sixty races between 1907-1950; wins included classic races such as The Oaks, the winner in May 1925 was Saucy Sue and his other horse Miss Gadabout was second, One Thousand Guineas, Two Thousand Guineas and the Saint Ledger, his horse St Germans won the Coronation Cup at Epson in 1925. Waldorf's horses came second in the Derby five times; his horse Buchen lost the race by a neck in 1919 which was a great disappointment, as it had been his wish to win the Derby, although he had many winners he never won that particular race. In June 1936 he had two winners at Ascot, Rhodes Scholar, (who beat Mahmoud the Derby winner) in the St James's Palace (one mile) and his other success was gained with Early School, one of the best youngsters in the Coventry stakes, distance five furlongs.

There were occasions when Nancy had special lunches or dinners at Cliveden that Waldorf, not wanting to be engaged in tittle-tattle with certain guests, would leave the dining table and escape to his favourite room upstairs and leave the ladies to chatter away whilst he would become engrossed in his world of horses. The room was affectionately known as the 'Munnings Room' where he could relax with the pictures and portraits of horses that had been painted by Sir Alfred J. Munnings (1879-1959) who later became President of the Royal Academy. In his early life Munnings painted pictures of East Anglian landscape and rural life including cattle and horses. He received his first commission in 1919 for an equestrian portrait and from then he went on to paint many famous racehorses, it made him the outstanding animal painter of his day and Waldorf's room was adorned with his paintings.

Waldorf's wealth did not deter him from giving a loving and supporting role to his beloved wife Nancy when she became Member of Parliament. The saying 'Behind every great man there is a woman' in this instance was to be reversed as Waldorf was to be her guiding star in almost everything she did throughout her life; his devotion to Nancy was complete. Waldorf was a kind man and highly respected; as well as good-looking, he and Nancy were complete opposites, he was intensely courteous and had personal charm, he was also a shy person, quiet and reserved, it was known that he also had a great sense of humour, he had wonderful patience and was most fastidious. Nancy, however, was quite the energetic extrovert. It is clear that Nancy would never have been the success she was without Waldorf; he was her strength and advisor, his love for her was passionate and their love was forged in unity and togetherness. He was, too, a very generous man, there was one occasion when he wanted to buy a particular horse, which was priced at one thousand guineas, and he had set his heart on buying the animal. However, that day he picked up the local paper and read that a rescue home for girls would have to close for lack of the sum of one thousand pounds. Waldorf did not hesitate he immediately sent the cheque of one thousand pounds to save the home, the young Lord Astor had shown he was a caring man for the community. Waldorf also looked after distant relatives of Nancy in Virginia who were considered poor; he paid the school fees for the children of other relatives who were poor in Virginia.

Waldorf always took a great interest in what Nancy was doing but on one occasion he was most concerned for her safety, as she loved fast driving and riding. One of her joys was riding pillion on RAF Aircraftman Shaw's motorbike. Known formerly as an Army Colonel and as Aircraftman Shaw (Lawrence of Arabia) he and Nancy became good friends, it was a unique friendship and she would often go on long distance bike rides with him, he liked it because Nancy could keep her balance without touching him, Waldorf was not too happy about the joy rides, and suggested that it would be best to stop. Her last ride with Lawrence was ironically two weeks before his fatal accident in 1935; he died on her 56th birthday 19th May 1935. Nancy was most distressed at his loss, she attended the funeral and the nation had lost a brilliant desert strategist. Viscount Astor's ill health meant that he was prevented from serving in the armed forces during the Second World War. On occasion there was criticism of Waldorf, first being accused of being part of the mythical 'Cliveden Set' and also because sometimes he was missing from Plymouth city, his health played a large part in those times he was absent. It has to be considered that the Astors as recognised leaders were under great strain and national security members would constantly issue instructions that had to be obeyed which on occasion involved moving to a quieter area until the immediate danger had passed. Those who knew him saw him as too much a family man to be coupled with fascism and knew his national pride of living in England, sensible people cast the doubt aside but there is always someone ready to think ill and condemn a person on a whim or a chance remark. During the war when taken ill with a very high fever Lord Astor had to be evacuated to Bray House, Rock, in Cornwall for six weeks, later he moved to Bickham on Dartmoor, until his recovery, occasionally he would rest at a Farm in South Brent. In the event of real danger, the Astors, as they were on Hitler's death list, would be moved to Treverbyn Vean Manor at Twowatersfoot, near Liskeard, Cornwall for security. The Manor house is now a Grade 11 listed Neo-Gothic building of great architectural and historic importance, located high above the beautiful Glynn Valley close to the Loveny and Fowey rivers. In the 1930's and 1940's the Manor house was owned by Lord Beaverbrook (1879-1964) and was used extensively during the Second World War for secret meetings.

The influence that Lord Astor was able to bring to bear in very important quarters will never be fully known among the ordinary public, he gave his all for Plymouth and without doubt his work rate affected his health. Waldorf ensured that Nissan huts for the YMCA were built during the war years for the servicemen; he considered their welfare as paramount. The Town Clerk Mr Colin Campbell (later to be known as Sir Colin Campbell) also worked extremely hard for the City of Plymouth. Waldorf Astor was a man of vision for it was he, when as Lord Mayor of Plymouth in 1941 after the savage bombing, invited Professor Sir Patrick Abercrombie (1872-1957) one of Britain's best-known town planners and James Paton Watson the City Engineer and Surveyor to oversee the design of Plymouth to plan its rebuild as a City of the future. Although started it was never completely fulfilled. Plymouth was the first city in the country to present its post-war plan for rebuilding the city centre. Waldorf lobbied Whitehall for a larger national grant for the city, local government funding was allocated on the total of their income from the rates and since the rates were levied on habitable properties Plymouth was being unnecessarily punished by the government for the extent of its suffering in the blitz. In 1944 the city was receiving only a quarter of the total income from the rates before the war. Lord Astor pleaded to the government for more help, but the politicians nationally and locally had their eyes on the spoils of peace. Just after the war Lord Astor could be seen driving in an old Austin Seven car around London visiting newspaper editors to ensure press coverage of The Plan for Plymouth.

There was a deep disquiet at the treatment Waldorf Astor received from the local politicians in 1944 as Frank Wintle pointed out in his book The Plymouth Blitz. Waldorf seems to have been a straightforward victim of political manipulation and the tale of his treatment in the closing months of the war is a narrative of exceptional shabbiness. The local authority was working towards the establishment of its Reconstruction Committee. The political parties had their plans for power dovetailed between the pages of their plans for Plymouth. The Reconstruction Committee met on 18th July 1944, in Camera. Shortly after the doors opened, reporters were rushing back to base with the story that a stunned city would read under the headline: Lord Astor Declines to Serve. It was an unnecessary euphemism. Lord Astor had been boxed into a corner. The Chairmanship of the Committee, which he had hoped to get, was never within reach. Later Lord Astor issued a statement, upon which the political parties declined to comment, the statement gave a bitter timetable of his ejection from the Committee.

In April 1944 Sir Clifford Tozer, leader of the majority Conservative group, together with the Labour leader Alderman Churchward and in liaison with other influential councillors, had approached Lord Astor and asked him to submit a proposal for an all party reconstruction committee. Each of the three main parties would nominate two members. Each political party on a municipal or county council has an organisation that is known as a 'caucus.' The caucus convenes secretly before each council meeting, peruses the agenda, and determines which way the party will vote en masse on crucial issues. The majority decision of the caucus is binding on all members of the party and enforced by the whips. The Tory caucus of 1944, according to Lord Astor, dismissed the proposal for an all-party reconstruction committee with an impartial chairman. Reaction to the controversy in Plymouth was swift and almost unanimously opposed to the caucus principle, on Saturday 29th July 1944 the Western Morning News carried a selection of letters supporting Lord Astor. One comment stated: such an ungrateful and short-sighted discourtesy is only another example of the folly of the illogical and unnecessary intrusion of party politics into municipal administration. It would be a tribute to him (Lord Astor) to offer him the chair. The final rebuff came for the wartime Lord Mayor four months later. In November 1944, Waldorf Astor was told that the Conservatives wished him to stand down from the Lord Mayoralty to make way for a party politician. It had been his hope to complete as Mayor the year of the final victory in 1945 and would thus have the honour of proclaiming it, but it was not to be. How sad that a man who had done so much for the people should end his links with Plymouth in such a shameful way. His death on the 30th September 1952 was to have a heart wrenching affect on Nancy. His last words were spoken to his son William who was to become the 3rd Viscount, he said: "Take care of your mother." His funeral was held on Wednesday 22nd October 1952. Waldorf and Nancy's love had been so strong and their bond of marriage an almost perfect example of what marriage should be. Admittedly their marriage went through a rocky period in her very later years and Nancy had been very possessive of her children and this did, for a while, put a strain on the closeness of the family. However, their mutual respect and love for each other and the love for their six children strengthened the bond between them. During that difficult time Nancy sought some solace in religion, as a Christian Scientist she had always read the scriptures from the bible every day and now took to reading them more frequently. She never really came to terms with Waldorf's death and Nancy lived until the grand old age of eighty-five, but for her they were the lonely years. With Waldorf's death Plymouth had lost a caring brilliant negotiator and as a man all citizens respected him. Being a Lord did not stop him from mingling with the local people and helping wherever he could, one must ask the question, will the city citizens ever find his like again? Waldorf Astor 2nd Viscount's most endearing memorial was the planning of Plymouth with Professor Abercrombie after the savage bombing of Plymouth in 1941.

Original plans had been drawn up to name the road that is now known as Armada Way to be called Phoenix Way to highlight the rise of the city after the tragic bombing, alas that too was not to be. Plymouth did however show their respect and ensured that Waldorf's name would not be forgotten by installing a beautiful, dedicated, stained glass window to him in Saint Andrew's church, Plymouth. It would go a long way towards easing the ache in many citizens' hearts to name the new Millbay highway being built as the Astor Boulevard. This new exciting development road that all generations will use, links Millbay waterfront to the city centre of Plymouth, this indeed would be a lasting memorial to both Waldorf and Nancy Astor. Every generation would then know its reason for the name it bears, there are many trusts and memorials still in perpetuity known only by the City Fathers or the higher echelons of education. The people need something obvious to all ages, status and lifestyles. Lord and Lady Astor were the best thing that happened to Plymouth in those historical years. Forward thinking, progressive, extremely generous with their own money to the citizens of Plymouth, it is hoped the powers that be will now give credence to the wishes of many people, to honour and in some small way make up for the disquieting manner in which Lord and Lady Astor were dismissed from the cities activities thus causing the senior Astors to sever their useful political links to Plymouth in 1945-1946. Waldorf and Nancy, disillusioned, sailed in the ship Eros for New York in January 1946 for a well-earned rest. Although Waldorf remained in touch with some friends in Plymouth and took an interest in various activities in the City, Waldorf's early death in 1952 severed the last link with Plymouth's political scene. Waldorf was buried at Cliveden in Marlow, Buckinghamshire, but his name is forever etched in the hearts of true Plymothians.

Photo courtesy Mr Geoff Rodd from a private collection. The Author gratefully acknowledges Westcountry Publications

Lord and Lady Astor in later years.
Lord Astor died in 1952 and Lady Astor in 1964.
Portrait taken it is thought at 3, Elliot Terrace, Plymouth.

CHAPTER FOUR
BLITZ MEMORIES

"Women have got to make the world safe for men since men have made it so darned unsafe for women." *Nancy Astor.*

THE SEEDS OF WAR

War was declared on the third September 1939, England had responded to the promise to Poland to protect her borders. Hitler's dream was to conquer the world and his Reich was to place terror in the hearts of many citizens. Reich refers to the union of German states; the first Reich was the Holy Roman Empire, which ended in 1806. The Second Reich was the united Germany established in 1871. The 'Weimar Republic' was established in February 1919 after the defeat of Germany in the First World War and lasted until March 1933. Historians called it Weimar Republic after the City of Weimar where a National Assembly convened to write and adopt a new constitution for the German Reich; this was a first attempt to establish a Liberal Democracy in Germany.

Adolf Hitler was born in 1889 on the frontier of two states in Austria-Hungary on the border between upper Austria and Bavaria in the little town of Braunau-am-Inn. He was the son of a customs official who changed his name from Schickelgruber to Hitler. When Hitler's father changed his surname little did he know that he had changed the family name to one that was to place terror in the hearts of many people. The name Adolf comes from old High German and means noble wolf and relatives and friends called him Uncle Wolf.

Hitler's party came to power in 1933 and, having been a soldier in the First World War and a house painter in civilian life, he was named leader of the Third Reich in the nineteen thirties and vowed that the Third Reich would last for a thousand years. The Nazi Party won almost half the seats in the ninth federal election of the Weimar Republic. Hitler made a former Weimar official, Dr. Hjalmar Schacht, Minister of Economics in 1934 and it was he who became the financial architect of the Nazis' rearmament programme. Germany in the 1930's was still reeling from the restrictions imposed on them in reparations that the country was forced to pay to France under the Treaty of Versailles at the close of World War One. Under this Treaty, enforced in December 1918, allied troops marched into Germany and took control of the Rhineland area for a period of fifteen years. The Rhineland, a key industrial region of Germany became a permanently demilitarised zone; this was to prevent it being a springboard for unexpected invasion of France. The severe reparation that ran into billions caused the economic instability that led to the rise of Adolf Hitler. In March 1936 Hitler marched 22,000 German troops into the Rhineland, in a direct contravention of the Treaty of Versailles. He offered France and Britain a twenty-five year non-aggression pact but the situation deteriorated and by 1939 war had broken out; however, Hitler's one thousand year regime ended in 1945. It had lasted twelve years.

PLYMOUTH'S ROLE

In the later part of September 1939, 20,000 evacuees arrived in Plymouth and Devon. Plymouth took a large proportion of the evacuees here as the city was deemed a safe area but little did the population know what was to come as those first heady days of the Phoney War drifted quietly by. During the terrible war years Lord Mayor Waldorf Astor and Lady Mayoress Nancy Astor were the main figureheads in Plymouth and they proved more than capable of holding that venerable position although at that time they were not recognised City Councillors, but they indeed left an indelible mark

Photograph by kind permission Mrs Mavis Hawken Plymstock Plymouth.

This photograph depicts Nancy, Lady Astor, helping to collect waste paper for the war effort with the Plymouth citizens in 1940. The bombing in 1940 had not yet reached its zenith and as those who wish to contribute had popped out of his or her homes to support the venture (it could be Trelawney Road Peverell) it is noted that nobody was carrying his or her gas mask. Mr Albert (Bert) R Hawken who worked at the Western Morning News Newspaper as official photographer for forty-seven years took the photograph and his mother Mrs Grace Hawken is standing on the right at the end of the queue.

on the City. During the war years the Astor's home in Elliot Terrace was to be a hive of activity and entertainment. Five of the houses alongside the Astor's home were occupied by the American Red Cross and were used as hostels for needy personnel. The American Red Cross Club in Elliot Terrace was opened in January 1944 by the American Red Cross Commissioner and Lady Astor and served the white American servicemen and on the day it was opened they presented Lady Astor with some beautiful flowers.

The Astors of 3 Elliot Terrace put maximum effort in giving support to the distressed war-torn population. They entertained King Haakon of Norway in 1941 as the Royal Norwegian family had escaped from Norway, now occupied by the Germans, to seek refuge in Britain. On 20th March 1941 they had the honour of entertaining our King George V1 and Queen Elizabeth at 3, Elliot Terrace, and during a tour of the city to see the bomb damage, the King and Queen spoke to some of the bombed out citizens. The king spoke to one of the ladies and said: "You are very brave, I have great admiration for you," The woman replied: "Well, Sir, there is one thing about it, I can go where I like, I can do what I like, and there is nobody in Germany that can do that!" The evening that their majesties returned to London, Plymouth was heavily bombed and the city suffered extensive damage. The Queen on hearing of the act of aggression wrote to Lady Astor on Saturday 23rd March 1941 expressing her distress at the terrible event. The Australian Prime Minister Mr Robert Gordon Menzies (later Right Honourable Sir Robert Menzies) came to Plymouth on the 27th March 1941. He was in Britain to discuss war strategy with Winston Churchill.

In May 1941, after the tragic bombing of Plymouth, the Military Authorities began concerts on Plymouth Hoe to keep the spirits up and to offer a couple of hours of pleasant music for the population and the citizens were pleased to have a little light entertainment to lift their hearts. Another distinguished royal visitor to Plymouth was King Peter of Yugoslavia (1923-1970) who was welcomed to the city by Lord Astor, the Lord Mayor. The young King Peter came to Britain in June 1941 after the fall of Yugoslavia in April, he was the last King of Yugoslavia (1934-1945) and Queen Elizabeth was his Godmother. King Peter completed his education at Cambridge and joined the Royal Air Force.

Lady Astor continued doing her public duties; in November 1941 as Lord Astor's representative she attended the funeral of Caroline Bond Beckly at Mutley Methodist Church. Mrs Beckly was the sister of Sir Frederick Winnicott; she had been vice president of St John's Ambulance and a member of the Ambulance Brigade. Her late husband had been head of the firm Messrs John Yeo and Company. The Town Clerk had notified the citizens that the blackout was in full force; blackout times were 6pm until 8am wintertime, and 9pm to 5.30am in the summer time. It had been decided that in future when members of the public boarded the buses the name of the destination would be called out at every stop. This was a good help as sometimes batteries in the torches would fail or, on many occasions, exhausted citizens through lack of sleep would nod off on the buses. Throughout the darkest hours of the war the Astors supported and fought for their constituents and their citizens; where they were needed they were always there.

CHURCHILL'S SECRET ARMY

Britain was alone fighting the Axis forces and in England secret units of men from all walks of life were building underground holes beneath normal recognised landmarks, rabbit warrens, chicken coops, sheep and horse troughs, underground country dugouts, converting them into liveable underground units, storing weapons, ammunition, food, explosives, chemical fuses, tilly lamps and cookers, and each man who did not live close by would have a bicycle to get to his unit. These units were known as the Operational Base, each construction had two exits for a quick escape. The underground country dugouts had grass and bracken covered trap doors and concealed beneath would be a metal ring attached to a wire which, when lifted, the lid or trap door would open. Winston Churchill's highly secret resistance army was set up in 1940 as the Second Corp Observation Unit to resist the enemy if German Forces ever landed on British soil. If the invader did come, the secret unit would hide themselves from the enemy and become fully-fledged saboteurs. Their brief was to obstruct the enemy at all costs, blow up bridges, destroy railway lines, cut fuel supplies, destroy communications and kill as many of the invaders as they could. Some of the men were taught how to use a Blacker Bombard Bomb Thrower; the men were specially trained and had never been short of weapons, equipment or goods, not like the home guard who only had perhaps one rifle bullet each. Should any member of the Secret Army be caught the survivors would commit suicide to prevent giving away their positions; their expected survival time was one month and every man knew it could mean giving their lives. Even to this day little is known who they were and that they had made the promise to fight to the bitter end, although it meant losing contact with their families. What brave men, the butcher, the young messenger, the postman, the labourer, the farmer and the home guard veteran. In Devon on the outskirts of Plymouth the beautiful Dartmoor countryside had to be protected and that task fell to the Moorside Battalion Home Guard, who patrolled the rivers, the moor and wasteland of Dartmoor on horseback. Winston was determined that the invaders would pay a heavy price before they marched up Whitehall.

Photo courtesy of Westcountry Publications

Winston Spencer Churchill with his wife Clementine visits war torn Plymouth 1941.
Seen here in the company of Nancy, Lady Astor, leaving 3, Elliot Terrace on the Hoe.
This great man united the population when appointed Prime Minister in 1940.
His leadership throughout the war years was of paramount importance to a nation almost
on its knees. Yes, he made mistakes! Does anyone know a leader who did not make mistakes
when at the helm of the nation?

GOOD NEWS FROM AMERICA

In November 1941 some good news from America cheered the British nation who had lost so many of her merchants ships bringing food and essential supplies to Britain. The House of Representatives in the United States of America adopted the resolution of the Neutrality Revision Bill by 212 to 194 votes, a majority of eighteen. Thank god they did for it was to turn the course of history, they were not to know then that they would be at war in December of 1941. It was good news for Britain, because the measure authorised the arming of United States Merchantmen, and allowed them to sail to any port in the combat zones to deliver defence aid materials in such volume to help achieve victory against the Axis forces. Their support was paramount and welcome. Stateside in November 1941 the Americans were giving a grand welcome to the crews of British ships being refitted in United States ports and wealthy estate owners arranged weekend parties. British organisations in the USA such as the English Speaking Union and the Union Jack Club established recreation centres. One favourite haunt was 'Nellie's English Restaurant' renowned for its English dishes especially roast beef and Yorkshire pudding. Men from the British

Navy were admitted free of charge to cinemas and theatres, so the ordinary Americans were doing their bit to support the British servicemen wherever they could, and a United States reporter wrote how they admired the excellent behaviour of the sailors and their quiet conversations in public.

ROYAL AND IMPORTANT VISITORS

On Friday the 20th March 1942 King Peter of Yugoslavia came again to the City, and on the Saturday he took the salute at the Plymouth Warship Week parade. That year more members of the Royal family visited Plymouth and on Saturday 31st January 1942 Princess Marie Louise, Granddaughter of Queen Victoria was at the YMCA in Union Street. Princess Alice of Athlone, who was the head of the Women's Auxiliary Air Force, also came to 3 Elliot Terrace. His Royal Highness Prince George, Duke of Kent, visited Plymouth in June 1941 and was escorted by Lady Astor to meet members of the public who were performing sterling service to the city and on Saturday 14th February 1942 he opened the Hyde Park Social Centre. He also performed one of the last public ceremonies when he attended the official opening of the King George V1 Officers' Club, close to the entrance of Plymouth Hoe, which was run by the YMCA, where officers could obtain a meal and night time accommodation. The Duke of Kent had been a Rear Admiral, but in April 1940 transferred to the Royal Air Force Training Command with the rank of Air Commodore. Sadly the Duke was killed on the 25th August 1942 in Scotland whilst on active service; although it has never been officially confirmed it is believed that he was on a secret diplomatic mission.

On 6th April 1942 the Duke of Gloucester made a private visit to Plymouth and on 9th April 1942 the Home Secretary, Mr Herbert Morrison, visited the City. In 1943 the American General Dwight David Eisenhower (1890-1969) was appointed Supreme Commander of the Allied Invasion Army for the Normandy Landings, and on his arrival in Plymouth was greeted by the Lord Mayor. Lord and Lady Astor and the citizens of Plymouth were delighted when the American forces came to Plymouth in 1942 for it signalled that a dramatic change in the outcome of the war could at last put Britain on the offensive. Nancy remarked: "I do not think I shall ever forget the year 1942 because it was in that year that the people of Plymouth were brought face to face with the Americans."

NANCY'S BUSY SCHEDULE

In 1941 General Montgomery said to Nancy, "I don't approve of women Members of Parliament" Nancy replied, "Well I don't approve of Generals, there is only one General I admire and her name is General Evangeline Cory Booth (1865-1950) of the

King Peter 1923-1970
The last King of Yugoslavia (1934-1945)
Lord and Lady Astor welcomed the young visitor to Plymouth

Salvation Army." In December 1941 Nancy, as Lady Mayoress of Plymouth, opened the Salvation Army Women's Hostel in Portland Square; the following day she visited the Christmas Cheer Fund depot at 2, Windsor Villas to speak to Mrs Hannaford who had been administrating the fund for many years. Nancy then called at the firemen's toy display at Plymouth and Stonehouse Gas Light and Coke Company's showroom at Mutley Plain. Later in the week she appeared at the Odeon and Royal Kinemas to appeal for the Lord Mayor's Christmas Fund and on the Sunday afternoon she attended St Budeaux Methodist Sunday School gift service and in the evening at the Palace Theatre concert for the Services. On this occasion she made a speech to the servicemen at the theatre saying: "Now that America is with us in this war you can rest assured that we shall not only win the war but that we shall win the peace, but we will make no peace with dictators, there are people who say that they dread the thought of the world after the war. I have no fear for the future while the English-speaking nations stick together there will be no room for class distinction and petty grievances, we shall all work to make a better living and better praying world." Whilst there she appealed to the servicemen to give generously to the Lord Mayor's Christmas Cheer Fund for old and unemployed families whose only hopes for a reasonable Yuletide depended upon this fund. The following Monday she attended the Virginia House Nursery Centre party. Nancy indeed gave much of her time to her beloved citizens. By day she would visit the sick and wounded in hospitals and evenings were spent supervising emergency rescue works. Nancy met local members of the Auxiliary Territorial Service and visited the mobile British Legion canteens, donated to the stricken city by the citizens of Cincinnati, USA, and Guelph, Ontario, Canada, the American and Canadian people were most generous to the Plymouth citizens and they gave help wherever possible.

THE SALVATION ARMY

Nancy, who was a great social reformer, thought highly of the Salvation Army and all that they did and spoke on occasion to Lieut-Colonel Soper. In 1930 the Salvation Army owned a local paper called The Deliverer, which highlighted their social workers achievements in the city of Plymouth. They operated from the Octagon, which had been opened in 1889, later new premises were opened in King Street and the building became a women's hostel. Lieut-Colonel Soper was a sister to Mrs Catherine Bramwell Booth, (1883-1987) OBE and Order of the Founder. Catherine became leader of the women's social services in 1926 and was the first woman who sat in the Plymouth Police Courts and to whom the magistrates began handing over the Refractory Girls for care instead of sentencing them to servitude or prison. She retired with the Salvation Army rank of commissioner in 1948. The Salvation Army's paper today is The War Cry. Lady Astor was again very generous with her money.

After the war the Salvation Army promulgated a programme called Marching Forward, the main objectives of which included helping the homeless with the provision of soup-kitchens and overnight shelter, the promotion of evangelism, the prevention of juvenile delinquency, aid to veterans and their families, extensions of services in police courts and prisons and programmes to end human suffering in countries devastated by war. By 1993 the Salvation Army was operating in 99 countries and using more than 125 languages and dialects to preach the gospel. World membership of the group totals more than 3 million people, of whom about 25,000 are officers, graduates of some 30 schools maintained by the Salvation Army in many parts of the world. The facilities operated by organization members throughout the world include schools, maternity homes, children's homes, and hostels, which give free lodging and serve free meals.

The Salvation Army was particularly active during World War Two, rendering a wide variety of services to Allied soldiers, so were the Women's Institute and the Women's Voluntary Service. Over the years these groups of caring people have been the butt of many jokes at their expense and many snide remarks levied at what they stand for, however, the Women's Institute and the Women's Voluntary Service have a likeness to the Salvation Army and Nancy Astor respected them all for their qualities. The

Women's Voluntary Service began its humble beginnings in World War Two when many Plymouth people were blitzed out of their homes and were unable to cook their own food and the Women's Volunteer Service for Civil Defence (later to become the Women's Royal Voluntary Service known as WRVS) provided food for these people.

A WARTIME RECIPE

Frederick Marquis, Lord Woolton (1st Earl of Woolton) (1883-1964) was appointed as Minister for Food in 1940. He had been the former Managing Director of the John Lewis group of retail stores. Food supply was crucial during the war, with food rationing and many ships being sunk at sea, food had to be home grown if the nation

Copyright Mr Albert (Bert) Hawken, photographer for the Western Morning News

A welcome cup of tea in wartime Plymouth
Volunteers gave sterling service

Lady Astor accepting presentation of a British Legion canteen in the 1940's

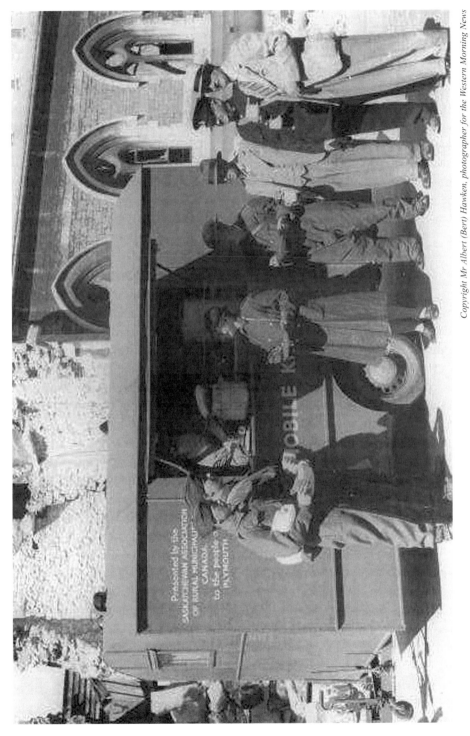

This mobile canteen was donated to the City of Plymouth from the citizens of Canada

was to be fed and avoid starvation. Everyone had to try and grow vegetables. Wartime recipes were to be the butt of many jokes, yet they kept the people fed and they were far healthier than today. Families would eat tripe and onions, bubble and squeak, where left over cabbage and potatoes were mashed together and fried, and lots of vegetables. The meagre meat ration allocated to each person did not allow for a substantial meal, and most wives would ensure that the men, or the breadwinner, had the meat as their main meal, whilst other members of the family ate corned beef. Carrots would also be grated and used as a sweetener (substitute for sugar) in home made cakes, housewives had to be creative to produce an appetising meal. In 1941 Lord Woolton advertised a recipe in the Times newspaper for the housewives to make. Although it was primarily a vegetable pie it was given the name of Woolton pie. Comprising of, onions, swede, carrots, potatoes, cauliflower and parsley, to this would be added small spoonfuls of oatmeal and vegetable extract, most housewives covered the pie with a wholemeal pastry to make it more filling, then it was baked in the oven.

Another of the wartime recipes by Helen Burke was Rabbit Pudding not a really appetising presentation but a meal nevertheless and wartime food was difficult to present as an exciting menu. The requirements were a packet of Spillers Albatross self raising flour, some suet, one small rabbit, sixpence-worth of bacon pieces, pepper and salt, chopped parsley and water. The name Meals on Wheels derived from the Women's Royal Voluntary Service (1938-2008) related activity of bringing meals to servicemen. In the year 2007 the WRVS Meals on Wheels celebrated their Diamond anniversary, and in 2008 have celebrated seventy years of service. These groups had the same ideas to help people in need; they were The Rocks, always there when needed, champions of the people.

NO CHOICE CONSCRIPTION

With conscription in 1940-1944 the young men and women were mostly joining the services, but there were some who were not allowed to choose the service they would have liked as the Government decided that an even balance of serving personnel would be distributed where they were needed. Women registered for war work as nurses, ambulance drivers, messengers, railway cleaners and porters, bus conductors, bus drivers and female pilots. Women groups were very special and important to the nation and made an enormous contribution to the country's war effort supporting vital industries. Two other very special groups were the Women's Land Army, and the Women's Timber Corp (nick-named Lumber Jills) and what a magnificent job they did keeping the nation fed, working long arduous hours on farms doing men's work and producing the food needed. They have never been fully officially recognised. However, in January 2008 their work was finally acknowledged with an issue of a special commemorative badge, although many have now passed on, but the few still left will be able to claim their badge. Citizens who lived through those uncertain years will always remember them and what they did. Then there were the canteen workers, Red Cross and the Women's Voluntary Service; some were designated to work on the railways or in munitions factories. Men were detailed for clearance of bombed areas, some men were kept in civilian work as they were needed and considered as being under War Cabinet Priority. Usually these men were Great Western Railway engine drivers and workmen engaged in secret work building the necessary defence protection projects. Others were designated as wardens, some formed rescue teams, and a body of men not to be forgotten, the Bevin Boys. The Bevin Boys scheme was introduced in 1943 by the then Minister for Labour and National Service Ernest Bevin in response to a shortage of labour in the coal mining industry. Recruiting men of 18 to 25 years to work in coalmines rather than serve in the armed forces did not please many of the men, but they had to go where they were needed. It is good to honour these men and be proud and grateful for their tremendous work for they, too, kept the homes fires burning.

FARMERS ROLE

Farmers, too, contributed to keeping the nation fed during the war years, farming was vital to the war effort especially during the blockade by German U-Boats, which were sinking our cargo ships containing food supplies, at an alarming rate. The National Farm Survey carried out principally between 1941 and 1943 in England and Wales, by the Ministry of Agriculture and Fisheries, produced a record of each agricultural holding. Across the country Agricultural Executive Committees were formed and were known as 'War Ags.' The Ministry had issued an order to make farm workers exempt from military service as many farm workers had been conscripted before 1941. The farming industry was to change dramatically as cultivation orders were introduced, and in some areas land was subjected to dispossession orders for military purposes. Other farms were given a small subsidy for every acre of land that produce crops as well as raising livestock, poultry and dairy farm assets. Local farmers had no choice about this change to their lifestyles and methods of farming. 'War Ag' supplied necessary machinery to put suitable areas under cultivation, whilst many farmers used shire horses and tractors, and employed Land Army Girls, prisoners of war, and their own employees to harvest the crops. The rich pastures of our countryside had to be ploughed and cultivated to grow the new output of crops. Fields of potatoes, swedes, turnips, peas, carrots, oats, rape, kale, corn, wheat, and in some areas where soil was suitable, sugar beet. Farmers were not allowed to grow flowers as all land had to be used to grow vegetables, but they could sell small bunches of wild flowers such as violets, primroses and bluebells. Most farmers were honest hard-working folk but there were also the profiteers as the black market flourished in selling, or swapping for other goods, eggs, meat, poultry, rabbits, hams and on occasion, half a pig. A Government directive to people who owned a pig was that, upon killing it, the owner may keep half but the other half must be surrendered to the Government for food processing to feed servicemen. The magnificent work that farmers did to keep the nation fed in those turbulent days must never be overlooked.

Photo by kind permission of Mrs Joy Wills

The fisherman risked their lives daily to bring fish to the population. With businesses bombed out little stalls set up their wares and fish became a substantial meal in the war years. Location unknown.

THE ORDINARY CITIZEN AND THE SERVICE PERSONNEL.

In January 1944 'Monty' General Bernard Law Montgomery (1887-1976) who had been appointed head of the Second Army and Commander of all British ground forces made a flying visit to Plymouth, and in May 1944 he addressed a meeting of United States Army Officers at the Odeon Cinema. He was later promoted to Field Marshall and he ended his career as 1st Viscount Montgomery of Alamein having won the title at the battle of El Alamein October 1942 in the Western Desert. Nancy and Waldorf however also entertained and met the every day ordinary citizen. The Astors made it their responsibility to look after the welfare and entertainment of the serving forces whatever their nationality. There were occasional moments of racial tensions and some street battles between negro troops and white troops. Civilians too became involved. Nancy thought of a simple solution to diffuse the scenario by entertaining a multi-racial selection of servicemen and treating them with even-handed generosity as her house guests. Nancy would often been seen in the YMCA in Elliot

Street (formerly the Hoe Mansions now the Astor Hotel) chatting over a cup of Maypole tea with the Commonwealth servicemen; the YMCA supplied meals, entertainment and sleeping accommodation for service personnel, no mean feat in those memorable years. What organisation must have been undertaken to achieve the possible from what one assumed would be the impossible. The population had to find their own ways and means of entertaining and the young people joined small groups of entertainers, which gave joy and respite for service units and the workers playtime. One little amateur group who entertained and who never received the acknowl edgement of their efforts was the Victory Revellers for no matter what happened in regard to the air raids they entertained all over the Plymouth area by giving concert parties to keep the spirits up.

We must remember, too, the wonderful work of the Toc H who provided much needed help; they also occupied the YMCA in Elliot Street and gave sterling service where required. The Toc H members had their own special message, 'to think fairly, to love widely, to witness humbly and to build bravely' On Saturday 1st February 1941 a new Toc H hostel for forty-seven men was opened at 46 Union Street, Plymouth. The cost was in the form of a gift from the British War Relief Society of America. Sadly, in the year 2008 there is no longer a branch in Plymouth. Toc H is an organisation made up of groups of people meeting together and serving their

Photo from a private collection

Salvage workers clearing up after a heavy bombing raid on Plymouth in 1941

community in worthwhile projects. Begun 80 years ago, spurred on by a world in turmoil, (The First World War) the original Toc H was in Poperinge, Belgium, set up to provide basic comforts to the young men going to and from the battle lines of the Western Front. Since then, Toc H has developed into a worldwide body, which has chosen to operate at the grass roots level of communities. It is now a movement of men and women who demonstrate their belief in breaking down the barriers that can divide people from one another. Toc H is a movement concerned with Christian values and from the day of its foundation, has made no secret of its Christian basis. In France during the First World War a ruined house was taken over and used as a rest centre for servicemen. Talbot House was named in memory of Lieutenant Gilbert W L Talbot, aged 23, who was the brother of Padre Neville Talbot. Gilbert was serving with 7th Battalion The Rifle Brigade when he was killed at Hooge in the Ypres Salient on 30th July 1915. His death came during a British counter-attack following the German Army's first use of liquid fire on the Western Front. Gilbert was the youngest son of the Lord Bishop Talbot of Winchester and left a career of brilliant promise unfulfilled. He is buried in Sanctuary Wood British Military Cemetery, Zillebeke near

Two lady salvage workers having a chat with Lady Astor.
Cleaning up after the heavy bombing 1941

Ieper. The name Talbot House soon became known to the soldiers of the Ypres Salient as 'Toc H'; Toc being the army signaller's code for 'T'. Now the Toc H was helping the generation of servicemen fighting the Second World War. Many servicemen from all over the world could be seen in the city and all played their part in fighting for freedom right up to the D-Day landings.

The Polish Air Force operated from a nearby fighter station, some were stationed at RAF Chivenor, others were billeted with families and the Polish pilots would often be seen in the skies above Plymouth shooting at the invaders. The Polish Navy had their warships manned by Polish men who had escaped from the occupation of Poland; many were to marry Plymouth girls, as were other overseas visitors. Polish men conscripted into the Polish services had to take work perhaps not suited to their capabilities and many of these men never returned to Poland, some went on to develop their own businesses, from nightclubs, to shop outfitters and builders. Others were employed by major companies becoming valued staff and obtaining good positions. Lady Astor frequently visited the Polish community at their own original club, Polski Klub Orzet (Polish Eagle Club) which was started on the Hoe and then moving on to the permanent home at Napier Terrace, Mutley Plain. The club stayed

Photo from a private collection – formerly Westcountry Publications

Lady Astor showing American, British and Commonwealth servicemen
The damaged church of Saint Andrew's Plymouth 1943

Lady Astor with dignitaries and police support watching the hard working ladies salvage team clearing up after a horrific bombing raid on Plymouth circa 1941. Note the housewife in the background watching the activity and The white paint on the kerb edge for pedestrians to see in the dark

Lady Astor showing Dorothy Thompson (Columnist for The New York Tribune) the bomb damage in Plymouth in 1941. A public relations arrangement to ask for help from America for bombed citizens.

opened until 2005 when it was sold due to lack of members. In May 1940 the Duchess of Kent accompanied by Lady Astor attended the inspection parade of the Plymouth and District's St John Nursing Division at the Plymouth Guildhall, these nurses were the unsung heroines as they gave sterling support during the blitz that followed and they tended to the hundreds of wounded and exhausted servicemen who were landed at Millbay Docks in those tragic years.

In 1940 the Canadian First Division in Plymouth embarked on board ship for France to join the British Expeditionary Force in the fight against our enemies, however they only got as far as Plymouth Sound when news came through that France had fallen. They disembarked again that night without sailing as all the ships would be needed to rescue our troops from Dunkirk. When the troopship Lancastria was bombed on 17th June 1940, after loading aboard approximately nine thousand men as she laid off St Nazaire, the damage resulted in her sinking with the loss of 5000 men. Some of the survivors were landed at Millbay dressed in all sorts of oddments of clothes and some with none at all. They had been through hell and not content with bombing the ship the German aircraft machine-gunned the survivors struggling in the water, including women and children. First to go to their aid when they docked were the magnificent Guild of Social Service and the Lord Mayor's Welfare Fund, the ever-reliable Salvation Army and the British Red Cross, (formerly known as the British National Society for aid to the sick and wounded in war. The first chairman of the Society was Colonel Robert Lloyd-Lindsay created Lord Wantage in 1885.) The exhausted survivors were taken to Stonehouse Town Hall to be fed and kitted out again. Many families to this day do not know how their loved ones were lost as, shocked by the massive casualty list, Winston Churchill put an immediate ban on making the news public as it could have undermined morale. Later the nation heard that the French troops were losing the battle and fighting without their customary ûlan, the French totally capitulated on 25th June 1940. During the month of June 1940 more troops embarked from Dunkirk on the gallant little boats and ships of the Royal Navy. From this time on the Lord Mayor's Welfare Fund, which had been organised to look after distressed citizens and servicemen, along with many volunteer workers, were to play a key role in supporting all troops that landed at Millbay docks or by train from North Road Station.

WELFARE FUND AND BRITISH RESTAURANTS

The women's voluntary canteen service run by the Lord Mayor's Service Welfare Fund at the North Road Canteen was magnificent for when the weary French, (nearly 80,000 French troops were rescued from the beaches at Dunkirk) and British troops finally reached our shores they were hungry, thirsty and demoralised, but the voluntary workers including the ever-reliable Salvation Army were there with a hot meal if they could, sandwiches, cigarettes, biscuits, buns, chocolate and even oranges (which was a luxury if you could get one.) Hovering and helping wherever she could was the irrepressible Lady Astor. The canteen was handled with such efficiency that one could be proud of how, in the face of such adversity, so many were united in the common cause. The canteen was opened day and night and would give a free cup of tea (or a jam jar as cups were short) and a bun; during its working time thousand of cups of tea were served. Nancy worked tirelessly in supporting the nursing fraternity and the Civil Defence Corp and continued to supply goods or food where she could. The blitz in 1940 damaged the Royal Fleet Club in Devonport when receiving a direct hit but thankfully it survived and became a refuge centre for families, whose houses were destroyed in the blitz, serving meals to 700 people in 1941. All over the city British Restaurants were opening to feed the beleaguered citizens. At the height of the blitz field kitchens were set up around the districts to help feed bombed out victims, civil defence workers and troops. Sometimes all these people would be working for hours day and night looking for victims, giving aid and support, and after the bombing raids, streets, houses, buildings and schools had to be made safe, buildings were so badly damaged that hardly a building above single story height was left standing. One or two schools that were not damaged had been taken over by the Army as temporary hospitals; others were used as temporary accommodation for bombed out families to sleep in. To make areas safe; bomb damage clearance workers did sterling work and here the women played their part as the Women's Salvage Corp would be called in to help clear the areas so that some measure of normal life could continue. Lady Astor's frequent appearances on the streets of Plymouth were a source of encouragement for the brave residents of the badly bombed city.

THE BOMBING BEGINS

With the fall of France in 1940 a French cynic declared that Britain's neck would be wrung like that of a chicken and that within six weeks Britain would also be occupied. Winston Churchill threw back the taunt and declared, "Some chicken - some neck!" Nancy approved and from this time her relationship with Winston found a more balanced empathy. Unity was paramount during this critical time, with our backs to the wall a firm leadership was needed if we were to survive. The German Heinkel bombers began in earnest their bombing of England, first it was the airfields and then the cities, soon Plymouth was to become a prime target. The first bombing to have a real impact were the raids on Saturday the 6th July 1940, which destroyed houses in Swilly (now North Prospect) and on Sunday 7th July 1940 when Cattedown became the target, and on Monday 8th July 1940 Devonport was bombed, two days later another raid destroyed property around the Hoe area. On one particular distressing day, Tuesday 12th September 1940, thirteen people were killed while queuing at a fish and chip shop on the corner of Emma Place and Chapel Street in Stonehouse. Some were marines on their way back to barracks with their girl friends who had stopped to buy fish and chips. Further raids were to continue into 1941 and

Scene of devastation in the centre of Plymouth April 1941. Taken after the salvage workers had made the area safe and cleared the roads for the population to commute to work and for transport to continue with their duties.

The devastating scene after a bombing raid on Plymouth March 1941. Spooners Corner /Bedford Street/Old Town Street. Note the wrecked 'Sun' design (top left) from the former Sun Assurance building later converted to Spooners shop. The spire bottom left corner could be the top of the St Andrew's cross. Unveiled 30th May 1895, it was a special feature until later; when it too, was bombed and destroyed.

Sun Buildings and "new" Spooners Corner; taken prior to the March 1941 bombing of Plymouth. Note the Sunflower face at the top of the building, it was a symbol for the building.

WINDSOR CASTLE

Saturday March 23rd, 1941,

Dearest Lady Astor,

Since early yesterday morning when I first heard of the savage attack on dear Plymouth, I have been thinking of you all without ceasing. I have been praying that the people may be helped to find courage, and ability to face such a terrible ordeal, and I am certain that they have all this spirit already.

Words are not invented to say even mildly what one feels, but having just left you after such a happy and inspiring day, one feels it all so bitterly, and so personally. My heart does truly ache for those good mothers and children and all the splendid workers.

That is one of the hard things about being King and Queen of a country that one loves so much. Every time this sort of murderous attack is made, we feel it, as if our own children were being hurt. All we can all do, is to do our very best, and leave the rest in God's hand.

I know how much you love the people, and how much you have striven to better their lives in Plymouth, and my sympathy is <u>very</u> deep and sincere.

I long to hear how Virginia House fared, also the Club and Toc H, as I fear they were in the shopping centre.

Oh, curse the Germans,

With love and thanks for your devoted service to humanity,

Yours affec.

ELIZABETH R.

A letter from HM Queen Elizabeth to Lady Astor written soon after the start of the Plymouth blitz

1943 when the Gasworks, North Road Station, RAF Mountbatten, the Ford Institution, and our historic Guildhall were bombed, our beautiful Lord Mayor's and Lady Mayoress' parlours were completely destroyed, however Lord and Lady Astor continued to function in their temporary quarters.

PIGEON POST

Lord Astor with his successful Welfare Fund ensured that Plymouth had a 'Wings for Victory' campaign in May and June 1943. With Plymouth's postal service being constantly put under pressure an unusual postal system was put into force, the Pigeon Post. Homing pigeons were being trained at RAF Mount Batten as early as 1942 and all were given a registration number just like the servicemen. Local breeders of the birds had homing lofts all over the city ready to receive the returning birds and became part of the National Pigeon Service. One particular local bird from Plymouth a Pied Hen racer had a test flight from London to Plymouth, the message the bird carried came from the then Chancellor of the Exchequer John Anderson, First Viscount Waverley (1882-1958) and the message was for the Lord Mayor of Plymouth, Lord Astor. Every evening the pigeons were put aboard the Sunderland Flying Boats flying out from Mount Batten as they were being trained to bring rescue messages from airmen if an aircraft was shot down and the birds were also being used to bring messages from other cities in England. Citizens were bemused seeing American Jeeps stopping at houses in the City whose back yards contained pigeon lofts; the pigeons were being collected for their duties to bring back messages from the Allied forces during the D-Day landings in France in 1944. Many living servicemen today owe their lives to what these birds did in the war years.

FIRE WATCHERS

Fire Watchers, including many elderly women, performed exploits of heroism in saving valuable property belonging to the Churches of Saint Andrew's and Saint Catherine's on the 31st March 1941. With the destruction of Spooners shop beloved by the Plymothians it seemed as though everything we treasured was being destroyed, however our morale was lifted when the defiant John Bedford O.B.E. Manager of Spooners, (1939-1949) placed a stirring advertising board displaying this slogan 'Smitten down but not destroyed' and the shop re-opened in various outlets across the city. There was extensive damage and many civilians were killed, large numbers of civilians were reported missing and no trace of them has ever been found, so the death toll was much higher than the official figure stated. In September and November the raids intensified and more damage to property resulted and sadly more civilians killed. The oil tanks at Turnchapel were set on fire and the Auxiliary Firemen fought a long battle to keep it under control with two gallant firemen losing their lives. The

National Fire Service was magnificent as they fought a losing battle with the raging fires. Tribute should also be paid to the Teenage Fire Fighters, young lads of sixteen to nineteen who helped tackle the flames as Plymouth burned in 1941. 'The Teenage Pump Team' manned the water pumps as their main task, and helped with clearing the damaged buildings, most of the young men were stationed at Stonehouse Fire Station. Many young men were volunteer cadets or scouts with the Auxiliary Fire Service and they, too, played their part and some paid the ultimate price in their efforts to preserve lives and property. In April 1941 just a year after the AFS had been formed a Saltash Taxi left for Devonport towing a trailer pump unit with the Saltash AFS crew aboard to assist in helping to fight the fires at Devonport. Unfortunately, on the way to Devonport the trailer hit an unexploded bomb and all the firefighters were killed.

FIRE, DESTRUCTION AND DEATHS

Incendiary bombs set fire to hundreds of homes and businesses and the streets became ovens as the air currents sucked the flames from buildings on either side to make ferocious tunnels of heat. Walls cracked and crumbled, glass melted and the liquid glass formed pools on the pavements, the stench of burning was nauseating. Further raids were to follow and the beloved Pier on the Hoe was totally destroyed, along with public buildings, churches, hospitals and schools. The raids on the night of 20th March and late April in 1941 caused such devastation as German bombers pounded Plymouth, almost totally destroying the City Centre, incurring many more deaths, and disrupting normal family life. Some raids lasted as long as six hours. The scene of devastation was beyond description, piles of smouldering rubble, burnt out shells of buildings, the stench and the grime, plumes of ash and not a bird singing. Hollow-eyed for want of sleep, grimly silent but still with an unconquerable spirit, the people of Plymouth set about the task of clearing up. Always in attendance Lady Astor looked to see where she could help and arranged emergency accommodation for the stricken citizens. There were miles of hoses strewn across the roads from gallant firemen's efforts to control the fires, unable to cope with so many fires the brave fire fighters had to leave many premises to burn themselves out whilst they tackled other fires. One particular business left to burn itself out was the once well-known furnishing stores of Jays in the Octagon, it was unfortunate that some of the fire fighters equipment would not fit the hydrants.

Plymouth's devastation was far greater than any other provincial City. The saddest episode of the bombing took place in seven nights of merciless bombardment in March and April 1941 which resulted in the total destruction of the close knit shopping district in Devonport. The whole of Fore Street Devonport was destroyed which included nearly sixty businesses, among them the much loved Tozers, Marks and Spencers, Woolworths, British Homes Stores, and the YMCA in St Aubyn Street. Plymouth as well as Devonport suffered and the historical and well loved hotels such as the Westminster and Hackers situated in the Crescent, the Waverley in Millbay Road, Farley's in Union Street and the Royal Hotel, Devonport, were bombed beyond repair. Demolition squads were out in full force pulling down dangerous burnt out shells of buildings and trying to keep the streets clear for some semblance of order. On Monday, 21st April 1941, during an air raid, which had continued for three days and nights, Boscawen accommodation block in the Naval Barracks took a direct hit, the bomb penetrating the basement before exploding. Ninety-six Petty Officers and other ranks were killed and such was the intensity of the explosion that only seventy-eight bodies were recovered for identification, which was extremely difficult because some of the naval men were not wearing their uniform; the grim task of recovering the bodies made even strong men cry. Many of the men were buried at Weston Mill Cemetery, others at Efford Cemetery, that week all the civilian dead were also buried. Because it was thought that it would take a costly toll on morale the dreadful number of servicemen killed was kept secret for many years.

From a private collection – original copyright local Plymouth photographer Dermot Fitzgerald, he had taken the photogrph by pure chance, when passing the scene, although the city buildings in the background of the photo had been censured out for national security.

Brave exhausted Plymouth Firemen clearing up after spending days and nights putting out fires all over the city 1941. Meanwhile two Firemen defiantly raise the Union Jack on an old lamppost to boost the morale of a war torn city and its population.

THE AMBULANCE SERVICE

The Ambulance service must be acknowledged for all the sterling work they did in Plymouth especially during, and after, the wartime bombing. The old equipment they were supplied with made completing their tasks efficiently very difficult. Mrs Flo (Floss) Ponsford reminisces about her experiences as a woman ambulance driver in Plymouth during the war and this is her story.

In 1942 I was an assistant driver in the ARP Ambulance Service and the lorries we used were the old time soft-topped style, which were fitted out with four iron stretchers. Not the most comfortable to ride. Lady Astor had contacted Cincinnati in America requesting a modern model. On its arrival, I was thrilled to learn that our post had been selected to have the beautiful new ambulance and my driver and I were taken on Plymouth Hoe to receive it. A few other vehicles were also lined up in front of Elliot Terrace. Lady Astor and Mr Colin Campbell, the Town Clerk, (later Sir Colin Campbell, knighted in 1952) accepted the gifts of the new ambulances from various cities in America. As they were all new vehicles we were able to perform our tasks in comfort. I shall never forget Lady Astor as she did so much for the people in the war years.

Photo courtesy of Mrs Floss Ponsford, Plymouth

Another new Ambulance, which Lady Astor accepted on behalf of the city in 1942 from the citizens of Cincinnati U.S.A. The gift presentation was made in the prescence of Mr Colin Campbell, Town Clerk. Front row: Mr Colin Campbell and Nancy, Lady Astor.

Ambulances assembled on Plymouth Hoe circa 1942. First left is the Ambulance that assistant driver Mrs Floss Ponsford and her team received from Lady Astor who appears second right with Mr Colin Campbell, Town Clerk third right. Residents of Wit Deep, Germiston, South Africa, donated an Ambulance in the USA also responded to the call for help. Aid came from our Allies and Friends overseas to help on the home front.

THE ORPHANS

On the night of Saint George's day 23rd April 1941 the Stoke House Orphanage was badly damaged and almost destroyed by fire which meant the children had to be accommodated at Montpelier School, Peverell, which had been turned into an emergency rest home, until their subsequent evacuation to Clovelly, North Devon, on 30th April 1941. Lady Astor had arranged with her friend the Honourable Betty Asquith to send the Stoke House orphans and the fostered out Scattered Homes children to the New Inn Clovelly. The children who remained in the city during the war played their part in putting out the incendiary bombs, which rained down on the distressed war torn city. The children had been taught to put them out with water and sand until the nature of the bomb changed. The enemy had become subtler in their techniques and mixed the explosives so that it caused delayed action so some children were injured and the authorities stopped the children from helping with their disposal. High incendiary bombs were modified and became the newest weapon comprised of oil and phosphorous explosives, the citizens had to be on their guard all the time with these new type bombs. Public transport was badly affected as the Milehouse Bus Depot was severely damaged by the raids in 1941 when fifty buses were destroyed and many more damaged beyond repair; it was indeed a nightmare time and many citizens still living today who went through those traumatic years try to block out the agony of that dreadful period of our history.

Photo: Evening Herald

Lady Astor pictured among a collection of children's toys. circa 1944.

UNITED IN THE CAUSE

The bombing of Plymouth brought out the worst and the best of people from the population. In October 1942 Plymouth police rounded up many draft dodgers and returned them to the military authorities. On the good side were our magnificent service personnel comprising of British, American, Canadian, New Zealand, Polish, Belgian, Czech, Norwegian, Colonial, Dutch and Free French. One thing was certain all were united in the cause to defeat the enemy. The spirit of Plymouth's defiance was expressed when two Royal Navy bluejackets produced their own 'Iwo Jima' flag-raising, it was a proud moment when they hoisted the Union Jack over the damaged historical Plymouth Guildhall. All over the city there appeared as if by magic small Union Jacks waving bravely in the breeze in pockets of damaged buildings and public areas, raised in defiance against the manic destruction of our city. Henry Patrick Twyford (1892-1964) Plymouth's war correspondent for the Western Morning News remarked in his book 'It Came to Our Door,' "Plymouth's physical wounds were terrible to witness. Its heart was torn out with violence beyond imagination, but Plymouth wiped away her tears, healed her wounds as best she could, and steeled her heart. It became another epic in her stirring history." Henry Twyford also covered all of Lady Astor's campaigns and public events and was a Special Constable for many years; he had spent most of his life in journalism.

OUR NANCY

'Our Nancy' was an inspiration to us all and she would tour the city to meet the bombed out citizens and her distress was clear to see as she met families who had lost everything in the tragedy that was the Plymouth blitz. Nancy was seen wherever there was damage to talk with the people and encourage them, which, in her own inimitable way, she succeeded in doing. Nancy, wearing her familiar long black coat with gloves and handbag, and black laced up shoes over socks and stockings, would be on the scene talking to bombed out families and the servicemen who were helping to clear the rubble. In her hand would be the notepaper and pen she always carried ready to jot down the needs of the family in distress. Determined to help practically as well as morally she would take the Housing Officer with her to ensure that he was aware of their immediate needs. After one particular bombing raid a taxi driver who lived locally had his livelihood taken from him when his car was destroyed. Lady Astor was so sympathetic she had her chauffeur drive down her Daimler for him to use so that he could continue his business. Another citizen who lost everything in a raid was very upset at losing her jewellery including her engagement ring. Lady Astor immediately took a five-diamond ring from her finger and gave it to her saying, "There, this may help to replace it." Nancy rallied all her American friends appealing for help for the distressed citizens and children as food was becoming scarce and housewives could no longer cook meals, gas and electricity being affected by the

Photo: Courtesy of Westcountry Publications. Copy by Trevor Burrows Photographer Plymouth

Lady Astor talking to bombed out Plymouth citizens 1941-1943

bombing. The population had plenty of vegetables and housewives learned to compromise and create recipes to make ends meet, greens and vegetables were the mainstay of our meals in those years. On occasion the City of Plymouth Corporation Depot at Mill Street had surplus supplies of vegetables and an advert would be put in the paper inviting the population to come and buy from 8am in the morning until sunset, one day an advert appeared: Surplus Savoy cabbages and potatoes available! The real heroines in Plymouth were the mothers, they have never been fully recognised for their refusal to be beaten during those terrible war years. Their loyalty and unselfish sacrifice, although reeling under the torment of the blitz to keep their families and children fed, kept some measure of stability to a war torn population.

Photo: Courtesy of Westcountry Publications

Lady Astor with an evacuee Plymouth 1941

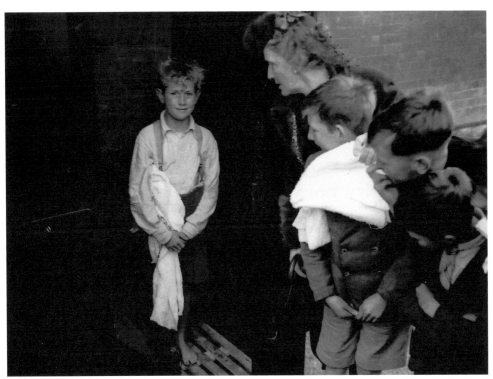

Photo: Evening Herald

Lady Astor and mobile baths in Plymouth - opened in November 1941 -
Lady Astor paid the sixpences for the children

BUNDLES FOR BRITAIN

The Americans and Canadians responded magnificently by sending food parcels, 'Bundles for Britain' which contained clothes and gifts for the citizens and children of our beleaguered City. Plymouth rest centres and hospitals received parcels from the Red Cross which supplied clothes, bedding and cooking equipment. One Plymouth gentleman can still remember Nancy bringing clothes parcels to his school and handing out long trousers to the boys, for some boys this was their very first pair of long trousers and they were quite proud to wear them as it made them feel more grown up. Such a gesture still lives strong in the memories of those war-torn children, as more families were left homeless and without any possessions their very existence relied on these very precious parcels. Nancy herself gave out dark chocolate caramels sent from America, whilst in England rationing was still in force. Nancy and Waldorf had a fierce argument about those chocolates that Nancy had had sent to Plymouth citizens from America. In 1942 the English court fined her £50 for ordering rationed clothing items and dark chocolate caramels from the USA; well that was certainly a human touch. Human nature being what it is, and understanding the self preservation code, most people in the war years trying to survive would, if they could, obtain items from the black market or friends who had access to rationed goods. Nancy exerted pressure on high society and the media in Whitehall and London to force Plymouth's plight to national attention. She wrote a very strong letter to The Times highlighting the six months of devastating bombing and the lack of Government organisation. In May 1941 after Plymouth had suffered the worst of the blitz, the House of Commons began the debate for the Emergency Provisions Bill. Lord Astor meanwhile had suggested early in 1941 to the Military Authorities that if a band were available it might give concerts on Plymouth Hoe. The response was immediate and a band played regularly on the Hoe promenade from 4pm to 5pm commencing from the 5th May 1941. What a great idea and how it raised the morale of a stricken city.

NANCY FINDS A NEW FRIEND

Nancy's workload was mammoth in carrying out her duties as Member of Parliament and Lady Mayoress. She attended the House of Commons regularly; she would catch the midnight express from London to Plymouth after participating in debates in Parliament to bring the needs of her suffering constituents to the notice of the Government. In the morning she would rise early and have a cold bath, put on her make up, usually a small amount of foundation cream and powder, still as enthusiastic as ever and with her Secretaries would work tirelessly from morning to night, one wonders where she found the energy from as she undertook her duties. There were others, too, who did much to enhance the quality of life in those dreadful years. One gentleman to be remembered was Ernest T English; he too became a friend to Nancy. London born he came to Plymouth in 1942. He immediately centred his

Lady Astor collecting clothing, July 1941 – van, Rowe & Sons,
7 High Street, Plymouth

efforts on helping the aged in the City, a kind man his selfless devotion to the well being of the Plymouth citizens made him widely known and loved. A fitting memorial was established to this man when in 1960, the two-storey Ernest English house was built on land given to the Guild on a ninety-nine year lease by the Plymouth City Council. Ernest English became General Secretary of the Plymouth Guild of Social Service and in 1956 he was one of the founder members of the Plymouth Barbican Association who fought to restore, and prevent the loss of, old buildings that survived the war. When Ernest died in August 1971 the city had lost another great friend of the people. Another staunch worker was the Food Officer for Plymouth who faced a mammoth task of feeding the population. Plymouth was fortunate to find men with such dedication to undertake these responsibilities.

PORTLAND SQUARE

Memories are still vivid in 89 year old Cathie Hunt of Yelverton, in Plymouth, as she scrambled out of the Portland Square shelter when it was bombed in 1941. A just-married twenty-year-old young lady and with a little flat in Portland Square, all looked rosy until that dreadful night when the area of Portland Square was devastated by the German Luftwaffe. It is hoped that soon a lasting memorial will be presented near Portland Square, now part of Plymouth University Campus, in memory of those civilians killed that night. Cathie stayed on in Plymouth and she remembers with intense pleasure attending many functions where Lady Astor was a guest speaker. Nancy's witticisms were par excellence! Often Cathie would attend the political campaign outside the Dockyard gates where Nancy was trying to win over the workforce. Once Nancy was challenged by a burly Dockyard worker saying, "Garn, don't suppose you know what a pig's trotter (pig's foot) looks like!" Her quick response was "Take off your shoe my man and I will soon show you!"

THE ASTOR'S FEELINGS FOR PLYMOUTH

For Plymothians the Astor's war record is something to be admired and many a bombed out citizen, bereaved war widow and orphaned child owe a debt of gratitude to both Lord and Lady Astor; let us not forget that the name Plymouth was written across their hearts. One Plymouth citizen Betty Britton (nee Tribe) who was only a child of five at the time remembers the effect that Lady Astor had on her family in 1940. Her father Leonard Tribe a stretcher-bearer with the Duke of Wellington's Hampshire Regiment had been killed at Dunkirk (Dunkerque) in May/June 1940. Betty's mother Elizabeth was twenty-nine years old and had two girls with another baby on the way. Distressed and without financial support she attended the War Widows Guild meeting which was being addressed by Lady Astor at a building near the old Corona Lemonade Warehouse. Seeking out Lady Astor after the meeting she asked for help and Nancy as usual gave her financial support until her war widow's pension could be arranged. Betty remarked that her mother did not talk about it much but always praised Nancy Astor for her kindness and it has never been forgotten; the sure testimony is that Betty from the age of five remembered Nancy's deed.

One senior lady, 101-year-old former teacher Mrs Edith Jury, remembers the Astors' many kindnesses to her school children who, during the time when the bombs were falling on Plymouth, were evacuated to Cornwall. After evacuation, parcels were packed for the children and sent on which included warm clothing and Wellington boots. As a teacher times were difficult but the Astors made life more pleasant with their generosity. They made sure that the children received games and many other things to help them while they were in Cornwall. Their thoughtful kindnesses were gratefully appreciated and Edith remarked in her letter to the local paper that she was very sad that no one thanked them for the good things they did for Plymouth. The terrible blitz exemplified everything that was good about Plymothians. The community spirit engendered during leadership and courage was admired and those who still survive from that era remember Nancy's efforts to the blitzed population. A photographer who took a picture, unbeknown to Lady Astor, of her standing in the ruins of Plymouth's Saint Andrew's church, shows a very distressed and forlorn figure in the bomb-ruined interior of the beloved mother church. It was a clear signal of her love for Plymouth that she cared so much at seeing its destruction. When Lord and Lady Astor walked around the smouldering streets after the bombing they were utterly drained and deeply saddened. Lord Astor made a statement proving the Astors commitment to Plymouth with this message.

Photo: from a private collection

The Supermarine Spitfire

"What is the spirit of Drake which still persists in Plymouth and the spirit of all our fighting men and women? It is a strange thing, invisible, intangible, imponderable and, as we know now, of an audacity well nigh incredible. It can hardly be analysed, it is neither guns nor armour, it is something which is nursed, nourished, and found where people live close together in daily, hourly peril of their lives. So close is our union with Plymouth that I have left instructions, in the event of disaster, for a communal burial along with my fellow citizens."

In Plymouth all over the city children were participating in displays and fancy dress parties to boost the fighting funds, as all proceeds collected would go to the Spitfire Fund, and in the summer of 1940 and late into 1941 the Spitfire Fund nationally was so successful that every other Spitfire off the production line had been donated.

THE ARP

Day after day Nancy and Lord Astor would meet members of the public and service personnel to encourage and offer help where they could. 'At home' meetings were arranged to offer support as needed and in addition Nancy arranged for food parcels to be sent to distressed families. Nancy chased all her relatives and friends in America to give aid and they responded handsomely, particularly sending clothes for the children. In July 1941 after the heavy bombing in March/April the Astors met Air Raid Precaution (ARP) personnel and shook hands with the hundreds of citizens who attended as they queued outside Home Park Football Ground. How their hands must have ached on those days, but they were determined to show that to them every member was important. Plymouth's Chief Constable in 1941 was Mr W.T. Hutchings and he was also Chief Officer of the Air Raid Precaution service, and he explained to Lady Astor in December 1941 that the ARP personnel were doing a splendid job and that they had their own monthly magazine called 'The Alert' and after the horrific bombing in March/April 1941 he placed an article in the magazine praising the service by saying: "Should necessity unfortunately again arise I have complete confidence in the ability of the men and women of the wardens' service, undeterred by the grim experiences of the past, to once more render a full measure of service." The magazine gave news from other divisions and valuable instruction hints. The Chief Warden was Captain A.S. Hicks, the Commandant of the Special Constabulary Mr Edgar Bowden and the First Aid Commandant Doctor R.J. Chatfield; Lady Astor had shaken hands with all these dedicated people.

FEEDING THE HUNGRY

The citizens were waiting for the arrival of the Queen's Messengers and the Royal Navy personnel to supply food. The Royal Navy provided stoves and Naval Ratings kept the fires burning in them to supply hot food and a lunch could be bought for one

Lord and Lady Astor with Miss Harriman at a British Restaurant in Plymouth, 6th June 1941.

Photo: From a private collection with permission from the owner

A wartime scene featuring a British restaurant set up in an emergency centre. Musical entertainment soothed the shattered nerves and a hot meal was welcome. Location not known.

Photo: from a private collection: Copyright, Westcountry Publications

Lady Astor at a Communal Kitchen. circa 1941-1944 Plymouth

125

shilling. A plate of hot sausage and mash, a hot cup of tea and a bun did wonders for the hungry stomach. After the April bombing food centres and British Restaurants worked together to feed the hungry citizens. A two-course meal was available for the sum of nine pence, many a bombed out and hungry person gratefully accepted the most welcomed hot food, many household tenants could no longer cook as gas and electric facilities were destroyed in the bombing. One could obtain at certain times a small meal of soup, bread, and potato stew (sometimes the grey coloured bread passing for white bread was not available, the alterative daily bread then was 'Turog' a brown bread offering stamina, energy and vigour) a cup of tea completed the meal for four pence (old English money.) Many food centres were set up at schools to serve the meals, these were to be found at Plymouth High for Girls, Treville Street, Barbican, Portland Square, Oxford Street, Morice Town, Sutton Road, North Prospect, King Street, York Street, Frederick Street, Salisbury Road School and others.

Nancy loved her food and lunches were always the highlight of her day, one favourite she adored on occasion was a lovely fresh crab. She had an arrangement with Cloads the Ship's Chandler on the Barbican for crabs to be delivered to her home. Fishing was one of the tasks the Ship's Chandlers would undertake and when Nancy knew the King and Queen were having lunch with her she asked the fisherman for a fresh crab. It was the custom in Plymouth, when royalty visited; Cloads always presented the edible shellfish as a gift. The crab was delivered in time for the chef to prepare for the very special lunch.

ON STANDBY

During the blitz, at Nancy's home in Elliot Terrace, every tub was filled with water and spades were on standby with sandbags to tackle the fires. During the bombing the explosions broke the windows of the house but despite being ordered to the basement shelter by the Warden, Nancy put on her tin hat, mustered the sandbags and buckets, and proceeded to run up and down the stairs to locate the burning incendiary bombs. She helped put out the fires on the roof of 3 Elliot Terrace with sandbags. Early in the morning Nancy, exhausted but defiant, retired to bed amongst the rubble in her bedroom, as so many other citizens of Plymouth did, without light and with no glass in the windows. She would not move out of her damaged home and vowed never to leave Plymouth.

WE WILL BUILD IT AGAIN

Then began the billeting plans to place people who had lost their homes and belongings to share with citizens who had rooms to spare or homes unoccupied and plans were initiated to evacuate the children. During heavy bombing raids Lady Astor would turn cartwheels in the passageway of the emergency rest homes to cheer frightened children and citizens, no mean feat as she was in her sixties then. She was still doing cartwheels at the age of seventy in the hallway of Cliveden when she visited her son there in 1950. When Nancy appeared on the scene in the shelters the blitz children sang war songs for morale purposes. Nancy frequented the shelters in all areas making the citizens laugh with her sense of humour and giving them encouragement and promising to help them. When the Luftwaffe started to bomb the city of Plymouth the editor of a German newspaper 'Völkischer Beobachter' wrote this comment: 'We will bring to England a revolution of blood and tears which as a punishment will reduce the British population to degradation and poverty.' A clear indication that it was not only military targets they were going to bomb but a deliberate act to kill as many citizens in every raid where possible. The very first large store to suffer the destructive bombing was the well-loved Spooners. Their reaction was to blow a raspberry at the German Lufftwaffe with their own message placed in the Tavistock Times on March 28th 1941 which said: 'We are troubled on every side, yet not distressed. We are perplexed, but not in despair. Corinthians, Chapter two, verse eight.'

Lady Astor with Professor Abercrombie and Mr. N. Grigg in the barbican area - Oct 1941

During the war the flower parterre outside 3 Elliot Terrace facing the front toward the Hoe was dug to plant vegetables for the war effort. Looking out of the window of her home Nancy witnessed the dreadful damage the German bombers had inflicted and she remarked, "We will build it again." Whilst taking the Australian Prime Minister Mr Menzies on a tour of the city, they were caught outside during an air raid and made a sudden dash for the Belvedere just under the Hoe (designed after Queen Victoria's wedding cake) and thankfully taking refuge in the Plymouth landmark saved their lives. Nancy did not win all her arguments as on one particular occasion when Lady Astor and the Australian Prime Minister were guests in the house of the Commander-in-Chief Admiral Sir Martin Dunbar-Nasmith VC, a bombing raid took place. They were looking at the panoramic view of the city lit by the flames. Lady Astor mentioned that she wanted to be there where she was needed and not in the safety of the air raid shelter. The Admiral stated that she would be safer remaining where she was, Lady Astor said, "I am a Member of Parliament and I demand my car." The Admiral replied: "I am the Commander-in-Chief and I order you to the shelter!" Nancy gave in gracefully.

PET CARE

The Plymouth people had not lost their spirit although many lost everything, their homes, relatives, animals and pets, belongings, and the peaceful happy environment they once knew. The Animal Rescue Squad organised by the RSPCA was very busy during the blitz and the rescue van would scour the streets to collect sick, frightened, lost and injured pets. During the war Animal Guards were appointed; they would register pets so that, in the event of bombing, animals found wandering could be re-united with their owners. The Guards were mostly women and were issued with a book of useful tips on how to deal with frightened animals. Imagine a slightly built lady trying to cope with a Drayman's frightened horse and these were likely to be powerful Shire horses. The Guard's instructions read: Coax the animal to lie down next to you, keep its head down, even if this means sitting on the head, wait until further assistance arrives. Well these ladies must have been tough, even the draymen had difficultly containing their horses.

A COMMON CAUSE AND THE LOOTERS

People, who lived in the same street for years and never spoke to their neighbours, began to speak to one another, the community united in the common cause. They experienced night after night of heavy bombing and some times there would be 'Tip and Run' raids. Catching people in the open, the planes would swoop out of nowhere and unload their bombs. Citizens saw shops, schools, cinemas, and homes, historical buildings, whole streets and hospitals burning, blasted and destroyed and many relatives and friends killed. The physical wounds were there to see and Plymothians, like citizens in other bombed cities, will carry the emotional and psychological scars to their graves. Despite the unity among the people many scoundrels took advantage of the bombed city's plight by looting and plundering evacuated and partially damaged properties, stealing furniture, bedding, clothing, jewellery, ornaments, and other precious goods; some citizens came out of their shelters to return home only to find their belongings taken and in some instances the looters had even stripped the kitchen stove. In 1941 three servicemen, supposedly helping the firemen to secure bombed properties, took the opportunity to help themselves, but a sharp-eyed fireman of the Auxiliary Fire Service spotted the act and they were brought before the court for looting. The same year a police constable with seventeen years service was sentenced to hard labour for stealing a doctor's car looted from blitzed premises, he had lost the respect of all and his family were to suffer from his actions. The war brought out the best and the worst of the human race. Vandalism was rife and the police could do little as they were already stretched to the full keeping order and communications secure. Schools were also targeted as schoolbooks, paints, panes of glass, school furniture, and slates from the roof were stolen and what items the thieves could not take they smashed to pieces. Two servicemen stole seventeen new typewriters from Pryors the Secretarial Training School at North Hill, Plymouth, however the police were on the mark and caught the offenders two days later in London, and they, too, received sentences for burglary. Con men and bogus contractors made their mark as they increased rents out of all proportion and delivered goods to large hotels and businesses bypassing the ordinary citizens to make huge profits, albeit, these acts were made only by a small minority but it rankled the honest citizen trying to survive in the war torn city.

RUBBLE AND DESTRUCTION

Citizens on waking one morning would go into town only to find the whole area completely devastated, only rubble, destruction and fire everywhere. Dust hung over the ruins and everywhere rescue squads were digging to get people out. Streets that appeared stable would have signs hung telling the population 'Unexploded Bomb - No Entry' and former tenants would have to ask permission to enter their premises to recover personal effects. For the residents of the city night time was hard, many will remember how the dust, sulphur fumes and smoke hung in the air and the strangest thing to come to terms with was that we could not see the stars. The Home Guard put on a brave face to try and keep the spirit of the population in focus but how shocked some of the citizens would have been if they had known the terrible truth in those grim years. The local Home Guard platoon whose duty it was to defend the Great Western Railway only had one bullet each and imagine the consequences if German forces had landed. The ARP rescue men worked tirelessly to prevent fires from incendiary bombs and to assist the local population. One local area known as Coxside had its own ARP rescue team because of the importance of their expertise, and what brave men they were. Their task was to maintain high security with the gas industry and the potential dangers associated with the gasometers at Coxside and all the gas mains running under the streets. They were a rapid repair team day and night and when Luftwaffe bombs struck crucial gas facilities they were the first to respond. Gas mains were being destroyed all over the city and when a gas main was hit it was like walking through the gates of a potential inferno. Through their efforts many lives were saved. The number of fires they had to tackle overwhelmed the fire-fighters and they sometimes had to stand hopelessly watching beautiful buildings burn to the ground. Their equipment either did not fit some of the hydrants or there was not enough water to quench the fires. The Canadian Fire Fighters based in the city between 1942 and 1945 were at Greenbank Road, Victoria Road, Tor House, and from March 1943, occupied a new large station at the Drive, Hartley, and they became a part of the community in Plymouth and were very popular. They and the Auxiliary Fire Service made magnificent efforts to save the city from being further destroyed; it was the Canadians who fought a huge fire at Timothy Whites the Chemist shop on Mutley Plain.

THE AFTERMATH

Soldiers, sailors and civilians joined the rescue services to help in trying to recover bombed victims. A sailor staggered grim faced toward a fireman nearby as another child's body was found knowing it was hopeless but wanting to help in extracting the little victim. An Air Raid Precaution Officer stood by a soldier crouching in the doorway in what had been a thriving shop, "I can't help much till the doctors and ambulance arrives," he said to the soldier whose arm had been blown off in the blast. Several bodies of sailors were nearby, caught in the bombing on their way back to the barracks. Rescue squads started digging to locate bodies but it was the ambulance drivers who were faced with labelling parts of bodies recovered; the drivers had to mark the body parts with their name, the name of the first aid post, and whether the remains of the body parts were male or female, the smell of death was dreadful. Then followed the acrid smell of burnt plaster, brick dust, burnt materials and paper, burning mattresses, blazing buses, and smell of gas from burst pipes. Clothes blown by the blast from the bombing hung from branches of trees and on the mantel shelves of houses damaged could be seen family photographs and mirrors still unbroken, yet the house destroyed and its occupants killed. Exhausted rescue workers and civilians worked tirelessly, they were dirty, unwashed, hungry, cold, yet they were magnificent! Full justice to the pain and heartache of the terrible nights of bombing and its after affect is impossible to erase from the minds of those stricken citizens who lived through its nightmare and who experienced the horror of it all. The screaming

Photo: Evening Herald

Lady Astor with American servicemen U.S. Thanksgiving Day 1943 at the Mayflower steps, Barbican, Plymouth.

noise of the bombs blocked all other sounds and citizens caught out in the open pressed closer to the walls of the houses and waited with bated breath, this sang froid seems incredible but it must be remembered that Plymouth had been the target for the German Luftwaffe destructive bombing campaign for quite some time. The bravest of all were the servicemen in the Bomb Disposal Squads who put their lives on the line every day to remove and dismantle hundreds of unexploded bombs. The red painted bomb disposal lorry would normally be seen dashing at full speed through the streets of Plymouth on its way to the moor, (where the bombs were safely detonated) their cool courage and utter disregard for the danger in which they lived rendered magnificent service. Some paid with their lives; in one incident five bomb disposal men were killed in Osborne Place on the Hoe when, on the point of driving the lorry away with an unexploded bomb on board, the time fuse triggered and the lorry was blown to bits and all five men died instantly. The sacrifices of the men of the Bomb Disposal Unit saved many citizens lives each day.

In 1943 Plymouth was host to servicemen from all nations and it must not be forgotten that we owe a debt of gratitude to these brave men, Czech, Dutch, Polish, Free French, Australian and American servicemen. Fighting men from India and Sweden, Naval personnel from Canada and the forces from New Zealand and Newfoundland and many others. Seventeen allied countries took part in the war. Lord and Lady Astor visited many of the men and met them in the YMCA huts or hotels and dined with officers and other ranks. The Royal Australian Air Force were based at Mount Batten Air Station as part of Coastal Command and many Plymouth citizens still remember seeing them taking off or returning to base in Sunderlands and Catalina Flying Boats.

MAGNIFICENT HELP

The Guild of Social Service provided magnificent help in the war relief of bombed out citizens and particularly looking after the older folk. Hot meals were served in the old Guildhall Civic Restaurant and the Lord Mayor's Christmas Fund ensured that distressed citizens were taken care of by issuing vouchers which could be spent in the shops for much needed food and goods. It also looked after the unemployed, war widows, and the aged. This was a wonderful help as the Guild of Social Service did not have any rations allocated for the Church canteen, everybody who came to the club brought something from their meagre rations, nearly all those who attended gave all they could spare. The old folk always paid for their refreshments and it proved to be a friendly contact for the war torn city folk. Lady Astor visited frequently to see if she could find any other means of helping. She would on occasion call in at the Old Folks Club in Saint John's Church, Devonport, which had been opened by the Archbishop of Canterbury Doctor Temple. Sometimes her contact man Mr Freddie Knox would attend if Lady Astor had other commitments and he would help and report back to Lady Astor if special needs were required; Mr Knox remained a lifelong friend to the Club and the Guild of Social Service. The WVS served in the canteen and the club was popular because it had a general-purpose hall where dances could be held and was also a very good Youth Club. During the war years the young people had to make their own fun as the bombing destroyed their clubs and premises. At Christmas time Lady Astor distributed from her home, filled Christmas stockings sent from America to Plymouth children who had lost their fathers at sea. Another group who did so much for the older folk and took an active part in helping where required were the members of the Inner Wheel, and the Wireless for the Housebound was a blessing for those confined to their homes. The Inner Wheel members would see that the old folk had a radio to listen to when they were unable to venture out into the bombed out City and groups such as the Guild of Social Service and the Inner Wheel quietly gave magnificent support and it is time that they were recognised for all their efforts. Nancy did what she could to support them and the unity that was forged from those dreadful years between Nancy and these generous and willing members will never be surpassed.

Photo: Western Evening Herald 15th December 1941

Nancy Astor visits the Lord Mayor's Christmas Cheer Fund office. Lady Astor seen here chatting to Mrs J. H. Hannaford who has been connected with the fund for many years. Small boy unknown.

Photo courtesy of Mrs Myra W.A. Stevens (nee Harkcom) and Westcountry Publications

Nancy, Lady Astor, about to give out bars of chocolate from the Americans. Given to the children in the infant class at Cattedown School 1942-1943. In the picture left to right: Audrey Harkcom and Myra Harkcom (twins) Lady Astor, who has her hand cuddled around Sylvia Clatworthy's (RIP) neck who died in her thirties. Extreme right is Lady Mayoress Mrs Mary Modley. The little girl front bottom right is Ann Mutton.

LOST EDUCATION

For children the war years were to bring so many changes and in some case the break up of family life forever. The children's education was to suffer dreadfully; most children of the war years who were evacuated to other areas were two or three years behind in their education when the war ended. Records show that one third of city children were receiving no schooling at all, and then it was too late for them to make up for lost time as most had to leave school at fourteen to start work. No blame could be placed on any one body because it was impossible to maintain the standards that operated before the blitz. Hundreds of schools were bombed and some were commandeered for Civil Defence Depots as rest homes and some schools were used as mortuaries. Salisbury Road became a wartime hospital. Children had to have lessons in churches, village halls, even pubs or, if the weather was good, in open fields. There were some who were taught in private houses. There was a desperate shortage of teachers resulting in classes of forty or fifty children and a shortage of paper and materials, which had a drastic effect as pencils had to be shared; with the paper shortage the education authorities agreed to do away with the rigid rule of the margin so as to make full use of the paper available. The dig for victory campaign meant that games were replaced by gardening and by following the troop movements we learnt our geography. Food now rationed meant that children's tastes were forced to change as the food fed to them consisted of Spam, corned beef, sprats, watercress, fish and meat paste, dripping, and even condensed milk sandwiches and with potatoes plentiful chip sandwiches became quite a favourite and all children were encouraged to eat lots of vegetables.

PROVISION OF FOOD

Because of government-controlled rationing, the provision of food was a constant worry and the various methods of making tasty meals for the population was a daunting task. Nearly always hungry for food the nation was forced to grow vegetables and everyone was conditioned by propaganda to grow as much as possible. Children would often been seen eating turnips and beetroot and a scraped carrot would appease the empty stomach. In April 1941 a government order allowed that rissoles and vegetable sausages could be bought for eight pence (old English money) what was in these rissoles and vegetable sausages remains to this day a mystery, but hunger and shortage of food hardened the most delicate stomach. Potatoes were to become the highlight of every meal as they were filling and recipe books were quickly circulated on the various ways they could be cooked. Ships bringing food to our Island were being sunk at sea daily and the gallant Merchant Navy crews sacrificed their lives in an effort to get supplies through, the Government looked to the home front to keep the children fed. Often children could be heard singing the song of the day, one song was called 'Song of Potato Pete' Memory dims the exact words but it went something like this:

Potatoes new, potatoes old
Potatoes in a salad cold
Potatoes baked mashed or fried
Potatoes whole, potatoes pied
Enjoy them all including chips
Remembering spuds don't come in ships.

Photo: Evening Herald

Lady Astor with the Duke of Kent on his visit to Plymouth, 20th June 1941 - Citizens gather outside the fruit, vegetable and florist shop - Note the home grown strawberries on display.

THE MERCHANT SEAFARERS

It must never be forgotten the sacrifice that was made by the Merchant Navy, the Royal Navy Reserve, and their ships in those dreadful war years because 32,000 merchant seafarers lost their lives in the worst sea battles in history. In June 2008 Plymouth City Council honoured the Merchant Navy and the Royal Navy Reserve by granting them the Freedom of the City. It has been long overdue. The council leader said, "The honour will allow them to march into the city with drums beating, colours flying and bayonets drawn, as an expression of the admiration of the citizens of Plymouth for their great and glorious achievements in the service of this country and of their long and historic association with the city." British sailors and seamen of all nationalities including Indians and Chinese were poorly paid yet loyal to the cause of the Red Ensign. Britain depended for her maritime trade and survival on these brave men; we had the largest merchant fleet in the world then, 1,900 ships with crews from throughout the Commonwealth. Along with ships of friendly nations they supplied all Britain's oil, half her food and most of her raw materials. They also exported goods from Britain to help pay for these imports. Whatever Britain had imported, or on lend lease, was paid for in full for the goods and continued paying until the year 2006 when we made our last interest payment to the United States of America. Without the lend lease agreement we were in dire straits particularly after the battle of Dunkirk, lend lease saved us and it proved to be the turning point of the war for our beleaguered nation. The first merchant ship to be sunk was the SS Athena, a passenger liner outward bound to America with one hundred and twelve passengers and thirty crew members aboard, the ship was torpedoed 200 miles west of the Hebrides on the day war was declared 3rd September 1939 and one hundred and twenty-eight lives were lost. The German U-boat U30 under the command of Capitan Oberleutant Lemp who was later in the war killed in action, sank her in the evening. Two wounded passengers were rescued by the freighter 'City of Flint' the surviving crew members remained prisoners of war until the war ended.

EVACUATION AND TRAUMAS

Children constantly asked questions as they were being moved from bombed out houses to emergency rest centres or being evacuated. Astor Hall, Stoke, was the main centre in 1942 for the Rest Centre Controller. "Where are we going to go Mum?" Mothers had grim features set on their faces as they faced the dreadful trauma of survival with the breakdown of all normal services. Some streets would be earmarked for evacuation and other streets overlooked, small wonder that there was anger and confusion. Plymouth had been deemed a safe area and no official evacuation took place until the City had suffered almost total destruction, the citizens were confused. Lady Astor sent a telegram to Herbert Morrison, who was then Home Secretary, as she had raised the issue in Parliament that the Minister of Health and the Home Secretary had visited other cities that had been bombed yet had refused to come to Plymouth. Lady Astor had requested in her telegram that news should be released concerning the Plymouth raids particularly to the press in America as Nancy was encouraging help from her friends across the sea. On the 26th March 1941 Herbert Morrison acknowledged Lady Astor's telegram with a letter.

> *Dear Lady Astor,*
>
> *Thank you for your telegram in which you urge that as much news as possible about the Plymouth raids should be released for the American Press. I sympathise with what you have in mind, but my main difficultly is*

that on security grounds it is out of the question to release to the press the outstanding feature about these raids, namely that there was systematic destruction of the central part of Plymouth (as the comments made by the German newspaper Völkischer Beobachter revealed) while practically no damage was done to the many legitimate naval and military objectives in the neighbourhood.

There is also the difficultly that there are liable to be protests if we release in respect of Plymouth information which we were not prepared to release in the case of other towns which experienced heavy attacks. At the same time, however, I fully appreciate the force of the suggestion that as much information as possible should be given and I have issued instructions that no objection is to be raised if the press wish to refer, for example, to the fact that the Mayflower Stone was damaged and also that St. Andrew's Church was hit. I am very sorry you had such a bad time; I hope and believe that my people did all they could to help.

Yours sincerely

Herbert Morrison Ministry of Home Security.

Children growing up in the war-torn city experienced traumas that were to remain in their memories for the rest of their lives. The huge barrage balloons floated above the rooftops in the hope they would bring down enemy bombers. Everyone could hear the sirens wailing and see the searchlight beams darting in the night sky in an effort to light up an enemy bomber for the gun crews to target. Overhead came the loud droning noise of large groups of German bombers and then the bombing began. After each explosion one could hear the shrapnel pinging off the roofs and walls. Everyone would run quickly to shelters and sit on cold wooden forms. Air Raid Wardens marshalling groups of people to hurry them along at the same time shouting "Keep closed up!" and after the 'All Clear' was given the warden would shepherd the frightened people out of the shelters. Then the worried faces looked toward their homes. Whose home still stood and whose home was bombed? Outside on the roads were huge pits with gas mains blown up, and one immediately smelled the burning sulphur. Plate glass windows from damaged buildings began to melt and the metal frameworks became twisted from the raging fires. Making their way through the streets strewn with rubble were the Ambulance and Fire Engines their bells ringing, and volunteers began to search the smouldering ruins. Men, women and children were trapped in the debris, grim faced rescuers worked unceasingly and appointed personnel began checking names, anyone missing? Tiredness was etched on the rescuers' faces and the musty, smelly dust from burning plaster; this was the children's heritage.

Lady Astor was appalled at the red tape and incompetence of officialdom. Elements of the local population moved out of the city at night as hundreds walked or cadged lifts to Dartmoor for peace and safety to avoid the bombing. Lord and Lady Astor continued to confront Whitehall for action and an evacuation order; they felt strongly that the Government simply had not done enough to help. There was increased tension between Whitehall and the Westcountry and it was not until Winston Churchill's visit to the City of Plymouth in 1941 when he and Lady Astor toured the stricken city (both of them in tears at the devastation) that the final official evacuation order from the Government was given. Winston announced the words the Plymouth population had waited for: 'Evacuate forthwith.' Children were to face emotional and distressing separation from family unity. To the younger generation of today it must seem like ancient folklore being constantly reminded by the older generation of its relevance, but how can it be forgotten? Should we forget? Or can it by our knowledge and sufferings prevent the next generation from experiencing total war? Winston's inspiring words, "We shall draw from the heart of suffering itself the means of inspiration and survival," gave hope to the beleaguered nation.

SAINT GABRIEL'S CHURCH

One officially designated Rest Centre that Nancy Astor visited was St. Gabriel's Church Peverell. Wally Hirons and John Bennet, both Plymothians, vividly remember the actual night when the first bombed out 'refugees' arrived at the church in April 1941. Saint Joseph's Home for the aged at Hartley Plymouth had been bombed and the residents were transferred to the Crypt of St Gabriel's church. On arrival, there was a hot pasty and a cup of hot tea for everyone and each person was issued with a palliasse, a blanket, and was allocated a space on the floor. The Vicar, Reverend Frank Oswald Irwin, was organising the food distribution and bringing comfort to the people, John Bennet was one of the helpers (average age of the helpers was 15-16 years) and he recalls what happened next. Suddenly, Lady Astor appeared unannounced, I did not know who she was but knew that she must be someone of importance by her deportment. She said, "Boy, that man is drinking! Take that bottle of beer away from him and give it to the Vicar!" She then swept on and the old gentleman who had the beer said, "Listen son, this is my only possession in the world as I have lost everything and I don't want to give it up," I said, "Let me borrow it for half an hour until Lady Astor has gone and then I will give it back to you and you can have an extra pasty!" The old gent accepted the offer with alacrity and as soon as Lady Astor left the old gent finished off his bottle of beer and the extra pasty!

John continues: Lady Astor was like a whirlwind, she spoke to everyone, the homeless and the helpers alike, and anything which appeared to be needed she made provision for, she really was an inspiration to us all. A little later I was on duty again and she paid us another visit and said to me "You look like an intelligent strong lad, would you do a job for me?" I was very flattered to be singled out from the rest but was not quite so proud when Lady Astor said "I have just put a can of Jeyes Fluid and a scrubbing brush in the toilet and I want it cleaned up - it's filthy!" I cleaned it reluctantly and she looked in every nook and cranny her motto was 'Cleanliness was next to Godliness' and when you consider her other official duties as Lady Mayoress one wonders just how she fitted it all in.

All this eventually culminated with a meeting arranged by Lady Astor and attended by Her Majesty the Queen that was described in our own number ten copy of the church magazine called 'Ye Plymouth Herald' dated June 1942. The Editor of the magazine was the Curate of Saint Gabriel, Reverend John (Joe) Ellis. In 1942 the contribution that Saint Gabriel had made to help the blitzed victims in 1941 was recognised during the Royal Visit of her majesty Queen Elizabeth to Plymouth. The OBE was awarded to Commander Perry, Chorister and Secretary of the Church Council and, at the Swathmore Hall Mutley Plain where a crowd of local Plymothians had gathered, Lady Astor told her majesty of what Saint Gabriel's parishioners had done. The Vicar and the Curate were presented to the Queen and it was a proud moment for all including the boys and helpers who assisted in those fateful times. It was not all heartache though as the young lads of Saint Gabriel not yet old enough to be called into the services decided to have some fun while they could and not let the war spoil everything. They managed to secure a tennis court at Beacon Park and form a tennis club, other activities included mid-week cycle runs to Cornwall, cubs and scouts, brownies and guides, everyone tried to live normal life.

Many of those Gabrielites who have forged life long friendships are still meeting today. 1942 saw many visits to Plymouth by Royalty, Aristocrats and Dignitaries, which enhanced the moral fibre of the stricken war-torn Plymouth citizens. On Wednesday 25th November 1942 the Archbishop of Canterbury opened St John's Centre at Devonport.

AN ELEVEN YEAR OLD IN 1941

Mrs Sylvia Bennett (nee Alcock) remembers vividly as an eleven year old the day she, and Stoke Damerel High School, was evacuated to Truro in Cornwall in 1941. She recalled that when they boarded the train to be evacuated Lady Astor was on the platform and as all the windows of the train compartments were open she peered through every one and spoke to the children. Hiding her distress at seeing children separated from their families she covered up her real feelings with her comments, speaking in a loud voice Nancy said, "Be good children and behave yourselves!" Sylvia's immediate reaction was one of fright with Lady Astor's abrupt manner and she thought is was another teacher barking out orders, but an older child told her who it was. Scenes that one hopes will never been seen again were being played out. Ashen faced, red eyed mothers holding on to the childrens hands through the train windows reluctant to let go, messages being issued, "Look after Johnny - Stay with your sister Janet - Keep together dears," Carriages move off - must let go - "Goodbye" they shout, mothers quickly turn away wiping tears of heartache from their eyes, suppressing feelings of guilt. And there alongside was Nancy Astor, whenever children were in difficulties she was always hovering in the background making her presence known and giving out sweets and toys. When the Hyde Park School near Mutley in Plymouth was bombed it was Lady Astor who had it partly repaired, using her own money, and through her efforts it was re-opened as a youth club funded by American funds, which Lady Astor had organised. Whenever youth required help she was there.

THE LADY MAYORESS

3, ELLIOT TERRACE,
THE HOE,
PLYMOUTH.

18th September, 1941.

Dear Plymouth Mother,

      The Lord Mayor and I are delighted that you and your children are going to get a chance to live out of the target area of Plymouth. We are glad you are taking advantage of this. We can't guarantee where you are going but the Government is doing its best.

      One of the most trying things of the whole war is the break-up of family life, but we who have not lost our children have much to be grateful for. I am perfectly certain that wherever you go you will realise how many problems billeting creates. It is as difficult for people to have strangers put into their homes as it is for strangers to be in them.

      I have great confidence in the Mothers of Plymouth, and I do ask you one thing. If you have any difficulty and things are not as you hoped, send me a line c/o The Billeting Officer, 15 Whitefield Terrace, Plymouth, and we will send someone to see you and try our best to make things right, but please don't return to Plymouth until we have had a chance to do this.

      Please don't let us down. We are taking great trouble to help you to get away. It has not been easy, and you, if you want to, can make it a great success, and I believe you will.

Yours sincerely,

Nancy Astor

Letter to a mother from Lady Astor in 1941.
Some mothers found that evecuated children were not happy in their billets.

THE ATS SCORE A HIT

The women of the Auxiliary Territorial Service (ATS) scored their first victory when an Anti Aircraft Battery firing Ack-Ack guns in London succeeded in bringing down their first German bomber. The ATS women were members of the mixed crew and were the first to go into action, they handled the secret instruments for finding direction and height to target the bombers. In June 1940 Lady Astor met members of the ATS in Plymouth and it boosted the morale of the women forces. With our nation struggling to survive and to continue the fight for freedom we needed help in what were our darkest years.

THE YANKS ARE HERE

In October 1940 a second group of American destroyers arrived in Plymouth to be manned by British crews to replace those ships which had been sunk at sea. Then in 1943 came the arrival of the United States Army and the GI's were to have an immediate impact on the citizens. Many United States forces were based in Plymouth during the war years including the Officers and Men of the 13th Port. The American Army 29th Division moved to Devon and Cornwall in the spring of 1943, in preparation of the build up for the Allied invasion of Normandy. Meanwhile, the area of Devonport, Plymouth, was in the process of annexation by the Admiralty for the Dockyard Naval Base, it was to have quite an effect on the Devonport citizens seeing their beloved suburb segregated from the unity that the community once held. On their arrival, the American servicemen were billeted at the Nissen hut encampment in Tavistock Street, near Marlborough Street, Devonport, others were billeted at Plumer, Seaton, Crownhill and Raglan barracks, there were also USA camps at Queen Anne's Battery, Coxside, and Efford in Plymouth, and more Americans were billeted in the village of Ivybridge.

The American Naval Headquarters was at Hamoaze House, Mount Wise and their advance bases stretched from the Cattewater including almost the entire frontage from Sutton Pool to Laira Bridge. Nancy and Lord Astor ensured they were made welcome and went out of their way to entertain and help in forging friendships between the American soldiers and the Plymouth citizens. Lady Astor often visited the American barracks and on one particular occasion she was thrilled and honoured as a battalion from her birthplace, Virginia, held a special parade in her honour, she was so proud when they marched along the promenade and she was given the rank of Corporal in the USA Army. She treasured that certificate showing her rank and her badges with great pride for the rest of her life - one wonders where those artefacts are today, are they in a museum or have they been disposed of lost in time?

THE BEDFORD BOYS

One tragic war outcome of the Second World War that deeply distressed Nancy was the loss of the Bedford Boys on Omaha beach, Normandy, during the D-Day landings on the 6th June 1944. Nancy had met many of the servicemen from the United States of America, including the men from her beloved state of Virginia. The Americans had spent quite some time in England training for Operation Overlord. The Bedford Boys were part of Company 'A' 1st Battalion, 116th Infantry Brigade, 29th Infantry Division USA. Bedford is an independent city in the county of Virginia and in 1944 it had a small population of 3,200 souls. The young men had gone to school together, lived and played together, and were brothers and friends. They were to land as a unit in Normandy and would stand side by side in the assault in what was to prove almost a suicide wave. It was indeed an oversight by the American Army not to realise that all these men would be going into combat together and the chances were that a lot of men would be killed, and that is exactly what happened. Of the thirty-five Bedford Boys who landed that day nineteen were killed in the first fifteen minutes including brothers, twin brothers, friends, teachers and sportsmen, two more were to die later, only fourteen men made it back to Bedford. Four of the survivors still live in the little town today and they attend the memorials to their friends each year. Bedford has its own special memorial monument called the 'Overlord Arch' and is dedicated to the one hundred and seventy soldiers who went ashore in the first assault. Virginian Allan Barber wrote a song about the Bedford Boys and it says, "Their faces are forever young." The United States military, remembering the fate of the Sullivans in the United States Navy and the Bedford Boys in the Army, ensured that in future, an only surviving son from a family who had already lost family members, would be allowed to return home to support and maintain the family name. (The five Sullivan brothers came from Waterloo, Iowa, and joined the United States Navy together. They were very close to each other and did everything together. All five were on the USS Juneau that was taking an important part in the battle of Guadalcanal, but on the 13th November 1942 the ship was sunk by a Japanese destroyer and all five brothers with 700 more of their shipmates died on board the sinking ship. The tragedy also changed the US Navy policy on family members serving together)

One former ATS (Auxiliary Territorial Service) girl then serving remembers vividly when the Americans came to the City. The first GI's arrived in their hundreds packed on double-decker buses to Plymouth on the 1st May 1943. They were all chewing gum. Nancy Astor also chewed gum but she hardly moved her jaw and was quite discreet when chewing in company. The first known American words to be used with regularity became part of the Devon dialect, as flirting girls would hear, "Hi Honey - what are you doing tonight?" or "Hello Guys" and girls would reply, "Got any gum chum?" They became extremely generous to Plymouth ladies, supplying nylon stockings and candy, giving food parcels comprising of tinned fruit and that luxury drink called Nescafe coffee. The Americans introduced Nescafe to Plymothians in 1943, as it was part of the GI's ration kit. The Brazilian Government had asked Nestles in 1930 to produce an instant coffee drink, it took eight years to produce but in 1938 Nescafe instant coffee was ready for the market and the known American favourite became a quality drink for Britain, whilst we in turn introduced our national drink to the Americans, a cup of tea which they thought highly amusing. The GI's would treat the ladies to meals at Genoni's, then a well - known high class Swiss Restaurant in Old George Street that was situated opposite the Theatre Royal; it used to have pristine white tablecloths and beautiful china, afterwards the escorts would treat the ladies to a taxi home, they were never short of money and many a British serviceman lost his girl friend to the visitors from across the sea. The GI's, part of the 116th Infantry 23rd Division were billeted with local families where possible and Crownhill Barracks, which became their home base. More American Troops including the 29th Armoured Division arrived in Plymouth in 1943/44 in preparation for Operation Overlord that would eventually lead to the D-Day landings on the 6th June 1944. Plymouth City had difficultly in finding suitable areas for their concealment. Eventually wooded areas were found at Mount Edgecumbe and Anthony Park in Cornwall and the Saltram woods in Devon. These hidden areas were given the code name 'sausages' and in the evenings all local pubs would be packed out with American visitors. All the parks in Plymouth had tents set up to accommodate them and what was once the beautiful Devonport Park was covered in American tents.

NANCY'S QUEST FOR PEACE

Cynics in the past have adversely judged Nancy's attitude to Nazi Germany. She hated all tyrannies and wanted to preserve the peace of Europe by negotiation. In 1933 Lady Astor had been most upset on hearing that Germany had withdrawn from the League of Nations. Too much emphasis has been put on blaming the Astors with rumours and innuendoes of sympathising with the German policies of that era and many blamed the Cliveden set for disquieting policies. The Cliveden set were as sharply divided, as many other groups of people were who sought appeasement. Even before the war there was always an undercurrent of hostility to the Astor regime. Yet the Astors were blameless for all the guilt of appeasement, most of the accusations levelled at them were merely myth. In 1938 Waldorf, Viscount Astor had written to The Times and clearly emphasised that they had entertained all members of all parties, all faiths and of all countries whatever their interests. As many anti-appeasers stayed at Cliveden as frequently as did the appeasers, the Astors were deeply upset at the accusations. Nancy was the last person in the world to engage in any conspiracy, her love of England was too strong and there is no doubt she would have disassociated herself from any indication of betrayal, she was too loyal and she would never let her Plymouth constituents down. It was publicly made clear when the Nazi black book was discovered in 1940, the names of Lord and Lady Astor were on Hitler's black list of people to be arrested and executed immediately as soon as the Germans occupied London. In addition over two thousand other Plymouth citizens were also on the list, this in itself was proof that Nancy was against Nazism. Every living person has the human touch and that means each and every one have opinions and if we believe in something sincerely, remarks we have made can often be taken out of context. Such was the case with Nancy Astor, perhaps she did make some most controversial remarks, but at its foundation was the fact that she cared so much for underprivileged people and had their interests at heart.

THE STIGMA OF INNUENDOES

It was said that Nancy had tried to stop allowances to sailors working under difficult conditions. Some old sweats of the services were unhappy at the intentions of Nancy to stop the payment to matelots as compensation for the discomfort of serving in small ships. The Royal Navy was in deep shock on hearing that the Jolly Jack's tot of grog should be stopped immediately. She was accused of having talked of the eighth army basking in the sun while people at home were being bombed; this and some other rumours may have been due to honest misunderstanding. Controversial indeed, was the remark reported that she had insisted that all men coming back from the Middle East should wear yellow armbands as a warning against venereal disease which was rampant in the nineteen forties. Some ex-servicemen still maintain that Lady Astor was responsible for demanding that Forces tea be laced with bromide. All these charges she vehemently denied, so it is left to the individual to assess their own opinion. Public opinion was divided; Plymothians were sometimes resentful of her but generally affectionately tolerant. Any one in the public eye is vulnerable to media judgement, press reporters were poised like cougars to strike out and innuendoes would be enlarged upon to increase the sales of papers to the readers. Once printed that innuendo registered a stigma that never went away so it was difficult to separate truth from myth. Another innuendo levied at Lady Astor, yet never proven, was that the RAF base at Mountbatten was labelled as Lady Astor's rest home, as any Westcountry mother whose son was posted to Northern England or Scotland could apply to her and she would try to arrange a compassionate home posting. We must never glorify war nor dwell in hatred but seek simply to remember that it did indeed place hopes and dreams on hold, and we must strive to promote peace so that war can never happen again.

NAUGHTY NANCY!

Nancy did unfortunately become involved in a black market scandal in 1943. In her desire to obtain clothing and sweets for her citizens she broke the rules; one can say it was a human touch as in the war years everyone survived the best they could and

Photo: courtesy of Charles Prynne

Lord and Lady Astor leaving Bow Street Court, London 1943. Lady Astor had been fined for a breach of the rules.

many a citizen was involved in black market activities, some were caught whilst hundreds more got away with it. Nancy was caught because she had written to the American Red Cross to send her some clothes from America and the censor on that day opened her letter and found the anomaly. Nancy was summoned to appear at Bow Street court in London, found guilty, and was ordered to pay a £50 fine with cost. Waldorf was displeased and a few angry words were exchanged. Undeterred she continued to try and get goods for her distressed citizens and once again found herself in trouble, oddly enough this time it was her own desire that caused an upset. The American Red Cross had sent to Waldorf Astor a large parcel with sweets and chocolates to be distributed among the population and Nancy saw the parcel, was tempted and demanded some of the chocolates as she had quite a sweet tooth. Waldorf refused saying it was for the people and she was to have none and accused her of being greedy. Needless to say there was an outburst of angry words, which caused quite a rift between Nancy and Waldorf; later Nancy calmed down and felt ashamed of her outburst but secretly resented the incident that caused disquiet between them for a long time. Shortly after this event Waldorf was taken ill with a heart complaint and moved to Rock, a small village near Wadebridge in Cornwall across the camel estuary from the fishing port of Padstow for a complete rest.

THE RAF IN PLYMOUTH

The Royal Air Force strove to keep the skies free of enemy planes during World War Two, to protect our homeland and to take the war to the enemy. In Plymouth during the war years the RAF were stationed at Harrowbeer airfield in Yelverton off the A386 between Plymouth and Tavistock. Granite stone boundaries often marked areas on Dartmoor dating back to the 14th century, and a former Plymouth Librarian William Best Harris wrote a book called 'Place Names' and he claimed the name Harrowbeer came from either Horra, which comes from the word Har, which means 'a grey lichen-covered stone' or a very old English word Hara, which means Hare. The place name Harrowbeer probably means either 'the hill of the hares' or 'the copse of the hares.' To avoid confusion with the Yelverton airfield it was decided to call the new airfield to be constructed as Harrowbeer. The Secretary of State had acquired the site for development in 1937, which meant many houses, and parcels of land in the area being requisitioned. Knightstone House, formerly Victoria Lodge, (now Knightstone Tea Rooms and Restaurant, which includes a small museum housing artefacts of the RAF) became the original Watch Office in April 1942. Ravenscroft House (formerly a boys' school) was at the beginning used for airfield defence units for a few months, but when Harrowbeer officially opened they were transferred to Down Park House and Ravenscroft became the RAF HQ Officers mess and quarters during the war and Harrowbeer eventually evolved into a Fighter Station. (When the Ministry handed over the houses Ravenscroft was returned to its original owner but they sold the property later. It became holiday lettings but is now a Residential and Nursing Home.) The airfield with its three runways was built in 1941 and on the 15th August 1941 RAF Station Harrowbeer was officially opened. The third runway, the first to be built, was possible because the Udal Torre sanatorium, formerly a large private dwelling house near the rock at Yelverton, had been closed in 1932 and was subsequently demolished between 1938/1939. Other buildings too were demolished and some of the village houses were reduced by one storey to allow the planes to come in and take off safely. It was operational between 1941 and 1945 and remained with the Air Ministry until 1962.

Flying from Harrowbeer were many types of planes and the roar of the Rolls-Royce Merlin engines could be heard over the city. The first planes to land at Harrowbeer were Blenheim bombers followed by Spitfires, Mustangs, Hurricanes, Typhoons, Whirlwinds, Walrus, Lysanders, Mosquitoes, Swordfish, Oxfords and Vengeance. Many pilots, of various nationalities, flew from this Fighter station, British, Canadians, New Zealand, Australian, Americans, (Army and Navy) French, Czech, Polish, Belgians, Rhodesians, Dutch and Norwegians. At Harrowbeer before the war documents show that Plymouth City Council began to look at future airfield sites for Plymouth in the mid 1930s. A report dated 1937 shows that three sites were being looked at, Chelson Meadow, Roborough airport, and Roborough Down. The report suggests that Chelson Meadow was not suitable as it lay in a hollow, and would therefore be awkward for planes taking off. Roborough was felt unsuitable because the main runway would be too short and there was no easy way to extend it, finally Harrowbeer, although not ideal, was suggested as the preferred option due to the nature of the land on which it would be built. The only drawback that could be foreseen was the probability of fog. In the aftermath of the early bombing of Plymouth the rubble from the city was used as the hardcore for the foundation of the three runways.

At the beginning of the Second World War it was assumed that Plymouth was too far from German air bases to be under threat of aerial bombardment. The bombers of the Luftwaffe, Dorniers, Heinkels and Junkers, did not possess the range to bomb targets in South West England and the air defence of Plymouth was not considered an immediate priority in 1939. The Air Ministry had decreed in 1940, that all new airfields would be equipped with tarmac runways, (because of the difficulties experienced by squadrons landing on grass airfields) and so it was that the rubble from the Plymouth blitz was transported to Yelverton to form part of the hard core for the new runways. Rock from quarries and mines near Tavistock was also used to form the base of the runways and the new roads in the area. The airfield construction provided welcome employment for local people, as the small village became a hive of activity as construction progressed. The shops in Yelverton were reduced to single storey buildings to reduce the risk to low flying aircraft taking off from, or approaching, the runways and several roads were diverted and new ones built.

The first operational unit to use RAF Harrowbeer as a base was 500 squadron (Code letters MK) on the 15th September 1941, who were flying Bristol Blenheims. The first machine to land was a Blenheim 1F bomber. The RAF had modified the Blenheim bomber as a fighter by the addition of four machine guns in a ventral position, and several days later a number of Blenheim fighters arrived at Harrowbeer. On the 6th October 1941, Hurricane fighters and Spitfires of the Polish 302 Squadron (Code letters WX) landed at the airfield. A rumour had arisen that Harrowbeer was a bomber base, after a Halifax was forced to land but the airfield was too small for bomber operation and Harrowbeer was therefore used solely as a fighter base. On the

21st October 1941, 130 Squadron, (Code letters PJ) flying Spitfire Mk II fighters, enjoyed a brief stay until December 1941, when the recently formed 276 Squadron (Code letter TQ) arrived. The latter unit was involved in air sea rescue and flew Lysanders, Boulton Paul Defiants, Walrus and Spitfires. In October 1941, the 302 Polish Poznan Squadron (Code letters WX) arrived at Harrowbeer, flying the Spitfire VB and Hurricanes under the command of Squadron leader Kowalski. Building construction of the airfield continued in 1942. Meanwhile, the Polish 302 Squadron was replaced in April 1942, by 312 Squadron (Code letters DU) a Czech unit flying Spitfire VBs under the command of Squadron Leader Cermak. Further squadrons arrived which included the Free French, Australians, New Zealanders and Canadians. The early missions involved shipping reconnaissance, as the fighters protected Channel convoys. With the advent of the new German fighter - the Focke Wulf 190 - Spitfires of 312 Squadron were detached to a satellite station at Bolt Head near Kingsbridge in South Devon. FW 190s were engaged in low level attacks in the South Hams and the Czech Spitfires were required to intercept the enemy intruders. Czech units were also engaged in offensive operations over the Channel in the destruction of German E boats operating from the Channel Islands. The Spitfires would also escort light bombers on sorties over occupied Europe. Pilots of the Czech squadron were posted to delivery flight duty after flying the required number of combat missions. New aircraft had to be delivered to RAF fighter stations and a Czech Flight Sergeant remembers flying the new Hawker Typhoon from Westonzoyland in Somerset. RAF 193 Squadron who flew Typhoon 1b aircraft (Code letters DP) was based at Harrowbeer in February 1943. They were in a section known on the station as Tiffy Corner in blast shelters, which still remain at Harrowbeer today. The Typhoon initially suffered from unreliability problems and could be a difficult aircraft to start. One of the main structural problems it suffered was that the tail of the aeroplane would shear off in mid air, some pilots lost their lives, however the plane was to play an effective part in the battle for Normandy in 1944 and was used principally in the ground attack role against German armour. One is reminded of Paul Nash's famous painting of Typhoons over Falaise.

With the airfield constantly shrouded in fog the pilots had to rely on guidance from the Operations room and the expertise of ground control. In support of their work the 'Ops' as it was known, would have been fitted with the accurate sector clock, these were installed in all RAF operation control rooms throughout the Second World War. Sector clocks were a vital part of the system devised to plot the position and strength of enemy aircraft. Their unique four colour segmented dial simplified and helped make fail-proof air operations control by showing time periods in a graphic way which made the work much less tedious for the often under pressure controllers and plotters. (On the walls of the 'Leg of Mutton Inn' in Yelverton, Dartmoor, are many pictures of wartime crews and a framed text plaque including a full description of the important sector clock. This was researched and written by Ken Johnson 2006) March 1943 saw the arrival of 263 Squadron (Code letters HE) flying the twin-engine

Whirlwind F1 fighter-bomber and Typhoons. The Whirlwind, escorted by single engine fighters was used effectively in strikes on enemy shipping. On the 25th May 1943, the 414 Squadron (Code letters RU) of the Royal Canadian Air Force commenced flying operations in Mustangs1b, a supremely effective fighter used, like the Typhoon, in a ground attack role. From 1943 until 1945, many U.S. light aircraft used Harrowbeer, and this airfield, as with all other RAF stations, was to play a key role in the forthcoming invasion of occupied Europe. Only the Allied High Command knew the proposed date of the invasion but all were aware that the greatest amphibious assault in the history of warfare was imminent. The Typhoons left Harrowbeer, to be replaced by many Squadrons of Spitfires whose function would be to defend against enemy air attacks. The end of Operation Overlord virtually marked the eventual demise of Harrowbeer as an RAF fighter station. By August 1944, the station became a satellite of Exeter and the Free French 329 Squadron (Code letters 5A) was the last operational unit to use the field, flying Spitfire IX fighters, until June 1945.

Nancy would meet some of the Free French ground crews and pilots from the airfield in the Y.M.C.A quarters in Elliot Street (now the Astor Hotel) and join them for tea where she would mix with all ranks from many nations. Waldorf and Nancy always ensured they helped wherever they could; comfort facilities were also made available for the RAF at Harrowbeer. Lady Astor frequently visited the aircrews and maintenance personnel, including the five original WAAF ladies serving on the base, later more ladies were to arrive serving as armourers, transport drivers, maintenance crews or cooks. Lady Astor attended a function at Harrowbeer on the 16th October 1943 where she was accompanying the Brazilian Ambassador in his capacity of supporting the war work in Britain. The British ex-pats group living in Brazil had bought half of the Typhoon aircraft that the RAF 193 Squadron flew. This group were known as, The Fellowship of the Bellows, and it was their way of helping the war effort and the Brazilian Ambassador was making the official presentation to Harrowbeer airfield, also attending the function was Under Secretary of State for Air assisted by Lady Astor. A fly-past was to be arranged as an additional welcome, but the weather was very bad and the rain came down so hard it was impossible to hold the event. Instead of a fly-past there was a 'taxi-past' as rain drenched visiting press and dignitaries made a hasty retreat from the airfield in a continuous flow of taxis.

Virginia-born Nancy visited Plaister Down camp, near Tavistock in 1943, where servicemen of the 29th Infantry Division were billeted. (Plaister Down can be found between the villages of Whitchurch and Sampford Spinney, it is a stretch of open moorland in the shadow of Pew Tor) The purpose of her visit was to 'Talk Southern' with Lt.Col. Fourrier of Louisiana, USA. Entertainment was the highlight for weary servicemen and on Monday 28th August 1944 the celebrated bandleader Glenn Miller landed at Harrowbeer with his AEF forty-piece Orchestra with a full entertainment programme. The band played at Harrowbeer then US Navy trucks provided transport

Major Glenn Miller (1904-1944) and the American Band of the AEF toured
The United Kingdom during 1944 performing for service personnel.
He and his band arrived at Harrowbeer in August 1944.
He was given a tour of Plymouth's badly bombed city centre.
Lady Astor had the pleasure of listening to his very popular band.
In December 1944 whilst flying from the UK to France
His plane disappeared and the plane and his body were never found.

to the Royal Naval College at Manadon, where the Band played to patients of the nearby United States Navy Hospital. Later they performed at the Odeon Cinema to an audience of four thousand British and American servicemen. Meanwhile a string section entertained two thousand servicemen, which included one thousand 'Seebees' (Construction Battalion Personnel) at Shapter's field, Cattedown, Plymouth. Jazz fanatics and local Jazzmen were treated to an improvised Jazz session at the Duke of Cornwall Hotel, these musical interludes were to bring, for a little while, some pleasure into people's lives. The Band was billeted at Queen Anne's Battery. Sadly in December that year Glenn Miller's plane was either shot down or crashed into the sea and his body and the plane were never found.

MEMORIES OF V.E. DAY

Mr Eric.R.J. Annis now living in Newton Abbot remembers vividly the celebrations of VE day (Victory over Europe.) He remarked that most of the population of Plymouth headed for Plymouth Hoe and things began to get out of hand as some over-enthusiastic celebrators started ripping up the temporary band stand and piling up the deck chairs and setting fire to them to make an impressive bonfire. The fire service and the council workers exhausted from six years of war were not prepared to cope with this unexpected event. There had been no organisation and everyone seemed to be doing just as they pleased. Suddenly Lady Astor appeared and she began to make moves to bring the crowd under control and to diffuse the situation. Enrolling the help of two burly sailors, they stood either side of her then lifted her up on their shoulders, and pushed their way towards the bonfire. Mr Annis recalls the force of her personality and the respect they held for her created an immediate response. She shouted to them to listen for a moment "Enjoy yourselves but please respect our property" she talked to them for a while and the crowd became calmer and then a voice shouted out from the background "Turn her over Jack she is done that side!" and the crowd roared with laughter, for Nancy had been side on to the bonfire and she and both the sailors were feeling the heat. The remark brought an instant response and, laughing with the crowd, she said, "Come on, let's all have a dance," the tension lifted and the crowd swept on to the promenade and began to dance. Mr Annis admired Lady Astor as she had always visited his youth club at Saint Andrew's Church between the years 1943-1945. Mr Annis was about fifteen years old in 1943 and the club met regularly at Prysten House and every time Nancy visited the club Mr Eric (Mick) Annis or another young lad would escort Lady Astor home from Prysten House to Elliot Terrace. Mr Annis was quite honoured at this task and he would chat to her on the way back to her home and he was quite at ease. He said, "She was a grand lady and we shall never have another lady Member of Parliament like her."

PRESERVATION FIGHT

When the war ended Lady Astor would be seen outside Underhills stationery bookshop near the Library lobbying citizens to fight to preserve some of Plymouth's architectural buildings which were being pulled down as part of the rebuilding of the bomb damaged city under the 1941 Abercrombie new town plan. She was near the end of her political career yet she refused to give up on any issue that affected her beloved Plymothians. Nancy's cut-out cardboard profile was seen for many years looking out from the window of the Museum in Drake Circus, alongside the cut-outs of Professor Abercrombie and Forbes Watson. Passengers travelling on the local buses would see if they looked up, the imposing figure of Nancy viewing her beloved Plymouth. The profile figures looked out over the University buildings, which had been one of Nancy's dreams, to see Plymouth as a University City. In January 2008 the Plymouth museum was closed for three months for a complete renovation and scaffolding was placed around the building. With renovations complete the Museum was re-opened in March 2008 and it was noted that the cardboard cut-outs had been completely removed from the window.

ENDURANCE

In those crowded years there were events enough to fill a lifetime. Would we ever forgive or forget those dreadful times? Over the years that generation has not forgotten, but they have come to terms with quiet retrospect, life seems to provide us with those little interludes even in the midst of adversity. The new Plymouth is indeed controversial, each generation sees it differently, and the older generation believe that the intimate has been replaced by the impersonal. In times of need and when a nation is on the brink of defeat there is always someone somewhere who can turn the tide of despair into a victory. For Plymouth when our greatest need looked for leaders it was met by the Astor family and we must ensure that the history Plymothians endured during those traumatic times will be remembered in school curriculums and that each generation should learn what the Astor family did for this beautiful city by the sea. To our American friends in that lovely county of Virginia, USA, we thank you for giving us one of your own flowers of youth in 1906 who was to give England such pleasure, enriched by her beauty, thrilled with her witticisms, and enthralled at her fire to fight for women's rights. Indeed a woman who gave so much of herself to the ordinary people of Plymouth.

Photo from a private collection. Courtesy Westcountry Publications
Digital copy by Trevor Burrows Plymouth Photographer

Lady Astor as Lady Mayoress escorting her Majesty Queen Elizabeth
(The late Queen Mother) around the city of Plymouth 1941

Photo courtesy of Charles Prynne, & Westcountry Publications. Digital copy Trevor Burrows Plymouth.

His Royal Highness Prince George, Duke of Kent, visited Plymouth in June 1941 and was escorted by Lady Astor to meet members of the public who were performing a sterling service to the city.

Photo from a private collection. Original photo thought to be Western Morning News. Digital copy Trevor Burrows Photography Plymouth

Lord and Lady Astor with the Duchess of Kent in Plymouth Circa 1943-1944. The Duchess is wearing the uniform of Commandant, The Women's Royal Naval Service

Lady Astor and Mr Modley Deputy Lord Mayor with Mrs Modley behind on right
Circa 1939-1944.
Taking a memorial wreath to Plymouth Hoe for a November remembrance service.

*Viscount and Viscountess Astor chosen as Plymouth's Lord Mayor and Lady Mayoress in 1939.
Right of Lady Astor the Deputy Lord and Lady Mayoress Mrs & Mrs Modley. Standing left of Lord Astor the Town Clerk.*

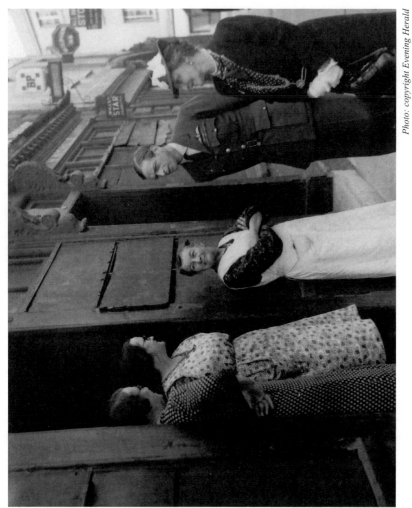

Photo: copyright Evening Herald

Lady Astor with the Duke of Kent and Plymouth citizens. 20th June 1941.

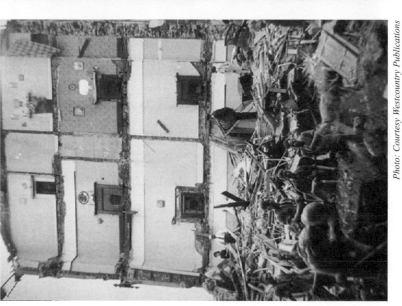

Photo: Courtesy Westcountry Publications

Blitzed Westcountry house 1941. Note the unbroken mirror on the mantelpiece and the photographs on the wall untouched. Yet the house was destroyed and the occupants killed.

CHAPTER FIVE
THE FOOTMAN - THOMAS CHARLES PRYNNE

Pioneers may be picturesque figures, but they are often rather lonely ones. *Nancy Astor 1879-1964.*

Charles, a young man of twenty-two years, took the post as Footman to Lady Astor in March 1957 and remained in her service until February 1959. Now in his seventies he comes from a time when words like duty, service, and loyalty, had more meaning than they do in today's modern irreverent Britain; he still admires and remembers her with affection and the impact she had on his life. He found it very easy, although he was a young man, to work for an older lady and he had been around old people for some time, more so than his own generation. In the RAF his wages had been three pounds a week. When he started work in 1957 for Lady Astor, Charles had full board and lodgings and was supplied every year with two new lounge suits made at Horne's the gentlemen outfitters in London, new shirts, ties and shoes, and every week four pounds pocket money. Lady Astor was a good employer and looked after her staff. When Charles left her employment, with the reference Lady Astor had given him, his life was to change. He only had to say that he had worked for Lady Astor, and that enabled him in later years to gain the position of every post he applied for. Here is his story as told, updated with facts and dates by the Author, and what a fascinating story it is.

My Grandmother over the years used to keep scrapbooks and if anything about the Royal Family or the aristocracy were in the papers or magazines during her lifetime, she would cut out the pieces and put them in a scrapbook. As a young lad of ten I used to read these and I would ask her questions, "Who is this lady or this person? Why have you got them in a scrapbook?" I read them frequently and I became very interested in history and my Grandmother admired Lady Astor for what she had achieved. I took an interest in this American lady being elected to the House of Commons and the things that happened during the war and I began to follow her life and career. In 1956, before I was demobbed from the Royal Air Force, I had come to the Royal Naval Hospital in Devonport, Plymouth, to have an operation on my distorted toe, which was extremely painful, and thankfully the operation was successful. I was in Plymouth for a few days when the Hospital Authorities sent me to Noss Mayo, which is a little hamlet near Plymouth to recuperate; sometime patients who were recovering were allowed to come into Plymouth on the bus and we would perhaps have tea somewhere or have a nice walk if the weather was good.

One afternoon I went up to Plymouth Hoe and saw 3, Elliot Terrace, which is where Lady Astor lived when she was in Plymouth. I was fascinated by it and thought what

Charles Prynne as a young man employed as Lady Astor's Footman
Photo taken at Wilton House summer 1957 (Whilst on holiday)

a lovely house, what a nice place to live, not thinking that within three months I would be actually working for the lady who lived there. She was lovely to work for and treated her staff as family; naturally on occasion she would complain about things if they were not right in her eyes, but she was never unkind with the things she said to her servants. Her maid Rose Harrison was a servants' champion because if she noticed that any member of the staff was unhappy about anything she would go upstairs and report it right away to her Ladyship and it would be put right immediately. As her Ladyship got older she became more tolerant and mellowed with age. She was in her seventies but her mind was failing. There is no doubt that the loss of her political career and not being in the centre of everything was deeply felt; she had lost the fire and passion that had been the pivot of her life. I thought highly of her because she was such a character. Lady Astor used to tell the story of her conversation with her maid Rose Harrison in the shelter during the bombing. Her ladyship would reminisce about Virginia and her childhood and the tobacco fields. Rose, her maid, and Lady Astor had been together for thirty years and her ladyship would say about Rose, "she was the only woman in the world who would put up with me," Rose declared once that Lady Astor is the kind of woman who takes understanding and it took her three years to understand her but despite her comments Rose Harrison was a loyal and reliable maid for the rest of her working life. Viscountess Astor was, however, still in demand, people wishing to interview her, attending meetings, and was frequently invited out to lunch.

If someone wanted to interview her on her political career she warmed to it because she loved talking about her time in Parliament. There were times when people came to her for lunch or dinner and she always enjoyed entertaining guests. One story she frequently told at the dinner table was the time when she went to church and there were quite a few black members in the congregation and a young girl stood up and said, "How come we got white folks and black folks?" The minister thought about it for a minute or two before replying, "Well, once upon a time all folks was black and God lined them up against a fence and started painting some of them and he ran out of paint, and that is why you got white folks and black folks." Then the girl asked, "Well minister, who put the fence there?" The minister now becoming exasperated said, "Child it's questions like that what's ruining religion!" Then there was a story when Nancy Langhorne was at school run by two maiden ladies. They said on a Friday that, "on Monday we are going to do an examination in a form of a mathematical test," and Nancy said, "I knew I was never any good at mathematics, so I went home that weekend and I prayed to God that he would burn down the school house, so of course when I went back to school on the Monday it was still standing, and I went off religion for a long time."

I had been demobbed from the Royal Air Force in the February and I went home to St Ives, Cornwall, not really knowing what I was going to do for employment. In late February I left St Ives and travelled to London primarily to seek employment. On the journey I had been reading the Daily Telegraph newspaper, in those days the paper had a column of household and domestic servants wanted. I came across an advert from the Hunt Regina Domestic Agency in Marylebone High Street, London and when I arrived in London I booked into the Union Jack Club at Waterloo and the next day went to Marylebone High Street to the agency offices. I entered this charming little office and there were two elderly ladies who were conducting the interviews and a few people sitting around waiting their turn. I was about the fourth in line and the lady who interviewed me was named Miss Phillips and she was something out of a Charles Dickens novel, very prim, very dainty, and as it was February she was wearing these little mittens where the tips of the fingers were exposed. When it was my turn she called me over and I sat down, I was quite relaxed, as I knew

A stunning autographed photograph of Lady Astor
Given to her Footman Charles Prynne
With a message referring to her beloved Virginia saying:
To Charles trusting he will like my native land of Virginia.

instinctively that she was a genteel person. She asked my name and particulars and said: "What are you looking for?" I replied, "I don't know really because I have not been trained for anything, when I left school I just went to work in the Post Office, but I did not like that and left, then I found another job at a factory where they made boxes for vegetables and flowers, and I was there until I was eighteen. From there in 1954 I went into the Royal Air Force to take up training as a Medical Orderly." Miss Phillips then said; "Well if you do go into service you know you will probably have to start at the bottom?" I remarked that I did not mind that because at least I would be learning something. She advised me that there was no vacancy at that time but if I gave her my home address she would let me know if a vacancy became available. I thanked her and made my way back to the Union Jack Club where I stayed for a couple of days to have a look around London and then returned home.

My next-door neighbour who had been the Manager at the factory where I had been formerly employed in St Ives no longer worked there himself as the factory had closed. He was not long out of work because he had been fortunate enough to be employed again and whilst we were having a conversation he mentioned that his employer was Mr Boyd. (Alan Tindal Lennox-Boyd (1904-1983) Conservative Member of Parliament for mid-Bedfordshire and at that time Colonial Secretary. He was also Deputy Lieutenant of Bedfordshire between 1954-1960. Later he became the First Viscount Boyd of Merton) My next-door neighbour was working for him during the week in Southampton where Mr Lennox-Boyd had a yacht and it was being fitted out for a cruise that summer to the Mediterranean and Mr Curtis suggested to me that I might like to take a job as there was a vacancy for a Steward, so I thought about it and as I did not have anything else at that time I decided to accept the post. I left for Southampton and was on the yacht for a couple of days, it was the absolute height of luxury, being a big racing yacht, and it was beautiful.

In the meantime Miss Phillips, the lady who had interviewed me in London earlier, had sent a letter to my home in Cornwall and my mother forwarded it on to me. The letter stated that Viscountess Astor was looking for a Footman to be trained in the way her household was run. I spoke to Mr Curtis and explained to him that I would prefer to be in private service rather than being a steward on the yacht because I was not quite sure how I would have managed on the ocean never having been to sea before. He very kindly let me go. I left Southampton immediately, travelled to London and booked in once again into the Union Jack Club. As soon as I could I phoned the number given to me at Hill Street, Berkeley Square, and I was told to come the next afternoon for an interview with the Butler and the Secretary. I duly turned up and met the Butler, Mr Arnold Harwood, and the Secretary, Miss Jones. The interview took place in Miss Jones' office and I must say that she was a perfectly mannered lady, exquisitely turned out and with a quiet sense of humour. Asked to wait outside while my future was being discussed, I waited with bated breath for their decision and they wasted no time in calling me back into the office to tell me that I had been employed. I was delighted and the Butler asked me "When can you start? Can you start tomorrow?" I replied, "Yes, splendid!" I went back to the Club, assembled all my belongings, and started my new job the next morning, when I told my mother to write to me care of Lady Astor she was so proud.

At ten o'clock the following morning I was introduced to all the staff and as they were about to have their coffee break I was invited to join them. Mrs Hawkins was the Head House maid; there were two daily cleaning ladies and William the 'Odd Man.' I thought that was a strange title, however, it was explained to me, his job was to look after the fires, do all the menial tasks around the house, and to do all the heavy fetching and carrying. Then I was taken along to the kitchen to meet the Chef, Mr Otto Dangl, he was an Austrian from Vienna, and had two staff, a kitchen maid and a daily maid. I could not meet Lady Astor at the time as she was in America with her maid Rose and would not be back for a month, this enabled me to learn some of my duties. As the footman my domestic duties would vary and involved me in cleaning Lady Astor's shoes, serving table, preparing and taking her breakfast tray to her bedroom in the mornings passing the tray to Rose her maid. Other duties were cleaning the silver (there were some beautiful pieces of silver I liked doing that) running errands, taking the dog for a walk and answering the door. I was only a young man of twenty-two but I loved the job and adored Lady Astor, she was wonderful to her staff. The thrill of meeting famous people was fascinating and I started to collect autographs and her Ladyship would always have my autograph book placed beside the visitor's book to ensure I got their autographs.

I was taken by Mr Harwood the Butler to the pantry into the silver safe where all the valuable silver items were kept; he filled a tray with a selection of spoons, forks, knives and condiment sets and also added a few glasses, and said," "I will take you up to the dining room and show you how we lay a table." He taught me how to set the table for lunch or dinner, I tried, and made a couple of mistakes, putting the salt cellars in the wrong place and I had not set the glasses correctly. He reassured me saying that I would get it right next time, as it was early days yet. We went down to the staff hall for lunch where the staff were seated, and we had a scrumptious lunch. For servants it was a wonderful lunch, in fact we were given always the same food as her Ladyship and her guests upstairs were having. After lunch the Butler said, "Come on Charles, we will take you around the house." He showed me all the rooms, the dining room already set for the evening meal. The Library was a beautiful room; the hallway went from the front door right through the house to a window at the end. Next to that in the corner was Miss Jones' office; in the hallway was a lift, which was regularly used.

We walked up the stairs which was a grand Georgian staircase and entered the first room on the right, that went right through from the front of the house to the back of the house and at the end was the ballroom. There hanging from the ceiling were two magnificent chandeliers, Queen Marie of Rumania who was the granddaughter of Queen Victoria had given one of them to Lord and Lady Astor. She was a friend of the Astor family, as Lord Astor had known her since he was a young man. I do not know where the other chandelier came from. Next to the ballroom at the end of the corridor was her Ladyship's sitting room, which was always referred to as 'The Boudoir.' Now this room was really lovely, very welcoming, the walls were all lined with blue satin and it had a lovely bay window that overlooked the houses at the back; being in London all the houses were built back to back. From there I was taken up to the private bedrooms where her Ladyship's bedroom and two guest bedrooms were; I think there were four bedrooms but it was so many years ago that I am not sure. The next floor up were the staff rooms, it was a six-floor house with the basement. My room was right at the back of the basement with a bathroom and a big storeroom where steamer trunks, goods and chattels were kept; I was never able to get into it because it was always kept locked. After the tour I had the rest of the day off and the Butler said, "Do you know London?" I said, "No not really, only the sights that I saw as a child with my Grandmother during the war, and most of that was bombed." Then he said, "I will show you around." Off we went to Berkeley Square, Piccadilly, St James's Square and along the Mall, it was a lovely afternoon and it was indeed a very pleasant few hours. We came back to the house and had another staff meal and then the rest of the time was my own, so I unpacked my bags and made my room comfortable.

The following day I was reminded of my duties and advised on the things I had to do and how her Ladyship liked things done and I was also given the task of looking after the family pet. I had been there about a month before Lady Astor and Rose came back from America. The day after the liner left New York telegrams began to arrive from Miss Harrison with various instructions; the first telegram indicated that her Ladyship would require a car to meet the boat at Southampton and they would drive up to London, the difficulty was she had a lot of luggage. The next day another telegram arrived saying cancel the earlier instruction as her Ladyship would now come back by train and would the car meet her at Waterloo. This changing of her mind went on for three days until the final decision was to meet her at Waterloo; everyone breathed a sigh of relief. On the evening they were due to come back there was bad weather and fog in the Channel, the liner was late in docking and by the time they got to Southampton, gone through the customs and got on the train, all was mayhem. To make matters worse the train was late at Waterloo. It was in the early hours of the morning when they finally arrived. William the 'Odd Man,' Mr Harwood the Butler, and myself, had been waiting in the hall for hours for the car to arrive. The night Lady Astor returned from America she had with her a lady called Miss Butterworth who was a Christian Science Practitioner. I do not know if she had come from America with her Ladyship or whether she had met her at Waterloo Station. She was a lovely lady, I liked her very much. She was always very gracious.

ON THE WAY
HOME FROM
AMERICA
1957

By kind permission Charles Prynne
Digital copy taken by Trevor Burrows Photographer Plymouth

Lady Astor on her way home from America in 1957
The photo has been autographed by Lady Astor

Her Ladyship had a Corgi dog, a pretty little thing called Madam a gift from her eldest son, Mr Bobby Shaw. Although not a keen dog lover she did treasure Madam but her ladyship did not like cats or spiders. I had been looking after the little dog for a month, feeding her, grooming her, and taking her for walks, and she had got quite attached to me. I had often taken the dog for a walk in the afternoons and I always took her around Buckingham Palace thinking that people would believe I was walking one of the Queen's corgis. I was quite a snob in those days but soon matured with age. When the car finally arrived at quarter past one in the morning the door was opened and her Ladyship rushed in, said "Good Morning Arnold," looked at me and then at the 'Odd Man' and said, "Good Morning William," and went upstairs. On the way up she called the dog "Madam come here," Madam remained motionless, "Come along Madam," the dog would not go she just looked at her Ladyship. The little dog sat beside me and refused to budge, her Ladyship carried on upstairs. In the meantime a taxi drew up behind Lady Astor's car absolutely packed with luggage, steamer trunks, suitcases, bags and handbags. Miss Harrison counted them all in and then we were told to take all the bags to her Ladyship's floor. The Butler received a phone call telling him to send the Footman up right away and to bring the dog. I carried Madam up the stairs knocked on her Ladyship's door and heard her say, "Come in." I said, "The dog my lady." "Oh yes, bring her in here," she said. Her Ladyship was at her desk going through the mail, at that time of the morning. She looked at me and said, "Now, you are the new Footman, what is your name?" I said, "Yes my lady, my name is Thomas Prynne," "Thomas? Thomas? Have you got another name?" I replied, "Yes my lady, Thomas Charles Prynne," Her ladyship said, "Yes that will be your name while you are here, we will call you Charles! Where are you from?" I said, "I am Cornish my lady," "Oh you are from Cornwall, I think I have Cornish roots, that's wonderful. Now, you know I was Member of Parliament for Sutton Division of Plymouth for twenty-five years?" "Yes my lady, I did know that," I replied. She looked at me straight in the eye and said, "Splendid! I hope you will be happy here, thank you very much and good night!"

Having wished her good night and grateful that my introduction had been quite pleasant, off I went. I started down the stairs and all of a sudden I heard someone playing a harmonica, bearing in mind it was now nearly two in the morning, and then I realised it was Lady Astor. Her Ladyship tried, I say tried, to play a tune. She was playing Carry Me Back To Old Virginia and while she was doing this the little dog started howling, really howling like a wolf. I thought my God, this is going to be an interesting place to work, and it was! During my time there she would often continue to play Carry Me Back To Old Virginia and everyone would be in fits of laughter. When she came back from America after one of her trips she would bring back recordings of songs of the Civil War, and songs of the Old South, mostly the songs by Stephen Collins Foster. (Foster (1826-1864) was known as the Father of American music who died at the young age of thirty-seven. A brilliant songwriter who wrote songs about the Deep South, some of the songs he wrote are remembered today, such as: Oh! Susanna, My old Kentucky Home, Beautiful Dreamer, and Old Folks at Home, (Swanee River) and many more.)

Photo by kind permission Charles Prynne

Autographed photo of Lady Astor age 78 yrs
Taken in the back drawing room at 3, Elliot Terrace on a visit to Plymouth 1957

Lady Astor liked music and she had a beautiful radiogram from the maker's His Master Voice (HMV) and she would play her favourite records, usually songs of the American Civil War. One song that she used to play over and over again was Eartha Kitt's 'If I Can't Take It With Me When I Go, I Ain't Going,' she really liked that one. Her Ladyship's friend, Mary Stocks, played the mouth organ, and it could be the reason that Lady Astor tried so hard to play the instrument, unfortunately with little success, as she was tone deaf; all the staff would run and find something else to do if they saw the appearance of the harmonica. Her Ladyship read her bible every day and we would on occasion be told of a quotation from her Christian Science beliefs if she wanted to emphasise a point. She would read the papers, usually The Times, Illustrated London News, The Sketch (now part of the Daily Mail) Punch and National Geographic Magazines. Her Ladyship was full of fun, witty, and very clever with mimicry and yes, she could be demanding, but champion to her staff.

I soon learnt how to do things correctly and I would take up her breakfast tray, which consisted of pure orange juice squeezed from a fresh orange, she had coffee, which she called Boston coffee, half hot coffee and half hot milk, toast and marmalade. She also liked ice cream and fresh fruit. I gave the tray to Miss Harrison the maid and went downstairs to the staff room for my breakfast. For breakfast the staff had the full whack to eat. I had the cooked breakfast each day, bacon, eggs, sausages, mushrooms, tomatoes, and toast with marmalade, lovely food. I particularly liked the kedgeree, which was made with rice and fish, the fish was cooked and then it was crumbled and mixed with the rice and served with hard boiled eggs cut in half coupled with mustard sauce; it tasted really nice. Her Ladyship would also like corn soufflé with vegetables and that was made with ground up corn and put in to the oven for a certain amount of time. If she was late coming back from church and the soufflé was in the oven the Chef used to get really up tight. If it was spoilt he would scrub it; he would never serve anything that was not perfect. Another favourite meal was saddle of lamb with roast potatoes and runner beans sliced very thinly; Lady Astor liked runner beans, sliced almonds were fried in butter and that would be poured over the saddle of lamb before it was taken to the dining room; it was a scrumptious dish, and her Ladyship loved to eat the old southern dishes. Her Ladyship would have whole smoked Virginia hams sent from America in the 1950's; they were covered in honey with sticks of cloves and she would also have a brace of pheasants sent down from Scotland during the shooting season, usually Lord Ancaster sent them. Lady Astor rarely had tea; teatime was usually between four or five in the afternoon. Tea would only be served when anyone was coming to visit her. Her Ladyship would not drink tea herself, instead she preferred to have a glass of Ribena or a glass of Dubonnet.

Lady Astor read her Christian Science books first thing in the morning and my first job for the day after breakfast was to lay the table for luncheon, this would be a daily ritual and I soon learned how things were done. The Butler would ring Miss Harrison, her Ladyship's maid, to find out how many people there would be for lunch. In the meantime the Chef had gone upstairs with the menu for the day, given it to Miss Harrison who took it into her Ladyship and everything was passed. The Chef returned to the kitchen to prepare the agreed menu. The Butler and I went upstairs to lay the table for lunch. Well I had forgotten everything he had told me and I was quite embarrassed, however, he told me not to worry as it does take time and he kindly showed me again how to do it. Usually the table would be set for six to eight people, her Ladyship liked a lot of people around the table. Then her Ladyship starts phoning. We had a telephone exchange down in the basement, one of the old-fashioned systems where you inserted cable pins into sockets and William the 'Odd Man' used to operate that, and she began ringing around and when she had finished there would be one or two more guests coming for lunch or dinner.

Lady Astor had three homes. There was the London home at 35 Hill Street and a very fine house in Sandwich, Kent, called Rest Harrow which was mainly used as her summer holiday home, and we used to go down there for about six weeks every year. The Dowager Viscountess still continued to swim and play tennis well into her late seventies when she was staying in Sandwich. Another home was 3, Elliot Terrace, on the Hoe in Plymouth; we would stay there about three weeks. The house on Plymouth Hoe was lovely and the views of Plymouth Sound were breathtaking. Miss Manning, the Housekeeper, spent most of her time in the basement where there was an old Morrison Shelter and it brought back some memories of the war years for her ladyship. Mrs Woods the Cook took care of the meals if the Chef did not come down to Plymouth. On the ground floor when you went in on the left would be the dining room, behind that was the pantry, and behind that again was Lady Astor's Plymouth Secretary's office. Her secretary was called Miss Knight, she did not live in but lived somewhere in the district.

Photo courtesy of Charles Prynne

Photo taken in the summer of 1957 at the house known as Rest Harrow, Sandwich, Kent.
Left to right: Miss Day, Housekeeper. Charles Prynne, Footman and
Arnold Harwood, Butler.

On the right hand side of the entrance hall was a beautiful antique Grandfather Clock and everything moved on the face, it was fascinating, you could see the moon, the stars, and the sun. The stairway of the house was special; it went up to a little landing and then one had to turn left taking in a few more stairs to the main floor upstairs. At the top of the first staircase on the small landing, hanging proudly on the wall, was a picture of her Ladyship entering Parliament. I do not know if it was original or a copy, but it was always on that wall facing you as you went upstairs. At the very top of the stairs on the left you walked into her Ladyship's drawing room. Years ago when Lord and Lady Astor were Lord Mayor and Lady Mayoress they also occupied the house next door where there was a small office there next to her Ladyship's drawing room, and a blocked up doorway which had led into the house next door where a lot of his Lordship's Mayoral duties were done by Miss Knight and a typist. The drawing room went right from the front to the back; I think there was a small toilet on that floor, then there was another staircase which took you up to Lady Astor's bedroom and guest rooms and above that were the staff rooms. Miss Harrison had one and I had the other. I used to spend a lot of time with Rose Harrison when we were down in Plymouth, more so than when I was in London. Rose was always working sorting things out and ironing; she always turned out her Ladyship looking immaculate, she would be dressed to perfection. I had the highest regard for Rose Harrison, she had a wonderful sense of humour, was very direct and I would say was a servants' champion. I know she was not very popular in some areas but to me, having worked with her, she was honest; true, Rose always spoke her mind (similar trait as Lady Astor) and got things done and I have always appreciated that, as you know where you are with people with that characteristic.

Elliot Terrace was my favourite place because I had a very fine bedroom right at the top of the house with spectacular views across Plymouth Sound to Drake's Island, Mount Edgecumbe and Mountbatten. During our visits to Plymouth Lady Astor often used to go down to the Barbican to look around the antique shops. Invariably she bought something that I had to collect later and bring back to Elliot Terrace. Her Ladyship would put it somewhere in the drawing room upstairs and she would have it displayed for a day or two and then suddenly I would be called to return the item to the shop in the Barbican, as she was not happy with the way it looked in the drawing room. Either her Ladyship or Rose Harrison would have contacted the shop to say the item was being returned and to expect me at the shop. This happened several times because Lady Astor would pick up something thinking it would be nice or she would buy something for a friend and then she would think about it and change her mind. Off I would go across Plymouth Hoe, down past the Citadel and on to the Barbican and I used to look forward to this little trip.

At Elliot Terrace we always had lots of people for meals, some I can remember. One couple I do remember because they were very nice people was Alderman and Mrs Modley who used to be the Deputy Mayor and Mayoress of Plymouth to Lord and

Lady Astor. He and Mrs Modley came regularly at least once a fortnight to either lunch or dinner. They were a charming couple and always very polite and they were friends, and remained friends, for life. Another visitor was the sister of the Earl of Mount Edgecumbe. The Admiral Superintendent of the Dockyard and his wife were frequent visitors, in addition one or two friends of Lady Astor who lived in the countryside would call on occasion for lunch on Sundays. HRH Princess Alice, Countess of Athlone, who was the last surviving grandchild of Queen Victoria, came to Plymouth and stayed at Elliot Terrace as the guest of Lady Astor, to attend the re-consecration of Saint Andrew's Church, the mother Church of Plymouth. In the afternoon on the 30th November 1957 she attended the blessing in the presence of the Lord Bishop of Exeter and the Bishop of Plymouth, also in attendance was the current Lord Mayor Leslie Francis Paul. In my autograph book I am proud to say I have Princess Alice's autograph there as HRH Princess Alice stayed for several days. Eventually the Princess, Lady Astor, and her staff departed Plymouth, to return to London on the train. Of course Lady Astor and her guest had a compartment to themselves, occasionally Miss Rose Harrison, her Ladyship's maid, would pop in and out of the carriage to see if they were alright or in need of anything.

In London her Ladyship continued to invite guests, family and friends to her home, during her retirement years she still entertained royalty, politicians, writers and invited anyone she fancied at the time. Her Ladyship's years of retirement from the political scene left her completely isolated from full time activity, so she would keep busy with meetings, interviews, sitting on trustee committees and entertaining guests at her home for lunch or perhaps dinner and frequently invited a last minute guest. This would anger the chef and words filled the air as he became quite cross with her, as it meant resetting the table and re-organising the food programme. Lady Astor loved her food and the Chef used to cook a lot of Southern dishes for her ladyship, she particularly liked cornbread, biscuits and French menus. Although her Ladyship and Otto frequently had words both had the highest regard and mutual respect for each other. There was a time when he got so cross about this he went to see her Ladyship, he always called her Madame and he handed in his resignation, however, 'Madame' never accepted it. Lady Astor had a very sweet tooth and she would have an endless supply of goodies sent to her from the United States, as American sweets were her favourite. She liked boxes of candies, pecan candies in purple boxes and peanut brittle. Chewing gum was another favourite, any sweet that she could chew and friends would send her boxes of chocolates and candy.

One of the nicest people I knew that I still remember with affection was her Ladyship's niece Joyce Grenfell, the comedienne and entertainer. She was also a very talented amateur painter and a confirmed Christian Scientist and she was charming and quite funny really, always with a powerful sense of humour. Joyce and her Aunt regularly played tennis and invariably her Ladyship won, and she would often tease Joyce about it but Joyce took it in good spirit. I remember on one occasion when Miss

Grenfell visited wearing an unusual hat, and her Ladyship immediately commented by saying to her: "Really Joyce, that hat you are wearing, wherever did you find it?" Miss Grenfell would say where she had got it from and her Ladyship replied: "I think it is terrible, you should wear something better than that!" Joyce would be telling her what she planned to do in the shows and her Ladyship tried, I say tried, not to laugh, but she couldn't help herself and eventually would burst out laughing. Although at times some bickering would take place Joyce was very fond of her. Despite her Ladyship's criticisms when she met other people she always remarked how proud she was of Joyce's success on the stage. Joyce was involved with theatre shows in the evening that is why she came for lunch during the day instead of attending the dinner in the evening. (Note by the Author. Joyce Grenfell, dearly loved and best remembered for her monolgues, songs, and comic writings, appeared in 1954 in her first solo show Joyce Grenfell Requests the Pleasure. (In 1964 and 1972 her television shows were to prove very popular.)

Another regular to visit and stay for lunch was Lady Astor's son, Mr Bobby Shaw, he did not come very often for dinner; he had two corgi dogs that he always brought with him. He had given his mother the Corgi bitch called Madam although she was not keen on dogs she took care of it, and when the Dowager Viscountess died in 1964 her maid Rose Harrison took care of the little dog. Other callers at her Ladyship's home were her family members, including her grandson and a great nephew, who was drowned in the Channel a few years later, also at the lunches was Lady Astor's daughter Phyllis Astor (known to the family as Wissie.) She had married Gilbert James Heathcote-Drummond-Willoughby 3rd Earl of Ancaster. Lord Ancaster and the Countess (Phyllis) with their daughter Lady Jane Willoughby and their son Timothy Gilbert Heathcote-Drummond-Willoughby (1936-1963) were regular visitors to her Ladyship's home; they were nice children typical of their class always very pleasant. (Between 1951 and 1963 Timothy was styled as Lord Willoughby de Eresby. Sadly he drowned in a sailing accident in 1963 at the age of twenty-seven when his yacht disappeared at sea between Cap Ferrat and Corsica. Lord Ancaster senior had been badly wounded in the Second World War and had lost a leg.)

I can remember vividly an incident, which occurred when they were staying in Sandwich one summer. Lord Ancaster came to stay for a short while and he always had his breakfast in bed. One morning I was taking his breakfast up to his bedroom, I knew he had a false leg but did not take any notice of his predicament. I knocked on the door and I heard him say, "Come in" he was up but not quite dressed but he did have a dressing gown on. Propped up against the bedstead at the foot of the bed was the leg. I looked at the leg and then at Lord Ancaster and he said quite casually: "Pretty good eh?" I said: "Yes my Lord," put the tray down and left. I always remember that, such courage, he was a nice gentleman with all their wealth they too had their pain and tragedies in their lives. Another very special lady that comes to mind, she was absolutely lovely, was Queen Ingrid of Denmark who liked to visit her

Ladyship in the afternoon. (Note by the Author. Princess Ingrid Victoria Sofia Louise Margareta of Sweden (1910-2000) married Frederik, Crown Prince of Denmark and Iceland, in May 1935, and became Queen of Denmark upon her husband's accession to the throne in April 1947. They had three children. While visiting Lady Astor, the Queen of Denmark stayed at a well-known hotel in Mayfair, Claridges. Film Actor Spencer Tracey, who had stayed at Claridge's once, said: "I don't want to go to heaven, I want to go to Claridge's." Royalty and celebrities frequented the hotel.)

The Danish Royal family had arrived in London in the Royal yacht and as King Frederik was a sailor he preferred to stay on board the ship in the pool of London while the Queen of Denmark and the Princesses stayed at the hotel. I was privileged to be working for Lady Astor to be able to see these famous people for there was always a constant stream of guests. Another visitor was King Gustav Adolf V1 and the Queen of Sweden, at the time of her marriage Queen Louise was the former Lady Louise of Battenberg, sister of Lord Mountbatten, her father took the name during the First World War. Their reign was from 1950-1973. King Gustav was a keen archaeologist and was admitted to the British Academy in 1958 for his work in botany. I remember quite vividly an incident from the King's visit when he and his wife came to tea on one occasion with her Ladyship. It was quite amusing really because the King liked to remain incognito and he did not want any fuss. On the afternoon that they were due to arrive for tea at five o'clock plans were made to ensure they were met and quickly ushered into the house. In the morning of that day her Ladyship said to Miss Harrison: "I think we had better send for a policeman to be on duty at the door from Western Central Police Station to see the King in," so at ten to five the policeman arrived and stood at the front door. Her Ladyship came downstairs, beautifully dressed. Meanwhile the offices were turning out and people were on their way home and, of course, they saw the policeman outside the house and their curiosity was aroused and a few began to congregate. As soon as the car drew up her Ladyship rushed out on to the pavement, the car door opened and the Swedish King and Queen got out and her Ladyship dropped a very deep curtsey and the policeman saluted. The look on the King's face was a picture that I remember to this day; he was obviously annoyed at being in the public eye because he stormed in with the Queen following him and her Ladyship rushing along behind to catch up to take them upstairs. It was clear the King was not very pleased and he told Lady Astor so. Later when I took tea up to them, tempers had cooled and everything was alright. Her Ladyship also had members of the Rumanian royal family visiting her for tea.

A very special occasion, which caused great excitement, was the dinner at 10, Downing Street, during the Premiership of Harold Macmillan, which Lady Astor had been invited to attend. It was decided that her Ladyship would wear her tiara, as were all the other ladies who had been invited to the event. A week before this event was to take place Miss Harrison said to me: "Charles, I want you to come with me, we are going to the Bank to collect one of Lady Astor's tiaras to take it to the jewellers Roods

& Company in the Burlington Arcade to get it cleaned because she is going to dinner at 10, Downing Street." So off we went and I was quite fascinated at the prospect of seeing her beautiful collection of jewellery. We took a taxi to Park Lane to the Westminster Bank; they knew Miss Harrison there so she was given the key to the vault, and we sat down at a table and Rose took a cardboard box out of the vault and in it were the big tiara with a beautiful diamond and a smaller tiara which her Ladyship wanted. I was most surprised to see it was only a cardboard box they were stored in as I had expected a locked security box. In the meantime Miss Harrison was showing me some of the pieces of jewellery and there were some beautiful pieces. For me it was quite moving to see these lovely items and eventually they were all put back in the box. I believe that when her Ladyship died Miss Harrison was left one of the brooches although I am not sure which one. In her retirement years Lady Astor often wore heavy bracelets. We took a taxi to Roods shop, Burlington Arcade, in Mayfair, London, with the tiara that her Ladyship was going to wear, to be left for cleaning, later during the week Miss Harrison and I went back to collect it.

It had been decided that Miss Harrison and I would accompany her Ladyship in the Rolls Royce to Downing Street and ten minutes before Lady Astor was due to leave I went upstairs. We were all asked if we would like to go up to the main hall and see her in her regalia, well when she came down those stairs she was a vision. Miss Harrison really turned her out beautifully and her Ladyship was seventy-eight years of age then but she looked gorgeous. If I remember rightly she had a pale blue satin or taffeta gown, a mink stole and wore the tiara and her hair was always done in a French roll and then pinned at the back. I still think today that she looked a million dollars despite her age. You could see the beauty that had been evident in her earlier years. Her Ladyship was always immaculately dressed; she had a fondness for pastel colours as well as darker colours, lilacs, pinks, greys, white and navy blue. When she went to church in the summer time she would appear wearing a tip-tilted white straw hat and a printed blue and white patterned silk suit. After she left Plymouth Lady Astor bought her shoes and hats in London and a London dressmaker made her dresses and gowns and her hair was done by Hairdresser Emile in London who came to the house to do her hair. Emile was the official hairdresser to the Queen and the hairdresser's business closed in the early 1960s.

We got into the car and off we drove. I was as excited as her Ladyship and I was only the Footman. When we arrived at the function we dropped her there and we came back to Hill Street with instructions to be back at the Foreign Office at ten o'clock. We returned to the Foreign Office precisely on time to collect her Ladyship but we had to wait about twenty minutes because they had a system, which had to be adhered to. The cars would park at the Foreign Office and they had loudspeakers. They would call the cars as required. Eventually we were called and Miss Harrison said to me: "Now Charles, when you have seen her Ladyship into the car walk around the back and then get in beside me," apparently this was the correct etiquette procedure, it was not acceptable to walk in front of the car, so I did as I was asked. I recall many hilarious moments and life was quite interesting, yet the human side always showed itself on occasion. One day there was a time when I was going upstairs to fetch her Ladyship's shoes and as I reached the top of the stairs I heard a commotion and realised that Lady Astor and Rose were having a bit of a barney and her Ladyship walked out of the bedroom, looked at me and said: "Charles do you think God ever made deaf and dumb maids? Because if you do, find me one!" and off she went. Miss Harrison came out shaking her head, looked up at the ceiling with a silent prayer and went upstairs to her quarters. There really were some funny times, but never dull, every day was different. After about a year at Hill Street it was decided that the house really was too big for her Ladyship and Lord (Bob) Brand who was living with her. (Robert Henry Brand, 1st Baron Brand (1878-1963) was a British civil servant and businessman. In 1917, he married Phyllis Langhorne, Lady Astor's favourite sister. Their son Lieutenant Robert James (Jim) Brand (1923-1945) was only twenty-one when he was killed in action in Western Europe in March 1945. In 1946 Robert Henry Brand was made Baron Brand by George VI and the title expired upon his death. Bob Brand and Lady Astor were friends for life and he particularly treasured a gift she had bought him fifty years earlier, a set of gold buttons for a white wasistcoat, whilst on a visit to Cartier's in Paris in the 1900s.)

Lady Astor moved to 100 Eaton Square, Belgravia. It was a very large flat comprising the first floor of number 100 and the next two houses alongside, it was a three bay wide building joined in regular terraces in a classical style. It had three bedrooms, three bathrooms, one reception and a lower ground floor and had been built by the Grosvenor family; the present Duke of Westminster lives there now. The flat was comfortably furnished with both Louis Quinze and Louis Seize furniture (1715-1793) a style perfected in France during the 18th century in furniture, architecture, and interior design. I had a very nice bed/sitting room in the basement; her Ladyship had a lovely bedroom, which was at the back of the flat and a sitting room with the walls lined in pretty pale blue silk. Lady Astor loved her china; she particularly liked the eighteenth century continental china and the Chinese hard stone carvings in crystal or jade. She also had portraits and Italian landscapes on the walls. Quality was the hallmark of her belongings and she was always interested in the Arts and frequently donated handsome sums of money to various charities and projects. Miss Harrison had a bed-sitting room beside Lady Astor's bedroom, where she did all her work and where she rested. Rose did not rest very often as she was always on the go but she would not allow Lady Astor to go out of the house unless she was dressed perfectly.

Once when Rose was away on holiday we had a French lady who was retired but would stand in to cover illness or holidays. She was called Mademoiselle Elise Gaubert and she came to take care of her Ladyship while Rose was on holiday. One afternoon Lady Astor was going to St James's Palace, which is the senior Palace of the sovereign with a long history as a Royal Palace, as she was attending a reception for American teachers and the Queen Mother was going to be there and, of course, the press. Lady Astor's shoes were usually of the same style, black or navy blue, I do not think she had any other colours except for her golf shoes which were brown. At the reception, photographs were taken, and one was of Lady Astor standing talking to some of the visiting teachers. A few days later Miss Harrison came back from her holiday and having seen the photograph she gave an impression that she was not happy with what she saw and was clearly upset. When I spoke to her she said: "Charles, those shoes were not right, her Ladyship had gone out with odd shoes, one black and one navy." There was only a slight difference in those shoes but Miss Harrison noticed it immediately. She remarked: "Fancy sending my Ladyship out looking like that!" It was good to have Rose Harrison back again because everything was once again back to normal.

The Chef always called her Ladyship 'Madame de Viscountess' which I thought was really nice. He said to her Ladyship that he was very annoyed and was thinking of leaving her service, she would say, "Well if you do you know you won't get another job anywhere!" and he said, "Why not Madame?" Her Ladyship replied, "Oh, I shall tell everybody you are a Communist and nobody will employ you!" The staff would be quietly smiling, as this was a regular occurrence and we also knew the high regard her Ladyship had for his expertise. After all that it all blew over. Then there were times, of course, when the guests, because he had done such a wonderful meal, would ask to see him and that pleased him very much because everyone likes a bit of praise and he indeed took great pride in his work. I always had the afternoon off, so in the afternoons after everything was cleared up which was usually about 3pm, off I would go around London, perhaps to see the museums, places of interest or just have a lovely walk. On my return to her Ladyship's home I would start again with my duties. Wherever she went her staff were devoted to her, they understood her perfectly, knew how to take her and loved her spirit. Of course her Ladyship had tiffs with her staff on occasion but surely that emphasises the human touch.

Sometimes Lady Astor would be going out for a meal herself and if she was we had to order the car to take her to wherever the venue was. Mr Harris her driver would fetch the car from the garage at the back of the house in the Mews. Mr and Mrs Harris lived in the flat above the garage, so he was called and told to be at the house at 5pm as her Ladyship was going out. She used to go out quite often because being the person she was everybody wanted Lady Astor, and sometimes her nieces would invite her for lunch or dinner. It was mostly nieces as, unfortunately, her nephew Jim Brand had been killed during the war. Lord Brand came up to the house at weekends as he had a permanent room there, and William 'Odd Man' used to look after him, Lord Brand was a charming man, a real gentleman. He very rarely ate his meals at Hill Street, only his breakfast as he preferred going to his club for the day and to meet his friends so he had his meals at the club. After dinner we would clean up and sort every

Photo courtesy Charles Prynne. Original copyright not known
Digital copy by Trevor Burrows Plymouth Photographer

Lady Astor in her golfing shoes (her favourite sport)
At Cliveden in the late 1950s

thing out, put all the silverware away and in the evening we would all get together in the staff sitting room and watch television, it was a lovely room; her Ladyship always ensured that we were comfortable. I remember in the cabinets around the staff room there was some beautiful china, lovely things; I do not think that any of that was ever used. There were wonderful Meisen pieces. Mrs Hawkins really looked after them when they were to be washed and she would not allow anyone else to touch them. At the end of the day, perhaps at half past ten, we started to disperse and most of the staff would go to bed but William and I would stay and clear up things for the Butler, Mr Harwood, as he lived out at Ealing. He had an invalid father to take care of so he would leave Hill Street and come back early in the morning. The staff always helped each other where they could. When finally I got to bed I was so tired that as soon as my head touched the pillow I fell quickly asleep. Most of the staff were up at six thirty in the morning to sort things out and organise the duties for the day. It was a most interesting job and Lady Astor was very kind to me, she was extremely generous and cared greatly about my welfare.

There was a time when my mother was not very well and I had been working for Lady Astor for about a year. I was very worried about my mother and I was serving lunch one day when her Ladyship sensed that all was not well with me so after lunch, when I went downstairs to the kitchen and I was helping with the washing up and clearing away the dishes, Miss Jones, the Secretary, rang down (Miss Jones had been Lord Astor's Secretary for years, and worked for him when he owned the Observer Newspaper and continued to work for him until his death in 1952) and asked me to come up to her office, which I did, and she asked me, "Charles, are you happy with us?" and I said, "Yes, Miss Jones very happy, Why?" she said, "Well, her Ladyship sensed at lunch today that you were not happy, do you have problems?" I said, "well I am very concerned about my mother's health Miss Jones, I have had a letter from my step-father saying that he is rather concerned because of some condition she had." Miss Jones said, "Alright Charles, thank you for letting me know." With that I went downstairs and twenty minutes later she rang down again at 3pm in the afternoon and said, "Lady Astor says that you are to go home right away, see how your mother is and you are to stay until you are convinced she is going to be alright." Well, I thought that was wonderful, how caring. Miss Jones asked, "What time is the next train to Plymouth?" I said, I thought there was a train about 4pm that would get me home in the evening, so I was allowed to leave right away. A week later I got back to Hill Street satisfied that all was well at home and I arrived at Lady Astor's home about five o'clock in the afternoon. That evening her ladyship was having some guests for dinner, she called me upstairs and said: "Now Charles, how do you feel about your Mother?" she was always concerned about my relationship with my Mother. I told her Ladyship that I was very happy now that my Mother was all right. In fact mother was on the change of life and was having odd moods, I did not understand then the problems that ladies had to put up with, she replied "Quite, Quite!" and for the rest of my working life with Lady Astor she would ask once a week how my Mother was.

Lady Astor often used to tell this tale at the lunch or dinner table to her guests, about the visit of the King and Queen in Plymouth. Lord and Lady Astor with the King and Queen toured the city just before the night of the terrible bombing in March 1941. The Queen Mother said to Lady Astor, "You know Aunt Nancy, (the Bowes-Lyons called her Aunt Nancy) you made history by being elected to the House of Commons and taking your seat." Her Ladyship replied, "Ah but remember, you Ma'am made a King." There is no doubt that England and the British Isles were graced with a wonderful King and Queen, the Queen Mother gave sterling support to her husband and we, the nation, were honoured that their daughter Queen Elizabeth followed in their footsteps, loyal to the people, a strength in time of adversity and true to their sacred promise. The Bowes-Lyons brought stability to the throne. King George V1 on his visit in 1941 said to one of the bombed out ladies of Plymouth, "You are very brave, I have great admiration for you." The woman replied, "Well there is one thing about it, Sir, I can go where I like, and I can do what I like and there is nobody in Germany that can do that!"

The Dowager Viscountess, during her retirement and into her seventies, continued to entertain guests such as Mary, The Duchess of Roxburgh, and the King and Queen of Sweden. Of course, Lord and Lady Astor's sons were made welcome, but it has to be said that Lady Astor adored her first son from her first marriage, but his lifestyle was so different to her Ladyship's other sons and Bobby's end was indeed tragic. When Lady Astor died he was a lost soul yet, in their lifetime, they would argue constantly and would upset each other. Another member of the family close to her Ladyship was Lady Ancaster (her daughter Phyllis) and they got on quite well, but her Ladyship did not particularly like her daughters-in-law so they did not come very often for lunch. Lord Ancaster, her son-in-law, carried war wounds from the Second World War, which he obtained by being run over by a tank. Her Ladyship loved to play tricks on everyone and, if at a lunch or dinner table, the conversation went flat she would turn her head to one side, slip in the plastic teeth, and start the conversation again making everyone laugh. She always liked a lot of people around her at meal times and she was a good conversationist but toward the end of my time there she became a bit forgetful.

One day when coming by train to North Road Station, Plymouth, Lady Astor asked us to wait. When we got out of the train her Ladyship was met by the Station Master, he always met her off the train and he would be wearing his top hat. We had to go down a flight of steps from the platform to the corridor before reaching street level. On this day as we came toward the steps there was a young mother struggling along with a baby and a pushchair, Lady Astor turned to me and said, "Charles, help that young lady down the steps with the pushchair." She cared about little things like that, always ready to help someone along the way. In the 1950's Mr and Mrs Modley were regular visitors at Elliot Terrace, they were very nice people and they were good friends, She had known them for many years; during the war years they had been the Deputy Lord and Lady Mayoress of Plymouth from 1939 to 1944.

Original picture taken by a Penzance photographer (unknown) (It is thought for the Western Morning News)
This copy taken by Trevor Burrows Photography Limited Plymouth

Charles Prynne in his seventies. Lady Astor's former footman.
Here holding one of his favourite photographs of Lady Astor

When in the London home frequent visitors were the General of the Salvation Army Wilfred Kitchen and his wife. (The General (1893-1977) served in the Salvation Army from the years 1954-1963 and was the seventh General of the Christian movement. He was 84 when he died) I remember that they never went away without a cheque; Lady Astor had a very high regard for the Salvation Army. She was still being extremely generous even in those days, to everyone and charities and the ordinary citizen. The Admiral of the Royal Navy in Plymouth and his wife were also frequent visitors for lunch as were the Commanding Officer of the Royal Marines and the Earl of Mount Edgecumbe. She would spend a lot of time on the telephone speaking to her nieces, family members and friends. Mrs Winn and Joyce Grenfell came regularly for lunch and her brother-in-law Lord Brand with his two daughters also came.

Next door to 3 Elliot Terrace the house had been turned into flats and in there lived a boy called Peter and Lady Astor would speak to him if he was playing outside when she went out the front door. She would say, "And how are you today Peter?" He always called her Miss Astor "Well Miss Astor, I got something wrong with my tiddyly," (Devon talk) Lady Astor thought that was quite funny and laughed. She loved children and, of course, later his mother explained to her Ladyship the problem, he had been to hospital to be circumcised. I happened to hear this as I had escorted Lady Astor out the front door. I wonder where Peter is now, no doubt a grandfather with a family. At Elliot Terrace Lady Astor would often go for a walk in the afternoons and on one occasion she came back with an American serviceman who was drunk, she had found him on the pavement and had said to him, "You should be ashamed of yourself, you are coming home with me!" "No I am not," he said, "because my Mother warned me about women like you!" Undeterred, she brought him home, and he stayed overnight, in the evening Lady Astor contacted his regiment's duty officer so that he would not be charged with being absent without leave. In the morning he was given a large cooked breakfast and sent on his way.

I left her service in 1959, I did not want to leave but there had been a change of staff and I did not want to work under this particular member, so it was with heavy heart that I left. The week that I left, Lady Astor wanted to give me a parting gift and offered me a choice of a pair a cufflinks or a £50 cheque so naturally I opted for the £50 cheque. When I left her service I continued to write to her Ladyship and she always replied. I enjoyed working for Lady Astor and I was privileged to meet people I would not normally have met. I travelled to the United States of America and made many long-term friendships. I recall when, later, I was working in America, receiving a Christmas card from her Ladyship and at the end of the card she wrote, 'always look after your Mother, Charles' and this was a thing with her Ladyship, she had a thing about me and my Mother, perhaps it was because then I was a young man. When she was older her ladyship wrote to me and her writing got difficult to read, but we continued to write to one another and she always sent me a Christmas card every year of her life. She wrote in a letter to me in her later years saying: "Dear Charles, I was so pleased to get your letter and thank you for remembering my birthday. I have been quite overwhelmed by all the letters, cards and telegrams I received. I was really surprised by the number of people who remembered me, I do appreciate it, ever sincerely Nancy Astor." I received a letter from her dated 16th January 1962 and it seems that her Footman then was called Leonard and he too wanted to go to America. Miss Margaret Jones wrote to me and asked me to put a word in to Miss Sterling who was Lady Ormsby-Gore's secretary at the time and, of course, I did what I could to help.

The next letter I received was dated 16th May 1963 when Lady Astor was living at 100 Eaton Square, London. (The author discussed with Charles the sensitive nature of the letter and not wanting to offend or give the impression of seeking publicity, it was mutually agreed that it should be revealed so that the people would know where her loyalties lie and that she cared so much about her citizens) This is what she wrote: "I was delighted to have your letter and I know you will always do something for other people, because you are so grateful for what little I have done for you. I have always noticed that grateful people are the ones who help others. Those who take things for granted seem never to bother about helping others. (Author's note. There were additional remarks here about the field workers in the South of America but with today's political correctness it is prudent not to include them. Lady Astor was an ardent supporter of Royalty and adored the Royal Family. However, she was entitled to her opinion and she expressed it with these comments) I was amazed that anybody should address the Duchess of Windsor as her Royal Highness, I crossed on the ship with the Duke of Windsor and he asked me if I would like to meet his wife. I said no, and he asked me why not? I said, because he had broken the heart of most of England. I shall never forget the night he went away, no doubt it was for the best because the Queen is wonderful, so natural and so good and loved by everybody. I am glad, Charles, that you like the other Lady Astor, she is very nice but quite honestly I do not like anyone in my place. That is not a very Christian spirit but it is true, but I lived at Cliveden for forty years and I adored it. My daughter-in-law is very thoughtful when I go back and my sons are as good as gold. I am sorry to write so dull a letter but I had many, many to write, people still seem to think I am in the House of Commons, how I wish I was. With best wishes Nancy Astor."

I still have that precious letter lovingly placed in my very special scrapbook. The letter gives a wonderful insight into her feelings in later years showing that she carried in her heart the need to mix with people and to be wanted. When I was asked why I was so grateful, as her Ladyship had said in her letter, I said, I was grateful because she was so kind. She was always asking questions about my mother, and was such a generous person, she really cared about people and she was a very good employer and I was so happy there. When she knew I came from Cornwall she was wonderful to me, I thought a great deal of her, such a vibrant woman. Having worked for Lady Astor completely changed my life and she had such an influence on my future years. I felt I was going up slowly in the world. When I left her ladyship I went to work at the Times Bookshop in Wigmore Street, London, a very old, lovely bookshop that was owned by her ladyship's brother-in-law, Lord Astor of Hever. From there I got another job through Lady Astor via Miss Jones her secretary. She found out that the Ambassador to Washington was going to be Mr Ormsby-Gore, and they were looking for staff, so Miss Jones, on behalf of Lady Astor, rang me at the bookshop and told me, because they knew I wanted eventually to go to America. (Sir William David Ormsby-Gore (1918-1985) Conservative Parliamentary member and created 5th Baron Harlech. He served as Ambassador to Washington from 1961 to 1965. He was killed in a car crash in England at the age of sixty-six.) I immediately contacted the Hunt Regina Domestic Agency that had got me my original post with Lady Astor, as they were handling the new Ambassador's staff recruitment. I went for an interview with Sir David; he had only just been knighted to take up his position in Washington and in 1961 John F Kennedy was elected as President of the United States. I got the post and was thrilled and I had the blessing of the bookshop, as they knew it was an opportunity for me not to be missed.

Charles Prynne in his seventies - Lady Astor's former Footman

Off I went to America and I was with the British Embassy for just over a year and a half; it was so interesting as it opened up a new world for me. Whilst I was there David Astor came to stay as did the Duke and Duchess of Devonshire. Mary, Duchess of Devonshire was very tall and graceful, a lovely lady. It was an amazing thing with important visitors coming and going. When I left the embassy I went to California and the funny thing is Lady Astor laughed when I told her as she had always said, "Go to Virginia!" I never got to stay in Virginia as my mistake was going to Los Angeles. I found Los Angeles was like a huge transit camp; always everybody was coming or going somewhere else. Later I went to San Francisco and I fell in love with that place. If I had made San Francisco as my base in the beginning I would have never come back to England. I needed another operation on my knee, which, in America, had cost me a lot of money, so I decided to come home and have the second operation free under the National Health scheme.

All this came about because I was her Footman and what a wonderful experience it was. Lady Astor will live on in my heart as I have had, and still have, respect for a very gracious employer.

When Charles Prynne heard of the death of his former employer Lady Astor he was deeply upset and wanted to ensure that her memory would always be remembered. In May 1964 he wrote to the Plymouth Lord Mayor, Councillor Harold M. Pattinson, CBE, suggesting that a statue of Lady Astor be placed on Plymouth Hoe, he offered financial assistance toward its cost. Below is a copy of the letter that the Lord Mayor wrote to Charles on the 12th May 1964.

THE LORD MAYOR'S PARLOUR
PLYMOUTH
Plymouth 68000

12th May, 1964.

Dear Mr. Prynne,

      I am interested to have your letter of the 8th May and fully endorse your statement as I was a personal friend and great admirer of Lady Astor. You may be interested to know that I was one of the speakers at the Freedom Ceremony to which you refer and was also an advocate of the giving of this honour long before it actually happened. You will see, therefore, that I agree with you in many respects.

      So far as a memorial is concerned this matter is under discussion and a Memorial Service will be held in St. Andrew's Church on the 19th of this month, the arrangements for which have just been concluded.

      Lord Astor is presenting us with a bronze head, which will be displayed in one of the rooms of the Guildhall and there is a possibility of a memorial on the Hoe, the form of which is not yet decided, but as you keep in touch with the City you will no doubt be au fait with what is developing.

      Your offer of financial assistance is much appreciated and if any form of public subscription is arranged my successor or I will contact you.

      It is very nice to hear from you and I thank you very much indeed for your letter.

Yours sincerely,

(Councillor Harold M. Pattinson, C.B.E.)

Lord Mayor.

C. Prynne, Esq.,
Hotel Clark,
426 South Hill Street,
LOS ANGELES 13,
California.

Photo by kind permission of Mr Charles Prynne

A smiling Lady Astor in her eighties - still wearing her beloved pearls

Photo from a private collection-copyright unknown.

Joyce Grenfell (1910-1979) Nancy Astor's niece. Queen of comic monologue and a talented film actress.

CHAPTER SIX
CITIZEN'S MEMORIES

"It was the people I wanted to get to know, not the fishes!"

Lady Astor circa 1912 when it was suggested that her husband Waldorf should buy a yacht. The Astors lived close to the Royal Western Yacht Club on Plymouth Hoe from the early 1900s. The Royal Western Yacht Club was destroyed during the war and moved to a new location.

Nelda Bridgeman, now living in Ohio, United States of America, used to live between Normandy Way and Penros Road at the start of the Second World War she was then six years old. Much later, she remembers Lady Astor in a polka dot dress and a large brimmed black hat going around the area in an open-topped car, with a megaphone, shouting, "Mothers and children must leave this city." Nancy organised other prominent ladies to do the same thing at the same time. The event Nelda was remembering was when Nancy Astor had been challenging officials in the Government to evacuate the children after the devastating bombing of Plymouth in 1941. A bright young Parliamentary representative had nominated Plymouth as a safe city and even evacuated children from London to Plymouth in 1940. Plymouth was a naval port; it had an Army Garrison and an R.A.F. airfield. Nancy vigorously prompted Winston Churchill to visit the war torn city and when he left, after his inspection, he continued to wipe the tears from his eyes and the following day his order from the House of Parliament was finally received, "Evacuate forthwith."

Jack and Amelia Davey, who recently celebrated their diamond wedding, graciously allowed the author to tell their story and to state their feelings about Lady Astor as, in their hearts, they have never forgotten Nancy's kindness to them. Amelia recalled her childhood home in New Street on the barbican. Her father had been wounded in the First World War and had lost a leg whilst fighting in the Dardenelles campaign (1915-1916) and so was unable to go out. Amelia's mother went out to work from 5am to 5pm and the family were very poor. Amelia's Aunt, her father's sister, concerned about his depression and his distress at being unable to provide for his family, went to 3, Elliot Terrace and asked to speak to Lady Astor whom she told about her brother, and how she wished to help him regain his dignity. Lady Astor listened and said, "Leave it with me and I will see what I can do." The next morning a man delivered a pair of crutches and Amelia remembers Lady Astor calling in to see her father. She asked him if he would like to live in one of her houses in Mount Gould, saying, "Why don't you come, bring your family and live on my estate?" As a small girl, Amelia remembers being the only girl in the family, having five brothers, and they were all thrilled because in their present house they only had three rooms but the house in Mount Gould had three bedrooms, a dining room, lounge, and a bathroom (real joy). There was also a lovely garden. "We were very excited, recalls Amelia, and we settled in very quickly. The bath was in frequent use." Lady Astor visited Mr. Davey regularly to see that all was well and, of course, he was delighted and thought how kind and caring she was. However, it still quietly grieved him that he had no employment but Lady Astor sensed that he was too independent to beg for work and she decided to do something about it. One morning on visiting him, Nancy said, "Would you like to be Chairman of the Housing Committee?" Amelia's father was surprised but said he did not feel he was the man for the job. Nancy would have none of it, because he did have a unique ability in how to organise, so he took the job and never looked back. Lady Astor frequently visited the Mount Gould Estate and would call in on families, stop and have a cup of tea and a chat, and inspect the Estate for litter on the streets. When she called on the Davey family her first question would be, "How are you?" and Mrs. Davey would reply, "Very well, thank you, your Ladyship." Lady Astor would always call Amelia's mother 'Mary' and her continuing interest in Mr. Davey's welfare, together with giving him a regular job, ensured that he regained his dignity and made him feel needed. On a later visit, Lady Astor invited Amelia's father and mother to the wedding of her daughter but they had to decline. It was a great disappointment to them but Mr. Davey did not have a proper suit to wear to attend such a grand occasion. On another visit to the Estate, the Duchess of York accompanied Lady Astor and they walked along the path to the Davey's house. Other visitors were George Bernard Shaw the playwright and Lawrence of Arabia. Living at Mount Gould, recalled Amelia, meant we saw people we would not normally meet.

One day a letter came for Amelia's father telling him to report to Queen Mary's Auxiliary Hospital, Roehampton. Lady Astor had arranged for him to be fitted with an artificial limb. (The British Orthopaedic Association founded in 1918, under control from the war office, passed from them to the Ministry of Pensions in 1919.) Having a new leg gave Mr. Davey the mobility he so desired and it was to open a new chapter in his life. He was offered a job making jewellery in Spooners on the Jewellery counter. This counter was on lease with Spooners and it allowed wounded servicemen from the First World War the opportunity to make and sell jewellery and thus allowed them to make a wage and support their families.

The families living in Mount Gould had a close connection with Lady Astor and she ensured that they became involved in activities and each year one grand garden show was held at the Astor Institute and many garden lovers competed in the competition. Everyone on the Astor Estate grew something and on the day of the competition the young Amelia was chosen to present a bouquet of flowers. Nancy would perform the opening ceremony and did the judging of the flower and vegetable entries, Amelia stated that Lady Astor was quite a generous lady and she always overawed them. Their peaceful lives continued and the years slipped past until the outbreak of the Second World War in 1939 when lives were to change as we began the fight for freedom. "One day" Amelia recalls, "mother and I were in the front room when a knock came at the door and a voice called out saying, "Can I come in?" It was of course Lady Astor and my mother was flabbergasted at her impertinence at coming in without waiting for her to open the door. However, my mother made her welcome with a cup of tea. Lady Astor said, "I have come to visit the heroes of the family" we were surprised that she knew. My brother John Davey had been awarded the British Empire Medal (BEM) for saving an RAF pilot's life from a burning plane during the Second World War at an airfield in Kenya. John was stationed on the airfield as pilots were sent to Kenya to be trained in flying and to learn complicated manoeuvres before going on to designated Squadrons."

Amelia's husband Jack Davey was awarded the Distinguished Flying Cross after his exploits on the Pennamunde raid in Eastern Germany in August 1943. Five hundred and ninety-six aircraft of Bomber Command with their crews took part, the bombing was done on a moonlit night and forty of the aircraft with their crews were lost. The Davey family had much to be proud of. Jack Davey, Amelia's husband, had never seen Lady Astor as he was away serving in the forces during the war. When the war was over Jack returned to civilian life and one day he was working on a loading ramp when he saw a woman talking to a group of people. "She had a most beautiful figure and she was shouting out political advice at an open-air meeting. I did not know who she was until someone said to me, that is Lady Astor, I thought what a figure! Yet she was in her sixties then. There were times she was canvassing on the barbican when the barbican hooligans would let down her tyres on her car and she would admonish them until finally they relented and pumped her tyres up again." During the Second World War Amelia was an Air Raid Precaution Officer (ARP) as women had to contribute to the war effort. "When the siren went we would drop everything and rush to our posts, my post was alongside the Astor Institute, of course it is all gone now. If we were on duty we had to stay there until the end of the raid and our charges were accounted for.

Lady Astor was really a lovely person; whenever she visited she was always immaculately dressed. I remember on one occasion when she visited my home my sister-in-law and I could not take our eyes off her skirt (we sat on a box at home when Lady Astor visited so she could have the chair and we would be sitting low down). Underneath her skirt was the most beautiful silk petticoat which came just below her skirt when she sat down, Nancy saw that we were looking at her petticoat and she said, "Yes it is pretty, it comes from America." Lady Astor last visited us in the very early 1950s and talked about the destruction of Plymouth and made enquiries about the health of our family, she was quite sad at the impending loss of the housing estate at Mount Gould in the 1950s. I admired her greatly and thought she was a very kind caring person and she was also beautiful. When she died it was quite sad and we knew then we would not see her like again. Yes, we had wonderful memories of Lady Astor."

Barbara Hogan (nee Gardner) had her first meeting with Lady Astor as a child of six during the Second World War. With the bombing of the City of Plymouth, a shortage of food, hot water, and essential amenities, her mother, like other families, was struggling to feed and keep her children. Barbara lived in the Rendle Street Flats in the centre of Plymouth and the bombing took a heavy toll of that area. During one of her tours across the city Lady Astor had spoken to Barbara's mother asking her how she was managing, she politely replied that she was okay, but Lady Astor sensing her distress knew otherwise. With water and gas services struggling to maintain necessary supplies the authorities could not keep up with the devastation. Lady Astor invited Barbara's mother to take her children to the Baths adjacent to Union Street, they were considered to be quite luxurious and Barbara said, "It was wonderful having a hot bath and each child was given a tennis ball as a gift, and I can still visualise the setting of a picturesque staircase just as you would see in a glamorous film set, and the base was set in marble." Most adults who used the baths would pay one shilling for the issue of a bath towel and soap, for children it would have been sixpence, which was a lot of money for families on short income. Lady Astor paid the bill for any child using the facilities at her request.

Barbara recalls that, "Lady Astor looked at me and said to my mother that she would like to adopt me, and my mother with polite indignity refused." Although Barbara states there were times she was afraid in the war, searching for shrapnel in the bombed out sites like most children at that time found it very exciting. Lady Astor organised food kitchens during the war and helped to provide cooked meals. "My mother was friendly with the Parker family who lived in the flat above us in Rendle Street and Mrs Parker was extremely grateful to Lady Astor because she had arranged to have her Royal Naval husband brought back from sea as it was thought that the eldest son was going to die and there would have been no man in the family to care for them. The highlight for me was when Lady Astor invited my family to her house for tea and that was special. My cousin also remembers Lady Astor but for a different reason, her mother as a young woman used to deliver tulle hats to Lady Astor at 3, Elliot Terrace, but she would not buy a new one each time so the Milliner had to re-design the same one for her. They thought of her as being stingy but those who knew Lady Astor would know that she was not mean, she was indeed a generous person, perhaps she was being what the older generation always did and that was being thrifty. Lady Astor was a friend of Dorothy Elmhirst of Dartington Hall, near Totnes, (see Chapter Women Feminists) and she had asked Dorothy for help in taking some of the children from the bombed out city. Dorothy responded and it was because of this that our family was evacuated and billeted at Dartington after the heavy bombing. It is strange how many years later the memory in the mind of a child still remains clear, now in my twilight years I can say that Lady Astor touched many people's lives."

Plymouth citizen, Dorrien Peake (nee Pittman), remembers with pride her conversation with Lady Astor. "I have carried that precious memory all these years because for just a few moments in time to Lady Astor I was someone special." On a Sunday morning sixty-six years ago in 1941, when as young married mother, Dorrien was walking down North Hill towards Sherwell Church, Plymouth, with her baby daughter in her pram, she saw Lady Astor in the distance. Just before reaching the Church Lady Astor with another lady friend came up the road towards her. Dorrien, who now lives on the Barbican remembers the conversation as though it was yesterday, she said, "They both stopped beside me and said could they please have a peep at my baby. They asked the baby's name and how old she was, I said a few months as she was born on Christmas morning." Lady Astor thought it was a lovely Christmas present and thanked me for chatting to her. I have always admired her and in my eyes she was a perfect lady and I have never forgotten how nice it was for her to stop and talk to me, an ordinary citizen, with no airs or graces." (Sadly since this interview was taken ninety-four year old Dorrien passed away on 22nd February 2008 (RIP) but her story will live on for her family in this book.)

Another citizen Mrs Glen Trude remembers with pride her connection with Lady Astor when in the mid nineteen thirties Nancy was at the Conservative Offices, Southwark, London. "As a young girl, I was known as Gladys Crawley then but as four other girls had the same name Gladys, someone called me Glen by mistake and it was decided that from 1941 it would be easier to answer to that name. I was a member of the 'Young Britons', which was a junior youth club of the conservative branch. We used to tour all the conservative clubs participating in concerts and I really enjoyed meeting different people, I was about eleven years old and I thought it was wonderful. I was chosen to present Lady Astor with a bouquet of flowers and in doing so I did not miss the opportunity of obtaining her autograph.

I have guarded my little autograph book all these years, although dilapidated and worn I treasure it still and when I see her autograph again I feel the warmth from that memory. I remember she had a great sense of humour and once a conversation started she put everyone at ease. After the event, when we were having tea, someone was teasing her about the fabulous fur coat she was wearing and they drew attention to the fact that she could afford to buy such luxuries whereas working class people couldn't. Completely undeterred she remarked, "I will tell you a secret, this is second hand! I keep the special one my husband gave me for special occasions. With one easy going reply she had made more admiring friends."

Jean Churchill has this story to tell, "Nancy very often shopped at the local shops in the area and one of her favourite was the one owned by my father-in-law which sold fresh fish, fruit, vegetables and poultry. The shop was called Churchills. The head of the family was Alfred Horatio Churchill and one of his task's was to ensure that locally caught sturgeon were sent by them to the Royal table. I married Alfred's son

Victor Churchill and I still remember vividly today Nancy coming to the shop at numbers 3 & 4 Westwell Street. (Both Westwell Street and Westwell Gardens were formerly known as Burying Place Lane as it led to the burial ground at Strayer Park which was in use from about 1700. Westwell Street took it's name around 1820 in memory of the Town's west well which had been filled in a decade or so earlier.) Nancy would inspect every item and would buy nothing until she was completely satisfied. The Churchill family and Nancy were always on good terms and each respected the other. After the terrible bombing of Plymouth the war years were to interrupt the friendly arrangement as in April 1941 the devastation was again to take its toll. Alfred Horatio Churchill's family lived at 4, St James Place, and during a bombing raid he had opted to stay in the shelter while his wife Betty and their daughter Mabel chose to return to the house and wait under the stairs. That decision was to save their lives. Alfred and the cat were in the Air Raid shelter when it took a direct hit and Alfred was killed instantly. Out of the shelter unscathed, walked Micky, the black cat, which lived happily for many years looked after by Betty, Alfred's widow. Westwell Street had been bombed and Nissen Huts were installed to keep the businesses running. The Churchill family stayed on at Westwell Street and Alfred's son Randolph from his first marriage succeeded to the shop; it moved again to Cornwall Street in 1951 when Westwell Street was demolished to accommodate the re-building of Plymouth. It soon re-opened selling poultry, fish, game, vegetables, and flowers to the city's elite, who affectionately called it the Churchill Club"

The Plymouth Churchill's, like their namesakes, can be traced back to the early Marlborough family. The link was wasted on Nancy, who in her early years detested Winston Churchill. She signed a photograph depicting herself to Alfred Horatio Churchill and on it she wrote this inscription, 'To the Plymouth Mr Churchill the nicest Churchill I know.' On one occasion Lady Astor being overdue at home, ended up hitching a lift in the shop's fish van, and quite happy despite her title. Jean remarked how Nancy would entertain everybody in the shop when she came in, she would light up the room and her infectious laughter put a smile on everyone's face. She shopped personally for her fish and fruit and she was very particular, every apple would be examined before she bought it and only the freshest of fish would be accepted. When Randolph retired his son Winston inherited the shop. With the change in marketing goods and with the onset of larger stores, little businesses were systematically being closed down and the little family shop of Churchills closed in 1980. Jean has a personal feeling about Lady Astor when she remarked, "I thought she was wonderful and I am still full of admiration for her, would that we had someone like her still rooting for the Plymouth citizens." In helping the people in the war years Nancy would often be seen on the back of a storage van clinging on to the tail panel at the rear of the vehicle. It is thought it was the property of Rowe & Sons, the registration of the van was CFJ 143, perhaps someone may remember, certainly many were bemused at a Viscountess hitching a lift on the back of a van, that surely is a human touch.

Sue Crocker still holds today a precious memory told to her by her Grandmother Nora Medland. She recalls that her Grandmother worked as one of the many cooks who prepared meals in the Plymouth City Guildhall for special functions and Civic receptions. Grandmother had told her about a very pleasant gift she had received from Lady Astor. It was during the preparation of one of these functions that Nora spoke to Lady Astor about her feet as she was suffering extreme soreness and was in dire need of a new pair of shoes, however, shoes were rationed so if you had no clothes coupons left you could not buy new shoes. Lady Astor was most concerned and remarked that it was a shame she had no coupons left. Nora thought no more about it until the next evening when she received a parcel from Lady Astor and inside was a brand new pair of shoes. Nora always thought highly of Nancy Astor and said that she was a very nice person. Susan recalls that her Grandmother never forgot that kind act and made sure the story was passed down through the family. Nancy also had a favourite cake shop, though Susan cannot remember where the shop was, and Nancy made sure that this cake shop received sugar sent from America to ensure that customers could have some cake with sugar in as sugar too was severely rationed.

Dina O'Connor Jones vividly recalls her contact with Lady Astor although she was only a little girl at the time, but she was sincere in her statement that she liked her immensely and always dreamed of one day being able to live near her in Elliot Terrace on the Hoe. The memory is still very strong in her mind because her mother and father were also acquaintances of the Astors. (Dina's father was the former PC 239 Terry O'Connor, later to become Inspector, who retired in January 1965) During the war when on a four-week shift turn around he was often detailed to climb the steps and occupy the lookout with his binoculars at the Naval War Memorial to fulfil his task as firewatcher and enemy plane spotter. He would have to climb to the top of the narrow stairs and would be locked in for security reasons. Usually about 8.30pm in the evening on his official break he would step out to stretch his legs and at this time Lord Astor would take a stroll along the Hoe promenade after having had his dinner with the family and PC O'Connor and Lord Astor would meet and have a friendly chat, eventually the friendly policeman and his wife became regular visitors to Elliot Terrace.

Dina said; "My mother regularly caught a bus at the bus stop located by the Nissen Huts near Portland Ope. We lived at Higher Compton then and on occasion we would walk down the street near the library where Lady Astor was always seen campaigning for some cause. I was about 3-4 years old and had blonde curly hair like Shirley Temple and whenever Lady Astor saw me with my mother the bartering would begin. I can recall the event with a clear mind as Lady Astor was fond of children and I knew my mother and Lady Astor would start the bartering. I remember to this day that Lady Astor's bubbling personality shone through and her generosity knew no bounds. "I want that little girl, I would like to buy her," Lady Astor would say teasingly to mother, "I will give you a book of clothing coupons" (which was like gold dust then). My mother replied, "I would want the clothing coupon book and a threepenny piece!" Lady Astor said, "No," as she could not afford the threepenny bit, as she was not that wealthy. Yet I can see her today as she talked to the GI brides off to America in 1945, one of the brides who had lost everything in the war said she would feel the cold in the area her husband was taking her as she had no warm clothes, without hesitation Lady Astor took off her fur coat off her own back and gave it to the GI bride with her blessing as a wedding gift.

So the friendship grew and Lady Astor would invite us to 3 Elliot Terrace and I always wore a freshly starched and ironed dress on the visits. Mother knew Lady Astor had a soft spot for me and still the bantering to buy me would go on. My mother was a beautiful looking lady and her rapport with Lady Astor crossed all barriers of titles. Lady Astor knew many of the citizens by their first name and she always greeted them warmly. How I loved Elliot Terrace and I would say to Lady Astor and my mother that one day I would live in Elliot Terrace, my mother smiled knowingly and did not spoil my childhood dream, she thought time would erase that wish. I have only happy memories of Lady Astor and how sad that she is no longer here for we could have reminisced on so many good times.

Dina trained as a Radiographer in Freedom Fields Hospital and during her life married twice. Her dream came true when in 2004 her second husband David, a retired farmer, bought a holiday apartment in Elliot Terrace as a present for her on Valentine's Day. Dina was over the moon and she and her husband have the pleasure of a beautiful view embracing the vista of the Hoe promenade and Plymouth Sound and they can tread the very ground that Lady Astor graced all those years ago.

Mr T. Griffey of Kingsand-Cawsand remembers a precious moment in time that endeared Lady Astor to him during the Second World War. He remembers her as 'The tipster.' Mr Griffey had this to say; "I was a contracting overseer on a housing estate at St Budeaux in Plymouth. Lady Astor, together with the Duke of Kent, was among the dignitaries for the opening ceremony and the date coincided with a very important race meeting. The workmen and myself found that we were acting as an unofficial guard of honour at the ceremony. Lady Astor with her impish sense of humour realised that the workers were more interested in the big racing classic. She deliberately dallied behind the Duke's entourage to tell the workers that it was to be a one-horse race and her husband was the owner of it. It proved a hot tip, for it was the winner and as we collected our winnings I vowed secretly that I would always remember her and I did."

A Brixton war widow was left without a pension for several months after the death of her husband. The widow asked Lady Astor for help and when she heard about the case she was angry and immediately set the wheels in motion to have it rectified. Within three days the widow had her pension. The widow said, "I can never finish thanking her, and may her memory last for ever." Another citizen recalls that during an election campaign a heckler at the back kept jumping up to interrupt. At last Lady Astor in desperation said, "Who paid your rent and fed your wife and children while you were in prison?" There was dead silence and no more interruptions.

Pauline Moore's (nee Hambly) first encounter with Lady Astor was as a baby in a pram being pushed by her mother in the summer of 1932. Lady Astor always went for a walk along West Hoe in the mornings and whenever she saw a mother with a baby she invariably would stop and talk to them. Catching sight of Pauline in the pram Nancy stopped her mother to admire the baby. "What a lovely Indian baby," she said. Pauline's mother was most indignant, as she was not an Indian baby although the baby had dark brown hair and dark brown eyes and her skin was tanned with the summer sun. Pauline's mother reiterated saying, "This is my baby!" Nancy peering into Pauline's face confirmed and apologised for the mistake saying, "I am so sorry I can see it is your baby now," they chatted for a while and parted with friendly greetings.

Pauline's second encounter with Lady Astor was in August 1943. As a child Pauline and her mother lived in Melville Road, Ford, Plymouth, and they had a very small grocer's shop. A bombing raid had taken place and Pauline with her mother was in the Anderson Shelter. Father, who was an employee in the Dockyard, was on duty that night at his employer's premises Fire Watching, so the family had to take care of themselves. Their house took a direct hit and was completely destroyed; debris had cascaded onto the Anderson Shelter causing partial collapse, which left Pauline's mother badly injured. Her face was in a fearful state and she had lost her sight and Pauline was left with minor injuries. At eleven years of age it was a frightening experience. Eventually she and her mother were taken to hospital to have their injuries attended to. "We were kept in hospital until our injuries had been healed. My bed was pushed up tight against my mother's bed, as I would help the nurses who were run off their feet dealing with the casualties. Being so near my mother enabled me to hold her beaker while she drank her tea and feed her until she recovered, thankfully mother's sight returned after six weeks.

During our stay at the hospital we often had visitors from various dignitaries and one day along came Lady Astor with another lady who toured the wards and spoke to all the citizens. When Nancy spoke to my mother and asked her to explain what had happened her ladyship noticed that I was there too. Lady Astor came over to my bed and chatted for a while and I felt quite special, then her Ladyship said to me, "Would you like a present?" "Oh yes please, could I have a doll with long hair?" Nancy replied, "I will see." Two days later a beautiful doll with long hair was given to me sent by Lady Astor, I called the doll 'Virginia' as that is where Lady Astor came from. I was so thrilled and I treasured that doll all my life, I passed it to my daughters and now they have families of their own and the doll is somewhere in my family possessions."

Pauline's third encounter with Lady Astor was in 1950-1951. As a young lady she was working then as a clerk in the Strathmore Hotel in Elliot Street. The Hotel had been commandeered during the war and used as the Expense Account Department for the Dockyard until 1952 when the Hotel was handed back to the next owner. "In the lunch break about five of us girls decided to walk down Elliot Street into town to see if any new clothes were on display in the shop windows. Suddenly there appeared in front of us, her arms outstretched to stop us passing, was Lady Astor. She spoke to us saying, "It does my heart good to see all you lovely young girls out enjoying a day like this" for a moment we were taken aback but she continued to chat to us and we felt then quite at ease as she was taking a great deal of interest in our activities. That was to be my last encounter with Lady Astor but I have never forgotten, nor will I ever forget her kindness to me in August 1943. I admired and respected her and wish we had someone with the same passion today who could communicate with the ordinary people. Wherever young people could be helped Nancy reached out and touched our lives."

In a booklet called Memories of Stoke Damerel 1908-1986 introduced by the friends of Stoke Damerel, they highlighted in an article of their booklet an incident that they still hold dear in their memories, it referred to an event in July 1930 which took place at Stoke Damerel High School for Girls and this is what the historical piece said, 'We take this opportunity of thanking Lady Astor, Member of Parliament for her generous gift of £10 pounds, whereby our reference library has been enriched by the addition of many valuable works.' Ten pounds in 1930 was a lot of money in comparison to what wage earnings were. Stoke Damerel High School for Girls was turned over in the war to the Ministry of Defence and most of the girls were evacuated to Truro in Cornwall. The girls who stayed on in Plymouth then transferred to the Plymouth (Emergency) High School for Girls at North Hill. Mrs Joyce Thomas (neé Tidball) who was a former W.R.E.N 1942-1944, having been a former schoolgirl at the Stoke Damerel High School suddenly found herself working as a servicewoman in the School and she was the only pupil who had that privilege. She recalls that it seemed so strange to see the transformation the school had undergone in its wartime role. The basement was the Ship's Galley and the Ground Floor was the Fair Ledger Office transferred from the Royal Naval Barracks and Stoke Damerel became affectionately known as FLO from the initials of the Fair Ledger Office. The old building has been earmarked either for renovation or for a new school to be built; the old building still remains but the school closed in 1986 and so ended the history of the school.

Bertram J. Terry recalled a story about Lady Astor that has stayed in his heart and mind for all these years. "In 1944 when I was fourteen years old I was in my first job as an errand boy for the firm W.H. Ham Limited, Printers and Stationers, trading in East Street Plymouth at the rear of the old Meat Market. About once a month a chauffer driven car would pull up outside the shop and Lady Astor would come into the shop and purchase a small pack of blank business cards about the size of a matchbox. She would then request that the errand boy must deliver them, so the delivery was passed to me and I would have to get on my heavy delivery bike and ride to Elliot Terrace to deliver the pack. On arrival at the tradesmen's entrance the maid would invite me in and ask me to wait, she would then go upstairs and pass the pack to Lady Astor who would then always come down in person and give me a grand tip of a half crown coin which at that time was twenty-five per cent of my weekly wage. This has been in my memory because of her generosity and contact with the people in her constituency that has stayed with me until the present day and I am now in my seventy-eighth year. To me she was a great lady."

Sprightly eighty-one year old Barbara Ostler from Modbury in Devon, a member of that sterling group of ladies the Trefoil Guild recalls that in 1940 she used to live in Saltash, Cornwall, but later moved to live in Plymouth where she joined the Plymouth Girls Junior Choir and sang at the Plymouth Central Hall where many religious faiths were united. So many churches had been bombed which meant that the Central Hall was being used for all denominations to meet with the exception of the Salvation Army who had their own Congress Hall. The fourteen-year-old soprano sang and rehearsed regularly with the choir and visiting musical stars would come from other parts of the country to listen. Barbara also belonged to the Central Hall Girls' League formed to help and assist wherever they could. On one occasion in 1941 Lady Astor heard her sing solo at the damaged Saint Andrew's Church, which had no roof after the enemy bombing, and Barbara received an invitation to sing for her. "I sang twice at the Port Missionary Hall on the Barbican for seafarers, which Lady Astor attended. I also sang at 3, Elliot Terrace where Nancy was entertaining the American servicemen and I was quite thrilled to be invited to a little party with food and soft drinks followed by a dance. To me it was a big party and I thought I was someone special and I have never forgotten that wonderful time. I also became a singer with the Plymouth Orpheus Choir and was a helper at the Central Hall, which was used partly as an emergency rest home for bombed out citizens. The floor would be full of young mothers with babies and children and it was what we would call organised chaos. Nancy would call in to ensure that enough blankets, mattresses, food and hot drinks, was made available for the Deaconess of Central Hall who undertook sterling work and even resorted to cooking meals on a Primus Stove to feed the distressed citizens. I thought Nancy Astor was a wonderful, caring woman and I have respected her all my life and I will never forget her in my lifetime."

Robert Tierney (Diploma in Art -1956) International Artist and Textile Designer from Modbury in Devon, has a great affection for Nancy Astor as she had a bearing on how his life was to change and the kindness she endowed on him has never been forgotten: My mother, Mrs Hilda Tierney, used to be received by Lady Astor at her home address at Elliot Terrace as my mother was her hairdresser and had styled her hair for many years. I met Lady Astor four times as young teenager and I remember her generosity and kindness to this day. The first time I met her was when I was twelve years old, I had a new autograph book and collecting autographs was a hobby of mine. Determined to get Lady Astor's autograph I walked to the Hoe and had the audacity to knock on the door of her home and ask for her Ladyship's autograph. Her Secretary Miss Knight answered the door and told me to wait, she returned and took me up to Lady Astor's sitting room on the first floor. I got her autograph written on the first page of my new autograph book, which I still treasure today, and the inscription read, I hope you will see Plymouth re-built to be a wonderful City and that you will become one of its best citizens, signed Nancy Astor 1948. Then Lady Astor asked me "What do you want to be when you leave school?" I said, "An opera singer although I love art and music." Lady Astor replied, "You will have to work hard then and learn languages." I was already a boy soprano and had been singing in church halls and at concerts in Plymouth, Torquay and Cornwall. Lady Astor on hearing this information said to me, "Would you like to come and sing for my people in Virginia House?" I agreed, and I sung at three concerts for Lady Astor in 1948, 1949 and 1950. I was very proud at being asked by her Ladyship to sing. I had the pleasure of meeting and singing with a wonderful lady who sang on the BBC. Plymouth's well-known soprano Gladys Nicholls. The songs I chose to sing were, Ave Maria Bach-Gounod's version, On Wings of Song by Mendelssohn, Count your Blessings words by Johnson Oatman Jnr and music by Edwin Excell. I also sang The Holy City (aka Jerusalem) words by William Blake and music by Charles Hubert Parry. (It should be noted that the singing of this rousing hymn would have pleased Nancy because it was, and still is, an anthem of the women's rights movements, now it is used as a patriotic song for the Women's Institute and various sporting venues.) Nancy gave me ten shillings each time I sang at her concerts and that was big money for a young lad.

At fourteen my voice broke and for some reason I did not take up the chance of being a professional opera singer as a man, my thoughts and ideas were leaning toward Art and Textile Design. I do not regret the decision for I have had instead an International Career as an Artist and Textile Designer my works have been exhibited all over the world. From what I recall of Lady Astor she had no snobbery and could talk to ordinary people, she spoke to everyone rich or poor and she helped the young and the old with their problems. I met Lady Astor again several times in the 1950's when I came back to Plymouth to see my mother. I was only 22 years old and was still a student at the Art College in London but on occasion I bumped into her Ladyship in the Royal Parade where she had been shopping. As a young man I was full of admiration for her and what she did for Plymouth, when she spoke to me again in town she said, "Hello Robert, How are you getting on?" and I told that I was studying for Art and she showed a great interest. I remember her beautiful silver grey hair and I realised how time was catching up on her, however, I have never forgotten her and her fire and passion is missed beyond words." (Sadly, Robert Tierney passed away on the 19th February 2008, but his story will live on in this book. R.I.P.)

Victor Hill a retired pensioner was reminded of a simple story his mother told him several times to make sure he did not forget: My mother rarely talked about the past choosing to leave the past events in her life stored away in a corner of her memories. One must remember the 1920s and 1930s were harsh years. In the early part of the twentieth century my family lived in Castle Street and later at Lambhay Hill both on the Barbican. My maternal Grandmother, Elizabeth Platt, used to clean Lady Astor's house at Elliot Terrace. Lady Astor was often away from home on Parliamentary duty and my mother, Doris Platt, used to accompany my Grandmother while she was working, during her school holidays, and Lady Astor had given permission, as it was not the normal thing to do leaving a child at home alone. My mother can remember clearly that she used to climb the rather grand staircase to the top of the house from where she had a good view of a painting of a large sailing ship sailing away into the sunset. Apparently seeing the picture made her feel good and she would sing, Oh, Oh, Antonio he's gone away. Left me alone-ee-o, all on my own-ee-o. This was I understand a popular song of the time which might help to date the story which I trust you will find an interesting snap shot of the period. (Note by the Author. The Australian singer Florrie Forde originally sang the song 'Oh, Oh, Antonio' in 1908. During the Second World War the music hall favourite song was sung by Vera Lynn and in the 1970s the British singer Jill Daniels sang the song along with other wartime songs in special remembrance shows.)

My Grandmother was born in about 1880, given that she died in 1954 and was, I believed, 74 years old at the time. My mother was born almost exactly 100 years ago, on the 6th October 1907, one of seven children, my mother being the only one to survive more than ten days, which was not unusual in those days. If that is all correct, as assuming my mother was about ten or twelve at the time she visited Nancy Astor's house we can date the story to about 1919. My grandmother adored Lady Astor and she was very fair with her staff and the pay was better than working for someone in the city. Nancy would always give a child in the house a gift; she was such a generous person, although my mother never said whether she had a gift. I had often wondered how my Grandparent's got together as my grandmother was living in Morwellham, and my grandfather in Plymouth which is quite a distance. Family members would never tell the children about their lives and in those days children were to be 'Seen and not heard.' So I have spent my lifetime trying to find out about my own family. Quite by chance whilst taking my parents for a ride in my car in the Tavistock area some thirty years ago I found out about the Morwellham connection. My mother noticed a signpost to the village of Morwellham and commented that it had been years since she was there. My heart missed a beat, at last all would be revealed - I hoped. She went on to describe the village starting with the Methodist Chapel on the hill and my Grandparents cottage where my Grandmother used to bake bread for the village, and she described the orchard at the back with steps at the side of the cottage leading up to it. My Grandfather was apparently a woodman on the Duke of Bedford's estate. I had never even heard of the place never mind part of my history being linked with it! I was of course intrigued, so I turned the car around and found the village as mother had described except the cottage was now a ruin although the bread ovens still remained in the wall. There were some people working on the site and they told me the village was in the early stages of being restored. It was fifteen years when I last visited Morwellham to find it tastefully developed as a tourist attraction - the ovens still visible.

I know directly from my grandmother, that at thirteen she became a scullery maid in Cotehele House. I do not know the exact dates but taking her age it is likely she was there in 1893. I have no idea how long she was there but somehow she must have come into contact with my grandfather John Platt a Hansom Cab driver. Perhaps his work took him to Cotehele and that would be how he met Elizabeth Watts, or it could be that my grandmother took up some sort of live-in post in Plymouth. It seems clear that Morwellham was in decline then and did not offer any kind of work or marriage prospects. Life was very difficult, albeit I did manage to get grandmother to admit once about a problem when I was in my early teens. They lived in one room in Castle Street for some time, my grandfather became one of the first Royal Blue bus drivers but he died sometime between the wars.

One citizen still remembers when Farley's Rusk Factory of Plymouth was holding an outdoor event and they had an obstacle course, fun loving Nancy was not averse to joining in fun activities. Holding her skirt in her hands she would be seen jumping and climbing the obstacle course, determined to match all the competitors in the hope of winning; she was certainly a very down to earth lady. On some Saturday afternoons Nancy would also be seen at the Alhambra Theatre in Devonport watching the shows and applauding the Geraldine Lamb School of Dancing. Sometimes there would be nearly 100 children participating in the Theatre and the shows were held in aid of charities. Where youth was so was Nancy. Geraldine Lamb's 'Starlights' performed in many ENSA shows during the Second World War and in peacetime provided the dancers for local carnivals and entertained at the Palace Theatre.

Joyce M. Searle taught history at Devonport High School for Girls in 1959-1960 but decided to go to the United States of America as an exchange Teacher, under a scheme sponsored partly by the English Speaking Union, to teach at the Judge John Handley High School in Winchester, Virginia. In the summer before departure, Lady Astor, hearing of this, invited me to tea. It was something of a 'royal command' and I was given the afternoon off School to go to Elliot Terrace. She seemed really interested in the exchange project and was a pleasant and gracious hostess. She very much approved of my going to Virginia of course!

Miss Joyce M. Searle -
taken Sept 1959

Plymouth born Mrs Shirley White (née Liddicoat), now living in Stoke Fleming, South Devon, remembers her father Mr Alfred William Liddicoat who stood outside Mount Street School, Plymouth, at every voting occasion. She said, "He would monitor all the voters coming to the school, to register their votes. He would greet every person and, as he was an hundred per cent Conservative member, would always say, "Vote for Lady Astor." He had quite a rapport with Lady Astor and she used to call him Alfie irrespective of the fact he was called Alfred. Lady Astor would often change people's names to suit her, perhaps it was because she could remember them easily, and she was always so friendly to the working classes."

Another connection with the Author was Lady Astor's visit as Member of Parliament to the Efford Community Centre in 1948 because in the group photograph is my Grandmother Harriet Helen Beatrice (Nell) Foster (nee Parsonage) standing front row first left. She lived then in Holmes Avenue, Efford and had been allocated the house on her return to the city from Buckinghamshire. She had been evacuated to Buckingham after suffering the total loss of her home and contents in the bombing and destruction of Buckwell Street Flats, Plymouth, in March 1941. Just ordinary residents, yet when looking at the photograph taken at the Community Centre in Efford, you can see the look of pride on their faces. The group shows immense pleasure at the thrill of having their photograph taken with Lady Astor; it really meant something in those days.

Westwell Street, 1959, showing Churchill's Fisheries, vegetable, fruit and flower shop

Lady Astor on a visit to Efford Community Centre in 1948. First left (front row adults) is my Grandmother Harriet (Nell) Foster (Nee Parsonage) who lived at 31, Holmes Avenue, Efford. Second left back row is her friend Sarah Reid. Lady in middle back row (behind baby) Mrs Northcott. Second from right (Front row adults) and person just behind are the Drake Sisters. Lady holding baby in middle row Mrs Hexter. Third from the left back row holding little girl is Mrs Gregory. Rest unknown.

CHAPTER SEVEN
SPECIAL MEMORIES

The only thing I like about rich people is their money.
Nancy Astor 1879-1964.

Pauline Trenerry (nee Cowan) recalls that as a family she had many occasions to be grateful to Lady Astor: In late 1926 early 1927 my parents moved into the third house to be built on the Astor Estate, at number 13, Mirador Place, Mount Gould, Plymouth, Devon, we were about the fourth family to move in. Mirador was the name of the country estate in Virginia USA where Nancy and her family had lived before coming to Britain. The rent paid was invested in more houses being built and the Astors did not receive a penny. In order to qualify for a house a certain criteria had to be met and a family had to consist of parents and at least three children. Whilst living in the house we had so much bad luck that we strongly believed that Triskaidekaphobia (fear of number thirteen) was to mar our happiness. We the family made the decision to alter the house number to 12A, from that time on our bad luck went away, perhaps it was only a superstition but we were much happier that it was done.

In September 1927 my fourth brother was born – the first baby boy on the estate and at his baptism he was given the names David Dennys WALDORF after Lord Astor and he received a silver tankard from Lord and Lady Astor. During the terrible air raids in the Second World War 1939-1945 this was kept in a tin box with other family 'treasures' and taken to the shelter for safety. David still has this tankard after eighty-three years.

I was born three years after David and was the only girl in the family. I have sketchy memories of Lady Astor's visits to my Mother, who sadly died in 1936. I can remember a big car stopping outside our house and a chauffeur opening the door for Lady Astor to step out and come into our home. She would be elegantly dressed with gold lorgnette caressing her trim bosom, her favourite colour was blue and she nearly always wore pearls around her neck. Both Lord and Lady Astor were very generous to needy families and we had many gifts of blankets and food. At the times when this big car appeared all the neighbours would come to their front doors and watch the goings on. Cars were rarely seen in those days as only the rich and perhaps middle classes could afford one. When election time came round Lord and Lady Astor arranged for coal to be delivered by horse and cart to the most needy families.

My father was a postman, when he was alive he used to enjoy telling me that when Lady Astor came to our home with gifts he would tell her "I am very grateful to you, your Ladyship, but I will never vote for you." He was a staunch Labour supporter and at election time he would display a Labour placard in the window of the house. Apparently, Lady Astor told him that she did not mind and would still call to see Mother. My maternal grandparents lived at 22, Southside Street, the Barbican, above the shop of Mr Blowey a Compass Adjuster, and they were great admirers of Lord and Lady Astor.

My second eldest brother, Bill, remembers the time when Charlie Chaplin and the Astors visited Charlie Cload's (Senior) Chandlery Shop in Southside Street and a photograph was taken outside the shop. Bill was among several other local people in the picture with the Astors and Charlie Chaplin, you can imagine the pride they felt at having their photograph taken with the elite. Lady Astor was a formidable woman but she really did care for the families in her constituency and as a family we had many reasons to be grateful to her and her husband, her kindness will always be in our memories. (The Author notes that the barbican folk, who did not suffer fools gladly, had a very special relationship with Nancy. They were fisher folk, shopkeepers, and hard-core workers, the barbican housewives in tenement rooms strived desperately to feed and clothe their families and many were to benefit from the kindness shown by Lady Astor.)

One person who remembers with affection the care shown by Nancy to her now deceased family is Mrs Pamela Rendall (nee Price): My Grandfather Mr Price had been wounded in the First World War, having received a bullet wound in the leg, which refused to heal, and left him with limited movement that meant he could not do any heavy manual work. Unable to find employment, in desperation, he appealed

Photo: Copyright unknown.

Photograph of the wedding of Mr Price's youngest daughter to a marine showing Mr Price the former barber standing at the back right.

to Lady Astor for help, she did not hesitate, she immediately set him up in his own business as a barber in Southside Street, investing the sum of twenty-five pounds from her own pocket to licence his trade. He was allowed in addition two rooms, a living room and a bedroom, above the barbershop to raise his a family of ten children there and his barber's shop traded for many years. The original facia board is still mounted under the current advert above the shop, which has in recent years been a card and gift shop. The Price family down through the generations have made sure that that precious gift, the gift of work and support in times of extreme hardship by Nancy has not been forgotten.

The years of the depression and unemployment were unpleasant times, yet people had time for each other and neighbours would rally round in times of tragedy or illness. Lord and Lady Astor did their own rallying around as they foraged and bought property to give the citizens a better time. Their contributions are countless, Prince Rock playing fields, Housing Estate Mount Gould, Hall of Residence at Devonport, nursery schools, College for Nursery School Teachers, day nurseries, convalescent home, children's welfare, and the Virginia House Settlement. These actions were living proof of her love for Plymouth and its population, my family will never forget her kindness and I have made sure that my children have been informed of what she did for our family. We came from the poorest to an increase of quality life and all prospered because of the Astor family and I hope that they rest in peace.

Those who were Astor supporters would hang on every word she said for wherever she campaigned hundreds of people would turn out in the streets to hear her; we do not see that today. Nancy loved the hecklers, as she was in her element ready to reciprocate with a reply in exchange and barracking was commonplace, she was expert at producing wisecracks and epigrams with a natural eloquence. When a working man shouted at Nancy "I never voted for you" "Thank heaven for that!" Nancy quipped; she could produce wonderful repartees that many politicians would envy today. Many owe a debt of gratitude to the Astor family, some keep that debt stored in their hearts, others will not tell, as family secrets would be revealed. There are those who will not admit that she touched their lives and of course the trouble makers who spend their time indulging in character assassination. Many tried to destroy Nancy Astor because she had the courage to challenge, it did affect her political career later in life but for the true Plymouth folk she will remain in their hearts. Whatever Nancy did, or said, it was sure to make history.

Mrs Sylvia Bennett (nee Alcock) as an eighteen-year-old was working for the Solicitors Nash, Howett, Cocks and Clapp in Sussex Street and she said: One particular day I and two other of my colleagues decided to go the Lecture Room, which was being used temporarily as a British Restaurant in the Guildhall, for a meal during our dinner hour. As we walked along Windsor Lane to Notte Street we were chatting and giggling as most teenagers did when suddenly we saw Lady Astor and she spoke to us in a loud voice and said, "And what are you lot laughing about?" Sylvia being the bravest of the three replied "We are on our way to lunch at the Lecture Room" "Ah! Wait and see what you have got then and see if you will laugh afterwards" we laughed with her, but thought her formidable and went quickly on our way. We realised that she always spoke to people and she would say what came into her mind at the time. One thing I remember though is that I was never conscious of any American accent, she spoke good English where as other Americans in the City could be immediately recognised when they spoke.

Mr Les Palmer (ex Royal Navy) has mixed feelings about Nancy, Lady Astor, after returning from serving on HMS Illustrious in the Mediterranean, which had executed a courtesy call to Norfolk Virginia USA in 1941. On his return to Plymouth Les had been promoted to acting Petty Officer and detailed to shore duty. He remembers distinctly the event in his mind as he patrolled Union Street, Plymouth. Nearing the slot machine building under the arches he was confronted by Lady Astor and she ordered him to immediately close the gaming and slot machines. Taken aback, he pointed out to Lady Astor he could only take orders from his senior officer and that he would pass on her request. Nancy, ever the rebel against gambling and a strong Christian Scientist, tried to persuade people not to waste their money but unfortunately, it was a lost cause.

Mrs Sheila Soroka (nee Martin) recalls an event during the Second World War when as a young child of eight years old she accompanied her mother on a shopping trip. After being bombed out of their former premises Spooners opened a shop in a Nissen hut at Drake's Circus. Mother and I visited the new shop, as she wanted to buy a new hat. In those days it was a most serious business and could take quite some time. After trying on several hats and not being able to make up her mind I saw an old lady dressed all in black and carrying a rolled up umbrella, coming towards us. She poked my mother in the back with her umbrella and said, "Don't have that one, it makes you look like a monkey!" and walked off. I asked my Mother, "Who is that? My Mother replied "Lady Astor." Mother pulled off the hat laughing and chose another one. As most Plymouth ladies knew, Nancy Astor was a fashion expert of hats, and during the war years hats were not on clothes rationing coupons. Although I was only eight at the time I have never forgotten it.

This story about the hat reminded the author how important the hat fashion was in the 1920s/1930s/1940s. Every time Lady Astor bought a new hat many ladies would raid the milliner's shops to obtain a similar item to keep up with the fashions, a pattern that today's ladies still indulge in although the item may be a different article of clothing. All through her lifetime Lady Astor's hats would be a subject of speculation, vulnerable to press reporters and sometimes-humorous news reports. An article in the Western Morning News in July 1936 was one such instance. Lady Astor attended the Plymouth annual meeting of the Sutton Conservative and Unionist Association in

July 1936 wearing a new hat! The article printed was titled 'Mother's New Hat.' Her son, the Honourable William Astor M.P. for Fulham, who was a speaker, pointed to it, and remarked: "Collective security is like Mother's new hat - very fancy looking in the front, but not much protection against anything at the back." One can only speculate what Mother said to son after the meeting. Clever advertising perhaps? Oddly enough sales at the milliners shop rose rapidly during the next few days in Plymouth.

In 1944 Lady Astor boarded a train at Paddington to Plymouth on a campaigning trip and sat in a carriage with eight ladies; one Plymouth sailor was also in the carriage and he knew Lady Astor. The group were complete strangers and after exchanging nodding greetings they settled down for the journey. The ladies started to discuss various problems among themselves unaware of who Lady Astor was, when suddenly her name was mentioned and they started to severely criticise her and were running her down. It must have been an awful situation for her but for once she held her peace and when the train stopped at Exeter she moved to another carriage. The sailor informed the ladies then who they had been sitting with and there is no doubt they were embarrassed, but the damage was done. That evening all the ladies including Lady Astor must have had food for thought, and one wonders how much damage it did to Nancy's confidence.

The copy of the letter inserted below this paragraph is a letter sent by Nancy Astor to the young widowed Mrs Mary Lebar after the death of her husband who had been badly wounded at Arnhem but died later of his wounds. He was in the 1st Canadian Airborne Division. Ninety-two year old Mrs Lebar adored Nancy and has kept this precious letter and treasured it all these years: I was left with a baby to bring up with no financial support as was synonymous with many of my generation in the Second World War. Mount Gould Road was part of the Astor Estate but now the street has been renamed as Beaumont Road. Nancy visited me and my baby at my home later and I remember how friendly and caring she was. Nancy made provision for the young mothers to visit the Astor Institute to help in forging friendly relations with others who had been left widowed, and constantly opened fetes and stalls to help the war effort. Lord and Lady Astor would be frequently seen at the British Restaurant having a meal with the citizens. Both were very kind people. (Mary also received a letter from King George V1 offering his condolences and stating that he hoped the country would look after her after the sacrifice made by the Canadian soldier. Mary received a pension to help support herself and baby son.)

3, ELLIOT TERRACE,
THE HOE,
22nd March 1945   PLYMOUTH.

Dear Mrs Le-Bar,

I hoped so much to come myself to see
you and tell you how deeply I feel your great loss.
If I can help in any way at all, I do hope you will
let me know.

I am so glad you will have the baby to
comfort you in your grief.

Yours very truly,

Nancy Astor

23 Mount Gold Road,
Plymouth.

Amelia Stephens (nee Davey) was another lady who adored Lady Astor, although now in her eighties she has never forgotten Lady Astor's kindness to her father and she has kindly allowed the Author to tell her story. John Davey lost a leg in the battle for the Dardenelles during the First World War and despite still being a young man found obtaining employment very difficult. The land fit for heroes did not financially support the disabled men leaving them without much hope and facing further hardships and most men struggled valiantly to obtain self-respect. With a young family to support John Davey was desperate for work. His family lived in New Street on the Barbican and one day he was sitting on the windowsill of his home when Lady Astor, who frequently visited the Barbican, stopped to speak to him. "Young man," she asked, "Have you any work?" "No your ladyship, I cannot get work in my condition" he replied. "Well now, I have plenty of work for you, please start right away." How precious those words for it gave him independence and self-respect. His task was to keep the grass cut at the Astor Housing Estate, and he would sit on the ground with a pair of hand shears and trim the grass, yard by yard, from the front doors to the pavements.

John Davey and his little family, five sons and one daughter, moved to number 37 Mount Gould Terrace. Keeping the grass trim kept him in full time employment and later when he went to Roehampton to have a leg fitted and was able to walk and move about more freely, he continued doing odd jobs for Lady Astor until he retired. Her Ladyship visited the family regularly and little Amelia was chosen to present bouquets to Lady Astor when she visited Astor Hall or any event on the Astor Estate. One day her Ladyship called when least expected and Amelia answered the door, as her Mother was busy in the kitchen. "It's her Ladyship," Amelia gasped, worried that etiquette was not being observed. "It quite all right," said Lady Astor, who marched into the kitchen and promptly sat herself at the table whilst Mrs Davey made a cup of tea. Such was the ease that a Viscountess could mix with ordinary people.

John Davey and his family were always invited to the functions held by the Astor family and they felt honoured. A working class family they found those times were very hard and John Davey could not afford new suits to attend the functions, so the family could not always accept the invitations. There is the special invitation to the wedding of Nancy's daughter Phyllis to Lord Willoughby de Eresby held at Cliveden in July 1933, unfortunately the little family could ill afford to go so they had to send a letter of regret. Lady Astor took the time to write back and her letter for all to see show how she cared about ordinary people. It has additional spice as a little rider was added after typing to mention that "It's all so sudden," so it would appear the marriage was hastily arranged. A further invitation was sent to John Davey inviting his family to the celebrations held at Plymouth Guildhall on Thursday 26th October 1933, which was the wedding reception for Lord and Lady Willoughby de Eresby, entertainment consisted of music from 8pm to 9pm and dancing from 9pm to 12 Midnight. The Davey family have treasured the link that they had with Nancy Astor all those years ago, and those treasures, which have been lovingly kept, will be passed on to the new family members so that Lady Astor's kindness will never be forgotten.

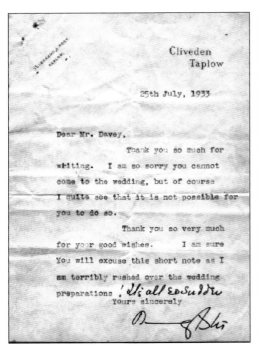

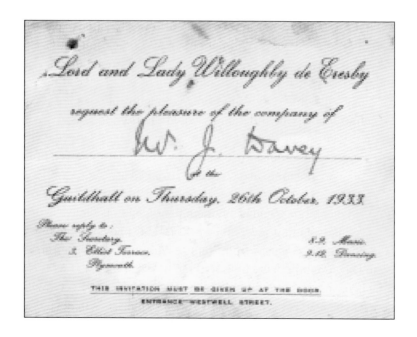

Winston Churchill and Lady Astor touring Plymouth, March 1941
after a heavy night raid.

Edward Clifton now a retired pensioner recalls an event that left a lasting impression on him as a boy when the Second World War was coming to an end: One day a Rolls Royce pulled up at Mount Gould Terrace and out of the car stepped this very fine lady. She started handing out packets and boxes of 'Candy,' she called out to the children in the Astor houses, front doors began to open and the children came running out delighted at the opportunity of free sweets. I hung back as I was quite shy and I had only recently returned from Tiverton where I had been evacuated, but my sister said, she is beckoning to you, go on over. Well this very fine lady I was to find out later was Lady Astor and she made a really big fuss of me and gave me a box of Candy, which was smashing! I remember my mother inviting Lady Astor into our house for a cup of tea as a thank you. Of course, out came the best china and we had to be on our best behaviour. Those were hard days but Lady Astor did everything she could to improve our lives. What a woman!

Vivien Pengelly, Leader of the Conservative Group of Plymouth city Council (2008) was frequently told the story about Lady Astor by her father. Vivien's Father Clifford Ronald Lynden (born June 1911 died March 2002 aged 91years) became a Telegraph Boy at the age of 14 years. In 1925 he delivered a Telegram to Lady Astor at the front door of 3, Elliot Terrace, and promptly got told off for not going to the back door. She then invited him around to the back door to have a cup of coffee, as he looked so cold. It was the first time he had ever tasted coffee, but he said it did warm him up!

Photo courtesy Vivien Pengelly

The Postman, father to Vivien Pengelly Conservative Leader for Plymouth City, who delivered mail (pre war) to 3, Elliot Terrace, home of the Astors.

Silver Tankard given by Lord and Lady Astor

THIS CUP WAS PRESENTED BY
LORD AND LADY ASTOR
5th SEPT 1927
TO DAVID DENNYS WALDORF COWAN
(FIRST MALE CHILD BORN ON THE
ASTOR ESTATE IN PLYMOUTH)

*Inscription showing the tankard as having been given to the
first boy born on the Astor estate*

CHAPTER EIGHT
THE ORPHAN'S FRIEND

"Vote for Lady Astor and your children will weigh more!"
Nancy Astor 1879-1964

Phyllis Baggott (nee Bartlett) tells her story:

When I read an article in the local paper that someone was going to write a book about Lady Astor and had asked for people to come forward to the Astor Hotel in June 2003 I was thrilled. I was determined to meet the lady to tell her my story of Lady Astor, for in my life she was someone very special and to this day lives in my heart. Came the day and I was taken very poorly and unable to attend as an Astor friend. Disappointed I thought my chance was lost but a friend gave me the telephone number of the Author writing the book so I tentatively rang her and the response was good. So now my story can be told.

I was born in 1924 and from the age of seven I was brought up, along with my sister, in the Devon and Female Orphanage in Lockyer Street, Plymouth. Near by was the Hoe Grammar School for boys run by Mr Diamond the Headmaster, and just a few doors away was the hotel that we now know as Astor Hotel. In the 1920's the hotel was called Hoe Mansions. We stayed at the Orphanage under the Poor Law Guardians, which was, a Board of Guardians for orphans, The Poor Law Act was abolished in 1930. When we became teenagers we were trained for service in the grand houses of the day until 1939 when war broke out and life styles were to change. However the Matron, Miss Durston, of the Orphanage kept me on for special service to her, by then I must have been the eldest girl, a couple of other girls were also kept on for training. When my sister was old enough she left the orphanage and eventually married an USA Navy Diver and went to America to make a new life for herself.

I can remember Lady Astor as though it was yesterday and I can tell you that she was a very kind and generous lady to us children throughout our stay at the home, as I truly know because I had to write many a thank you letter to her. Why I was picked I do not know, but now I look back with pride that I was chosen. Lady Astor brought a lot of happiness into our lives, which we would not normally have had, we would be so excited at times to see her as she was so special to us all. She remembered us for lots of little things like birthday gifts, little treats, and that is why she is so special in our hearts. She would send bottles of sweets bought direct from the factory to the orphanage for us and on occasion we all had a bottle each. All paid for by Lady Astor, of course, we must remember this was in the nineteen twenties and early nineteen thirties before the war and sweet rationing. It was Lady Astor that gave the children in the orphanage the very first Mars bar when they came out in August 1932. Another special event was the yearly pantomime trip to the Theatre Royal and each child was presented with a picture box of chocolates supplied by Nancy to have while we watched the show. This would be followed by a tea party with waitress service at a hotel and we would be served from the best silver and while we were tucking into our tea the orchestra would play music and we were so thrilled. I always remember the beautiful cake stands and the cakes were scrumptious. We were a little nervous when selecting our cake as we had been warned by the matron not to be greedy or gormandise and to remember our manners, so we were afraid to take more than one cake, but most of us could have tucked in to the lot! Miss Durston the matron was strict but fair, she had her good days and bad days, of course, she had her favourite girls and they would receive little extra treats. We who were not the favoured ones would have to just look and say nothing. Miss Durston had rescued a stray dog that kept turning up at the orphanage, finally she adopted it and the children were pleased. It was given a bath, brushed and combed and always wore a bow of red ribbon. Each girl was told that when we crossed the road in crocodile one of us was to carry him across the road, I did this once or twice so the matron delegated me to regularly feed it. In the evening when I used to give Bubbles her Sprat biscuits I put them in a dish

Photo: Copyright unknown

Miss Durston the Matron with pet dog Bubbles and the orphans of Devon & Cornwall Female Orphanage on the steps leading to the garden of the derelict Pencalenick Mansion former home of Lady Trelawney circa late 1930's. Phyllis is in the second row from the back first right and her sister Joan is sitting behind her.

under the table and I would crawl under the table and eat some of the Sprat biscuits myself. I was big for my age and I was nearly always hungry, we had good food at the orphanage but only the minimum to survive, there was no such thing as second helpings.

One very special occasion I shall always keep in my memory was when her Ladyship invited us to her daughter's wedding reception at Elliot Terrace and we all had to toast her with a small glass of champagne during the celebrations and it made us feel all grown up. We worshipped her because we knew she cared and did everything she could to make the quality of our life better and then there were her voting days, high excitement and anticipation. That was the only time our dormitory lights would be switched on, that was done by using a special key, as we children could not switch the lights on and off. We children always went to bed in the dark and got up in the dark so having the lights on was quite an event. As Lady Astor's entourage passed by we looked out of the open windows and sang at the top of our voices because we meant it. "Vote, Vote, Vote for Lady Astor." As the participants went down Lockyer Street she would look up and wave to us and we cheered her like mad. When the voting public had passed we would be treated with an oatmeal biscuit and a cup of tea; orphans were always ready for drink and food.

But the best present she ever gave us was the month's August holiday in the summer, our first holiday camp in the nineteen thirties was Prince Hall near Two Bridges Dartmoor. It was derelict then but now it is the Prince Hall Country House Hotel and has been completely renovated. What I remember most is that we used to be bathed in a hipbath; we thought it was quite special, although I was so young it is amazing how memories stay with you. Following that, our monthly holidays were spent at a place called Pencalenick, Tressillion, near Truro in Cornwall, the former home of Lady Trelawney. Plans were made to assemble the things we needed to be used and these were transported by Pickford's removal van and we slept on mattresses on the floor and ate off tin plates and drank from tin cups. But for us children it was great once we got used to the bats flying in and out of the windows at night, we would duck underneath, some of us giggled, some were frightened but we were happy. We wore sandals and print dresses, the dresses were paid for by Mrs E Dingle of Dingles shop, she was another kind lady, the dresses can be seen in the photograph taken in the garden. I remember we got really sunburnt, the summers seemed better in those years. During the Second World War the mansion was used as a billeting base for the Americans, it was the Headquarters of the 1st and 5th Engineer Special Brigades, and it was in quite a state when they left. Pencalenick House in 1997 was a school for children with special needs and it was planned to apply for a lottery grant to restore the old mansion to its former glory.

Thanks to her Ladyship, Nancy Astor, who had arranged and paid for the holiday, which brought great happiness into our lives, because otherwise we would not have

Orphan Girls and Bubbles on summer holiday at Pencalenick
circa 1938-1939. Phyllis is fourth from the left back row from girl waving hand.
sister Joan standing behind. Phyllis's friend Ruby first left front row.

had a holiday. All the girls had a purse with money in it, she would think of everything. I am so glad this book is being done to let everyone know what she really did for the people and she worked so hard for the children, the Barbican folk and the fishermen. She was an angel of kindness to us all. I would always be ready to defend her and to shout out loud all the good she had done for the girls in the orphanage and many others. I know I can speak on behalf of all former orphans of the Devonport and Female Orphanage of the nineteen twenties, nineteen thirties, and early nineteen forties who remember the little gifts of love and Lady Astor's kindness. Our generation have an undying love for this lady who did so much for so many underprivileged citizens. For the children of her era she had the very special human touch. All we can say, those of us who remember her is, God bless her and may she rest in peace.

When I was due to start work it was not my choice to remain at the home to work for Matron, I wanted to go out into the world and be independent, so secretly I wrote a letter seeking other employment and obtained a post with Taylor's Clothing. Unfortunately, I was not happy so I moved on to another job with a business and licensing family who I was with for seven years looking after their children. I was very happy with this family and my employer gave me a good home and was very

The Orphan girls in the swim

Devon & Cornwall Orphans in the Garden of Pencalenick late 1930's
with pet mascot dog Bubbles Phyllis is in the second row third from left.
Sister Joan is in the third row second from the right with the girl's arms around her.

Devon & Cornwall Female Orphanage
Before the bombing in 1941

The bombed Devon & Cornwall Female Orphanage
Locker Street Plymouth 1941

good to me, then came the war and we were bombed out of Fore Street, Devonport, and had to relocate to Teignmouth, Devon. I stayed there for seven years but my heart was in Plymouth so I left and returned to my city and managed to acquire a post in the NAAFI. In 1947 I met a young handsome man, he was an apprentice bricklayer and after a courtship of two years Charlie and I were married in October 1949 and we have been happily married for fifty-four years. We have one son and two lovely grandchildren. My last job when I finally retired from work was as a school dinner lady at Widey Primary School, Crownhill, Plymouth.

Sadly Phyllis Baggott (nee Bartlett) died on Saturday May 7th 2005 not having seen her story in print, but she will live on in this story as a permanent memorial. This former orphan girl defied all obstacles to achieve a hard working life and a happy marriage and her genes will live on in her children.

The Duchy of Cornwall purchased Pencalenick Mansion overlooking the Fowey estuary in the 1930s. Lady Salusbury-Trelawny lived at Pencalenick from 1918 until her death in 1932. The house was the former home of the Williams family. During the late 1940s it was used as a base for American servicemen. It is now a top class Residential Special School for children aged 11 to 16 years.

In researching the history of Lady Astor it revealed how caring she was toward children. Nancy and her family, right from the beginning of her love affair with Plymouth, had done everything within her power to improve the lives of children, and sick children, particularly, were given extra help in an effort to restore their health. There is a quote by an unknown person in 1928 that said, "Through her runs a golden thread of loving kindness toward young children." A convalescent home for children was acquired at Dousland called Wissiecott named after Lord and Lady Astor's daughter Phyllis, known as Wissie to family members, The home was used for children in need of special care because of poor health and tuberculosis and in the late 1900s an after care committee had been set up to give support to the children. The Astor family financed it themselves and had the home decorated and furnished to a high standard. In 1922 Queen Marie of Romania sent £100 for the poor of Plymouth, a lot of money in those days, she was a friend of Nancy and proved over the years to be a friend of Plymouth. However, funds from other sources were at an all time low and it was impossible to keep the home going solely on the Astor's money and sadly the children's home had to be closed in the 1920s.

The Scattered Homes and Stoke House Orphanage were to face a better future, as in 1930 the duties of the Board of Guardians were transferred to the City Council. Throughout their lives the Scattered Homes children were to experience the generosity and kindness of Lord and Lady Astor. Without their caring attitude the children would have been 'out of sight - out of mind.' In the late 1920's Lady Astor became aware of just how many orphaned, unwanted and abandoned children there were in care in homes across the city. One special occasion never forgotten by the surviving children from Scattered Homes took place on June 7th 1927 when eighty Scattered Homes children were treated to a party and entertained at Virginia House. That same year the children were treated again to a Christmas and New Year's party where the children sang carols for Lady Astor.

BRIEF PRINCE HALL HISTORY

This historical information is submitted by kind permission of Adam and Carrie Southwell the former tenants of Prince Hall. Prynse Hall or Prynchall, as it was originally called, is one of the ancient tenements of Dartmoor and a property has stood on the site since 1443. It was likely that the original house was destroyed through vandalism during the Civil War. With the planning of the Trans-Dartmoor road in the 1770's additional farm buildings were built. The present mansion as it stands today was built for Mr Justice Buller later to be Sir Francis Buller, who at thirty-two was the youngest High Court Judge ever to sit in the British Courts; he was also the first judge to send convicts to Australia. Born in 1746 he was just seventeen when he married the last of the line of the family of Yarde. Susannah was the only child and heiress of Francis Yarde of Churston Court near Brixham. Francis Buller

Photo by kind permission of Adam and Carrie Southwell former tenants.

Prince Hall Country House Hotel Two Bridges Dartmoor

promptly started to spend her fortune and whilst living at Prince Hall, sometime in the 1780s, he built the local public house the Saracen's Head, now known as Two Bridges Hotel. Sir Francis made the sitting room at Prince Hall available to local people as a place in which to worship, there being no local church. It was not until the early 1800's that Princetown was constructed and eventually a new church built. The mansion passed in turn to the Gullet family who were then succeeded by the Fowler family, but the Lamb family then lived at the mansion, who, appropriate to their name, introduced the black-faced sheep to Dartmoor and later followed this with the introduction of Galloway cattle.

At the end of the nineteenth century the house became the private home of the Barrington family, who were stewards to the Duke of Cornwall. The current Duke, His Royal Highness the Prince of Wales, still controls much of the surrounding moor and is the Landlord of Prince Hall. Although purists may challenge it as a myth, around this time it is thought that Sir Arthur Conan Doyle stayed at Prince Hall and was inspired by the surrounding countryside to write The Hound of the Baskervilles. In 1906 the house became a hotel and offered full board, garaging of motor vehicles and carriages, all for two guineas a week! In 1913 a golf course was constructed to the east of the tree-lined drive. The hotel closed during the First World War, opened again in 1918 but in 1922 the Petherick family sold the property and once again it became a private house. The next tenants were the Alder family; unfortunately, they let it fall into disrepair and in January 1931 the roof collapsed under a heavy fall of snow and it remained in a state of disrepair for some years. The children of the Devon & Female Orphanage, Lockyer Street, Plymouth, used the dilapidated mansion as a summer holiday residence in 1934 with the courtesy of the Prince of Wales, for them it was a real adventure paid for by Lady Astor, the children's friend. Nancy was a good friend to the Prince of Wales and had often entertained him and with her persuasive powers she would usually have favours granted.

Early in 1935 the Prince of Wales (1894-1972) (who later, from January to December 1936, became King Edward Vlll) used the property for stabling his string of forty-two Arab horses while he and Wallis Simpson stayed at Tor Royal near Princetown. In June 1935 HRH the Prince of Wales leased Prince Hall comprising three acres, two roods and twenty-nine perches of land in the manor of Lydford and Forest of Dartmoor in the County of Devon to Army Captain Griffith Robert P Oyntz Llewellyn. The house had a ninety-nine year lease, which expired in 2005. He moved into the mansion with his second wife and new baby along with his two daughters from his first marriage. He did extensive repairs to the house and gardens and had some fine wrought iron gates made which carried the words 'Here bloom the sweetest flowers and here cabbages are kings.' The gates were found buried during the renovation in 1984 and still survive today. Captain Llewellyn is remembered locally by a characteristic action. He found a party of picnickers throwing their litter on the Moor. When he approached them they drove off, but Captain Llewellyn took their car number, traced them and sent their rubbish to them in Yorkshire in two large tea chests, marked postage payable on delivery! Reminiscing with Lady Daphne Maynard, daughter of Captain Llewellyn and wife of Air Chief Marshall Sir Nigel Maynard, Bicester, Oxon, of this incident brought back vivid memories of her father. She remembered that it was typical of his characteristics, as he was a fierce supporter of keeping the moor in its natural state.

Mr and Mrs Cooper tenanted Prince Hall Farm with their son and two daughters, the family having moved from Nuns Cross Farm and Mrs Cooper helped out the Llewellyn family at Prince Hall when there were staff shortages. During the Second World War an army searchlight battery was based at Prince Hall Farm. When Captain Llewellyn left Prince Hall it remained empty for a short period of time and as Plymouth had been heavily bombed Lady Astor was offered the opportunity of buying the house. In 1945 Lord and Lady Astor bought Prince Hall as a summer residence, using the main sitting room as a billiard room. The following year they handed the house over to the Virginia House Settlement for deprived children and it was used as a holiday home, remaining with the charity until 1956. A lady, Doctor Bentley, from London who came to recuperate after an illness, tenanted the house then. She lived at Prince Hall for twenty years and did a lot of voluntary work at Princetown Prison. Then she sold the hall to a Torbay accountant who had plans to convert it into a hotel but his domestic problems proved too difficult a situation to overcome and he was forced to sell the lease to someone else. The hotel became a thriving business with Adam and Carrie Southwell as the leaseholders, they upgraded and refurbished every room in the hotel and have won several awards for hospitality and cuisine. Prince Hall certainly has a fine and varied history and its success will ensure the precious building remains a part of living history.

In June 1931 negotiations were underway for acquisition of a site at Newquay from the Duchy of Cornwall for a holiday home for the Royal United Services Orphan Home for Girls at Stoke Devonport. Governors and Subscribers attending the meeting were the President the Commander-in-Chief Admiral Sir Hubert Brand who was accompanied by his sister the Hon Alice Brand, President of the Ladies Committee, also attending Lieutenant Colonel F.L. Alford Hon Sec, the Mayor and Mayoress of Plymouth then Mr & Mrs J Clifford Tozer. This home was a very good home supporting 132 girls who were the orphan daughters of sailors and soldiers lost in battle or accidents and the home was designated as a real home to educate and train them for a useful life and to mould them into good citizens. The officers and men of the Royal Navy, Royal Marines and the Army financially supported it, and many civilian citizens also supported the home. Prominent subscribers to the Orphanage were his majesty the King, the Prince of Wales, the Bishop of Plymouth and Lady Astor, who always fought long and hard to improve the quality of life for children in institutions.

Picture courtesy Miss Jean Tozer JP (Daughter of Sir Clifford & Lady Tozer)

This Western Morning News and Mercury newspaper photograph was taken on Friday 19th June 1931 and depicts six orphan girls from the Royal United Services Orphan Home for Girls; typical of that era is that not one of their names is mentioned. Taken prior to the annual meeting, included in the group are the Mayor Mr J. Clifford Tozer (standing right behind three orphan girls) and Mayoress Mrs J Tozer (centre front with flowers.) Also in the picture the Commander-in-Chief, Lieut-Colonel F. Alford (Hon Sec) the Hon Alice Brand, and a member of staff in the background wearing the white apron. Front row left and right, three each side, the orphan children. Whatever hairstyle they previously had, children on entering the orphanage were given the typical institutional haircut, the regular fringe and short cut above the ears, as seen in this newspaper photograph.

Queen Mary and Lady Astor on a visit to an Orphanage in London circa 1920's/1930's.
Many orphans experienced their kindnesses.

CHAPTER NINE
CLOVELLY LINK

Photo courtesy of Vicky Norman. Copyright Baths Photographic, Bideford, North Devon

The porter having collected the empty beer crates and bottles from the New Inn Clovelly, takes the fully laden Donkeys up the High street. Today manpower and sledges push and pull this transport both ways.

FOREWORD
BY THE HONOURABLE JOHN ROUS CLOVELLY

Vicky Norman's lifetime association with Clovelly arose as a result of the friendship struck between my Great Great Aunt Christine Hamlyn and Nancy Astor MP, and this followed through to Christine's niece and heiress Betty Asquith.

Faced with the challenge of rehousing evacuated children from her constituency Nancy appealed to Betty. Accommodation in Betty's village was offered, and a relatively benign war experience followed for the children in our small fishing village.

It has been a source of pride to the residents of Clovelly that evacuee's reunions have followed, and indeed some have come back to live in the village they had been introduced to as a war time necessity.

The Honourable John Rous Clovelly Estate

A thing of beauty is a joy forever; It's loveliness increases; it will never pass into nothingness. *John Keats 1795-1821*

Lady Astor's friendship with Christine Hamlyn-Fane (1856-1936) (later the last name was dropped) was long and binding and when Christine Hamlyn died her niece, the Honourable Betty Asquith, (1889-1962) inherited the Clovelly estate. Nancy's friendship continued with the Asquith family and she would frequently visit Clovelly and it was because of that link that led, in 1941, to the orphaned, unwanted, and abandoned children of the Stoke House Orphanage and Scattered Homes in Plymouth, who had been bombed out of their Institution, being evacuated to the beautiful little village of Clovelly in North Devon during the Second World War, where they were to find a safe haven. Lady Astor had fought to house the children in the New Inn, half way down the cobbled High Street and from 1941 to 1945 the Plymouth City Council paid the rent for the hiring of the former hotel.

Photo by kind permission Hon. John Rous

The Honourable Betty Asquith Clovelly (1889-1962)

CLOVELLY'S HISTORY

The Clovelly Chronicles reveal a fascinating insight into some of Clovelly's history. The village is unique in that the cliffs around the bay are of soft sandstone with the exception of the cliff on which Clovelly stands, on an unexpected spur of solid rock. In the old smuggling days this rock appeared to the Clovelly folk as an admirable trait, and undeterred by the difficultly of constructing the village on an almost perpendicular slope, they set to work to make a harbour and a Main Street. The harbour was built in the14th century and underwent repair in the 16th century at a cost of two thousand pounds. Clovelly Court had been occupied since 1738, but at the time of its inclusion in the Domesday Book, which was commissioned in the year 1085 by King William the Conqueror, Clovelly Manor was owned by, and remained the property of, the King from the 11th Century until 1242 when the Giffard family acquired it. They were of Norman origin and later Sir Roger Giffard sublet the Manor of Clovelly. The first recorded Rector of Clovelly in 1262 was also a Giffard. Through various marriages the names in the mid and late 1300s were Staunton and Mandeville. The Carys were one of the great Devon families and cousins of the Grenvilles. Sir William Cary was the builder of the original pier or breakwater at Clovelly; it is unusual in that it is based still on massive boulders slotted together rather than mortared or cemented. His elder brother, Sir John, was a Judge and Baron of the Exchequer in 1370 but owing to dynastic intrigues was banished to Ireland and his lands confiscated. Clovelly provides a contrast, having been associated with only three families since the middle of the thirteenth century, nearly eight hundred years ago.

His son, Robert, was brought up in Sir William Cary's household and Sir John's fortunes turned when, at a Royal Tournament in 1413, Robert defeated the Knight Errant of Aragon who had hitherto been unconquered throughout Europe. Robert was immediately knighted by Henry V and his father's land restored to him. The Cary arms to this day include the 'three roses argent' of the Aragon Knight. The Carys lived in Clovelly for the next eleven generations; one of its sons, George Cary, married and had seven children, although his grandchildren proved childless through the sons not marrying and the daughters being without issue. So in 1738 Robert Barber, the widower of Elizabeth Cary, sold the Clovelly estate to Zachary Hamlyn and it is the Hamlyns and their descendants, who still own the village and much of the surrounding land. Modern history of Clovelly (Clovelleigh) started with the acquisition of the Clovelly Estate by the Hamlyn family in 1738. Zachary Hamlyn originally built Clovelly Court circa 1740 and in 1789 following a fire; the house was rebuilt incorporating parts of the original house. The house contains many interesting pictures notably one of Clovelly by Turner and many charming pieces of 18th Century furniture.

Clovelly is set in the parish of the Hartland Hundred, the Archdeaconry of Barnstaple, and the Diocese of Exeter. Zachary Hamlyn, who was born at Kennerland Farm in Higher Clovelly, made his fortune as a lawyer at Lincolns Inn and purchased the estate for £9,438 in 1738. He died unmarried and left the estate to his nephew James, on condition he changed his name from Hammett to Hamlyn. James married Arabella Williams, heiress of the Edwinsford Estate, Carmarthenshire in Wales. He was created a Baronet for public services. Their son James (2nd Baronet) married Diana (née Whitaker) whose share of her father's fortune was used to improve the estate including the construction of the Hobby Drive. Work started during the Napoleonic wars assisted, it is said, by French prisoners of war, the project was to create a scenic road; it was completed between 1811 and 1829. The drive and other coast path carriageways were completed in the period of high unemployment after 1815. The 3rd Baronet, also a James Hamlyn, married Mary, daughter of the 1st Earl Fortescue; another distinguished neighbouring West Country family. They had three daughters. The eldest, Susan Hester, married Henry Fane of Fulbeck Lincolnshire. The family assumed the surname Hamlyn-Fane. Their son, Neville Hamlyn-Fane aged 26, died in 1884. In 1934 it was still the seat of Christine Hamlyn.

H. Verne in his 'Song of Devon' in 1930 immortalises Clovelly in song.

Clovelly - Ah sweet Clovelly
Beside the Western Ocean sleeping
Thy rocks and woodlands the noontime sleeping
In golden ray
And when I wander sad and friendless
In lands a thousand leagues away
I long and long for my returning
But never more will come the day.

CHRISTINE HAMLYN - DOYENNE OF CLOVELLY

Constance Edwina Adeline Hamlyn-Fane (1861-1920) inherited land at Ringwood, the Avon Tyrrell estate and Christine Hamlyn-Fane (1856-1936) was given the Clovelly Estate. In 1889 she married Frederick Gosling. She requested him, firstly, to change his name from Gosling to Hamlyn because of the long association of the name Hamlyn with Clovelly and secondly, to devote his not inconsiderable fortune to the restoration of all properties on the estate. Christine Hamlyn who inherited the village in 1884 must be mentioned in Clovelly's history as she truly loved the village and cared for it intensely until her death in 1936. She had fought a hard and long battle to keep her beloved village solvent; there is evidence in the Clovelly Chronicles that show in 1925 she was constantly receiving letters from Land Agents, Surveyors and Auctioneers to sell the village, farms and surrounding land. Times were difficult as she struggled to maintain the village and its community and one must give credence

Photograph taken in 1927 at Dunster Castle. In the photograph: Left to right. (First left anon) Mr R. Tree, Mr Waddington, Mrs Christine Hamlyn, Lady Astor, in fur coat, Mrs Tree (behind Lady Astor's head), Mrs W. Pennant (tall lady with black short coat) and Miss Kindesly with top hat, and Mrs Landery Hobson.

to her courage to hold firm and to hold on. Christine had a strong belief in doing what was right for her villagers and she held out against all the profit-seeking agents. Mrs Hamlyn had paid for water and drainage to be installed into Clovelly village. She also had thousands of trees planted, restored the cliff paths and enhanced the scenic road which winds through woods and offers spectacular cliffside views of the sea and Clovelly's harbour. A tiny woman, she fervently fought against any external modernisation or commercialism in Clovelly, and it was she who was largely responsible for the unspoilt character and nature of Clovelly today.

Christine Hamlyn was also one of the best English hostesses in the West Country and on her trips to the village she always looked delightful in her old world style of black satin dress and a lace cap on her snowy white hair. She could always be heard coming down the cobbled steps of Clovelly with her long stick or sometimes carrying her gold staff. Christine always wore a crinoline dress, white gloves, and a wide-brimmed hat, but at times would favour an old-fashioned poke bonnet. This was large and draped with priceless antique lace and with this she would wear a stole. Every year she held tea parties, with entertainment, set up in the long passage at Clovelly Court for all the children of the village and the teachers at the school were invited too. What wonderful teas and entertainment the village children and orphan children from the surrounding area experienced, Christine Hamlyn was such a generous and gracious lady. When visitors came to the village she allowed them to walk the three mile Hobby Drive and on their return would entertain them on the lawns of Clovelly Court with a cream tea. This was followed by a tour of the house when she would explain the history of many of the interesting pictures and curios and on to view the lovely little Church. Every member of a visiting party would receive a bunch of beautiful flowers as a memento of their visit; Christine's general hospitality was to have a long lasting effect on visitors to the beautiful little village.

Photo courtesy of the Clovelly Estate

The beautiful Hobby Drive

Plymouth's link with Christine Hamlyn of Clovelly meant that many citizens from Plymouth visited the village; in August 1926 the Devonshire Association held their meeting at Bideford, North Devon, and Christine put Clovelly Court at their disposal and permission was granted to allow the cars to drive through Hobby Drive, which was a rare event in those days. The Honourable General Secretary from Thornhill Road, the Plymouth branch of the Devonshire Association, wrote to Mrs Hamlyn expressing their gratitude at her kind hospitality. That same year Christine Hamlyn was a special guest of the Flag Lieutenant at Admiralty House, Mount Wise, Plymouth under Admiral Sir Montague Edward Browning (1863-1947) Knight Admiral KCB. GCMG. MVO,(Commander-in-Chief Devonport 1920-1923) who retired in 1927. There amongst the high-ranking officers Christine Hamlyn was treated to a tasty dinner. The Admiral's house was beautifully furnished and it must indeed have been a wonderful occasion.

Christine was known as the Queen of Clovelly, it is due to her restoration work that many of the old cottages and much of the old village still exists; her love of the village and her generous nature ensured that charities gained from whatever function she organised. When groups of visitors to the village and guests arrived, invariably the vehicle owners would pay for fuel at the Clovelly Garage. The income from these sales were, or should have been, clear profit but Christine Hamlyn would have none of it. She refused to keep the money for her own benefit and insisted that all the proceeds from Clovelly Garage would be sent to various charities. Money went to the

Photo courtesy of Hon John Rous Clovelly

Photo taken 1927 during a luncheon meeting
In the photo left to right:
Miss Kindersley, Mr R. Tree, Mr Waddington, Mrs Christine Hamlyn,
Mrs Tree, Lady Astor (front) Mrs Hobson and Mrs W. Douglas-Pennant.

Middlesex Orthopaedic Hospital, Barnstaple Hospital, Devonport Orthopaedic Hospital for Children, various Church funds and the Rotary Ambulance.

Lady Astor always gave lovely presents to her family and friends, when Christine Hamlyn reached her seventieth birthday she received a beautiful moleskin coat, which in those days was very expensive. The Astor family always called her Auntie Chris and Christine had been a friend of all the Astor family for many years. Lord Astor gave her a Chelsea figure and the Astors together gave her a birthday dinner held on the 1st December 1925 at St James Square. Among the guests were the Marquis of Salisbury, Lord Cranborne (1893-1972) General Asquith, Captain (Navy) Hon. Sir Seymour John Fortescue, (1856-1942) Lord Islington, who was in charge of the National Savings Committee (1866-1936) and the Earl of Cary. When the Viscount and Viscountess Astor held a dinner at St James's Square in March 1927 to meet their Majesties King George V and Queen Mary, invitations were sent out to have the honour of meeting them. One invitation requested the pleasure of Mrs Christine Hamlyn from Clovelly to a dinner to be held on Wednesday March 9th 1927. Advice was given to the guests on what attire to wear, for the men knee britches and decorations to be worn; it proved to be a brilliant evening and enhanced the friendship between Christine and Nancy.

Research revealed the close link that Christine Hamlyn had with the Astors and Plymouth when she was presented with an invitation for a special occasion on 23rd October 1928, in which the President, The Earl of Crawford and Balcarres (1871-1940) (he was the 27th Earl of Crawford and the10th Earl of Balcarres, one of the most extant titles in the British Isles) and the Council for the Preservation of Rural England, invited Christine to attend a conference of Lord Lieutenants' representatives of local authorities and the Duchy of Cornwall. Others invited were the Societies and Universities, including the South West Exeter University and the Lucas Society. Land Owners and other interested parties in preserving the amenities of the Counties of Devon and Cornwall were also in attendance, notably the Ministers of Health, Transport and Agriculture, His Majesty's Office of Works, and the county branches of the National Federation of Women's Institutes.

The Chairman for this auspicious occasion was the Right Honourable the Viscount Astor and the venue was held at 3pm in Plymouth Guildhall. The purpose of the conference was to consider the advisability of setting up a Devon and Cornwall branch of the Council for the Preservation of Rural England. A widespread curriculum was discussed from the survey of landscapes, beauty spots, viewpoints, control and appearance of buildings, new roads, industry, quarrying, mining, tree planting, advertisements and that dreaded situation that exists (even worse today) litter. The subject of litter created quite a debate. It was mentioned that it was not only strangers who contribute to the daily litter and rubbish in streets and roads. The younger generation who always seem to be eating, smoking or drinking, are very careless in throwing about sweet and crisp papers, fruit peel, cigarette boxes, cigarette ends, chewing gum and general rubbish. (This was in 1928; if our forefathers could see our world today they would note that little has changed in the year 2008).

Christine Hamlyn, like the Astors, had an affinity with the Royal Navy. In 1929 she invited one hundred officers and men from the Long Range Escort Destroyer (D56) H.M.S. Wolfhound to Clovelly Court. The ship's complement were treated to a scrumptious cream tea in the Long Passage and all the officers and men were entertained and most were involved in the activities of tennis, squash, football and dancing. H.M.S. Wolfhound was launched in 1918 and served the fleet for many years. Long after Christine Hamlyn's death the destroyer and its gallant crew played a significant part in the rescue of troops from the beaches of Dunkirk in May 1940 under the command of her Captain W.G. Tennant and they rescued one hundred and sixty British and French servicemen. The ship, however, had an ignominious end as her splendid service ended when she was sold for scrap in 1948.

Christine Hamlyn was held in high esteem for her determined stand to preserve the village from Land Agents and to protect the farms and surrounding land. The villagers came to love Christine Hamlyn as she worked hard for her beloved estate and dedicated herself to renovating the ancient cottages. Her initials CH can be seen carved into the stones over the doorways of the village houses to this day. Any organisation that appealed for financial support for the betterment of the social conditions of the poor people or drew attention to the distress or suffering of citizens in need of help, received special support, and this included hospitals, nursing associations and children's care. Christine Hamlyn, like Lady Astor, held in admiration the Queen Alexandra's Nursing Corp and both supported them financially, giving to the Nursing Fund. Christine also supported the Royal National Lifeboat Institution and the Society for the Prevention of Cruelty to Children.

Nancy Astor organised another party and this time held an evening at home for a special dinner followed by dancing and once again the doyenne of Clovelly was invited. On this occasion she was to meet H.R.H. Edward, Prince of Wales. There were many important people in attendance. The ball had a very special significance in that it was held primarily for the Rhodes Scholars, people from Johannesburg, Alberta, Canada, New Jersey and the United States of America. The Scholars were thrilled at meeting the future King of England. On September 3rd 1935 Christine Hamlyn of Clovelly Court spent her 80th birthday at Cliveden, Buckinghamshire, as the honoured guest of the party given by Lady Astor. Beloved by all her Clovelly tenants Christine Hamlyn took a great and personal interest in their welfare and all joined with a host of other friends in wishing her a continuance of good health for many years to come; sadly Christine died the following year. Nancy Astor had been a staunch friend and spent many hours with her until her death in 1936 and it was a bitter blow when she died, on her death the Asquith family then inherited the estate.

Recorded in the Clovelly Chronicles is this article from The Times, dated November 13th 1936. The paper covered the obituary of that wonderful lady Christine Hamlyn, the mistress of Clovelly, who died after a short illness at the age of eighty. 'Christine Hamlyn will be missed by Clovelly because she knew every man, woman and child, and felt responsible for their welfare; she was a remarkable little figure and would be seen toiling sometimes three or four times a day up and down Clovelly. During girlhood her growth had been stunted by a desperate attack of typhoid fever and she stood five feet tall with a slim body, tiny hands and feet, and with the face of a Roman Emperor with masses of fair hair, bright grey eyes and an imperious American chin. The strength of her personality, her infectious vivacity, and her delight in life attracted everyone of every class and age; old and young confided to her their joys and sorrows, sure not only of sympathy but also if needed, her help. Her intense interest in men, women and children and in all their works made the slightest details of importance.'

Christine even thought of her beloved villagers in her Will to ensure that instructions were given not to incur expenses for her village folk. Such was the feelings for the purses of her villagers that she had insisted that no flowers were to be bought so everybody supplied posies of flowers from their own gardens. She was a courageous lady who faced the approach of death quite simply and calmly and would constantly speak of it saying, "Did I not have quiet confident trust in God's word? The summons would be accepted, the summons from the Lord, which says, Come, for all things are now ready." Selected members of her estate watched over the grave, which was lined with laurel and fern, throughout the night as a measure of their respect, for she was really loved. Clovelly the steep, straggling, rose-festooned village, where Devon seemed to turn to Malta and where Donkeys were used for transport was in mourning, Mrs Christine Hamlyn, who had ruled Clovelly, was dead. Throughout the village blinds were drawn in every house, the villagers whispered and spoke quietly, lost in their grief, for she had been a wonderful patron to them and with her death they were most apprehensive about their future. She had served Clovelly for more than sixty years; she preserved the beauties of her lovely Court and village and took care of her tenants by improving hygiene conditions. As the Lady of Manor she guarded jealously the characteristic beauty of that famous village and what Clovelly owes to her generosity, will probably never be fully told.

CLOVELLY DONKEYS

The Clovelly donkeys have been synonymous with Clovelly village for many, many years, but in July 1927 an anonymous complaint was received about alleged cruelty. Christine Hamlyn was deeply distressed at this accusation as Clovelly valued and loved their donkeys. In the Western Times newspaper printed on the 22nd July 1927 it was proven that there was no justification to the complaint of cruelty. That year

Photo by kind permission of the Clovelly Estate

Clovelly Donkeys 2007

Christine Hamlyn enforced the rule that visitors to Clovelly who were to ride the donkeys had to be weighed and no person over nine stone three pounds was allowed to ride. The donkeys were well fed and lovingly looked after and the R.S.P.C.A. confirmed that there was no case to answer for the anonymous complaint. Clovelly donkeys mentioned in the Clovelly Chronicles 1934 were well loved as this written article states. Each donkey was considered a civil servant, there was a donkey hotel porter, and there were donkeys who put Clovelly on the map. No one could live at Clovelly if it were not for the donkeys plodding patiently up and down about a mile of cobbled staircase on a cliff; the donkeys are Clovelly's means of communication with the outside world. They carried everything from baskets of fish on the way to market to tired holidaymakers on their way home. They had special rules made for their comfort by the Lady of the Manor, Christine Hamlyn. One donkey, Lipstick, was well known at the New Inn, in 1934 he was already thirty-two years old, he was the designated hotel porter and he simply had to live up to it and he did! In 1934 his coat was almost snow white. He had walked some 40,000 miles up and down the cliff and he still does his journey up the hill. Next to him comes Billy classified as the Civil Servant who carries mail bags to the Post Office. The Donkey Man of Clovelly said, "We are not ashamed to call the donkeys our greatest friends." Donkeys were to play a very significant part in making children happy and gave them delightful joy to ride on their backs up through the cobbled street. In 1941-1945 during the Second World War the orphan children from the Stoke House Orphanage and Scattered Homes billeted in the New Inn, were to experience that wonderful treat of riding on the backs of the donkeys which brought so much pleasure into their harsh life.

NEW ESTATE OWNERS

Christine and Frederick had no children and the estate was left in 1936 to Christine's niece, Betty Asquith (née Manners) who was the daughter of Lady Constance Manners (née Hamlyn-Fane) and Lord Manners. Betty Manners married Arthur Asquith (known as OC.) Amongst Lord Manner's claim to fame was that he had won a bet that he could, in 6 months, buy, train and ride a Grand National winner; this he achieved on Seaman in 1882, and to this day he remains the only peer to have won the Grand National. Betty's husband, Arthur (son of Prime Minister Asquith) was a distinguished and brave volunteer soldier in the First World War. His full title was the Honourable Arthur Medland Asquith who was the third son of the 1st Earl of Oxford and Asquith, former Liberal British Prime Minister Herbert Henry Asquith from 1908 to 1915. Arthur was the first of the sons to volunteer, enlisting as a Royal Naval Sub-Lieutenant, but was seconded to an Army Unit, and eventually in three years was promoted from Lieutenant to Brigadier General. It was indeed a remarkable achievement. He left 'A' Company, of the Hood Battalion Infantry Brigade, with the rank of Brigadier-General and had, during his service, won three Distinguish Service Order Medals and two bars. On 20th December 1917 he was wounded in the leg, which necessitated its amputation three weeks later and his military career was over. After the war he became a Director of several companies and died in 1939. He is buried in the churchyard in the village of Clovelly. His brother Raymond Asquith, who was in the Grenadier Guards, was killed in the battle of the Somme in 1916. When Brigadier General Arthur Melland Asquith (1883-1939) died, the Honourable Betty Asquith became the doyenne of Clovelly Court. Betty Asquith and Angela Asquith were twins, but Betty was older by five minutes so she inherited the estate. Lady Manners was the Grandmother of the present Honourable John Rous who now has control of the Clovelly Estate.

Betty and Arthur had four daughters of whom Mary April Asquith, (1919-2002) the eldest, married William Keith Rous (1907-1983) Earl of Stradbroke from the Henham Estate in Suffolk in 1943; she was his second wife. As a girl Mary Rous studied music in Vienna, and was told that she was capable of becoming a professional pianist. On her father's death in 1939, however, she decided to train as a nurse at St Thomas hospital. Her mother was amused by a report of her progress, which recorded, "Nurse Asquith treats the ward like a garden party." She became a close friend of Dame Cicely Mary Strode Saunders (1918-2005) founder and mother of the Hospice Movement, and later Mary regularly spent time working at St Christopher's Hospice, South London. Mary married in 1943, Keith Rous, the younger son of the third Earl of Stradbroke, who succeeded as the fifth Earl four days before his death in 1983. Mary Rous never used the title and is survived by her son the Honourable John Rous, Deputy Lieutenant of Devon, albeit John's elder half brother inherited the title of Earl of Stradbroke; meanwhile the Honourable John Rous who has owned the Clovelly estate since 1987, has dedicated his life to keeping Clovelly as a thriving village.

Mary inherited the Clovelly estate on Betty's death in 1962. Ironically Nancy Astor died in 1964 and the Clovelly link with Plymouth was broken. Mary April Rous, Countess of Stradbroke, died at the age of 83 and had been the guardian of the Clovelly estate. Mary Rous's interests lay in religion, philosophy, music and gardening, and she became exceptionally good at all of them. Always involved in various activities in the village she organised theatricals and poetry festivals and was a very active person and loved the outdoors, swimming in the Atlantic breakers and often arranging meets for pony clubs. Whilst in her seventies she trekked in the Himalayas. Clovelly had indeed been very rich in their history in having wonderful guardians of the estate. Clovelly was quite used to having a woman in charge as her mother Betty Asquith, the owner from 1936 to 1962, preceded Mary Rous and before that by her great Aunt Christine Hamlyn, whose suzerainty dated back to the 1880's and who compiled an eight-volume village scrapbook, known as the Clovelly Chronicles. Mary Rous discreetly ensured that Clovelly did not fall victim to metropolitan buyers of second homes. This meant keeping the estate solvent, while giving priority to providing homes and jobs for the families who had lived there for generations. She achieved this difficult task with infectious warmth, which brought her the devotion and loyalty of the entire village. Mary's son, the Honourable John Rous, took over the running of the estate in 1983 and what a challenge he has faced, but with determined resolve he has continued to preserve as much as he could whilst making the village financially viable and bringing it into the 21st Century.

From Elizabethan days, fishing for herrings was the staple activity and the village prospered on this basis until the shoals began to move away in the 1830s and the season was much shortened and most of the villagers found work on the surrounding farms or the Clovelly estate. On occasion a shoal of herrings can still be caught in Clovelly bay and they are known to be some of the finest herrings in the region and in the year 2007 Clovelly held its first annual Herring Festival. In keeping with modern living and adjusting to the 21st Century Clovelly has moved into the new era of the modern world whilst still keeping its unique identity. Lady Henrietta Rous, whose family are the current owners of the historic Clovelly estate, recently spent time with a high profile celebrity chef who was visiting the village to prepare for a forthcoming television show on banquets, in which the finest herrings will be sampled, Clovelly is quite at home with visiting television and camera crews who constantly record events in the historic village.

CLOVELLY HUMOUR

From the Victorian era Clovelly became a tourist attraction and now most of its income revolves around the tourist trade. The Devon fishermen and villagers had to adjust to seeing hundreds of visitors in the village and the inns; the Clovelly folk are well known for their tales, their folklore and their longevity. One visitor to the village saw an old fisherman lounging on the sea wall. The visitor said to the old man; "You are a wonderful old man," the Septuagenarian replied; "Not half so wonderful as my old father!" "How long has he been dead?" said the visitor. The veteran replied "Dead? He is not dead, he is at home putting Grandfather to bed!" The visitor smiled and walked off with a bemused expression. The Clovelly village has not been spoiled as no vehicle can enter its streets and the Clovelly Estate Company, which owns all the buildings in the village and a few thousand acres around it, takes responsibility for all the maintenance and is thus able to ensure that the results are a unique village, standing still in the midst of the 19th Century in terms of its buildings and streets (and its donkeys) but with a community of the 21st Century.

BEAUTIFUL VILLAGE

The beauty of the North Devon village still fascinates the hundreds of visitors who trek their way to the beautiful place of Saxon origin, an ancient and picturesque little fishing village on the North Devon coast between Hartland Point and Bideford, whose recorded history originates from the eleventh century. Nearby is a very special three-mile scenic route, a rich mosaic of colours whatever the season, known as the Hobby Drive. Hundreds of trees of every type planted by Clovelly folk who treasured the countryside and treated it with the utmost respect. Some of the trees, when you stand close to them and look up, give the impression that they almost reach the sky. There are oak, ash, birch, pine, beech, maple and London plane, many covered in ivy attracting wild life, mosses, navelwort and polypody ferns. Little streams of water run down the valley and in the spring would be seen glorious groups of flowers such as the deep blue bluebells, crocuses, cowslips so pretty with their apricot yellow and orange umbels, affectionately known to Devon folk as the tisty-tosty plant; there were tulips, snowdrops, buttercups, forget-me-nots, thistle, London pride, primroses, and Creeping Jenny another member of the primrose family. Also to be seen were the prolific violets, cyclamen, small groups of wild garlic, and clumps of pink purslane and not forgetting the honey-scented, wild honeysuckle and strong green ferns and golden hawkweed. In Wrinklebury lane the hedges would be a profusion of wild flowers with ragged robin, hollyhock, forget-me-not, pink campion, wild garlic, and the dainty sky blue speedwell.

Clovelly is rich with common speckled wood butterflies and the beautiful birds, blackbirds with their bright yellow beaks and the spotted song thrushes, the little blue and yellow blue tit which mates for life and the finch family, bullfinch, chaffinch, greenfinch, and the delightful tiny yellow and green siskin with its black markings on the wings and head. The little plump dunnock and the beautiful yellow hammer with its distinctive song, 'A little bit of bread and no cheese!' Flocks of starlings with their glossy plumage and the sheen on their feathered wings producing an illusion of glorious multi colours, and the pied wagtail wagging its tail and skeeting along on its little legs. The pheasant or game bird at it was sometimes called and the common hedge sparrow, the cooing of the ring-collared dove and the call of the wood pigeon. Magpies swooping down from the trees, their black and white feathers flashing in the daylight, The raucous cawing of the carrion crow and rook, and the dainty little ruddock (robin redbreast) with its pretty red breast, a shy bird and always alone, the darting redstart with its red tail and white patch on its head and not forgetting the call of the cuckoo.

FAMOUS VISITORS

So many famous names past and present have made their way to this beautiful village on the North Devon Coast of England. Visiting Clovelly in July 1926, H.B. Morton, the author said, 'That the quaintness of Clovelly is unique and Clovelly's motto is, or should be, every day and in every way and in spite of myself I become quainter and quainter and Clovelly is quaint. The village is so beautiful and has been beautiful for so long that it can well afford to take any knock at its self-consciousness.' In August

1935 Lawrence Whistler wrote a few lines while he was in the village. The very last paragraph could be used to honour Christine Hamlyn, it sums up the way people felt for what she did for Clovelly.

For who with love like hers
Whose hand preserves the beauty of this land
Could ever show the imperial sea
That strict and sweet authority

An Artist Mr O.A. Marxer wrote from North Wales on the 10th June 1928 to Christine Hamlyn saying, "A month ago I spent a few happy days at the Red Lion Hotel in Clovelly, three years after my previous visit, having travelled along supposed pretty places on the coast of Wales, Somerset and Devon. I was everywhere horrified at the extent and unsightliness of modernisation, and I am writing to you from an artist's point of view to compliment you on your successful efforts to preserve the charms of Clovelly, also to thank you for the privilege extended to visitors to explore the beauty spots towards the Gallantry Bower. Yours truly." (Gallantry Bower is a sheer precipice; the dramatic headland drops from a height of 387 feet to the sea and has breathtaking views over Bideford Bay.)

Other famous people to become part of Clovelly's history over the years were the noted poet, preacher and novelist Charles Kingsley, (1819-1875) who loved the village and wrote many poems and was rector of Eversley and Canon of Westminster; Charles Kingsley's father was rector of All Saints Church, Clovelly (1832-1836) and the celebrated English artist, illustrator and muralist, Rex Whistler (1905-1944) who had been a friend of, and a frequent visitor to, Christine Hamlyn, was commissioned by the Hamyln family to develop his sketches into a design for fabric and then printed. Samples of his Clovelly Toile de Jouy can be found today in the Fisherman's Cottage Museum situated half way down the famous cobbled street. Also in 1934 the Clovelly view ware, which had been designed by Rex Whistler and potted by Wedgwood, was on view for sale at the Clovelly Estate. There is no finer artist than Rex Whistler and no finer craftsman than Wedgwood could have been found to produce the Clovelly view ware. On it is printed a selection of some lovely little scenes for the beautiful Clovelly chintz, it carries the very spirit of the ancient flowering village of sea-going Devon folk that pitches downhill into Bideford Bay. The designs are in black and crimson on Wedgwood Kingswear.

Famous husband and wife musical stars Ann Zeigler (1910-2003) and Webster Booth (1902-1984) were frequent visitors to Clovelly in the 1940s. They were at the height of their careers and were known as the Sweethearts of Song. The former Irene Frances Eastwood changed her name to Ann Zeigler in 1934 and married the handsome Webster Booth in 1938. They appeared together in shows and later toured the United Kingdom performing in variety acts. Ann had a passion for crinoline dresses, Norman Hartnell designed most of them, and many admirers would watch to see which dress she wore next. After the war, their type of song was considered outdated, and they moved to South Africa to continue their singing career. In their retirement years they returned to the United Kingdom to live in Wales. Vernon Watson (1886-1949) was a music hall entertainer and comedian and he, too, loved Clovelly village, his pseudonym was Nosmo King and he had obtained that name whilst travelling on a train and seeing a railway poster on the door saying 'No smoking' with a slight deviation it became Nosmo King a very popular variety artiste who toured music halls and was also a clever impressionist. He died very peacefully in his sleep. Present day theatre star Joss Ackland lives in Clovelly and high profiled chefs who appear on television have visited the unique village, camera crews frequent the village to make documentaries and visitors from all over the world are mesmerised by its lifestyle.

WARTIME HELP

Lady Astor's relationship with both Christine Hamlyn and the Honourable Betty Constance Asquith (nee Manners) (1889-1962) who was the wife of Arthur Melland Asquith, led to a lifetime of friendship and she would often visit Clovelly. She had been a frequent visitor for many years; Nancy and Betty would play tennis together at Clovelly Court. Lady Astor would take the opportunity to have a couple of days rest and study her parliamentary notes. She was the saviour of the Stoke House and Scattered Homes orphaned children from Plymouth who were evacuated to the New Inn Clovelly 1941-1945. In April 1941, the night the orphaned children from Stoke House in Plymouth were bombed out of Montpelier School, (then being used as a emergency rest home) having already been burnt and bombed out of the Plymouth Stoke House Orphanage, Lady Astor rang the Honourable Betty Asquith to make a desperate appeal to house the orphan children to which she agreed.

Christine Clark (nèe Asquith), states her mother, the Honourable Betty took the call and Christine was standing at her mother's side and remembers vividly the telephone conversation her Mother had with Lady Astor. When Nancy rang she only heard one side of the telephone call, but by her Mother's replies knew what the subject matter was about. Christine recalls the conversation. Lady Astor, "You must help me with my orphan children, there are fifty boys and girls and they have no where to go! We have had a terrible night and now we are having a terrible day, the bombing is awful, I wonder if you can help me, can you manage to give me some way of housing my Scattered Homes children, and the orphans from the Stoke House Orphanage? They have all been saved from the bombing but they have no-where to sleep tonight except in the shelter at the moment, we have got to get them away. I thought that your New Inn might be empty. Is that true?" My mother replied, "Well, yes, the New Inn is empty and I shall see Mr J.C. Hilton (the estate agent) and I will ring you back." True

Lady Astor (Plymouth's MP and Christine Hamlyn doyenne of Clovelly)

to her word Betty Asquith rang back to make the New Inn available to the Plymouth Orphans who were eventually evacuated on the 30th April 1941 where they were to stay until 1945. Mr James Hilton MC arranged the financial costs between the Plymouth City Council and the Clovelly Estate.

Mrs Christine Clark (nee Asquith) recalls as she reminisced those years that, 'Nancy Astor had a large rich brown/black Rolls Royce Landaulette and always made her chauffeur wear brown to match. I had a goat called Josephine, which followed me everywhere like a dog. The children from the village and the New Inn would often play with the goat on the lawns of Clovelly Court. My great Aunt Chris (Christine Hamlyn) treated my mother and father as her children. Ever since they were married in 1918 they were welcomed to the Clovelly Court as a second home and Betty knew she would inherit since our eldest sister Mary died tragically of diphtheria at the age of seventeen in India, when travelling with my great Aunt. My mother (Honourable Betty Asquith) inherited Clovelly Court and estate in 1936 when my great Aunt (Christine Hamlyn) died.'

VILLAGE LADIES ACHIEVE A WIN

Lady Astor's friendship with Clovelly was a long and pleasant love affair. Her cemented friendship with Christine Hamyln and the Asquith family was to span many years. Sometimes she would spend three or four days at the big house in Clovelly Court and on occasion would work at Home Farm, which belonged to Clovelly Court. Bessie May (née Perkin) former Land Army Girl in Clovelly Court would be joined by Lady Astor and they would spend the morning picking fresh fruit. Bessie also had the privilege of playing tennis with Lady Astor, the Honourable Betty Asquith, Sheila Ellis, (the daughter of Paul and Gladys Ellis owners of the village shop) and Mrs Cavendish the Rector's wife. Nancy was known to favour playing close to the net and was a fierce competitor and nearly always won. One day the village ladies schemed that they would play with maximum effort to try and beat Lady Astor and they did! Credit due, Nancy took it in good stead. Nancy's favourite games were tennis and squash and she would take any opportunity she could to have a game. Every day she would take a cold-water bath followed by a Christian Science lesson so the ladies who played tennis with her would have to make arrangements to suit Nancy's availability.

ORPHANS REMEMBER

Lady Astor always wore colourful hats, and was rarely seen without her jewels; she favoured sapphire, diamonds and pearls, but did not particularly like emeralds. In later years she dressed in black, villagers and evacuee children, still remember her striding down the cobbled street to visit the orphans and staff in the New Inn. Every orphan child received a sixpenny piece from her and some sweets and the children really loved Nancy. The evacuee children in Clovelly would often see Lady Astor and the Honourable Betty Asquith paddling in the sea at Mouth Mill beach with their dresses tucked into their pink bloomers, of course, girls being girls they giggled hilariously. After the terrible fire at Clovelly Court in December 1943 most of the social events used to be held at Clovelly School, Wrinklebury Lane, and the evacuees remember vividly Lady Astor bringing sweets (on ration then) and again gave each girl sixpence to spend. The Ellis Tuck Shop did a roaring trade next day.

As the Author, I have connections with Lady Astor, in that I was one of the Plymouth Orphans (A fuller account can be found in the Author's first book Scattered Homes - Broken Hearts.) We were to benefit from her friendship with the Honourable Betty Asquith and we never forgot the kindness, also, of the Clovelly villagers and the Lifeboat men who made us so welcome in those dangerous years. Many of the children and evacuees, now in their twilight years, have made they way back to Clovelly to recapture some of those memories. In 1998 the children of Stoke House Orphanage had a re-union in Clovelly and once again the villagers gave us a warm welcome. This unique village will live on in our hearts. R.R. Thompson's poem sent to Christine Hamlyn in December 1930 reflects the beauty of the little village by the sea and expresses what visitors admire.

Oh tiny village by the sea
Clovelly honoured thou shalt be
For greatness cometh not with wealth
And beauty only lives thy stealth
The cliffs-the Sea-the wealth ashore
The downward butt – the Fleur-de-lis of change
And if clouds doth still shalt be
For weary souls a sanctuary

> **The President**
> (The Earl of Crawford and Balcarres)
> and
> **The Council**
> for the
> **Preservation of Rural England**
> have the honour to invite
>
> *Mrs Hamlyn*
>
> to attend a conference of Lords Lieutenants, Representatives of Local Authorities, The Duchy of Cornwall, Societies and Universities, Landowners and others interested in preserving the Amenities of the Counties of Devon and Cornwall.
> The Chair will be taken by
> **THE RT. HON. THE VISCOUNT ASTOR**
> at
> **THE GUILDHALL, PLYMOUTH**
> (By kind permission of the Rt. Worshipful the Mayor of Plymouth)
> on
> **OCTOBER 23rd at 3 p.m.**
>
> R.S.V.P.
> Council for the Preservation of Rural England,
> 17 Great Marlborough Street,
> Regent Street,   Patrick Abercrombie,
> London, W.1.   Hon. Sec.

The invitation to Christine Hamlyn of Clovelly from the President The Earl of Crawford and Balcarres for the conference on the Preservation of Rural England to be held at Plymouth Guildhall with the Rt. Hon The Viscount Astor taking the chair.

THE DAILY EXPRESS
APRIL 3, 1935

EXCEEDED SPEED LIMIT. FINED

The Hon. Mrs. Betty Asquith, of Sussex-square, Paddington, was fined forty shillings at Feltham yesterday for driving motor-car and trailer at more than 30 m.p.h. on Great West Road, at Bedfont, Middlesex. It was stated that her speed was between fifty-six and fifty-eight miles an hour.

Article by kind permission of the
Honourable John Rous Clovelly

The Daily Express picture and article featuring the Honourable Betty Asquith in 1935 who was fined for speeding.

COUNCIL FOR THE PRESERVATION OF RURAL ENGLAND.

CONFERENCE.

DEVON AND CORNWALL RURAL PRESERVATION.

October 23rd, 1928.

GUILDHALL, PLYMOUTH, 3 p.m.

(By kind permission of the Right Worshipful the Mayor of Plymouth).

Chairman :
THE RIGHT HON. THE VISCOUNT ASTOR.

The following have been invited to attend the Conference :

- (a) Representatives of the Local Authorities and Joint Town Planning Committees.
- (b) Representatives of the Ministries of Health, Transport and Agriculture and H.M.'s Office of Works.
- (c) The Duchy of Cornwall.
- (d) Landowners and Residents.
- (e) The University of the South-West (Exeter).
- (f) Approved Local Societies.
- (g) County Branches of the National Federation of Women's Institutes.
- (h) All Constituent Bodies of the Council for the Preservation of Rural England which include the National Trust.

SUGGESTED OBJECTS OF THE CONFERENCE.

1. To consider the advisability of setting up a Devon and Cornwall Branch of the Council for the Preservation of Rural England.

2. To discuss a programme of Preservation and Development which may be adopted as a common policy for the two counties :—

   i A general landscape survey, with the object of noting beauty spots, view points, antiquities and their surroundings, etc., including a broad analysis of their composition and of the ordinary beauties of the countryside.

   ii The survey also to note where disfigurement has taken place, in order that remedies may be applied and repetition may be avoided.

   iii Broad zoning to ensure that the right type of buildings are placed in the right kind of situation and with a view to the health, comfort and convenience of the inhabitants of users and to economy in public services.

   iv The control of the appearance of buildings, now possible under the Ministry of Health Model Clause.

   v Suggestions for new roads and bridges or the widening of existing roads, so that the convenience of traffic may be furthered on lines that pay full regard to the amenities of the countryside and the safety and comfort of its inhabitants.

   vi Industry, quarrying and mining.

   vii Tree Planting.

   viii Advertisements.

   ix Litter and Petrol Filling Stations.

E.L.P. LTD., LONDON.

Document by kind permission of the Honourable John Rous Clovelly

The invitation to Christine Hamlyn to attend Plymouth Guildhall in 1928 for a conference on Devon & Cornwall Rural Conservation.

Taken at the New Inn Clovelly North Devon May 1941. The Stoke House orphans and Scattered Homes children had been evacuated from Plymouth on the 30th April 1941 at Lady Astor's request. All rows read from the left.

Front row. 1. Betty Bennett. 2. Veronica (Vicky) Norman. 3. Dorothy Sabine. 4. Margaret Bailey (Head turned) 5. Violet Ray. 6. Margaret Ray. 7. Pat Richards (slightly behind).
Middle Row. 1. Miss Holly Penna. (RIP) 2. Gwendoline Tyrell. (RIP) 3. Barbara Baker. 4. Sheila Hanson. 5. Pat Roberts (RIP) 6. Ellen Saul (RIP) 7. Margaret Pester (Tall girl) (RIP).
Back Row 1. Betty Newham. 2. Dorothy Saul (RIP) 3. Rosemary Buckingham. 4. Ethel Gerry.

By kind permission Honourable John Rous and the Clovelly Estate.

Clovelly beach 1997

Photo: courtesy of Vicky Norman

Wrinkleberry lane Clovelly 1998. The children of the New Inn walked this lane to and fro four times a day in the 1940s on their way to school.

CHAPTER TEN
DANCING AND BUTTERCUP JOE

Dance is the hidden language of the soul.
Martha Graham. Goddess of Dance. USA. (1894-1991)

Copyright Westcountry Publications

Viscountess Astor dancing
with a sailor on Plymouth Hoe

All her life with the exception of her later retirement years Nancy loved to dance, she danced with servicemen of all nations in both World Wars, waltzed with civilians, reeled with the workmen, jigged with children, twirled around the floor with orphaned children and danced with the ordinary man in the street, but the best dance would always be with her beloved husband Waldorf Astor. There are many who remember dancing with this remarkable woman. George Bernard Shaw (1856-1950) once said: "Dancing is a perpendicular expression of a horizontal desire."

In December 1940 Nancy organised a Christmas party for the three hundred walking wounded Canadian soldiers in the hospital at Cliveden and to liven the party up a local Jazz Band was invited which was a real treat. Nancy delighted in trying different dances at these events and on this occasion she danced with a Canadian soldier, singing as she danced, 'The Cake Walk,' a traditional African American form of music and dance, featuring exaggerated imitations of the ritual which originated among slaves in the US South. A similar dance was known to originate from the Seminole Indians. At the end of the 19th century it became popular among white and black people. The cakewalk involved couples linked at the elbows, forming in a circle dancing forward in an alternating series of short hopping steps, and then continuing with very high kicking steps. Another presentation saw the couples forming an aisle, down which each pair would take a turn at a high-stepping promenade through the others. The name comes from the cake that would be awarded to the winning couple. The form was originally known as the Chalk Line Walk, taking its name from competitive slaveholders and slices of hoecake were offered as prizes for the best dancers.

Another dance Nancy loved taking part in was the 'Lindy Hop' and she was a lovely dancer. Swing dancing was very popular in the 1920's/1930's and one of the most famous was the 'Lindy Hop' and people at every party and ballroom event would dance to the movements. It swept across America and Nancy ensured the dance was recognised at her dancing parties here in England. During the days of slavery in the United States of America the African Slaves entertained themselves with musical and dance forms. Some of the swing dances went on to become recognised National Dances, most popular were the Lindy Hop, Cake Walk, Black Bottom and the Charleston. The Lindy Hop emerged in the authentic style in 1926 when it was first performed at the Savoy Ballroom, Harlem, United States of America. Then it was danced in a rigid, upright manner, angular bending of arms, legs and torso with shoulder and hip movement accompanied by stamping and hopping steps, sometimes performed in lines or in circles.

However, in the mid nineteen thirties, new steps were born every day and the styling became so refined that the dance was a joy to watch as well as to do, and this style soon swept through the ballrooms in America. In the 1940's swing dancing became known as the Jitterbug, Boogie Woogie and West Coast Swing. Those who knew Nancy Astor could easily visualise her kicking her heels and high stepping it out with her partners. Plymouth citizens remember vividly the wartime dancing on Plymouth Hoe in the 1940s. The blitz had taken a heavy toll on morale as night after night of bombing had devastated the city and there was no doubt that Plymouth began to lose its nerve as the intense bombing forced thousands of citizens to leave the city, moving out from urban streets and going to rural areas to find peace and quiet. Nancy had a brilliant idea for restoring morale, public dancing on the Hoe in the evenings, and it worked. Many citizens returned because now there was open entertainment. Henry Havelock Ellis, English psychologist and author (1859-1939) once quoted: 'Dancing is the loftiest, the most moving, the most beautiful of the Arts, because it is no mere translation or abstraction from life; it is life itself.'

Kathleen Scarlett in her 88th year remembers the wartime dances held on Plymouth Hoe as vividly as yesterday. She said: They were well attended and remembered with pride by all the now elderly people who, for a short while, forgot the war and danced to erase the memory of the devastation of the blitz and the trauma of the war years.

The title Lady Astor did not prevent her from relating to the ordinary folk; one wonders what Waldorf would have said if he knew all the things she used to get up to, she was full of fun. Once she was seen on the Hoe in an egg and spoon race with the children and sometimes children joined in the dancing. Dancing on the Hoe, in daylight hours, brought strangers from all over the world and they would pair off to dance together. Favourite band leaders were Ted Coleman, Frankie Fuge and not forgetting the Army Pioneer Corps who regularly played on Plymouth Hoe to please the dancers. Popular then was Glenn Miller music, and the wartime dance 'The Blackout Stroll' without the lights though, so as not to attract the German bombers. The dancing folk would take four steps forward, three short steps and a hop and then change partners. Of course if held indoors the lights in a dance hall would be switched off as partners changed but there were no lights on Plymouth Hoe in the war years, so everyone had to improvise. Everyone would join in the chorus:

'Everybody do the blackout stroll
Laugh and drive your cares right up the pole.'

Kathleen recalls that Lady Astor was often there. To get to the dancing she would climb over the railings outside 3 Elliot Terrace, select a sailor or a soldier and dance away, she danced regularly with my brother who often boasted that Nancy liked dancing with him. In those days he was slim and very light on his feet and he was a very good dancer, but I remember him most for his sense of humour and the way he could sing and speak in the Devonshire dialect when he had drunk a few pints of beer. There were times when he sang a song to Lady Astor and she would laugh at his rendering of this Devon folk song and would try hard to emulate him but the words were too difficult to roll around her tongue. Although she spoke good English her Virginian accent could not cope with the unique Devonshire accent. It was one of his favourite tunes and he would sing it in broad Devonshire dialect of course, the title was 'Buttercup Joe' and if I remember rightly it went something like this, although I cannot remember all the verses."

Oi can drive a plough an' milk a cow
An' Oi can reap an'zow
Oi'm as fresh as the daisy that graws in the vield
An' they calls Oi Buttercup Joe.

Now 'ave you zeen that young 'oman
They calls 'er udder Mary
'er works as buzy as a bumble bee
Down in Zir John's dairy.

An' doan 'er make them dumplin's vine
By Jobe you ought to try 'em.
Oi'll ax 'er if 'er'd loike to wed
A country chap loike Oi am.

No doubt, someone who remembers the whole song and probably sings it to this day will correct me, but my brother earned himself the nickname of 'Buttercup Joe,' which stayed with him throughout his life. I even attained a little fame as 'Buttercup Joe's' sister. I do not know if Lady Astor called my brother by his nickname, but I do know that my brother always spoke of her as 'Our Nancy.' If there is a heavenly equivalent to Plymouth Hoe, and surely there must be, perhaps Nancy and 'Buttercup Joe' still enjoy a dance or two together.

Terry J. Bickford as a nipper regularly went up on the Hoe and bunked into the closed Tinside swimming pool in the evening for a free swim and on occasions when he made his way home, he could hear the band playing for the dancing folk on the promenade. He watched the service personnel dancing with their young ladies, practicing their fancy steps, and he also noticed that Lady Astor was dancing in gay abandon. He said, "She was not in the least reserved in her enjoyment but was totally relaxed and at complete ease with all the ordinary folk. It was hard to believe that she was Viscountess Astor, Lady Mayoress of Plymouth, no one before or since has mingled with the common folk with such panache as Nancy Astor."

Sixty-five years later from those dancing years of nineteen forty-three, two ladies reflected on the effect that the dancing on Plymouth Hoe did for that generation. Pamela Trudie Hodge wrote the lyrics and Denise Couch of Mad Rush wrote the music and performed the song, on the CD 'Music of Time.' The song is indicative of those special years and pleasurable indeed to see that Lady Astor was included.

MUSIC OF TIME

He walked on the seafront in the late summer evening
an old man whose footsteps were halting and frail.
The daylight was fading, the mist softly creeping
to hide the calm sea in a grey cobweb veil.
He sat on a bench with his coat wrapped around him
and memories came stealing from out of the mist,
the band playing waltz tunes, the searchlights, the bombing,
the dancing and laughter, the girl he had kissed.

They had danced to the music of time.
Around them the houses lay shattered and broken.

They had danced to the music of time,
refusing to cry, not a sad word was spoken.
There were soldiers and sailors and V.A.D. nurses,
the girls from the factories, the lads from the Yard,
there were land girls and airmen and 'young' Lady Astor
and they danced to the band on the Hoe Promenade.

He remembered the last time he'd danced to the music,
the lovely young WAAF he had held to his heart.
He could still smell her perfume and see her eyes shining
as she whispered she loved him and they'd never part,
but orders for sailing come early next morning
and soon his destroyer sailed out from the Sound
away from the laughter, the dancing, the kissing,
to fight the grim fight on war's merry-go-round.

But he'd danced to the music of time
and how do you know when the songs fill your mind
and you dance to the music of time
who the grim reaper gathers and who leaves behind?
There were polish men, lawyers, and mothers with children,
there were ARP Wardens, men from the Home Guard,
there were little old ladies with headscarves and handbags
and they danced to the band on the Hoe Promenade.

Stealing out of the grey mist, the old man heard music,
the strains of a waltz drifting over the Hoe
and stepping toward him, her gentle eyes shining
the lovely young WAAF he had loved long ago.
The air was alive with soft music and laughter
as couples danced by them she held out her hand,
from out of the old man a young man stepped lightly
and they danced the last waltz to the beat of the band.

They danced to the music of time.
and the long, lonely years fell away without sorrow.
They danced to the music of time
their yesterdays lost in a shining tomorrow.
There were kids from the back streets and girls in white sandals,
there were fishermen, Yanks, and an old railway guard,
there were girls from the canteen and a WAAF and her sailor
and they danced the last waltz on the Hoe Promenade.

To be sure 'Our Nancy' had she lived would have approved and she would have loved to acquire this song! In the spiritual kingdom of our creator, maybe, just maybe, Nancy is dancing on the clouds. Those who love dancing will know, that we do not stop dancing when we grow old, we grow old when we stop dancing!

Dance, then, wherever you may be,
I am the Lord of the dance, said he,
and I'll lead you all, wherever you may be,
and I'll lead you all in the dance, said He.

Mr John Hoskin now living in Hampshire remembers with affection those dancing years as he first met Lady Astor at the Astor Institute in 1936. He was a young man of eighteen and his memory of her recalls vividly that she attended regularly the dances held on Saturday evenings at the Institution, although Nancy's husband Waldorf never attended. John had this to say: As her car waited for her she always left before the end of the evening, usually about ten o'clock. The dances were organised by a Mr and Mrs Jewell who were themselves excellent dancers but I believe Nancy had the say as to the type of dance for the evening. Two dances that she favoured were; The Military Two Step and The Lancers, and I know she also enjoyed a waltz. Another favourite dance was the Palais Glide when the dancers all linked arms and sang while dancing to the songs "Hometown" and "Little Angeline." I can see her now, kicking her legs out as the routine followed through; always full of fun she reminded me of Katherine Hepburn, the American actress, tall and slim and so light on her feet and a very good dancer, in fact a very attractive woman.

In those days the girls sat around the dance floor and Nancy used to sit among them conversing and enjoying the normal banter that went on. I saw her on two occasions having a motherly chat with tipsy young soldiers about the evils of drink! However, she still danced with them so she was no prude. She really was a lovely Lady. I feel very sad when I think of her now because we lost a very good caring person, those were lovely days made happy by her contact with ordinary people; God Bless Her! At one event I nervously asked her for a dance and happily the answer was yes, as we danced she spoke to me stating she thought she had seen me before and as we talked it came to light that she was at the gym a week or two before and she could remember me having a dressing on my head from an injury I had sustained in an accident at the gym. She said, "Were you the boy who had the accident recently?" "Yes," I replied, and she quickly ushered me to the nearest seat before the dance finished, "I must apologise for the lack of transport to hospital, but we are living in difficult times." I replied, "It is quite alright Lady Astor as I am recovering well."

My feelings for the Astors were as strong as many of the population in those early years; she could speak forcefully on any subject close to her heart. Today's politicians have never equalled her campaign for the working classes to have a better quality of life. I left Plymouth in 1939 having volunteered for the RAF on the day war broke out. I went to the Astor Institute in 1958 after returning from Malta still in the RAF. It looked so forlorn and cheerless, I only stayed for fifteen minutes, somehow those years could not be recaptured. I went again to Plymouth and stayed at the Astor Hotel for a holiday in July 2003 and that was only the fourth occasion I had been back to the City since 1939. It was there that I found out that the Author was looking for Astor memories and I know for sure there are hundreds who still hold memories of her for not many writers think about the ordinary folk when they produce biographies; how nice that a book is to be written that will tell our stories.

Nancy's dancing on the Hoe spurred the population to make merry wherever and however they could. Lady Astor took special care to dance with the servicemen and dockyard workers and it brought a little light relief to the war torn Plymouth population. Dancing not only with officers on the Hoe but also with ordinary ranks, too, at the regular dances in Seaton Barracks, and at another dance with the Polish Airmen at a venue in Yelverton, Plymouth. When dancing with the American sailors they would give Nancy chewing gum and she would chew away as they danced, her gaiety was contagious. Dances were being held all over the city, dancing on the Pier in 1940 had been very popular, they were held on Mondays, Wednesdays and Saturdays at the Pier Pavilion Ballroom. The couples performed on the large maple floor to the music of The Pavilions Ladies Orchestra and the Fred Hill Dance Orchestra but sadly the Pier was destroyed by enemy bombers in 1941 and was never rebuilt.

Proms! Proms!! Proms!!! Dances organised by the Entertainments Department, Plymouth City Council were held at the Plymouth Guildhall in 1940 until the Guildhall was bombed in 1941. Not to be defeated by this act of aggression the dances were re-organised and the venue opened at the Corn Exchange in East Street, still entitled Proms! Proms!! Proms!!! Music played by the Waldorf Dance Orchestra, admission sixpence, also playing would be the BBC accordionist Reg Manus and all the proceeds went to the Lord Mayor's Services Welfare Fund. The Royal Hotel at the Royal Assembly Rooms held a dance every Saturday 8pm to 11pm in 1940; tickets were two shillings and sixpence; music by Stanton Wicks and his band. Another venue was at the Co-operative's large hall where Mr Jewell's dances were held every Saturday, entry ticket nine pence, music by Miss Looney's Orchestra. The people's social club held weekly on Thursdays at the Co-operative Hall in Frankfort Street and Courtenay Street danced to the Norah Looney's Orchestra. St Peter's Conservatives popular dances took place every Saturday at the Co-op Café Courtenay Street 7-15pm to 10pm, music by the Rhythm Rascals. There the entrance fee was sixpence.

The Paramount, opposite the Gaumont Cinema, with the Leon Shortt Paramount Orchestra as broadcasted by the BBC, had a dance event every evening at 7pm and a Tea Dance on Saturday afternoons. Holy Cross Hall had dances some evenings but theirs were mostly for learners. The Mikado Café, in Saltash Street/Old Town Street, whose parent management business was S. Stephens & Risdon Limited, the high class bakers and confectioners, of 55, Ebrington Street, also had premises in Devonport, Crownhill and Plymouth. In the Mikado Café downstairs they had select learner's dancing classes every Tuesday, Wednesday, Thursday and Friday from 7pm to 10pm at one shilling for the evening, music by Archie Collins. Unfortunately bombing in 1941/1942 destroyed the Café. Other dancing venues were: The Astor Institute at Mount Gould, admission one shilling and sixpence, all proceeds to the Co-operative Employees Comforts Fund, the Railway Institute, Pennycomequick, from 7pm to 10pm, music played by Ted Coleman's Band, or the Martini Orchestra. Here the entrance fee differed, ladies paid nine pence and gentlemen paid one shilling. St Michael's church hall in Devonport in 1940 had select Flannel Dances entrance fee one shilling. St Gabriel's Church Peverell held a dance every Saturday evening from 7pm to 10pm, by Hillier and Whitaker admission one shilling and sixpence; music by the Waldorf Orchestra, Master of Ceremonies Mr Frank Hillier. The Duke of Cornwall Hotel held dances every Monday, Wednesday, Friday and Saturday, from 7pm to 10pm, Stanton Wicks and his band played the music; it was more expensive as the admission fee was three shillings. (In the war year's venues had to close early because of the blackout and civil defence regulations.)

On Wednesdays and Fridays from 1940, Flannel Dances were arranged at the Mutley Assembly Rooms, Mutley Plain, music played by the Paramount Orchestra. Flannel Dances came about because men had to wear civilian grey flannel, wide bottomed trousers at the dances. The ladies had to wear dresses to look attractive and some would have had a new permanent wave by the Callinan method, no electricity used and these were called the ARP safety perms by M Dingle, Tavistock Road, Stoke; the cost would be reduced to encourage more trade. Because women had to wear trousers and turbans when doing a man's job for war work it was nice to dress up and feel like a woman again. Twirling their partners during the Flannel Dances the men's trousers and the Ladies' dresses would flare out with the movement making it all look so light-hearted and carefree. Where she could, Nancy would attend the dances at various venues to mingle with her constituents to boost morale and to join in the fun.

On with the dance! Let joy be unconfined.
No sleep till morn, when youth and pleasure meet
To chase the glowing hours
With flying feet! (Lord Byron 1788-1824)

CHAPTER ELEVEN
BARBICAN ANTIQUE SHOP

The greatest glory of a woman is to be least talked about by men.
Pericles C494-429 BC.

Ninety-five year old Jack Hermon was born in Plymouth in 1910 and little was he to know how his life would be entwined with that of Nancy, Lady Astor, in his adult years. His father was an Army man posted to Yorkshire, which meant the family had to leave Plymouth. He grew up and was educated at Warmgate in the City of York. His mother managed a public house and a shop in the area and his sister, who was ten years older, was a semi-professional singer, so the family had a reasonable quality of life. In the late nineteen twenties they moved to Bedford to be nearer other family members, and Jack, now a young man, opened a small Art and Craft shop until 1932 when they moved back to Plymouth.

JACK'S STORY

I was out of work in Plymouth for several weeks until one day I happened to read on a notice board outside Virginia House that there were art lessons for the unemployed. I duly signed up, later finding out that Lady Astor had set up various projects for other men out of work, and from that day I blessed her for what she had done. I studied hard and then opened my first shop in Plymouth selling old books and antiques, leaving mother to run the shop until four in the afternoon when I would return to take over. This allowed me the opportunity to attend college to improve my art skills. I also liked ironwork and with practise became quite proficient and one task I was asked to undertake was to repair the crest over the large fireplace at Drake's House at Yelverton after it had suffered damage from a fire in the nineteen thirties. I repaired and repainted the crest to its original state, this in turn brought other residents of various manors and mansions to have their ironwork done to standard and suddenly I was on the ladder to success.

The shop that I owned, and the fact that my mother operated there during the day, meant that mother and Lady Astor became good friends. Her many visits to the shop resulted in me having many of Nancy's aristocratic friends as more customers, who were financially well off, and even the not so well off, visiting the shop buying antiques which gave me a good income. This meant I could visit different auctions and buy more stock. On several occasions Lady Astor would walk into the shop, when mother and I were both present, and buy items from me. Once she spotted an antique group of small elephants on a table, which she immediately bought, she loved buying Victorian cups and saucers; I found out later that she gave the items away as gifts. The cups and saucers would be used at teatime to entertain her American visitors; they loved anything that was unique, Lady Astor said they were Victorian, they would then remark how beautiful they were and she would give the china set to her visitors. They would openly boast how wonderful a gift is was to take back to America which they could show to their friends, I think the lovely antique elephants were given away at some time.

On a very wet day Nancy Astor made a quick visit to the shop as she had been in the vicinity visiting someone and when she came in her eyes fell on a beautiful Venton Vase." "I will have that," she whispered to my mother. "Little does he know I have the other matching one at Elliot House." I came from the back of the shop and said to her, "I heard that Lady Astor, but the price is still the same!" She smiled, and bought the matching vase. Lord Astor had expressed concern at Nancy dodging around the Barbican on her own and had insisted that in future she was to have an escort at all times when in the Barbican area. Because of this instruction Lady Astor would call in on my mother and ask her, "Can I borrow Jack, he is such a nice young man?" I would escort her around the Barbican; this pleased me as I met people I would not normally have met. Then came the war and whole life styles were to change.

On my return from India, when the war was over, I went to Kelly College, Tavistock, as a teacher to teach students painting and drawing. My large watercolour painting is placed somewhere in the civic centre building of Plymouth City Council; my painting of Lady Hamilton, which I am very proud of, is hanging in the BBC building in Delhi, the capital of India, which stands at the western end of the Gangetic Plain, its population is approximately thirteen million. I enjoyed my stay in India, as it was full of formidable mosques, monuments and forts, and some wonderful bazaars in narrow streets and exquisite antiques. New Delhi, the imperial city created by the British Raj, is composed of spacious tree lined avenues and many government buildings. A former pupil of mine at Kelly College, David Weekes, was commissioned to paint the ceiling in the Guildhall, Plymouth, it took him two years to complete and he was paid by the City Council. I can honestly say that my influence in art has touched many corners of the world.

One of the projects I got my students to undertake was to make a large version in wire mesh and paper of Sir Francis Drake and Elizabeth 1, when finished they were painted and placed outside Saint Andrews Church on the Royal Parade. They proved a great visitor attraction for days, but one day they were removed and burnt on orders of Commander Westhall, the Principal of the College, for what reason I was never able to establish. I was also responsible for setting up the modelling classes and the photographic section at the college, and I am pleased at the way the two sections have progressed today. I do have accolades after my name, the main one being the Royal College of Art award; I spent some time in Paris, France for a short time. My pride and joy is the artwork at the gates of Kelly College for it was me who designed the iron gates and the crest and had them made in a foundry at the back of Ebrington Street, Plymouth, for the princely sum of sixty pounds. I remember that the finance officer of Kelly College thought at the time that it was very expensive. He reluctantly paid the bill, and I did not even get a thank you to boot!

Later I re-opened a shop on the Barbican, Plymouth, renewing my business in antiques. I had a secret desire to revive the Cookworthy Pottery so took the plunge and my first attempt out of the kiln was a figurine of a white cat, and having renewed my contact with Lady Astor I gave it to her as a present in thanks for her past custom. Nancy was so pleased that she wrote a letter of thanks to me, which I have treasured all these years and still hold to this day. Another of my regular customers was the Countess of Edgecumbe, she was known as Effy. She came from New Zealand and some of her purchases, including some of the porcelain I made at my shop, are still at Mount Edgcumbe. I feel I have the spirit of Lady Astor in my system, as I am one of the rare breeds of people that dare challenge authority and win! My fight came when arriving at my shop one day I noticed a gang of workmen putting up an electric light over my shop. The powers to be had not asked my permission or had the courtesy to notify me. Challenging the indiscretion and the inconvenient location I started the campaign to have the lamp fixed to the corner apex of the shop to overlook the Ship Inn and Southside Street to stop the area being desecrated by late night revellers. I won the day; with common sense and compromise from the authorities the lamp was placed in the most useful position.

Another proud record that I hold dear is that my name is the first one in the visitors' book at 3, Elliot Terrace. All the royalty, politicians, judges, comedians, film stars, clergy and aristocrats that passed through these famous doors follow on from my signature; ironic indeed that an ordinary person is top of the list in the visitors' book. Nancy held a great deal of respect for me, the ordinary man. In retrospect I had friends in all stations and one of my friends was Mr Hector Sterling who had supplied the chandeliers hanging in the hall of the Guildhall, Plymouth. Hector had to go to France to receive the Gold Medal awarded for his design of the flats opposite the church in Notte Street.

One day the Education Minister the Earl Dillaway came to Plymouth. I was not very impressed at his application toward the post; however, the Earl was the Minister of Education so everyone had to accept his decision. Lady Astor gave a party for him at the Duke of Cornwall Hotel and I attended the party. That night, Nancy Astor was dressed in a pale blue satin dress trimmed with old ecru lace, and she looked beautiful. I loved and admired her and she is irreplaceable. She turned my life around with that first chance of breaking away from poverty at Virginia House all those years ago and from that chance I went from strength to strength. I miss her to this day, the warmth, and yes, even her brash remarks, for when she walked into the shop, she lit up the day, and everyone jumped to her attention. Yes indeed! She had the human touch.

Jack Hermon's Antique Shop on the Barbican Southside Street where
Lady Astor often bought antiques. Photo taken in the 1950s.

Nancy Langhorne Astor
circa 1900s

CHAPTER TWELVE
BANQUET TABLECLOTH

Truth always originates in a minority of one, and every custom begins as a broken precedent. *Nancy Astor 1879-1964*

When sixteen year old Joyce Srodzinski married her Polish sailor boy friend in 1943 little did she know that a thoughtful suggestion contributed by Lady Astor was to remain as a memory with her all her life, the gesture offered in kindness by Nancy Astor was one of many pleasantries that Plymouth citizens were to appreciate from this formidable lady. The Polish Navy had been living aboard a former British ship loaned to the Polish Navy. The whole crew comprised of Polish sailors who had come here to fight the cause of freedom. Later they were accommodated at the former United Services Orphan Home for Girls at Stoke, as all the girls had been evacuated to Cornwall. Being married at the very young age of sixteen to a Polish sailor in the war years was a risky gamble, but Joyce's beau Zbigniew Pajak had escaped from the terror of Poland which had been occupied by the Nazis and he made his way to England to serve in the Polish Navy.

On her wedding day, and with war rations severely restricted, food had been miraculously supplied by family and friends, in spite of the catering rules set by the authorities that only forty people were allowed to be catered for at wedding receptions during the war years. Usually charges would be 4/6 per head and the hire of a hall 12/6. There was also a restriction on photographs as, by the rule, only six photographs were officially allowed to be taken of the wedding event. A wedding dress meant forfeiting a month's clothing coupons so any second hand bridal dress was worth a fortune. The young couple to be married held their reception at the bride's mother's home at Connaught Avenue, near Mutley Plain, Plymouth, thus keeping the cost within close family and friends. Lady Astor had loaned them her beautiful white tablecloth from her home at 3 Elliot Terrace, which would fit a thirty/forty foot dining table. Damask tablecloths were in short supply during the war years and Joyce could not help but point out the setting on the table to her family and friends, and she was pleased that her Ladyship had loaned her the use of the item.

Unfortunately, Joyce's marriage to Zbigniew Pajak was to be a failure, and ended with a divorce. She married again and her second marriage was to be successful as she and Mr Bartczak lived a happy life until his death. Widowhood made life lonely for Joyce but she found contentment with her present partner Bert Symons who worked for Shephard and Bone in New Street, the Barbican; they were Shopfitters and Joinery experts. Bert would often pop in to Perillas café for a bite to eat during lunchtime and he would frequently see Robert Lenkiewicz the painter in there and on occasion they would sit together and have a friendly chat. Bert recalls that in 1984

Robert spoke to Bert and asked if he would be prepared to make him some frames for his artwork and recent paintings as he had no money but would be prepared to barter. In return for the frames he would paint a picture of Bert's choice. Being a kind man he agreed and he chose to have a portrait painted of himself and his friend Joyce Bartczak. It was one of Robert Lenkiewicz earliest oil paintings on canvas and it is a beautiful portrait, arguably one of his best works, which is displayed with pride in Bert's home. From then on Bert continued to make the frames for Robert until he (Bert) retired.

Photo: By kind permission of the owners. Digital copy taken by Trevor Burrows Photography
- from the original Lenkiewicz painting

Joyce Bartczak with her partner Bert Symonds painted in 1984. Bert made the frames for Robert Lenkiewicz's artworks and paintings.

Back Row. Florian Srodzinski (Father) Nora Srodzinski (Mother)
Joyce Pajak (now Bartczak) Zbigniew Pajak.
Bottom Row. Eliza Boaden (Grandmother) Margaret Peak (Bridesmaid)
John Boaden (Grandfather).

Krakowiak crew with German booty.

Polish Destroyer Krakowiak 1943

Polish Destroyer Krakowiak 1945

CHAPTER THIRTEEN
THE COURT HAIRDRESSERS

Say not goodbye but in some brighter clime, bid us good morning.

ROBERT TIERNEY

Robert Tierney remembers the shop his Mother and Aunt owned as being the recognised commissioned hairdressers for Nancy Astor from 1921 until 1950 in Plymouth. They were known as the Misses Hilda and Gladys Prout and both were the daughters of well-known publicans in Plymouth from the 1920's to the 1960's. Hilda later married Cyril Fortescue Tierney (Robert's father) and Gladys married Mr Ralph Fielden. He was a Naval Submariner Officer and was killed in the war in 1941. The family's hairdresser's shop was located in the old Drake Circus in the Margaret Summer's Hairdressers Salon and they were the first hairdressers in Plymouth to use the Marcel Wave hairstyle, which had started in London. A wire contraption was used in which tongs were heated, hair curled and then set and waved in the fashion of the day. Both my Aunt and my mother would go to Elliot Terrace to do her Ladyship's hair or on occasion Lady Astor would visit the hairdressing salon.

The two sisters bought the shop as the then owner was retiring and Hilda and Gladys decided to keep the name of the shop during their ownership. In the 1950's my Aunt became Manageress of the Hairdressers in Pophams and sometimes Lady Astor would call in at the department store, as she was not living in Plymouth then, but would often visit the city for a while. My Mother died in 1989 and my Aunt in 1990. Throughout their lives both would often say what a wonderful woman Lady Astor was, kind, knowledgeable and humorous. One particular story they would often tell was about Lord Astor. Whilst Nancy was having her hair styled at Elliot Terrace, Lord Astor came into the room and he jingled some coins in his pocket, Nancy heard it and said:" Waldorf, if you have so much money give me some!" Lord Astor was amused and left the room, Lady Astor could always say amusing things and she did so much for the people of Plymouth. (Robert Tierney died on the 19th February 2008. RIP)

JOY WILLS (NEE HOSKIN)

Meeting Joy Constance Kathleen Wills (nee Hoskin) a vibrant and warm hearted woman in her eighty-ninth year, revealed a wealth of information that would produce a wonderful book in itself, featuring all that she has achieved in her life time, for Joy, too, was a great giver to various charities and took a very keen interest in youth. Joy

Photo courtesy Mr Robert Tierney (RIP) Modbury, Devon.

The Marcel Wave hairstyle
The Misses Hilda and Gladys Prout hairdresser's shop was located in Drake Circus
Plymouth. Between 1920-1950 they were the first to introduce the
Marcel Wave hairstyle in Plymouth.

had been quite an active woman in her time and apart from her hairdressing business she had been a member of the Masonic Lodge. On the 4th May 1949 she was part of the group of ladies whose ritual it was to be of brotherly love, belief and truth. It was their consecration event and was the second Plymouth Masonic Lodge under the British Order admitting women. They became the daughter lodge of the Golden Hind and are number sixteen on the register at Queens Road, Lipson, their Headquarter address. Named Causa Causans (Craft Lodge) Ladies could make the advancement to Devonia Mark Lodge and later advance to the Royal Arch Chapter and finally on invitation, only, to the top Lodge, which is of the highest degree The Rose Croix.

Joy spent many years as a member of the Bickleigh Women's Institute and sang in the Yelverton Church Choir. Joy formed the Girls Nautical Training Corp in Tavistock in the 1950's and was their Commanding Officer. However, as the theme of this book is to link the human touch with Nancy, Lady Astor, so it must be, for here was a person whose link with the aristocracy and Lady Astor, was that of Court Hairdresser. No mean feat for she was a top of the range hairdresser sought by all the aristocratic

Copyright unknown

*Photo taken 4th May 1949 at the Ladies Masonic meeting. (From the Joy Hoskin collection)
Forth from the left front row standing, Mrs Mary E Modley, Plymouth. First right standing
back row (with black hair) Mrs Joy Wills (nee Hoskin).
Second left back row standing, Mrs Gabriele Pearce (Or Pearse)
Also in the photo is Mrs Alice Hamley. Mrs Winifred Priest. Mrs F. A. Crosse.
Mrs E Holmes. Mrs M Blackburn. Mrs E Charles. Mrs D Osborne.*

families who came to Plymouth, although there were underlying murmurs about her high prices, she was nevertheless a real professional hairdresser and she gave a far superior service. Her commission as a professional hairdresser came about with her mother paying a fee of thirty pounds in 1931 to apprentice Joy to a Miss Parsons the Hairdressers of Weston Park Road, Peverell, Plymouth. This meant three years as an apprentice and two years as an improver. She was bound, as it is said, and in her own interest to complete the required five years. No one could say then that it was for money, for her pay was meagre and the work hard. Two shillings and sixpence a week for the first year, five shillings for the second year, seven shillings and sixpence for the third year, ten shillings for the fourth year and fifteen shillings in the final year. Joy recalls working like a little skivvy. "I had to wash the front doorstep, sweep the surrounding areas, scrub the floors, clean mirrors, clear singed hair from gas brackets, put combs in containers of dehydrated solution of formaldehyde and polish the taps. Then I had to help the assistants sweep up the cut hair and get the permanent

267

waves ready, fold towels which had been washed the previous evening, and when time permitted I had to practice Boardwork, that is the art of wig making. I had to learn how to cut, set and perm whilst making sure the customer was properly looked after. The worst job was cleaning and destroying the nits from hair bought from the wholesalers. In the nineteen thirties hair was being imported from China and India. By the time it reached Heathrow it was alive and it would be left to the businesses that purchased the hair to clean it. After cleaning, the hair would be tied with strands of silk cotton and laid between drawing brushes, and then I would weave the hair into party pieces, at the time the fashions of the day were the bouffant and pin curls.

I was privileged to be Lady Astor's hairdresser intermittently when she was in residence at 3 Elliot Terrace, which overlooked Plymouth Hoe. I was known then as Joy Hoskin Limited Court Hairdresser. I used to charge Lady Astor much more to have her hair done if she asked for me to attend her personally. My assistants who did not have the specialist care charged the normal rate and there was quite a controversy at my charges. Well-known business socialites such as Mrs Mumford and Mrs Dingles and all the elite of Plymouth used to meet in Dingles of Plymouth for tea or coffee and they used to discuss my prices, and articles would be written to the newspapers deriding my charges. For just a cut in those days I used to charge fifteen shillings, which was a lot of money as the majority of hairdressers were charging one shilling, one and sixpence, or two and sixpence for a cut. I would charge fifteen pounds for permanent waves, which was very expensive in those days, but I gave extra service and the customers came to me because I was a top professional in my field. When asked by the author, "Why did you charge so much?" My reply was, "Because I had a special way of cutting, I never let them see the mirror, I used to put a towel over the mirror, and I took half-an-hour or even an hour to do a cut. I used to layer the hair; I was also a beauty culturist and therapist. I could do infra-red and ultra-violet ray and I had a doctor's certificate, which allowed me to prescribe any of these treatments.

After my apprenticeship and my improvership of five years, I applied for a job at Hender's Corner. This was with a lady called Miss Ethel Hodge and it was called Anne's Boudoir. She came from Noss Mayo, Devon, and used to motor in each morning to Mannamead and she offered me thirty shillings a week and one week's holiday with pay; that was a princely sum to me. Miss Hodge taught me much more about Boardwork, and how to assemble the false hairpieces, which was called Postiche. Because of the ladies hair styles in those days the postiche that we used to get out of customer's hair was excessive and a firm in Brighton and London use to take a lot of our postiche that we used to make at Anne's Boudoir. Of course when I used to take the postiche into the college they were highly delighted because Boardwork was a big thing then. Whilst in employment at Anne's Boudoir, Miss Hodge introduced me by letter to her old employer in South Molton Street who was Miss Atkins, and a Mr Law who was later to become the father of Trichology. When

I had my week's holiday I would stay at the Young Women's Christian Association Hostel and Mr Law used to take me to the Great Ormond Street Hospital to see how the children fared. Some of the children would have great horns growing out of their head, which was a disease associated with Trichology, and their plight was dreadful to see. There was a great deal of snobbery among the upper classes so how did I get to know Lady Astor? It was through attending the hospital on my week's holiday that I met the Honourable Helen Mildmay and she told Lady Astor that I was her hairdresser and that was the beginning in receiving further bookings for hair treatment among the aristocracy in Plymouth.

Finally I made the decision to buy my own business and in 1938 I bought the premises at 93 Mutley Plain in the rooms above Dilleighs Shop. I was happy there and I built up my list of regular customers. Then came the war and everything changed. I was registered and trained as a firewatcher and Air Raid Precaution Warden. When the incendiaries dropped and property was set on fire one or two Wardens disappeared into the shelters and it was left to the women to put the fires out. In December 1941, the day after Boxing Day, I married a Corporal in the RAF but I kept my business on as he was away quite a lot and my first daughter was born in 1943. The businesses in that area were close knit and very generous and we helped the war effort and charities by collecting spare change from our customers. Customers and businesses laid miles of pennies along Mutley Plain and when the pennies joined from end to end the money would be picked up and given to charity. My business, Joy Hoskin Limited, had the honour of winning the cup three times running for collecting the most money in 1943.

Like many other businesses in Plymouth, my shop suffered damage from the heavy bombing during the war but managed to survive, after the war I decided to seek other premises to expand my business. Over the years I had businesses at 69 Mutley Plain, Plymouth, Devon, and 7, Market Street, Tavistock, Devon, and 3 Portland Ope, Tavistock Road, Plymouth. Plymouth City Council had been granted the go ahead given by the Government for Professor Patrick Abercrombie and Paton Watson in 1943 with the 'Plan for Plymouth' to clear the rubble and rebuild the City. This meant that temporary Nissen Huts made of corrugated iron could be built to house some of the hard-pressed businesses that had suffered from the devastation. I took the opportunity to take out a five-year lease as Messrs Joy Hoskin Limited on one of the huts at 3 Portland Ope in August 1946.

Once established, people began to recommend me to various customers and I built up quite a clientele. The customers loved having their hair combed to stand large and tall and with the sides backed combed and some customers still used pin curls. Lady Astor was no exception and one-day I was doing her hair when she told me of one of the past incidents in her career. Nancy Astor always walked tall and well disciplined, elegant and precise, and one of the reasons she walked like that, was because of the hair fashions at the time, as she did not want to spoil the hair set. One had to walk

with a modicum of decorum to keep it neat and tidy. She said that at the time she was a guest of honour at a very important banquet and ball given by the Lord Mayor of London that was regarding her position as first lady Member of Parliament in the government and, as you know, she was a very exceptional person. She would move her body in such a way, perhaps to turn and speak. Sitting at the table about to eat a bowl of soup Lady Astor became aware that one of her pin curls, that she had had fixed by her hairdresser in London, fell into her soup. That was a most embarrassing experience and when I asked her "What did you think your ladyship?" Because it had not had time to become saturated and being the person she was she promptly took it out, dusted it off with her serviette and rapidly pinned it back into place with an invisible hairpin into her bouffant hair and carried on talking. Well of course, I nearly fell about with laughter when she told me this story. I said, "A pin curl falling into the soup, what a dreadful thing, didn't you feel terrible?" She said, "Why should I? I had something false on me, if you have something false on you, you must take the consequences," and that was Lady Astor direct and to the point.

The Honourable Helen Mildmay White and her husband had been detailed to entertain Queen Elizabeth and the two Princesses for lunch at Mothecombe House, as Lord Mildmay was unable to entertain the Royal persons at Flete House because Lady Mildmay was very ill and in a respite home. I was fetched by car and taken to Mothecombe House to prepare the Honourable Helen Mildmay's hair and I was able to see Queen Elizabeth and the two Princesses; however, I was not called upon to treat their hair but was at least on stand by. I used to go to Admiralty house, Mount Wise, to Lady Burnett who was the wife of Rear Admiral Robert Burnett to cut and set her hair; I was also on standby for Princess Alice, Countess of Athlone. This aristocratic link introduced me, as I said, to Nancy, Lady Astor and one day her Secretary rang to make an appointment for me to attend to her hair and of course I naturally accepted. She would only have her hair done occasionally, she would flit in when in Plymouth and then she would rush off to London again, she was a well-travelled lady.

Joy Hoskin's Hairdressing staff.
Front row second left Joy Hoskin (Joy was 44years old
when this picture was taken in 1960). Man at back Mr Jack
Whiting. In front of the man is the cleaning and towel lady,
Mrs Eileen Gilliyer. Bottom right hand corner Jean Clark.
Rest unknown.

Lady Astor spoke to me about her son 'Jakie' (Sir John Jacob Astor V11) who had married the daughter of the President of Argentina. Her Ladyship said to me when I was setting her hair one afternoon "I think it is morally wrong that she dyes her hair." I said, "What do you mean, she dyes her hair, what colour was she?" "Oh," she said, "She was dark but she wanted to go an auburn colour." I said, "Ah, she is not dyeing her hair, because she has normal dark hair, she is bleaching her hair because she is taking colour out!" She said, "What do you mean?" I said, "You must think of me as morally wrong because I am very dark and I wanted to go auburn and I am putting colour back, I am bleaching my hair not putting colour in." She answered, "Well I think it's disgusting, I do not believe in it!" Lady Astor hated the colouring that was used on some customer's hair and she refused to use it. It was called Paraphenylenediamine which was liquid para dye used for colouring hair in those days. I replied, "But you are modern, look what you are doing for the people, really you should not talk like that!" Lady Astor retorted, "I talk as I want!" Aware of her sharpness I said gently, "Well you have got to go with the times." Nancy replied, "I am going with the times, I am modern, first lady in Parliament!" I knew I had to pacify her, as I did not want to lose her custom so I said, "Don't we all know it! And we do believe in you so, and we love you for it, how you got the Astor Institute going and the Macmillan School underway."

 I waited with bated breath for her reply and when it came I was quite surprised. She said, "Ah, now that is where I want to take you, I have been going to your little kiosk Tea for Two round the corner." (Portland Ope Tea for Two closed in 1952) I said, "Well now, that kiosk really should not have been there, the City of Plymouth said

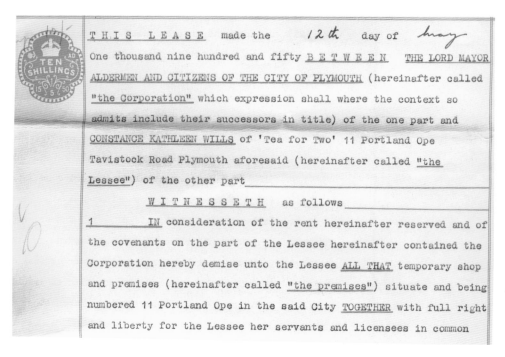

THIS LEASE made the 12th day of May
One thousand nine hundred and fifty B E T W E E N THE LORD MAYOR
ALDERMEN AND CITIZENS OF THE CITY OF PLYMOUTH (hereinafter called
"the Corporation" which expression shall where the context so
admits include their successors in title) of the one part and
CONSTANCE KATHLEEN WILLS of 'Tea for Two' 11 Portland Ope
Tavistock Road Plymouth aforesaid (hereinafter called "the
Lessee") of the other part

    W I T N E S S E T H   as follows
1   IN consideration of the rent hereinafter reserved and of
the covenants on the part of the Lessee hereinafter contained the
Corporation hereby demise unto the Lessee ALL THAT temporary shop
and premises (hereinafter called "the premises") situate and being
numbered 11 Portland Ope in the said City TOGETHER with full right
and liberty for the Lessee her servants and licensees in common

Mrs Joy Wills lease for the 'Tea for Two cafe

that the space never existed. I wrote three times to the City Council and asked if I could please run a little kiosk there so that I could help the builders who are clearing all the rubble before they start on the rebuilding of the City of Plymouth. The workmen do not have anywhere to go to have a cup of tea, coffee or a sandwich." I told her that I had pleaded with the City Council to let me have this kiosk, and it would bring extra rent and rates into the City, which was so badly needed at the time, and in 1950 I obtained the lease for the premises. Lady Astor said, "Yes, I think that is a wonderful thing and I will certainly go there and in fact I have already had tea and sandwiches there. I did not realise it belonged to you, but you can now take me along and we can have a bite to eat and then I will take you to see the Macmillan Nursery," which was at the top end of Hoegate Street on the Hoe.

This particular day when Lady Astor had come to have her hair done at the Nissen hut, number 3 Portland Ope, she had not come in the usual official car but had brought her little run-about car. She said, "I will take you up to see the children who will be having their siesta during our lunch time." I got in the car with her and oh dear! It was dreadful; I was clutching the seat and hanging on like grim death. I thought my God please let me get out. Well, we reached Hoegate Street and she took me into Matron and showed me the children, meanwhile she had disappeared for about half an hour and when she came back she said, "Ready to go Miss Hoskin?" "Oh no please!" I said, "I would rather walk." She retorted, "I brought you here therefore I will take you back." I again said, "No, I would rather walk. You are such a dreadful driver Lady Astor. I have never been driven by any one so bad as you." She said, "For Gods sake Miss Hoskin get in the car and shut up!" Which I promptly did as I secretly thought that I had just about pushed her too far with my differences of opinions, and could I afford to lose her trade? I got back into the car and when she let me out she said, "Not so bad was it?" Determined not to be bullied I said, "Its shocking! You have no business to be on the road." She said, "I told you to shut up! - shut up!" and this is what Lady Astor was like.

The little snack kiosk was popular with the workmen; they could buy their cigarettes from the counter as well as enjoy their snack with comfort. When she had had her hair done Lady Astor would pop into the little café, number 11, Portland Ope, and talk to the workmen. They loved her because she used to talk to them and get down to their level and ask them how their families were getting on and how did they manage and really draw them out in such a way. Oh! they thought it was wonderful. Lady Astor reminded me that she always enjoyed my sandwiches so much and that I made them so much better than my assistant Edna, who I employed to serve the customers. She said." I think you put more butter on, and butter is so scarce these days with the rations. As for the workmen these poor men don't get very much money and they have to work under such dreadful conditions. If I can do anything for them or help them in anyway I shall do so. It is just like my Macmillan Nursery, there are so many poor citizens and underprivileged children and I will fight, and mean really fight, to try to get better help for these poor unfortunates." She was so sincere and during her lifetime she did these sorts of things and I applaud her and I loved her for it, I think one could say a person either loved Lady Astor or hated her. We, the ordinary people, would be on her side and I really think, this is only my opinion of course, that the Royal Parade should have been named Astor Parade. So many people thought so at the time but of course it is what the local council says and you have to obey the law.

I was only Lady Astor's regular hairdresser for a short period of time. I was very ill during my pregnancy and had to have an operation, which meant I was away for a very long time from the business. My secretary had to come to my house to sign cheques and read all my business details because I was confined to bed, so I never knew who took over as Lady Astor's hairdresser after I did. I kept my company Joy Hoskin limited on until 1960 when I was appointed as a Lecturer in 1960-1963 at the Department of Education and Science and my first appointment was in Farnborough, Hampshire. In those days hairdressing was not considered a top enough subject but because I had been a manufacturer, making hair cream, hand cream, dandruff lotion and face cream and was also able to practice infra-red and ultra-violet ray the Science department wanted to know what made me tick. I held a poison licence and a weights and measures licence. I stayed in that position for three years and when I left the principal said that they had never collected so much money to give a parting present as they did for me. Naturally I was most pleased. I then went to the only other college in England, Scotland and Wales, which was the South Shields Marine and

Technical College, which the Duke of Edinburgh opened. When I was at Farnborough College I had a very lowly position, which use to be then as Assistant Lecturer, but now there is no such thing as they now start as Lecturer 1, Lecturer 2, Senior Lecturer, Deputy Head of Department and Head of Department. In later years I became the first lady president of the Hairdresser's Federation and in 1951 when Mrs J. Marshall was the very first Lady Lord Mayor of Plymouth (1950-1951), they gave a ball in my honour. My business in 1955 was at 69 Mutley Plain and well established. I bought the premises outright in 1961 for ten thousand pounds.

Copyright unknown

National Hairdressers' ball 14th February 1951 at the Duke of Cornwall Hotel.
Seated left to right Miss B. Barker (Secretary) Mrs George, Alderman Mrs Jacquetta Marshall, (first lady Lord Mayor) Miss Joy Hoskin President, (first Lady President)
Standing: Mr W.L. George (National President) Mr C.P. Brown J.P. Mrs Black,
Mr Colin Campbell (Town Clerk) Mr A. Sanders (Vice President)

My most exciting experience was in 1956 when I was selected as a hairdresser model to walk down the catwalk, displaying a classic hairstyle, my hair was black and I had rainbow hues and wore a beautiful cream suit. This took place in Paris, France, and I stayed at the Hotel D'Albret, 16, Rue Pierre-Semard, Square Montholon. I had the pleasure of being a member of the National Hairdressing Federation and I often wrote an article in our magazine. The Editor wrote on one occasion: "Joy Wills (neé

Hoskin) is a well known craft personality in Plymouth and in the South West generally. In addition to being a Director of Joy Hoskin Limited with a staff of thirty-five in four well established salons, she is a member of the National Hairdressers Federation, the Incorporated Guild and the Hairdressing Registration Council. She has taken a great interest in the Technical Education of young people and was herself an entrant for the Gold Cup in 1948. (Premier award of all apprentice's works). She has also appeared in a ten-minute spot on the Home Service of the BBC giving a talk on Hairdressing as a career." I was one of eighteen people chosen from the Westcountry to represent the Hairdresser Bill and we used to meet once a month and I remember vividly the trips to London. We really worked hard to get this Act through Parliament and in 1964 (the year Nancy Astor died) we succeeded. It meant hygiene was a top priority, everything was to be sterilised and staff had to be fully trained because you were handling sometimes unclean hair and dangerous instruments, hairdryers, scissors, and in those days open razors were used and razor cutting came in, and all electric items used in the proximity of water. We also fought for better conditions and pay for trainee hairdressers. Today we have mobile hairdressers, in the eyes of our generation, hairdressing today is not considered to be one of the top professions and I think the profession has gone into the doldrums.

Despite my career I still remember my days with Nancy, Lady Astor and my personal relationship with her as customer and business contact. I always called her 'M' Lady.' I think the different subjects we discussed, pin curls, hair dyeing, Great Ormond Street, Macmillan Nursery, my cheek at challenging her driving, and the trade with my little café all brought about a mutual understanding and respect, albeit, I was never on intimate terms with her. Nancy's abilities were widespread and I recall one particular incident that increased the respect I had for her. Rumour had it that many of her servants were ill at Cliveden, Buckinghamshire, and Nancy had to commute frequently between Cliveden and Plymouth. There was a very bad bout of flu round about that time and lots of her servants were absent and could not carry out their duties. The scullery maid was absent which meant floors could not be scrubbed and Lady Astor had a policy that she would not give her staff any job that she could not do herself. One of Lady Astor's guests at Cliveden was looking for Nancy and after a careful search found her down in one of the rooms scrubbing the floor. The friend said, "Whatever are you doing Nancy? She said, "My servants are away, the scullery maid is away, and I am holding this banquet tonight and everything has got to be spick-and-span so I am scrubbing the floors that they would normally have done, so you come down and join me!" Which she promptly did because she dare not refuse being a friend and one of the Cliveden set.

It is great to be able to put on record my memories and impressions of a wonderful person. Lady Astor had a wasp like waist and she often wore beautiful embroidered tops and the embroidery was remarkable, but the actual skirt seemed to be plain. She was always in the height of fashion with her hats and that is why she had the bouffant style hair to match the style of the day. Ladies would watch to see how Lady Astor was dressed for special occasions and the focus would be on the hat and milliners stock would take a dip as the ladies kept up with the height of fashion. At the Hospital Fair in July 1931 Lady Astor wore a dove coloured coat with a brown picture hat trimmed with rose beige velvet, many weeks later ladies would be seen wearing picture hats. These were the experiences that links me to Lady Astor, I supposed she trusted me, she confided in me, during the time that I knew her we really got on well together. Both of us would speak straight and direct, she had a wit that was second to none and was so spontaneous, as I was similar we jelled and this gave us a common bond of mutual respect. I suppose taking me for a motor car ride was in her eyes special, albeit, it was a scary event that I will always remember. One could look back at it now and laugh. Who was to know that one day I would relate these memories into a book? So one can say that each of us met in our lifetime and experienced the human touch.

What stands out in my memory about Lady Astor was that she was so pretty, oh, she was really pretty, and she used to look you straight in the eye. With her slim waist and her long skirts and her little buttoned up boots that she wore, she walked so elegantly. People these days slouch when they are walking but she would not. With her hair supported by many invisible hairpins although why they were called that I do not know for how can you have invisible hairpins? I used to call them very fine hairpins. She did a remarkable job and her heritage is such that we all appreciate what she did. I have one little reminder today that links me still with her after all these years and that is the regular supply of Macmillan Christmas Cards that I buy every year. I will stand up and be counted because I loved Lady Astor, she made everyone feel alive and her love of Plymouth and Plymothians stood out like a beacon for the entire world to see, indeed, a very kind and gracious lady and I know that when she died it was the end of an era."

Joy Wills (nee Hoskin) died on the 22nd of March 2007 ninety years of age. RIP; all her family and friends will sadly miss her. Her family in their bereavement announcement honoured Joy with this comment: "Say not goodbye but in some brighter clime, bid us good morning." Plymouth, with the deaths of Joy Wills and Robert Tierney, has lost two more links with the Astor history.

DATED   1961

M11

JOY CONSTANCE KATHLEEN WILLS

and

WESSEX BUSINESS BROKERS LIMITED

of 1st and 2nd floors
69 Mutley Plain, in the
City of Plymouth.

Arthur Goldberg,
Solicitor,
PLYMOUTH

The lease that Joy Hoskin took out for her business
at Mutley Plain

*Lady Astor in her younger years. Note the hairstyle and wearing
her favourite pearls.*

CHAPTER FOURTEEN
VIRGINIA HOUSE SETTLEMENT

"The main dangers in this life are the people who want to change everything.....or nothing." *Nancy Astor.*

VIRGINIA HOUSE

In the 1900's Mary Danvers Stocks (née Brinton) (1891-1975) academic, feminist, radical and college head had, on the basis of her Manchester experience, given Nancy Astor advice on setting up a Social Settlement in Plymouth. As a compliment to Nancy it was called Virginia House. Mary Stocks wrote with some forethought from 22 Wilbraham Road: "Some day Plymouth will be linked up with a University of the West and then it would be a thousand pities if there is not a Settlement to work the practical side of a social studies department." Mary and Nancy would have been proud to learn that eighty years later there would be a Plymouth University. From Nancy's meeting with Mary Stocks the embryo of Virginia House was sown. Lord and Lady Astor bought the premises. Mary and Nancy became good friends and Mary was able to handle Nancy's personality and became quite sisterly over the years. Mary had been Principal of Westfield College from 1939-1951 and broadcasting brought her a peerage (Baroness) in 1966, she had a dry humour and a terse speaking style; she had appeared with Issac Foot in what was billed as a 'Younger Generation' question time from a Plymouth Youth Club. The Westcountry featured regularly in the 'Any questions' sessions of the BBC. Nancy Astor and Mary Stocks were both philanthropists in a changing world.

40 Looe Street, Bretonside, on the Barbican, Plymouth, was built in 1720 and it included the first 19th Century Presbyterian Church built in the City. The Church closed in 1923 and was sold to Lord Astor to extend the work of what was then the Victory Club. Lord and Lady Astor purchased Virginia House, numbers 38, 39 & 40 Looe Street along with the old Batter Street Chapel and the Victory Club in 1924 with a sum of £40,000 pounds and endowed the Virginia House Settlement. When it had been converted for public use they gave it to the City in 1925, for all the young and the older generation to have as a meeting point. It was used as a club for all age groups, a Mother's Club and a Young people's Club that included football. In 1932-1933 the Virginia House football team were the winners of the United Churches League and more winners were to follow in later years. Other sporting activities were gymnastics, boxing, dancing classes, boating, rowing and sailing, camping and judo. Virginia House also featured a library and music room. Nancy had a wonderful affinity with the Barbican folk and despite the barracking she sometimes received from the hard working Barbican fishermen and women during her political speeches as she toured the City, over the years she earned their respect.

Located near the Barbican, Virginia House had a catchment of a possible one thousand members; the club facilities also included a cinema, library, carpenter's shop, gymnasium and a printing press for the settlement to use. Opened in December 1925 the first New Years Eve parties were held there for youth and senior citizen alike and were to be the forerunner of many more events to follow. The large hall would be decorated with flags and bunting, dancing would continue until 11pm and an orchestra made up from the Virginia House members, played the music. It was the beginning of a wonderful facility for the Barbican folk and other citizens who chose to attend. Dancing continued throughout the year and the monetary profits were saved until enough funds were accrued for the Maker Camp holidays held in Cornwall for children of the poor. Other activity groups who used the Virginia House settlement were Senior and Junior Boys, Senior and Junior girls' club, Mothers meeting, Nursery afternoon, and Scout and Guides. Membership was very popular as over fifteen hundred children attended the Virginia House activities in the 1920's. For seventy years the Virginia House Settlement managed care, training and advice projects, and provided a home to various organisations.

At Maker Camp in Cornwall hundreds of children enjoyed a wonderful holiday that they would not have normally had. It only lasted for a fortnight but what fun they had and many still remember that event. The children were grateful because it was Nancy Astor who began Maker Camp in 1918 at the end of the First World War for poor and underprivileged children to have a holiday in a country area near the sea. The holidays continued throughout the Second World War and Nancy Astor was still paying for the orphan children's fees. The camp later closed as the social lifestyles changed and in the year 2007 efforts had been made to form a trust by fifteen trustees to apply for a grant to establish a museum, it has proven difficult and now it may be turned into an educational tourism and arts haven. Maker Camp's history is not only military as the 18th Century military base at Maker Heights is now a project to make the area more accessible to the public. The Grade 11 listed guardhouse that is part of the original artillery barracks built on Maker Heights in 1796 recently won an award for its restoration and contribution to improving the local environment undertaken by the Rame Conservation Trust and Plymouth based Architects Design Group using traditional workmanship and materials. It is a project for the future, which will hopefully involve all the community.

Research has shown that in 1928 Lord and Lady Astor made an appeal on the BBC Radio asking for funds to give needy children a holiday. Some parents or guardians could not afford to pay for the holidays, as it was already a struggle to keep families fed. For its time it was a wonderful appeal and it proved that Nancy would use any means to get what she wanted for the children. Lady Astor bought an empty factory and the Batter Street Chapel to be converted and used it as a play centre cum club for children and young people. At a mothers meeting in Virginia House she gave a speech, she did not make long speeches what she had to say was straight and direct and on this occasion she boldly said "The world is a far better place than it was in the time of our Grandfathers." One former club member remarked, "Yes, we thought secretly but not for the poorest of the poor." However, credit where it is due, Nancy fought more for improving the quality of life for the working class than any other politician. Junior members of the Virginia House were always specially treated by Nancy as she adored children, there was a junior members club where children from three years of age and upwards would often take part in entertainment, Nancy never missed a session. The nursery children would open the entertainment with songs and dances, giving dramatised versions of 'Three Blind Mice' 'Pat-a-Cake' and quite charming the audience by their naiveté. Children followed them from the youngest section of the Play Centre, looking very becoming in the crinolines and brightly coloured frocks made for them by members of the Senior Club. They took part in a series of dances, the Minuet and Curtsey Dances proving especially attractive and culminating in the Maypole Dance. The programme would end with more songs and folk dances given by the older members of the Play Centre.

In March 1941 during the King and Queen's tour of the City along with Lady Astor they visited Virginia House Settlement. Their Majesties visited the men's clubroom and Lady Astor introduced them to Mr C.R.Cload with the words "He always gives you a nice fresh crab to take home with you." Later the royal visitors were presented with a nine-pound fresh crab. But the women attending Virginia House had their own way of making the royals welcome as they expressed their loyalty in their typical barbican tradition. "All the nice girls love a sailor," sang the mothers at Virginia House as the King was in Naval Uniform, they followed with another song The Navy, the British Navy and Three cheers for the Red, White and Blue. For the Queen they sang a Scottish Air and the royals were quite amused and proud. When her majesty the Queen asked Plymouth bombed out citizens if everything was broken, Lady Astor who accompanied her interjected, "Not quite Ma'am, their spirit is unbroken." Meanwhile the Virginia House Devon Minor League Football Team (First Team) had a fixture with North Down, soccer games were taking part in places all over the city and at Home Park the Royal Air Force played representatives of Plymouth City and that drew a large crowd, it was a little light relief and the entertainment boosted everyone's morale, also all the proceeds of the matches were being devoted the City Distress Fund.

In 1942 Nancy met Mr Ernest T. English who was staying at the Warden's Mr J. Judge's flat, who was Honorary Secretary of the Civil Guild of Help. Lady Astor insisted that Mr English take a walk with her and have a chat, albeit, Ernest did not do much talking, Lady Astor did all the talking. In his book Pilgrim to Plymouth published in the Plymouth Guild of Social Services Jubilee Year in 1967, Ernest English said "It was obvious she loved every brick and every person in this adopted City of hers, she walked me through the Barbican, up Hoegate Street and across Plymouth Hoe and into the YMCA" (Before the war the YMCA had been known as

Hoe Mansions, now it is the Astor Hotel) Ernest continued by saying, "She lifted up hearts wherever she went, her love for people was manifest in everything that she did." Plymouth Guild of Social Service was formerly known as Council of Social Service and before that as the Civic Guild of Help.

In 1943 four wonderful Christmas parties were arranged for Virginia House providing food, ice cream and entertainment for the children and the old folk. Most of the parties were for children and they attended in groups with supporting teachers, many members of the other Virginia House Settlement Clubs also attended and sailors from a United States Naval ship came to listen to the children sing carols. Junior girls performed tap dances and sang American songs to make the servicemen feel welcomed and they in turn took some of the children out for a ride in an American Jeep, ensuring that Santa Claus was in attendance. The American troops were very kind to the children always giving up their chocolate rations or sweets and the U.S. Navy were not going to be left out, a visiting U.S.A. ship's crew had collected £500 to give to the orphanages and children's institutions, a lot of money in those days. The American Wives of the serving United States sailors visited Virginia House and were made most welcome; they did not mind the girls from Virginia House dancing with their husbands for the hands of friendship were extended. The older girls had a dance in the evening and were able to dance with the sailors and the Hyde Park Centre Band

Lady Astor at a childrens' party circa 1943

Lady Astor giving sweets to a small girl at a children's party at Virginia House 1952

provided the music. Nancy, as Lady Mayoress, attended the dance after having heard the Nursery Children in their singing and distributing sweets with the aid of some sailors and then she joined wholeheartedly in the dancing. Other parties were taking place in the City, notably the American Red Cross in Elliot Terrace with gifts and boxes of candy for the children, included in this party were fifty children from the Devon & Cornwall Female Orphanage.

Virginia House was still going strong in the 1960's; this decade was to change the music world and the introduction and fame of the Beatles singing group were to change young people's social life, dances were still held but the music had changed dramatically, very different from the nineteen fifties. Sports were still very popular and particularly boxing, in fact it was the highlight of their lives for the Virginia House Boxing Club, its young boxers produced some quality fighters and one or two boxers reached the last eight of the Amateur Boxing Association Championships. The boys who boxed at Virginia House had a former naval man as a top class coach who brought the best out of the young men with his enthusiasm and instruction. In those days boxing tournaments were held at the Plymouth Guildhall. The Virginia House settlement amalgamated with the Guild of Social Service in 1974 in an effort to keep the community together for it had become noticeable that after the Second World War and the coming of the Welfare State it had led to a gradual decline in the uses of Virginia House in the style that it had known during the 1920's/1930's when it played a leading part in both the Barbican and community life. New ideas and new projects were tried such as, teenage clubs, mother's and toddler's groups, activities for the elderly, neighbourhood work and a resource centre to provide information.

Lady Astor must have been looking down from her parliament in the sky with disquiet at the crisis and proposed closure of Virginia House Settlement, for which she and Lord Astor had generously contributed a huge sum of money to its opening for the citizens of Plymouth. Virginia House had always been a source of worry as in October 1951 workmen were repairing war damage in the dance hall of the settlement when they found three strange brick mounds a few inches below floor level. The mounds interfered with the laying of the new floor so the men started to demolish them. They found two coffins lying on brick ledges, rotting and falling to dust, more were found and the workmen realised that they were in the roof of a burial chamber. The hall had once been the Batter Street Congregational Church built in 1704; the vaults could have been constructed during the Church's early history. When the floorboards of the former church building were taken up seven coffins were found from the 1700's, they had to be reburied with respect before work could continue. In 1984, once again, there was serious concern for the safety of the building as the main hall was in danger of falling down, hundreds of people who used it for social functions, who had no where else to go, were deeply worried at the prospect of losing their precious centre. A major scheme was launched to raise one hundred thousand pounds to renovate the building. It was a daunting task and it was a case of 'All hands to the boat' and the population responded, everyone organised different functions to raise funds and the 41st Virginia House Girl Guides, Brownies and Cubs held jumble sales to help save the stricken building.

The Virginia House Settlement created many friendships and the volunteers who worked so hard to keep Virginia House as a going concern over the years will never be properly recognised. Lady Astor's influence came to bear on so many genuine citizens; The Western Evening Herald reported in an article in 1987 of a lady Winifred Sampson then in her eightieth year who had started her duties in Lady Astor's time and was given an award for her community work at Plymouth's Virginia House. Receiving a Dartington cut-glass vase with cards and flowers from the chairman, Mr Alistair Tinto of the Virginia House Management Committee in 1987. They commented that she had run the Mother's Club for forty years and the Friday dance club for twenty-two years, she had organised national and international outings and holidays for groups. Such was the dedication of this kind and caring woman, just one story of a volunteer for it is known that there were many who will never be acknowledged for their efforts.

A strategy to raise and promote the profile of Plymouth's Virginia House in order to ensure it's economic survival in the twenty-first century, brought about the appointment of the charity's first Marketing Director in 1989. It was clear the wind of change was blowing away the social structure of the times that the working class Barbican folk knew. Virginia House tried to survive and new groups used the building, the homeless were made welcome and refugees were advised of benefits and counselled to help support them to settle in their new country of choice. In the 1990's Virginia House again became a centre for voluntary work, the base for such organisations as Shelter and the Citizens Advice Bureau, and the precious links with Nancy remained as her granddaughter Alice Astor still sits on the management council and the current Astor Family gave a donation which enabled Virginia House to have a revamped courtyard and garden area. How kind of the Astor family to still uphold the generous nature of their indomitable Grandmother Nancy Astor. The legacy of the little Barbican garden donated by Nancy in the 1930's has once more been brought to life as it has been refurbished and made accessible to the general public, how proud Nancy would have been seeing her Granddaughter perform the opening ceremony.

Into the 1990's and the year 2000 the trust strived to maintain Virginia House for general use but it was clear they were losing the battle as new Health and Safety Regulations meant finding large sums of money to upgrade a listed building. New ideas were introduced to bring Virginia House into the 21st Century. It was one of the leading voluntary sector agencies which provided a wide range of services. Different groups use it as their base, Carers Service, a caring environment, Advocacy Service, a place where young people could discuss their problems, Domiciliary Care Services, Counselling and Training, People's Support Service, Detached Youth Project, interest in young people and their families, The Lighthouse Club, for the over sixties and pensioners, sports for the older generation to keep fit, gentle exercises, indoor bowls, table tennis, short tennis, games such as, bingo, scrabble and cards; dancing, modern, sequence and new dances, craft groups, art classes, home visits for the lonely living on their own, foot care where registered Chiropodists provided an inexpensive service, and arrangements could be made for a Hairdresser to visit disabled seniors in their homes; entertainment with coach trips and holidays. Of all the events that Virginia House stood for, it will be the elderly who will be lost without the social contact they desperately need.

Other events were Social and Leisure Activities, offering occasional holidays and Family Learning, a drop in centre where young adults are helped to manage independently in the community. Redwood Under Eights Centre with parent and toddler sessions, befriending and counselling, crisis counselling, training programmes, building services, conferences and meetings and the Plymouth Citizens Advice Bureau; looking after older people in the Sutton Area, an Out Youth Project and a new plan named, Refugees First. Young people and pensioners could get a free lunch, prepared and cooked by the young people. The training facilities varied, one particular group was the Ridley Courtlands Centre a 'drop in' Centre where young adults with mild learning disabilities were helped to manage independently in the community. They were advised on shopping, household budgeting, job seeking, current affairs, home seeking, personal hygiene and food hygiene. Classes and craft courses were available such as, numeracy, puzzles and games, handcrafts, walks and picnics, visits, computer training and supervised activity holidays.

In April 2001 a one hundred strong Gay Community organised by the Plymouth Pride Forum attended a 'Pink Saturday' conference at Virginia House, its aim was to bring together lesbian, gay and bisexual people. It included workshops, speakers, stalls, information and an Art Gallery. It was designed to bring awareness to the population of the isolation that the gay community experienced and to try to combat homophobia in a bid to make the city a place where the gay community could live and work without prejudice. Virginia House as it is, on the cusp between the past and present, became a dilemma that seemed insuperable to everyone and it was agreed that provision of services from the building was 'economically unsustainable.' In June 2003 eleventh hour talks were being held in a desperate attempt to save Virginia House from total closure, the decision to axe all services was taken because of a funding crisis, and in July 2003 the board of trustees took the decision, with great reluctance, to stop the services provided. Care services were particularly vulnerable and the Virginia House Settlement had talks with the Plymouth Single Regeneration Budget Company and senior members of the Plymouth City Council.

The Princess Royal Trust for Carers, UK, who had used Virginia House as a Centre, had to close down its regular meetings at the site, which put the Care system awareness project in jeopardy. The Citizens Advice Headquarters Bureau was located in Union Street and used Virginia House as another base; the Agency was allocated a yearly grant by the Plymouth City Council. It provided a level of service of help and advice for the needy and vulnerable people; however, it too had to relocate to another area. It was hoped that a new board of trustees could work together with the keepers of the public purse to keep the famous clubhouse open. All the young people who used the centre and the senior citizens clubs will see a seventy-nine year relationship draw to a close. Under threat is the domiciliary care protection for the vulnerable adults, services to refugees and day centres for young people with learning difficulties including all youth work and community activities. It had been in financial difficulties for some time; albeit it was partially funded by a European Social Fund. It is distressing for everyone concerned because it has been made difficult by the new regulations surrounding the costs of maintaining the listed building and adapting it to meet the new requirements set out by the Disability Discrimination Act in 2004. A frustrating time for all genuine Astor trustees and for the Plymouth City Council, choked by the unavailability of funds and the consternation it has caused with Plymouth citizens who have reacted strongly to its threatened closure.

Eighty devastated employees were issued with redundancy notices in May 2003 and told that the building would be put up for sale. The Councillor portfolio holder for social services and other council members and the Virginia House trustees had several meetings to try and save the dying facility. Staffing costs could not be met from the money received from funding organisations. Trustees of Virginia House said that demand was not strong enough to meet running costs. Enquiries by the Charity Commission into how the finances were run totally exonerated the Bretonside Charity, which ran the Virginia House Settlement, and in August 2003 after years of service to Plymothians Virginia House was closed. Lady Astor would have been deeply saddened that her pride and joy and the promised commitment to Plymouth citizens had been completely lost. Now begins the disquiet and the infighting, who to blame? Whilst trustees are not paid, their personal possessions and assets are always vulnerable to sequestration, if they act imprudently, so the decision to close was not taken lightly. Plymouth City Council itself now face an uphill battle to recover hundreds of thousands of pounds paid in grants and contract fees, but it will be an impossible task as no one can get blood from a stone.

In October 2003 the historic Virginia House was sold for more than £1 million to the housing developer Cedar Homes Limited in Plymouth; if pleasant homes are built for the local families that will still honour Lady Astor's dream, however, whether the local people could afford to buy the homes is another matter as with earnings in the region of £8,000-£10,000 here in the South West they could ill afford the asking price of £90,000 per flat. That could mean well off purchasers buying the flats as second homes being so close to the waterfront. Lady Astor's idea was to donate Virginia House for the use of underprivileged people. Listed buildings can often cause great difficulties in planning and incur more than the normal building costs. To keep within guidelines which the Disability Discrimination Act in 2004 required would involve employing expert craftsmen at prices not suitable for a return of the investment. The Virginia House board of Trustees is hoping to keep part of the building open to community groups, which have used the facilities for years.

It could not have been easy for the trustees to have to take this momentous decision but they were faced with an impossible situation and with no rich benefactor to give them financial support, the end result was inevitable. Discussions had been held with a city council Cabinet member, responsible for social services and health, in a desperate attempt to rescue the dying facility to no avail and in the end financial expediency was once again the overall winner. Mounting anger amongst the population, who could not believe that this was happening, only exacerbated the already frustrated board of trustees. Only a short time before the decision to close Virginia House a gentleman called Mr Jean left £10,000 to the Virginia House Dance Club, he and his wife had spent many happy hours dancing at Virginia House and when his wife died he still continued to go to the dance club for company and a little pleasure. On his demise he made this wonderful contribution for the dance club members to have funds for their little social group. When the dancing club had to move out some members queried the missing sum, was it misspent? Was it swallowed up in with the trustee funds or had it been utilised for another project? One has to sympathise with the board for their cause was hopeless; finally it was accepted that it was an end of an era. The board of trustees did everything to ensure that the historic house was sold for the best possible value as there was indeed a very high level of interest following the national marketing campaign carried out in compliance with the Charities Act 1993. A great Plymouth institution has come to an end on the Barbican, at Virginia House settlement, and with it goes all the fond dreams and memories that Lady Astor held dear to her heart, which was to serve the local population. Now lost forever are the harbourside roots that the barbican folk embraced with its history of fisherman and the sea, the real barbican folk who lived, worked, married and raised families have lost a quality of life that can never be replaced.

A refurbished room in the Virginia House area has now been made available for groups who wish to meet to further their activities. In March 2008 friends and members of the Fifty Plus Carers' Support and Social Group were invited to meet at the new venue to enjoy the warm and informal atmosphere and the opportunity to relax over a cup of tea or coffee. A new centre for carers staffed by volunteers and paid for through fund raising has made Virginia House its meeting point and will be the home of city charity Friends and Families of Special Children and the Plymouth branch of the National Carers UK and Active8. The cash was raised from grant-makers, business sponsorship and events. The part of the Virginia House Settlement lying idle for four years is now a hub of activity as the carers manifesto to form a base for sixty families in the Friends and Families group supporting other carers needs is well underway. In addition to a huge central room, there is a large office and a multi-sensory room named after Sheila Olive, who worked tirelessly in her lifetime to create a unique centre at Bretonside (sadly Mrs Olive died in March 2008). Also available in the building is a 'quiet room' for counselling, and kitchen and toilet. Furniture was donated from generous benefactors, and to link with its past, pictures from the glory days of the Virginia House Settlement, found in a cupboard, adorn the walls. It is hoped the charity's mission is successful for their dreams match those of Lady Astor.

The redevelopment of part of the historic Virginia House building in March 2008 into apartments once again revealed historical artefacts in the complex when workmen discovered unusual anomalies. They had, in fact, unearthed more ancient tombs containing human remains. This involved the police and crime scene officers attending the site on the corner of Batter Street and Looe Street to ascertain if a crime had been committed. Investigation revealed that the remains were very ancient which allowed the Church representatives and the council's Historic Environment Officer to survey the area. It was agreed to allow the bones to remain and to leave the tomb untouched. They could, of course, be part of the original tombs found in 1951.

FORMER MEMBERS REMEMBER

Mrs Lilian Becker recalls "My mother attended the Mothers Club for over fifty years and served on the committee with her friend Mrs Winifred Sampson arranging outings and holidays, in England and abroad. One highlight was to have tea at Lady Astor's home at Cliveden, Buckinghamshire, which was a trip everyone wanted to go on, as tea with Lady Astor was special. Although Mother and her friend were not dancers themselves, on Wednesday, Thursday and Friday they use to sit at the door and collect the entrance fees and mark the register, they both had made so many friends over the years but sadly most have passed away. As the club was near to the Barbican it had a great following from the local people; the wardens during part of the war years 1940-1944 were Mr and Mrs Howson. Every one pulled together in those years and the people were proud of Virginia House and all that it stood for. In 1940 when France fell to the German Invaders the French refugees were seen standing around the wireless set in Virginia House, many of them in tears heartbroken at the news. Virginia House made them welcome and the Lord Mayor's welfare fund came to the rescue in supplying their needs and Nancy would speak to them and make them welcome. Lord and Lady Astor did a lot for the people of Plymouth especially the young. They bought land at Prince Rock and had it converted into playing fields. It is still there today in the year 2008, albeit, it has been modernised, part being a playing field and part as a play park for the very young children. I remember going there in 1933 for our sports activities once a week from school, and each year we held our annual sports day, as did many other schools in Plymouth. During the war the Royal Air Force also used the Astor playing field as a balloon station. Lord and Lady Astor had property built at Mount Gould (Plymouth) and a new housing estate was created and it became known as the Astor Estate, which included the Astor Institute, a kind of club also for the local people on the estate. The houses were for working class families with children, today in the year 2008 many have purchased these houses and have modernised them with newer facilities."

Edward Clifton, a Plymouth pensioner, has always remembered his happy days at Virginia House by saying, "I benefited a great deal from Lady Astor's kindness to Plymouth, at Virginia House where I boxed as a young lad. In later years even my children went to Virginia House for judo classes. Nancy kept many generations of children off the streets and out of trouble, so she has left a lasting impression on me."

Mrs Gladys Trewin (nèe Ford) remembered her early days at Virginia House; born and bred in Batter Street her father was a fisherman who, with his brother Jack and nephew Bill, was the boat owner of a large Hooker named Silver Dart. Gladys tells her story, "Bill lived in Bates Building, which was in Palace Street, with his wife Jasmin and his family. Jasmin was for many years a good worker at Virginia House and she was well known. My parents had a large family and we all attended Sunday school at the church, which is now Virginia House and the gym underneath was a cemetery. There were hundreds of children in Sutton Ward in those days, with nowhere to go in the evenings. Then Lady Astor bought the Bennett's Flour premises and had it changed into a club, which she named the Victory Club in Peacock Lane. Children flocked to join and I was one of them. We were kept occupied every evening. For the girls there were classes in dressing making, cookery, dramatics and a choir. For the boys there were classes in drill, gymnastics, boxing and carpentry. At the opening and naming of the Virginia House by Lady Astor (who was well cheered) she spoke of her love of children having a week's holiday away from home. Mrs Victor Winnicott and all her friends formed the Ways and Means Committee and decided to have a country fair in the large hall, with fruit and cream teas. Through hard work they made hundreds of pounds and the country fair continued every year for many years. When the war broke out in 1939 it made quite a change to the attendance, quite a lot of people lost their homes, others left the area, but some still came to Virginia House. Then the new housing estates were built well away from the city and community centres were being built near them so that people stopped coming to Virginia House, also a good many of the older generation had passed away and the younger generation did not express such an interest in Virginia House. I shall never forget the fun I had and those memories will live on in my heart, as will the memories of a grand lady who did so much for the people of Plymouth - Lady Astor."

Seared into the mind of Enid Ware, a young one hundred years old in 2007, is a very special memory that will, in her lifetime, never be forgotten. She recalls the event, which forever held Lady Astor dear to her heart. "It took place in the late nineteen twenties one Christmas, Nancy Astor had given a big party to local war orphans of the First World War at Virginia House. There was an enormous Christmas tree laden with presents, Lady Astor saw me looking at the tree with bright eyes and then she picked me up and asked me what I would like from the tree. I had my eyes on a very pretty doll and I pointed to it wistfully, she called to a helper and asked her to get it down for me, it was lovely and Lady Astor held me in her arms for a few minutes talking to me and then she gave me a big kiss. My view today is that Lady Astor did so much for the people who were part of Virginia House settlement, taking people from the slums and putting them into nice houses with gardens. Barbican folk still hold in their hearts the affection they feel for Nancy and for what she did for them."

Mrs Jean Willis remembers Nancy Astor from when she was nine years old as she belonged to the Virginia House Youth Club. Jean states that, "Nancy was a vibrant person and you always knew when she was about. My mother belonged to the Ladies Thursday Dancing Club, which Nancy used to attend regularly. The ladies used to do old time dancing and Nancy would partner any lady, I saw my Mother dance with her often. It was the Astors who gave the club a mansion house called Prince Hall at Dartmoor for the children of the Barbican and the Scattered Homes orphaned children and children from other areas. They would have the chance to go there on holiday for

£1 or 25 shillings a week (depending on the age of the child.) Nancy always paid for the orphan children to go there on holiday. It was a lovely place and for just a little while the children ran free. Nancy had parcels sent from America with clothes, sweets and chocolate powder. My niece (then Jennifer Tapper) won a prize for an essay she wrote on a famous American General. The prize was presented by Nancy herself at Martin's Gate School. It was for the whole of Plymouth and the prize consisted of a concise Oxford Dictionary, an Oxford world Atlas, and an Oxford book of quotations."

Spoken word by a lady who wishes to remain anonymous. "Nancy attended the Virginia House Settlement in 1929 to open a country house fair in aid of the children's holiday fund and received an enthusiastic welcome. For the ladies, they were really interested in the fashion of the day, curious to see what Nancy would wear. She wore a gown of navy and figured crépe-de-chine, with a navy straw hat relieved with a touch of pink. During her visit she remarked; "Politics may come and go, but character remains, and a nation depends for its quality upon the character of its children." On another visit she wore a silky drapery of dark blue and white, with a group of matching carnations. Nancy, on her frequent visits to functions, would always call at Virginia House where Mrs Alice Fiddick held her sequence dance class on a Tuesday afternoon. Lady Astor purposely called in for a cup of tea and a chat with the barbican folk. When she made an entrance she filled the whole room with her presence and she generated vitality, everyone would be aware of her being. On one such occasion Nancy took off her coat and put it on a chair and one of the weekly regulars at the class, as a dare, picked it up and put it on. Without hesitation she said "Your coat fits me perfectly, are you going to let me have it my Lady?" Lady Astor replied, "Not bloody likely, that coat was the first present my husband gave me and I am keeping it!" It raised quite a furore; as Nancy was quite capable of changing her language to suit the common folk and she could on occasion drop the odd swear word as well as any trooper." The spritely, dancing ninety-three-year-old, who still attended the dance every Tuesday at Virginia House until her tired legs gave out and Virginia House closed, remembers that incident as though it was yesterday.

Lady Astor's dream has finally come to an end. Perhaps it is the wind of change and the social structure of our society today indicated that this type of facility is no longer required and as Robert Greene (1560-1592) quoted, 'Time is…Time was…Time is past…'

LADY ASTOR AT VIRGINIA HOUSE COUNTRY FAIR

THE large hall of Virginia House Settlement was packed for the opening ceremony of the Country Fair, which is held annually to obtain funds for the children's holiday weeks at Maker Camp.

Lady Astor, who opened the Fair, said that she thought everybody must know by now what Virginia House had done and continued to do. And if anyone knew nothing about the Holiday Home, she would advise them to go to Maker Camp and to see for themselves the way in which the children enjoyed themselves there.

Mr. E. Stanley Leatherby (chairman) thanked all who had helped in connection with the Fair, paying a special tribute to the work of Miss Lippert, the Warden.

Lord Astor was also present, and a vote of thanks to Lord and Lady Astor was proposed by the Mayor and seconded by the Hon. Alice Brand.

Many attractive stalls, gaily decorated with coloured festoons, were arranged in the hall, and the billiard-room had been converted into a café, in which prefects of the Girls' Club did their part as waitresses.

A special stall—the work of the Cripples' Handicraft Class—attracted many admirers.

Music in the afternoon was played by Miss Vera Budge and Miss Freda Mee.

Over £100, including donations, is the happy reward of the effort.

M. F. W.

Photo: Courtesy Western Independent & The Plymouth Reference Library

Lady Astor at Virginia House Plymouth July 1932.
A great champion for the children of the poor.
The working classes had great respect for this
formidable lady. John Boaden (Grandfather).

Senior Citizens Christmas party at Virginia House 1952. Photo courtesy of Virginia House trustees

known for her role in ...ath, Stephen Ward.

Lady Astor wearing a musical print dress and tilted hat. Her neatly pinned hair and radiant smile exudes the warmth she had for people.

CHAPTER FIFTEEN
THE ASTOR HOMES

The penalty of success is to be bored by the people who used to snub you! *Nancy Astor 1879-1964*

The first Viscount William Waldorf Astor (1848-1919) set eyes on the 13th Century Hever Castle in Kent in 1901 and immediately fell in love with it, subsequently, he bought the medieval Castle of Hever and 640 acres of land in 1903. William Waldorf Astor's immediate desire was for the restoration of the Castle, which he undertook with great enthusiasm. Ever the perfectionist with energy and foresight he completed the restoration to his liking during the years 1901-1903, he had built a Tudor style villa which contained one hundred rooms. His visionary dream involved altering the bed of the river Eden and a public road was diverted to enable the project to be completed. In 1916 he was created first Baron of Hever Castle and in 1919 became Viscount Astor. He died in the same year and his title went to his eldest son Waldorf. In 1981 the Astor Family and their trustees decided to sell Hever Castle and the whole property was bought by a Yorkshire based private company. The Astor Suite Exhibition contains the memorabilia and possessions of four generations of the Astor family and this is due to the generosity of the present Lord Astor of Hever.

Colonel James Elliot bought the Plymouth Hoe Fields in 1820 and soon the land was developed and the soldier is remembered today in the naming of Elliot Terrace and Elliot Street. He died, unmarried, in 1892, and the property passed to his cousin Tracey Elliot, the property stayed in the family into the 20th century. In 1907, Waldorf and Nancy Astor had previously lived for a few months, at the Grand Hotel on the Hoe and had rented one or two houses during their first visit to the city. They bought number two, and number three Elliot Terrace, a five storey Mansion, on Plymouth Hoe as a permanent home in 1908. The Astor's later sold number two Elliot Terrace.

When Waldorf, toured the City of Plymouth in 1910 as Conservative candidate with a view to adopting the vacant seat of Sutton Division, having already been chosen by the City Selection Committee, he decided that he liked the city and its people. He became Plymouth's Unionist Parliamentary Member of Parliament in 1910. Nancy, meanwhile, immediately fell in love with Plymouth and openly declared "Waldorf, it is here that we must pitch our tent." Nancy later became the first woman MP to sit in Parliament. 3, Elliot Terrace, was to be their Plymouth home for many years as she and her husband Waldorf lived there until his death in 1952. The building of the beautiful Elliot Terrace houses took place towards the end of the last century by leading Victorian property developer and Architect of the time (Honest) John Pethick

(1827-1904) 3, Elliot Terrace, is considered to be one of the finest examples of a Victorian Mansion in the city. It commands a fine view of the Hoe and has a wonderful vista of Plymouth Sound. In 1898-1900 John Pethick became Mayor of Plymouth. He was also responsible for the building of the Duke of Cornwall Hotel and in 1880 the construction of the Grand Hotel on the Esplanade. The manner of his death was tragic as, at the age of seventy-six, his horse drawn carriage ran out of control with him holding the reins. Eventually the carriage overturned in Lockyer Street, Plymouth, and the injuries he sustained led to his death shortly afterwards.

The modest staff at Elliot Terrace, in comparison to the number of staff employed at Cliveden were content with performing their duties and the relationship with the Astors was cordial, so all in all it was a happy household. Nancy's daily ritual of a cold bath, winter or summer, followed by a Christian Science reading and then departure to her various duties was programmed with precision. Converted to Christian Science in 1914 she was a strong believer and when taken ill on one occasion John Grigg author of the book 'Nancy Astor' first published in 1980, noted that she quoted from her sick bed. She said, "Whenever a soul is ready for enlightenment, and awaits it humbly, I believe that the answer is somewhere to hand: The Teacher comes." Christian scientists have a strong belief in the healing power that comes from God, albeit, they do support the works of doctors and others in the medical profession. Nancy found Christian Science practical and fulfilling.

During their marriage Waldorf and Nancy bought number 4 St James's Square, Westminster, London, which remained their London home until after the Second World War. From 1912 to 1942 the house was owned and occupied by the second Viscount Astor. In 1942 it was requisitioned, and from 1943 to 1945 was used as the London headquarters of the Free French forces. From September 1947 it had been occupied by the Arts Council of Great Britain: in 1948 Lord Astor sold the house to the Ministry of Works at a low price on condition that it should be restored and preserved as the headquarters of the Arts Council. It is now the Naval and Military Club.

Waldorf Viscount Astor, during the Second World War in 1942, gave the Astor home at Cliveden to the National Trust and endowed it, so that it could be maintained forever at his expense. His sole condition was that he should be allowed to live there and his heirs if they wished to do so. They continued to live there until Lord Astor died in 1952 and their son William (Bill) Astor, the third Viscount, lived there until his death in 1966 when it ceased to be the family home. Waldorf Astor opened the house and gardens to the public and preserved in perpetuity the Cliveden Woods. He also expressed the hope that, if later on his descendants decided to leave the house, the Government would use it, as he had used it, as an International meeting place. Waldorf had been elected again as Lord Mayor of Plymouth on 9th November 1942, which was to be his fourth term of office in that role. It would have been difficult to maintain Cliveden whilst still living at 3, Elliot Terrace. Cliveden Hotels Ltd turned it into Britain's only five red stars AA Hotel with a Michelin Star restaurant. In 2007 new properties are to be developed on the Cliveden Estate in Taplow, Buckinghamshire, in liaison with Countryside Properties to provide eco-friendly homes of quality and to create an environmentally sustainable development. The new Cliveden Village is to be built on the 367-acre estate overlooking the River Thames on the former site of the Canadian Red Cross Memorial Hospital. The profits from the properties will help the National Trust to preserve and protect the Cliveden estate.

The Astor family home at Cliveden, Buckinghamshire, consisted of 370 acres and for nearly four generations the Astors had the longest tenure of any of the families that have occupied the house. Chatelaine Nancy, Lady Astor, gave the house and the land to the National Trust and Nancy stipulated that the land should be used to generate income and the mansion today is a thriving hotel. The Daily Telegraph newspaper 2003, in a published article, stated that the National Trust was accused by some of its members of fostering a Disney like attitude towards Cliveden by deciding to lease fifteen acres of land to build houses on the estate. Objectors had stated that the National Trust is more interested in making money out of the historic site and described the decision as the 'antithesis' of the organisation purposes. In its defence the Trust stated that the houses would be environmental-friendly family homes and some would be managed by Housing Associations, they also pointed out that the proposed site is separated by woodland from the Grade 1 listed mansion. The National Trust intends to put the proceeds from the housing agreement into an endowment fund to maintain Cliveden. It must be difficult to safeguard an historic site that requires huge sums of money for its maintenance, the land is held inalienably by the trust, which means that it has heritage value and can never be sold. To keep it for future generations it is important to embrace modern living with the beauty of this lovely site and all aspects of securing the financial funds needed by the National Trust to maintain what is a huge commitment must be considered.

Waldorf died in 1952, and Nancy continued to live in Elliot Terrace, but found it hard without her beloved husband so decided to move to a smaller home. On the 3rd February 1958, Lady Astor gave 3, Elliot Terrace, to the City of Plymouth as a residence for future Lord Mayors. In October 1959 the Town Clerk Mr. S. Lloyd Jones, told the Special Purposes Committee of the Council that if they accepted Lady Astor's offer of the house, she would allow it to be used for a fair period as a house of reception for distinguished visitors and for accommodating them for their stay. If after a trial period the Council found these arrangements were not practicable, she would leave it to the Council to deal with the property as they may think advisable. One city Councillor Mr Gerald Wingate thought that the imposing building should be put to more constructive use. One has to remember that the upkeep now falls on public expense and whatever Council is in power it is a formidable task to keep the house in tip-top condition bearing in mind the ozone environment in which the house is located. Mr Wingate suggested that a national competition might be organised, to bring the name of Plymouth to the whole country. The idea suggested was an essay writing contest, the prize being a week's holiday as a guest of the City and using the house as accommodation. The trial period for its use as a reception centre for civic visitors was ended in 1961. There was a suggestion that no decision about the future of the house be made until it is known whether Plymouth will have a University, then perhaps it could be used possibly as the Dean's Residence or for members of the faculty.

3, Elliot Terrace, opened its doors for public tours in August 1994 on the 75th anniversary of Nancy's election to Parliament. Some furniture, ornaments, personal photographs, books and other family mementoes are just as Lady Astor left them. It is now used for Lord Mayor's functions and cabinet meetings for the local council, also for special conferences. The Lord Mayor is allowed to use the house twelve weekends a year as a residence. The interior of the house has been beautifully re-furbished and the rooms have all been named after places in the Astor's heart. Bedrooms and guest rooms hold the names, Langhorne, Mirador, Lady Astor's room and the Duke of Kent's room. The house has been tastefully decorated and all the furniture kept in pristine condition. Only one piece of furniture shows a damaged area, a writing bureau which still bears the scorched mark from an incendiary bomb in March 1941 from the bombing during the Second World War, the bureau is now in the former Duke of Kent's room. The re-furbishing of the house is a credit to the Plymouth City council for maintaining such an historical Grade 1 house, which is very difficult at public expense, as any alteration must obtain full approval from planners being a listed building. The exterior of the house does require painting as the weathering conditions takes its toll; the City Fathers have a difficult task in finding the funds to complete the project on a regular cycle.

Today the building is used to entertain civic guests, or as a temporary stay for circuit Judges who stay overnight in the Lady Astor Room. The visiting circuit judges stay at the house with their entourage when they have special court cases. In February 2007 a welcome dinner was held at 3, Elliot Terrace, hosted by Tudor Evans the leader of the Labour Council, Plymouth, with guests from the City Council, Regional Agencies and from Plymouth University. The function was held for the representatives of the Chinese United Kingdom Science Parks training programme, the group stayed at the Duke of Cornwall Hotel. The former Astor home building still holds some of Plymouth's most valuable Astor historical memorabilia. Outstanding among the books that Nancy once read is 'The Analects of Confucius' translated by W.E. Soothill of Oxford University. Inside the cover is an autograph, Nancy Astor, it is clear that she had read most of the classics. Having read the books she would sign her autograph inside the front cover; another author whose books she read was John Bunyan. Nancy was a great reader and there to be seen on the bookshelf in 3, Elliot Terrace, is the book 'Daily Readings from the Moffatt translation of the Bible' In

1992 the decision was taken to remove the portrait painted by F.H. Shepherd, of Nancy entering the House of Commons, from the Astor Room in the Guildhall and place it in her former home 3, Elliot Terrace, where it would be viewed by more visitors and could be kept under better security arrangements.

In June 2007 a citizen wrote to the local newspaper to express his disgust at the current state of 3, Elliot Terrace, now the property of the Plymouth city council. He stated that the exterior of the once magnificent building is desperately in need of redecoration and it is the shabbiest building in what is a beautiful terrace of Victorian Houses. He wrote to the Lord Mayor to bring it to his attention in the hope that such a generous legacy to the city should be maintained in the manner Lady Astor would wish and not appear so neglected. It is considered as one of the valuable and historic assets we have.

FAMOUS GUESTS

The Astors entertained many famous guests during their time in the building, King George V1 and the late Queen Mother, former Prime Minister Winston Churchill, writer and playwright George Bernard Shaw, young John F. Kennedy (in his twenties) who was in later years to become President of the United States, and England's own Lawrence of Arabia. In later years the civic dignitaries entertained Sir Francis Chichester in the former Astor residence. In 1931 Plymouth was a port of call for the transatlantic liners from New York, the arrival in May of the Cunard liner Mauritania disembarked the popular comedian and former silent screen movie star Charlie Chaplin. Greeted by the media and the press Charlie was also met by Nancy Astor who welcomed him to the city. Lady Astor accompanied Charlie Chaplin on the Great Western Railway Tender the Sir Richard Grenville to Millbay Docks. Mindful of the fact that he would be boarding the ocean passenger train to Paddington and thus deprive many Plymothians of seeing this world famous celebrity in person, she persuaded Charlie to visit her new Virginia House project. He agreed provided it was a quick visit with a fast car, the occasion was a success and he rejoined the boat train at North Road Station. Such was Nancy's persuasive power to create an occasion to please many local people.

Norman Hine a Plymouth resident recalls another opportunity that arose in November 1931: Whilst Lord and Lady Astor were dining with Chaplin in London, the Astors invited Charlie down to Plymouth as their guest for the weekend. A hectic round of visits was arranged, first to the Ballard Institute, delighting hundreds of boys, including my brother who reminisced about the antics Charlie performed for the boys who were absolutely thrilled. Next they visited Virginia House and the Palace Theatre. Wherever Charlie Chaplin went the cheering crowds welcomed him right up to the final send off at the station. A lot of happy citizens had to thank Lady Astor for creating such an event, they would never forget, proof indeed that the memory is still so fresh in the minds of those who remember seventy-two years later.

Another famous guest was Aircraftman Shaw, (formerly Colonel Lawrence) otherwise TE Lawrence (Lawrence of Arabia) known as a man of letters, and, on occasion, he visited Elliot Terrace as guest of the Astors. The Plymouth Radford and Hooe Lake Preservation Association's newsletter by Gerald Wasley in September 2003 refers to Lawrence and literary friends and recalls his many attributes. This conservation group is dedicated to the history of Hooe and Radford and it is remembered that when Lawrence was stationed at RAF Mountbatten he spent some of his free time translating books in his attic office above the station's workshop. Lawrence was an avid reader of classical books and earned extra income translating Homer's Odyssey to pay for alterations to his cottage at Clouds Hill, Dorset. There were many occasions when literary friends and publishers visited him and he would take them out and Nancy Astor would often accompany them. The literary genius and socialist George Bernard Shaw, a Nobel Prize winner for literature, was also a friend of Lawrence and Nancy Astor. She entertained her friend George Bernard Shaw at Elliot Terrace when he came to Plymouth to open Astor Hall in October 1929.

Another well-known writer who visited was E.M. Forster, whose fame is associated with his novels Passage to India and Howards End. Forster had a relative living in Plymouth and he would combine his visit between his great aunt and Lawrence. In good weather the two men would go out in Lawrence's speedboat, crossing Plymouth Sound to Mount Edgecumbe and, using a key given to Lawrence by the Earl of Mount Edgecumbe, they used a private entrance to wander around the beautiful gardens. The two men visited the Barbican, and sometimes Nancy Astor would join them, examining the old buildings. Lawrence, Lady Astor and E.M. Forster would, on occasion, have lunch at Mount Batten at the Wing Commander's residence. It was Lawrence who read and corrected the printer's proof of Yeats-Brown's book the Bengal Lancer. Later the rights of the book was sold to Hollywood which resulted in the popular film 'Lives of a Bengal Lancer.' Controversy would always follow Nancy wherever she went or whatever she did as Nancy was seen in the company of Yeats-Brown who was reputed to have fascist sympathies. He was at one time Editor of the Spectator and some believed that he was drawn to communism, and as Nancy mixed with these people doubtful citizens would express an undercurrent of disquiet. However, her love of England and America could never be challenged and it would indeed be a travesty if the rumours were allowed to blight a lady whose loyalty to Plymouth was second to none.

It was clear that Nancy was fascinated with Lawrence; he would often give her a lift on his Brough Superior motorbike, between visits to Cliveden and Plymouth. Cocking her leg over the seat with inelegant aplomb, the bike would whiz along, but Lawrence and Nancy were quite unperturbed at the public dismay for her safety.

Waldorf Astor often remarked that he was quite worried at Nancy's wild venture but had come to accept that she enjoyed the thrill of the ride, however, he was to be proved right when Lawrence was killed in a motor bike accident in 1935. Nancy was saddened by his death as they had become good friends and he would often cheer her up when she was worried or stressed, now his laughter was no more and one of England's heroes was gone. From then on the Astor's two favourite cars, the Phantom 11 Rolls Royce or the Humber Landauette were used.

Lady Astor had three homes in her retirement years; the London home at 35 Hill Street, Berkeley Square, London, which Waldorf had bought her when he sold 4, St James Square, to the Arts Council in 1945 and which is now the premises of the Naval & Military Club, then in 1958 she moved to 100 Eaton Square, London, a large flat comprising the whole of the first floor of number 100 and the house next door. Nancy had never lived in a flat before and found it strange to begin with especially as her staff did not have their own entrances. The furnishings were top class with Louis Quinze and Louis Seize furniture that made the flat comfortable to live in. Surrounded by her beloved 18th Century continental china and Chinese hardstone carvings in jade or crystal, on the walls hung her favourite English Old Masters Portraits, she was a great lover of the Arts. Nancy spent most of her time at the very fine house at Sandwich, Kent, called Rest Harrow and she would only meet Waldorf for public occasions. Rest Harrow was mainly used as her summer holiday home, and Charles Pyrnne her former footman remembers going down to Sandwich for about six weeks every year. Nancy had moved to Eaton Square after she left Hill Street and she wrote a letter in May 1961 to Charles Prynne who was then in America as a staff member to the British Embassy in Washington. In the letter she wrote that she moved into this apartment, which was the first floor of four houses so it was a very big apartment, she decided to move to make things easier for the staff as it was on all one level, whereas Hill Street had five floors.

During her retirement years Nancy's close friend Joan, Lady Altrincham (1897-1987) (formerly Lady Grigg) played an important part in the happy social life of Rest Harrow. Mary Stocks was also a frequent visitor, and she would stay for a while as a guest. The Marchesa Casa Maury who stayed at Rest Harrow (and had been the former mistress of the Duke of Windsor before Wallis Simpson arrived on the scene) was a comparatively new friend and during the long summer weeks took charge of the comings and goings of guests and indeed of Nancy herself. One particular evening the three resident guests staying at Rest Harrow, Baroness Stocks, Marchesa Casa Maury and Lady Altrincham, who all liked a glass of whisky as an evening drink, and whisky was then one of the few amenities not provided for guests, thought to have a quiet drink together. Nancy's temperance faith relaxed somewhat when she had visitors when they discreetly were given a small Dubonnet. Nancy too would be given a glass of Dubonnet believing it was not an alcoholic drink and convinced that it was a teetotal beverage. Nancy discovered that she liked it very much and friends were careful not to tell her it's real potency. Nancy's bedroom was immediately over the big sitting room where the guests had assembled for the evening, when retired to her bed she was in the habit of turning on the radio sufficiently loud to be heard in the room below. This would usually mean that she was not likely to return to the company and would soon be retiring for the night. Quietly the Marchesa fetched a bottle of whisky from her own bedroom and they indulged in a quiet drink. The women felt as though they were waiting for the head teacher to come through the door and they could not help but giggle at their indiscretion.

As Nancy's health began to deteriorate it was not possible for her to live alone, although her staff were very loyal and caring, it was prudent to advise her to live with a family member so as they could monitor her safety and finances. Nancy's last home was with her daughter, the Countess of Ancaster, at Grimsthorpe Castle, Lincolnshire. As she lay dying, the formerly vibrant woman, defiant to the end, and surrounded by all her children at her bedside said to her son, "Jakie, is it my birthday or am I dying?" She died on Saturday 2nd May 1964, 84 years of age. The 'Sunshine of Sutton' was gone, and in Plymouth many broken hearted people cried at her passing.

Photo: copyright Tony Knowles Design

2008, Plymouth City Council funded the redecoration of the exterior of the former Astor home at 3 Elliot Terrace, The Hoe, Plymouth. Now restored to its former glory it enhances the splendour of the Hoe Promenade.

CHAPTER SIXTEEN
ASTOR INSTITUTE & ASTOR HALL

"Change is not made without inconvenience, even from worse to better."
Samuel Johnson (1709-1784).

Lord and Lady Astor bought the Astor Institute and gave the Astor Youth Club Institute at Beaumont Road at the eastern end of Mount Gould, Plymouth, to the people who lived in the area. Nancy, Lady Astor opened it in 1929. The Mount Gould area was named after Colonel William Gould who died of wounds received during the Civil War after the Sabbath Day Battle. Lord and Lady Astor had arranged for the gift of the Astor Institute to be given to Plymothians 'in perpetuity.' It was to be linked with the Astor Housing Estate for all to use. The Plymouth Corporation and Lord Astor had hoped it would provide the foundation in which to encompass the community. Sadly the Institute was demolished in 1988 after falling into disrepair and attracting vandals. Over the years the Youth Club proved to be a lifeline for the working classes of Plymouth where friendships and social activities were formed and enjoyed. During the war years it was valuable to the citizens as a meeting point and kept up the morale of the worn torn citizens suffering bombing and destruction of our beautiful city.

Edward Clifton, now a Plymouth pensioner, remembers vividly as a young man the Astor Institute being used as an emergency rest home during the Second World War when the area of Mount Gould had been bombed. He tells his story, "The bombs had landed on Beaumont Road and the allotments that is now part of Mount Gould Hospital. My family home at 33 Mount Gould Terrace suffered badly as the whole front of the house was completely blown off and several of the adjoining houses were also badly damaged. My mother, father, and two older sisters, were accommodated at the Astor Institute while the houses were being repaired, and another seven families from the same area were also billeted there. The gymnasium had been converted into temporary rooms by hanging curtains hung at intervals between each family, for some measure of privacy. There was a canteen where hot food and welcome cups of tea were available. A luxury we were able to enjoy was a shower and everyone made a beeline to be first to the shower while the water was hot. We were all very pleased when our homes were repaired and we could get back to our own houses, however, with the bombing likely to continue I was evacuated to Tiverton, but homesickness and missing my family meant that I came home back to Plymouth before the war ended."

Edward reminisces about the Astor Institute by saying, "At the rear of the building there was a hut where RAF men were billeted to look after the barrage balloon permanently floating over the Institute, there were times when it would break loose and seeing the servicemen trying to recover the floating menace often led to peals of laughter. Lady Astor bought the RAF hut in 1944 and it was for some time used by the scouts. The Institute was a hub of the community when I was growing up; there was a great deal of sport and other activities for the young people to do. Some of the rooms were used as offices and in one of the offices was the lady in charge of the Astor Housing Estate and having her close by meant that our damaged houses would be taken care of fairly quickly. At the Astor Institute I did gymnastics, played table tennis, became a player in the football team winning many trophies and played snooker and darts. I even learnt ballroom dancing with my older sister and dances were held with live bands. At the end and just after the war dances were held for the doctors and nurses of Mount Gould Hospital and they also played tennis on the Astor Institute tennis court."

LADY ASTOR HOUSING TRUST.

FOUNDED BY VISCOUNT AND VISCOUNTESS ASTOR ON DECEMBER 30TH, 1924

OBJECTS

The provision of Houses for large families under conditions which secure to the Tenants as a community

(1) A share in the administration of the Estate on which they reside.

(2) An interest in the efficient maintenance of the property comprising the Estate.

(3) The use of Social, Educational and Recreative facilities.

Note.—The Deeds of the Trust provide for elected tenants becoming members of the Court of Governors of the Estate.

TYPES OF HOUSES.			Rental per week. (Exclusive of Rates)	
			s.	d.
A3	Ground Floor. First Floor.	Living Room, Scullery 3 Bedrooms	Bath, W.C. ..	8 9
A4	Ground Floor. First Floor.	Living Room, Scullery 4 Bedrooms	Bath, W.C. ..	9 6
B3	Ground Floor. First Floor.	Parlour, Living Room, Scullery 3 Bedrooms	Bath, W.C.	10 6
B4	Ground Floor. First Floor.	Parlour, Living Room, Scullery 4 Bedrooms	Bath, W.C.	11 3

Note.—The Standard Garden area allotted to each Tenant is approximately 300 yards super ; area in excess of this may be rented by arrangement with and consent of the Governors of the Trust.

By kind permission of a former resident

Document of the Lady Astor Housing Trust 1924

The Astor Housing Estate at Mount Gould had been a blessing for the poor people of Plymouth, rescuing them from the slums and giving decent homes for children to live in. The Astor Housing Estate was sold in 1952 and the article in the Western Morning News on the 13th August 1952 revealed how heartbroken Nancy was at the loss of the housing estate and what it stood for. She said; "It had been started as an experiment, we thought for life, but has failed because of the blindness of a few. During the war, when costs were going up, the governors of the Astor estate asked the tenants if they would voluntarily pay higher rents to save the estate, alas, it was not to be. The majority would do it, but the minority would not, so it is that minority that has made the whole of this estate come into the hands of other people. Lord Astor was deeply upset but we could not do anything else. A dissatisfied minority could spoil the conditions for the majority. That is what is happening in public life today, they generally are the people who want to change everything - not for the better but for the worse. I am truly sorry, because I have seen such happiness out of the Astor Housing, many of the people came from rooms, with four or five children, I have seen those children grow up."

In 1954 Lady Astor spoke at the Astor Institute saying, "Plymouth would never have been rebuilt without my husband and he gave his life for it." Nancy had thought that the Astor Institute would survive for future generations in the same format, yet times were changing and social entertainment was taking a different tack and the wind of change had made the Astor Institute outmoded. The Institute continued into the fifties and sixties and in 1956 members of that generation had a new roller skating rink at the Astor Institute. What fun the members had, and often youth bands performed at the Institute and many a potential musician gained experience by playing there.

Another sporting club utilising the Astor Institute in the late 1960s was the Bushido Karate Club now known as the Plymouth Shotokan Club. At the Institute they practiced their traditional Shotokan Karate moves that originated from the Far East and the Karate club in Plymouth proved to be very popular. Because of its popularity notable specialist Karate Instructors visited the club from the Japanese Karate Association and two of the top Karate instructors who visited the venues were Sensei Kanasawa and Sensei Takahashi. Later in the 1970's the Club changed its name and called itself the Civil Service Karate Club and events were held at the Civil Service Sports and Social Club in Beacon Park, Plymouth. The Club moved again in 1974 when they practiced their sport from St Simon's Church Hall in St Judes, Plymouth; there they were registered as the Plymouth Shotokan Karate Centre. The popularity of the Astor Institute began to wane in the 1970s and the building was becoming derelict so sporting clubs were looking elsewhere to hold their meetings. The building was eventually sold to Mount Gould Hospital in 1977 with the agreement of the Charity Commissioners.

Former members remember with affection the happy times they had at the old Institute particularly in the war years when many friendships were formed. Club members remembered their meetings several times a week. There was a very successful Girls Club and they loved dancing and on occasion Lady Astor asked some of the young ladies to teach the sailors how to dance; of course the girls were quite pleased to oblige. The Institute had a superb gymnasium and it was always in full use.

Such happy memories recalled, being able to spend the evening doing what they liked best and the cost being so reasonable, sixpence (old English money) was the entrance fee. Sandra Monaghan of Plymouth was a regular at the Centre in 1963 she remembers that there was a sports hall where five a side football and netball was played and roller skating took place; a snooker room with a full size snooker table, a table tennis room, a tuck shop, a television room where occasionally cards were played (sometimes for money) and a room with a record player where members could bring their own records to play. New single records were frequently bought so the members could dance or jive to the latest hits and many parties were arranged. The Astor Institute held many happy memories for those who passed through its doors; many met their future wives or husbands at the venue.

The Astor Community Centre in Mount Gould championed by hard working organisers still keep alive Nancy Astor's ideas in providing facilities for the ordinary people. In 2005 they supported a charity campaign for 'Do it for Devon' with various entertainment on offer such as, bowling, circus skills workshops and cream teas, among other attractions, Nancy would have approved! Plymouth has received many benefactions from Lord and Lady Astor. The Astor Institute, which cost £10,000 pounds, provided recreation amenities; these sums of money in the 1920s/1930s could be measured in hundreds of thousands of pounds in value today. Near the site of the old Astor Institute are two Venton memorial stones, one under the other, which were placed by Plymouth Age Concern in memory of William and Patricia Venton, the second stone was laid by Mrs Patricia Venton in memory of her husband and the centre was officially opened in November 1992.

In March 2008 Plymouth's former British and Commonwealth middleweight boxing champion Scott Dann launched an appeal to encourage local businessmen and women in Plymouth to consider replacing the former Astor Community Centre in Mount Gould with a multi-purpose fitness suite, housing martial arts, boxing and aerobics, he is also hoping to launch a fitness academy project sporting a gymnasium. The remaining dilapidated hut will require a lot of investment for the refurbishment before the building would be fit for use again. The crux of the matter would be making it financially viable whilst keeping the price of using the facility to a reasonable level. The Plymouth city council gave a favourable response to his appeal with a ninety-nine per cent certainty for planning permission to be granted. Scott's reasons for the suggestion was sound as he wished to have a venue which would keep youngsters off the streets thus avoiding the possibility of getting into mischief. It is hoped a two-storey building with the gym, dance studio, boxing ring and other facilities, that has received permission to go ahead, will be successful; the plan is to have volunteers to get it built for nothing, with good will, hard graft and friendly tradesmen and a local college has promised to send a group of trainee bricklayers to kick start the project. Nancy Astor had the same dream of making things happen for generations of youngsters.

On the 6th May 2006 when a reunion was held for ex members of the former Astor Institute Youth Club at the Elm Community Centre in Plymouth organised by Sandra Monaghan, many people attended and were very enthusiastic and stated that they wished it was still in existence, for its closure was indeed a sad loss. As the writer of this book I was thrilled to be invited to the reunion to speak to many of the citizens and when I questioned them of their feelings for Lady Astor, all stated they were full of admiration and extremely fond of her. Their spokesperson in the opening speech said, "So thanks to Lady Astor for providing me and many others with the opportunity to spend my formative years meeting people and learning social skills which I have carried with me throughout my life." What a lovely comment considering that Lady Astor had been dead since 1964, and it proves that she still lives on in their hearts today

The Astor name is still linked with some youth of today as the Wrigley's Junior and Minor Football League show that one league is remembered by the Astor name, that is the under-13 Astor football league. The Astor under 13's youngsters, playing in the Junior Football league, carries a famous name under their colours and they represent a wide area of the sport. SB Frankfort, Morley Rangers, Tamarside Junior Football Club, Plymouth Kolts, Woolwell Juniors, Ivybridge Town, Torpoint Athletic, YMCA 'K' & Parkway, Staddiscombe Colts, Tamerton Foliot and Manstow Football Club all play in the Astor under 13 league. In 2008 the proud winners of the Astor Cup were the Under-13 Plymouth Kolts team. The table tennis players have several teams playing in the District and Table Tennis League under the Astor name.

Peter Osborne from Canada remembers vividly former great players for Plymouth Argyle who started their football careers at the Astor Institute or Virginia House, names such as Reg Wyatt (centre half) 1955-1965. Peter Anderson (left Wing) born in Devonport in 1932, studied at the Astor Institute beginning his career with a local side Oak Villa, he signed for Plymouth Argyle in July 1950 and in December 1962 transferred to Torquay United. Brian Jasper (full back) former Astor Institute player signed for Argyle in the season 1956-1957 and then was transferred to St Austell, Cornwall. Graham Adams (full back), Pat Jones (left back) both played for the Astor Institute in their boy-hood years. Another Argyle favourite, Johnny S. Williams (left midfield or today known as midfield forward) played for the Virginia House football team. Who can forget some of the super goals he scored for Plymouth Argyle? They were usually spectacular long-range efforts and when he scored, the fans would roar in appreciation. He played 448 games for Plymouth Argyle between the years 1955-1966 and he scored 55 goals.

An announcement in a local paper in 2007 declared that the Astor Hall was to be closed. George Bernard Shaw had spoken to students of Exeter's University College at Astor Hall when he came to Plymouth to open Astor Hall, in Stoke, in October 1929, and at that time Lady Astor entertained her playwright friend at 3 Elliot Terrace. In the late 1920s Astor Hall was being used as a residential hostel for students. In

1945 it was converted into an orphanage under a new scheme with children being housed as a family unit. In recent years it has been home for people with physical disabilities, it is currently up for sale through the Exeter office of an agent specialising in business property sales. The home comprises of a detached property set in an acre of grounds, and provides care for up to twenty-six residents in single room provision, it also supplies day care facilities and fellowship club facilities for people in the city. It is the wish of the Astor Trustees of Astor Hall to maintain the arrangement of the club for the foreseeable future, post sale, until such time as they can source alternative premises or wind down the club facility. The trustees released a statement saying, "To ensure the continuation of Astor Hall as a care home for the future, we have made the difficult decision to sell the care home as a going concern. Plymouth City Council did agree an increase in fees to assist the home, however, for the long-term stability of the care home and the benefit of the residents and staff, we believe that this is the best way forward. By making this early decision, we are confident that the right buyer will be found and this will enable the residents and staff to have a secure future." Lady Astor's projects have been completely shattered as nearly everything she created has been lost. What now for her beloved ordinary citizens? Giant businesses with money beyond the pockets of the working class devour all the beautiful areas of waterfront and buy all the buildings, ostracising the working class from living in the areas that should have been replaced with homes for the rightful citizens born in Plymouth. If Nancy were to be looking down from the Parliament in the Sky, what would she do and say now? She was a rich woman but her money was always spent on the poor and needy. In Plymouth the poor and needy no longer have a champion to fight their cause.

On a cold night in January 1949 at Astor Hall, Stoke, Plymouth, thirty-seven people with disabilities, who were full of enthusiasm to succeed, founded the Fellowship and have belonged to the Fellowship since its full working capacity in 1958. Their motto was and still is today 'Help Us To Help Ourselves'. To ensure the continuation of Astor Hall as a care home for the future the Trustees and Directors have made the difficult decision to sell Astor Hall as a going concern. Astor Hall provides residential care for people with physical disabilities over the age of 18. Facilities include respite care, annual holidays and Fellowship events. It is a Residential Care Home and a Fellowship's Community Centre, which caters for up to twenty-six residents, the majority of whom are from Plymouth, but some from further afield. The Residential home has three qualified waking staff on duty through the night with additional qualified staff during the day. The Fellowship has three vehicles, all able to carry wheelchairs and fitted with electric lifts, and is a registered charity (number 1087327) and membership provides support from a visiting welfare officer, use of Astor Hall facilities and assistance to maintain independent living. Its aim is to support each member with a level of independence, according to his or her capabilities, that allows them to lead a life as full and satisfying as possible. The Fellowship programme is distributed to all members.

Astor Hall summer outing 1948 on the beach at Port Isaac. As the war had ended Astor Hall Plymouth was the new Headquarters children's home on return from Clovelly North Devon 1945 and the Scattered Homes name was dropped and was lost in time. The Matron Mrs Nunn had invited the retired former Matron of Stoke House Miss Holden and the retired sisters Nurse Audrey Penna & Miss Holly Penna to the outing. Miss Holly Penna is third from the right. Nurse Audrey Penna is fifth from the right. Miss M. Holden is seventh from the right (with large black hat).

A group from an R.N. Ship entertain the children at Christmas in the day room, Astor Hall

Christmas dinner in the dining room, Astor Hall.

Dressed up for a Carnival - Astor Hall veranda

CHAPTER SEVENTEEN
CHILDREN'S NURSERIES

"A true friend would always tell you of your faults but love you just the same." *Nancy Astor.*

During her early years in Plymouth Nancy Astor was very concerned about the children of poor mothers who were compelled to work. In April 1912 in Plymouth a day nursery for twenty-six children was established at number 19 Whimple Street, where, in the first six months, nearly 2,000 children were placed in care. Later the nursery was moved to Looe Street near the Barbican. In December 1912 another nursery was opened at number 18 Cecil Street, which was financed by Nancy Astor and named Francis Astor Nursery after her son. An additional nursery was opened at number 49 Embankment Road in August 1913.

In October 1918, Nancy's daughter, Miss Phyllis Astor, opened a convalescent home for delicate children from Plymouth, in a large house near Dousland Station on Dartmoor and called it 'Wissiecott Children's Convalescent Home.' It cared for twenty very delicate children and was fitted and fully financed by the Astors. Mr J. J. Judge, Miss Champness, Miss Olive Adams and Miss Phillips supplied practical assistance and served as trustees. However in 1921 it was to close as the Astor family could no longer bear the full cost to support the home, this caused much distress to the Astors who had given so much, yet could not find anyone else prepared to help in financing the project; so it was with heavy heart that Nancy agreed to its closure.

Inspired by the ideas of William Morris, Margaret and Rachael McMillan devoted their lives to helping children living in Britain's slums. Margaret McMillan and her sister Rachael founded a nursery school in Deptford, London in 1908 to care for slum children under school age left to play in the streets whilst the mothers went out to work, for many mothers had lost the breadwinner in the family and financial allowances for children were not available. They were motivated and helped by their alliance with socialist politics and Margaret's activities in Bradford and began a campaign to improve the health of children by arguing that local authorities should install bathrooms, improve ventilation and supply free school meals. Margaret McMillan changed the thinking of England about children, yet she could not get a grant from the London County Council, however she continued tirelessly in her quest.

Nancy Astor's love of children drove her to make conditions better for them. On hearing about the nursery school she paid a visit to Deptford with Lord Astor; it was then that Nancy had a moment of inspiration, why not have a centre where Nursery

School Teachers could be trained? In November 1929 the foundation stone was laid. Nancy did everything in her power to support the McMillan Nursery and was involved with the opening of the Nursery Training College in Deptford, London. This was a charity funded by the Astors and was to prove the most constructive enabling the nursery school movement to develop over England and in proving to be Nancy's favourite charity. Now nursery schools have been recognised by the state and are in receipts of grants. Nancy's love of children never faltered as she strove to obtain quality of life for them.

In 1934 the Astors bought land in a secluded area on Plymouth Hoe, number 24 Hoe Street, including the Holy Trinity Vicarage with its enclosed garden, as a nursery school for children, and it was named the Margaret McMillan Nursery. Nancy took full responsibility for the new project and had the old vicarage converted to enable the nursery to function. Maternity and child welfare were always top of her list. The generosity of the Astors helped establish the nursery school and pay its running costs; the aim was to provide quality day care for children from the age of two to five years coupled with first-class education. Her love of children embraced every effort she could muster to seeing to their welfare. In 1935 a voluntary committee was formed, which was intended to finance the project, with the aid of fees. The children received a well-cooked mid-day meal and the fees were two shillings and sixpence per week, including food. The staff consisted of a trained Superintendent, a voluntary helper, a cook and a cleaner. Eleven children first attended the school and by October 1936 there were forty children, the agreed maximum. Lady Astor opened the gardens of McMillan Nursery School in 1937.

Because the McMillan nursery was such a success Nancy initiated a scheme for a second nursery school at Valletort Place, Stonehouse, in 1937. She had received permission from the Plymouth City Council to continue after discussion with the Parks and Recreation Committee. Lady Astor gave the building to the City and she visited the site and discussed with the architect how the building should be built to accommodate the children; the site had been intended as a playground, however, another area was found in the brickfields for a playground to be provided. The architect agreed with Lady Astor to travel to London to see the Nursery School there so that the new one in Stonehouse would be of good standard. Nancy worked tirelessly for the Board of Guardians seeking always to improve children's welfare.

When the bombing of the City increased during the Second World War it was decided the children should be evacuated. Some of the nursery school staff went with the children to Dartington Hall for several weeks, but this proved very difficult and finally the children and supporting staff were evacuated to Dunley House in Bovey Tracey, which was made available by the Minister of Health, and the Evacuation Account met all expenses. After the war Lady Astor wished to re-open the nursery school at 24 Hoe Street but the City was using the building rent-free for another project. She did not succeed in re-opening it again until 1948 when Miss Truscott took charge and a general committee was formed. The nursery school resumed and it flourished.

The school continues today as a very efficient Independent Nursery School; it is a fitting memorial to the Astors who did so much for their adopted City of Plymouth. How proud Nancy would be in knowing that the nursery still thrives today offering excellent services in the year 2008. It is now self supporting by the nursery fees and, with assisted grants from the Government, operates as a non-profit making charitable trust with a board of trustees who meet regularly to support the staff and oversee the aims and ethos of the nursery. There is always a waiting list because the nursery school is so popular. The most experienced nursery school has been given the highest possible praise by education inspectors and now provides facilities for children from the age of three months to five years and is open for fifty weeks of the year and has first class staff to support its running. Every penny is re-invested; the curriculum covers a happy and homely environment with enclosed walls for safety and security. The nursery provides freshly cooked food on the premises, accepts vouchers and Government grants, and teaches literacy, numeracy, creativity, gymnastics, ballet, French, baking, role-play, music and drama, and the children learn how to mix with friends, but most importantly they learn consideration for others and good manners. A top class nursery school with hard working staff and well done the generations of trustees whose love for children has kept Lady Astor's dream alive.

This postcard photo was printed the year after Nancy Astor became MP for Plymouth, Sutton. (Printed 1920) From the time of her duties as MP in 1919 she was to become the children's champion

With grateful thanks to 'The New Illustrated' paper, November 15th 1919 (No. 40 volume 2)

CHAPTER EIGHTEEN
A CANADIAN EXILE REMEMBERS

Peter Osborne at the age of nineteen designed and made the Virginia House badge for the boys' football team which was then adopted as the Virginia House official logo. In the design of the badge notice the slightly raised lighthouse in the centre as this had a significant meaning because the lighthouse represented the hopes and future of the Club itself. The lines on the badge are an indication of the rays of light emanating from the lighthouse, which represented the influence that the club had on its members. At the time Peter was in the club there was a rowing club with their own boats, a boxing club, wrestling, billiards and snooker, table tennis, a dance club and they also had their own library. Inside Virginia House there used to be a higher balcony which one could walk around but it has since been taken down. Sometimes the football games were played at the Astor Playing Field, which is still in use today.

Peter remembers that his dad was in the navy serving on board on HMS Norfolk in 1939 and during that time his Grandmother lived in Crownhill and he lived with his Mother in Milehouse. Peter had this to say: We would walk to visit Grandmother and one particular day we were on our way home when it started to rain, a black car pulled up alongside, it was Lady Astor. She called out to us and invited us into the car, my mother, my brother Colin, and myself, saying she would take us to Milehouse. I was so excited having a ride in a car with a Lady and although I was only six years old at the time I can still remember it clearly. I sat between my mother and Lady Astor and she reached across and said, "With those lovely legs you should join the navy." She took us all the way home to our door and we were most grateful, as had we walked that distance we would have been extremely wet. In later years as I became a man I thought she was a very unusual person for her time, in my opinion class was irrelevant in her eyes which was a unique personality for that time as class distinction was prevalent.

When my school days were over I worked and completed my apprenticeship in Plymouth with a company called Auto Body Works in Saint Judes. My trade then was as a Coachbuilder, later I went into the Army (with a character reference letter from the warden of Virginia House) as a serving regular in the Royal Electrical Mechanical Engineers (REME) and completed three years service. My Army number was 22959536 perhaps someone reading this story will remember me. On ending my service I was only out for 28 days when I was recalled for the Suez Canal crisis in 1956. During that time I made two major life decisions, one to emigrate to British Columbia, Canada, and the other to marry an English girl. On my decision to leave England my thoughts turned to Canada as the country appealed to me. In 1957 we moved to the city of Penticton, British Columbia, the name of the city derives from the original American native name (meaning a place to stay forever.) I missed the football in Plymouth, as the English football style was not played in Canada.

Previously to that I had been posted to Germany for two years and then returned to England on embarkation leave and after my leave I was sent to Libya for eleven months. During my service I was discouraged from fraternising with German girls or Libyan girls. When I signed for three years it meant that you also signed up for seven years in the colours, which was an Army reserve, and I did not want to be in the position of being recalled again. It was at this time that I decided to emigrate to Canada. I had been working since I was fifteen and was now 23 years old and realised that in all my working days in the Army I had never earned a full day man's pay, needless to say I was frustrated at not making any progress. In Canada, I immediately went into the building trade where the standard of living was better, and I have been in the building trade ever since and am still working. Now I oversee building work and I build models for Architects and am involved in community development.

The thing I can say is that of all these different phases of my life over seventy years I kept records of only one particular phase in Plymouth, and that was my involvement with Virginia House and its association with Lady Astor. Because of her generous gift of Virginia House we boys had the opportunity to join clubs and meet new friends. In June 2003 all the Virginia boys' football team surviving had a reunion in Bovisand, near Plymouth, where one of the boys now has a chalet. If you looked at the lighthouse on the badge, and call it the Astor family badge, one can accept that the rays were her influence. There was chemistry between members of the Virginia House club, which kept us connected to each other. I will always remember that time when Lady Astor gave my family a lift, as it was in those days considered very special, an act of generosity not expected. There were links that connected us, the first one touching my knee to say join the navy, the second a two year link with the club at Virginia as an eighteen year old, and the third one was the reunion at Bovisand as a seventy year old with former members of the club. Of course I cannot play football now, instead it will be a meal, a pint, and talk over old times.

Peter Osborne's niece Susan Crocker remembers with pride her Grandmother who, whilst working as a cook in the Guildhall with many other cooks to prepare the special luncheons, did on one occasion meet Lady Astor: Grandmother was struggling when carrying items into the luncheon room and Lady Astor had noted and had said to her, "Why are you walking like that?" Grandmother replied, "Well, my shoes are well worn and they are very uncomfortable and I am short of coupons so I cannot buy a new pair yet." Shoes were rationed in the war, as were clothes, and the only items not on ration were hats. Shortly after this conversation she received a parcel from Lady Astor and inside was a brand new pair of shoes. My Grandmother never forgot that wonderful gift and Nancy's kindness, she thought Lady Astor was a lovely Lady and spoke highly of her for the rest of her life. To some it might appear that it was only a small gift but the reason behind had a meaning that came from Christian values in giving to those who did not have the luxuries enjoyed by well off people.

The badge was designed and made by Peter Osborne at the age of nineteen for the Virginia House boy's football club. It was officially adopted as the Virginia House Logo.

VIRGINIA HOUSE SETTLEMENT

FOUNDERS :
VISCOUNT and VISCOUNTESS ASTOR

WARDEN :
~~Marshall~~ ~~Blakeley~~
Mr. S. HOWSON

PALACE STREET

PLYMOUTH

Telephone : PLYMOUTH 2778

TO WHOM IT MAY CONCERN.

PETER OSBORNE.

Peter Osborne has been a member of the Senior Boys section of the
above Settlement since January 1951.

He has taken a prominent part in all the sporting activities of his
section, and has for two seasons played football for our under 21
team. He has at all times been willing to help in any project undertaken
by the Settlement.

He is of the highest Character, honest and trustworthy in every respect.
He is smart in appearance and bearing, and I would have no hesitation
in recommending him for service with H.M.Forces.

Signed.

S Howson

Warden.

19th. May, 1953.

CHAPTER NINETEEN
NEW YORK FAME

"I attribute my victory to the hard work that I have done for Plymouth and my personal connection with the people."
Nancy Astor December 1923.

LADY ASTOR CHEERED BY A HUGE CROWD

This article was sent by wireless from England to the New York Times on 6th December 1923 and was published in the New York Times newspaper on the 7th December 1923. The Author wishes to thank the newspaper for its use. The article reads:

HER VICTORY THE SIGNAL FOR A GREAT DEMONSTRATION BY THE PEOPLE OF PLYMOUTH. PROMISES TO WORK HARD AND TEACH HER CONSTITUENTS TO SING GOD SAVE THE KING INSTEAD OF THE RED FLAG.

Plymouth, England, 6th December 1923. Lady Astor 'Sunshine of Sutton' as she is popularly called here, has retained her seat in Parliament after one of the bitterest fights in the history of the division. Her vote was 16,111 against 13,438 for Captain G.W. Brennan, Labour. Her majority was about four hundred less than in the last election. The declaration of the result of the poll, in conjunction with the two other Plymouth seats, was made in the presence of a crowd of thousands which packed the main street in one dense mass. About eighty per cent of the electors voted, the women and ex-servicemen supporting Lady Astor strongly. A few ballot papers were spoiled by enthusiastic supporters writing on them messages of good luck. After the declaration Lady Astor addressed the crowd, estimated at ten thousand, from the balcony of the club. Hoarse voiced and tired but happy, and surrounded by her family, she said: "You cannot possibly know what it means to me to be the member for this division. I don't know what I should have felt like if you had sent me away. You say I have courage, but I doubt whether I should have had courage enough to face that. I believe some of you had the 'wind up' well, now you have 'sails up' I can promise you I will work for you in the future in the best way I can, and I shall try to teach you to sing God save the King and not the Red Flag."

Lord Astor said: "You can well imagine how proud I am of my old constituents. I am proud of my wife. She is a good wife, and a good Member of Parliament." Somebody in the crowd shouted, "and a good mother" whereupon the Honourable Phyllis Astor,

Lady Astor's young daughter, took up the megaphone and shouted, "Thank you very much" while her younger brother in a shrill voice shouted the same words. Then the immense crowd escorted Lady Astor in triumph to her home on the Hoe. Interviewed by 'The New York Times' Lady Astor said: "I attribute my victory to the hard work that I have done for Plymouth and my personal connection with the people. I am a social reformer, and Plymouth prefers people interested in socialism and communism. I go back now to carry on my work where I left it and I hope to find many more women there to help me."

AS TOLD BY MRS LILIAN BECKER (NEE RICKETTS)

My mother (Mrs M Ricketts) had an aunt and uncle (Mrs & Mrs W Andrews) who were the licensees of the Swan Hotel, 15 Saint Andrews Street, Plymouth, where the photograph shown in this chapter was taken outside the Hotel when Nancy Astor was campaigning for votes in 1919. Nancy Astor at this time was canvassing for a seat in Parliament, and that was why she was here. Her taxi driver came in to the hotel and asked if anyone would like to meet her and the soldier said he would, this was my father Musician Herbert Ricketts of the Royal Artillery Band stationed at the Royal Citadel Plymouth. The sailor in the picture (name unknown) also went with Herbert to meet Lady Astor. The servicemen were certainly bemused by their sudden rise to fame and Herbert always talked of the experience, he remembered particularly the velvet hat worn by Nancy Astor in the photograph, as the colour was deep purple. The style was quite chic for its time; she did in fact always wear colourful cloche hats or smaller hats tilted at a rakish angle. A photograph was taken outside the Swan Hotel (later known as the Pen and Quill) in Saint Andrews Street Plymouth.

Sometime later my father received from his brother W. Ricketts a newspaper cutting of the New York Times dated November 1919 with the photograph prominent in the front page. He was at that time serving as a Royal Marine, during which the ship he was on called at New York where he bought the paper and to his surprise found it contained his brother's photograph. To our knowledge it was never printed in our local paper (Plymouth) it was such a surprise to my father too. For many years we have treasured and kept the photograph for safekeeping to pass on to our heirs. We carried it to the shelter every time there was a raid during the bombing with other precious artefacts, we were determined that our piece of history which linked us to Nancy, Lady Astor, would not be forgotten. We were indeed very proud that she thought a Tommy Soldier was worthy to be seen with her.

Photograph courtesy of Mrs Lilian Becker

Left to right: Nancy, Lady Astor
Soldier, Musician Herbert Ricketts, Royal Artillery Band
Stationed at the Royal Citadel Plymouth
Sailor unknown. Photo taken in 1919

Photograph: copyright Nancy Astor with kind permission Mr Charles Prynne
Digital copy: Trevor Burrows Photography

Photograph taken after her book 'My Two Countries' was published in 1922/23. Lord and Lady Astor with a group of citizens in the USA.

CHAPTER TWENTY
PROUD WORKERS

I refuse to admit that I am more than fifty-two, even if that does make my sons illegitimate. *Nancy Astor.*

ARNOLD L SAYERS

Arnold L Sayers CBE (denotes the middle rank of the order in the category; Commanders of the order of the British Empire) recalls the life of John Robert Damerell, as he was not only their butler but also a close friend, and he had also worked for Lady Astor. (The Sayers were a very well known family during the 1940s and 1950s; and as John Damerell had worked before the war for the Sayer family at Alston Hall, Holbeton, Devon, John was asked to stay on as butler to the Sayer family after the war ended, which he accepted) Arnold tells his story: John was born in one of the Feoffee's Cottages in Harberton on 26th December 1904. He was one of eleven children and his father worked on the neighbouring Belsford Farm for fifteen shillings a week. Thus discipline at home had to be very strict if they were to survive, all the children picked primroses in the spring to send away, and the cash thus earned bought them footwear for the year. John went to work for a local baker during the Great War and soon afterwards was engaged as a footman to Squire Oxley Parker who lived at Sharpham House on the river Dart. He was promoted to butler in due course, but about 1935 Squire Parker died and his widow and daughter had to leave Sharpham and move to a house at Strete Gate, which was subsequently destroyed in the practice landings at Slapton in preparation for D-Day. Mrs Parker then found she could not afford to keep Arnold, so in 1938 he came to work for my parents Mrs and Mrs Sayers who still lived at Alston Hall, Holbeton. My parents and we five children immediately grew very fond of him and he was the perfect butler, but willing to do all sorts of other jobs as well.

Then came the war and he went off and joined the Army, travelled all over North Africa, Italy, and finished the War at Graz in Austria, by which time he had been promoted to Mess Sergeant and had been appointed batman to Major General Freeman-Attwood (1897-1963) of the Army and had been with him in the North Africa campaign. Unfortunately, General Freeman-Attwood had given away sensitive information to his wife in a letter that he had written to her, which was picked up by the censor, and subsequently the General was recalled but Uncle John stayed on as batman to the replacement officer. My Father died in 1940 and we wondered whether John would want to come back and work for us again. Working for a family was not thought of as a desirable job at the time. Anyway he did come back and really became the rock of the house and family, and enabled my mother to immerse herself in public work for which she was awarded the CBE in 1952, and a DBE (Dame) in 1956. John Damerell had always watched what the cook was up to in the kitchen and quickly became a proficient cook as well as an enthusiastic gardener. He became very interested in old things and on his days off used to potter around the old shops of Plymouth, and became very well known by their owners. He used to spend every penny of his salary, and when we said he ought to be saving he said spending was good for trade and employment. I was married in 1954 and John attended the celebrations. My mother died in 1959 and he came to live with us until his death in 1966. During his last years he suffered from diabetes and high blood pressure, which made life difficult for him. He was quite a remarkable person, he always use to say, "You are never too old to learn if you are not too big a fool to be told." He

This photograph depicts some of the guests at Arnold L. Sayers wedding in 1954. First Right John Robert Damerel Butler in the service of the Sayer family and trusted by Lady Astor. Lady first left Mrs Cunliffe, second left Mrs Milne and Lady third left unknown.

assimilated a great deal of knowledge, but above all was a very kind and generous person. He used to visit Mrs Mapp every week for lunch, always took her a gift. We used to deliver him to her address, as he did not drive. Hers was the only front door brass that was polished in the Crescent! I seem to remember him saying that Lady Astor was very kind to Mrs Mapp via her Secretary Miss Knight. After John's funeral we spread his ashes in a field above Harberton in an area that he loved so much.

VICTOR MAPP

My name is Victor James Mapp and I was born on the 9th August 1945 and given these particular Christian names by my mother with a little influence from Lady Astor because it was VJ Day (Victory over Japan) and the initials VJ were very appropriate. I have many memories of Lady Astor because my mother spent fifteen years working for her Ladyship as maid cum cook, working for her before, during, and after the war, my mother had a lovely relationship with her and took great pride in her work. Lady Astor's full time cook Mrs Woods apparently could not do a certain food dressing, which she liked, but knew that my mother could. Because she could prepare this particular dressing Lady Astor, who often held special functions at Cliveden House in Buckinghamshire and at Sandwich, Kent, asked my mother to go with them and as a special thank you allowed my mother to take two little children with her as a treat. That meant that my brother and I could go as we were the youngest, but the girls (my sisters) had to stay behind. Sometimes Lady Astor would also ask for my Uncle John Damerell, he was frequently called upon to help the Astors out on special occasions. When they needed him they would say "Could we please have Damerell for the day?" He would also go and help at Mothecombe House when the Queen Mother came to visit.

I remember the excitement of going to Lord and Lady Astor's home, for me it was very special and I remember it vividly to this day. What stood out in my mind as a child was sitting under the big kitchen table with my brother eating chicken legs, in those days chicken was a luxury food, what a treat. Another thrill was playing out the back garden by the tennis courts and thinking what a lovely place it was, to me it was open spaces and paradise. I can also recall as a child having the pleasure of going on board one of the American ships in Devonport Dockyard, and whilst aboard being given a train set which had been supplied by Lady Astor. She was wonderful to children and there are many citizens still living that remember her kindness and the gifts she bestowed on the poor children. Throughout the years my mother worked for Lady Astor, she always said to my mother, haven't you got rid of that awful man yet? Meaning my father, because he was a devoted labour supporter whereas Lady Astor was a staunch conservative. It was a remark only to tease my mother because despite being a Tory Nancy Astor would speak to all people irrespective of their political views. Every time Lady Astor was in Plymouth she would make a point of calling in to see Mrs Sparrow who lived at Beacon Park and she, too, was a serious labour supporter and they would banter frequently about their political differences but remained friends.

During the time my mother worked at 3 Elliot Terrace, my eldest sister Diana (born 1937) used to go there at weekends and during the school holidays to help the secretary cut anything out of the national newspapers. No matter how small, all relevant material about the Astors was saved, the cut outs were placed into large leather scrapbooks, this went on until my sister left school at the age of fourteen. Diana still reminisces about those days, as a spritely seventy-one year old in the year 2008, her admiration for Nancy Astor remains as strong today. Her very first impression of Lady Astor was frightening until she spoke and then the situation was totally different, she was warm and friendly and Diana liked her without reservation. Diana had this to say, ("Nancy was an extremely attractive woman and I enjoyed every moment of company I had with her and I wished secretly that I could be like her, beautiful, rich and able to meet important politicians, royalty and film stars.") During the war my mother fell pregnant with my brother George and Lady Astor, always caring, arranged for her to go to the Fleet Nursing Home to give birth. This was indeed a privilege seeing as this was a Maternity Hospital for service personnel; he was the only one born in hospital out of the whole family. Lady Astor suggested to my mother to send all of the children to the Christian Science Sunday school at Mutley Plain, I can remember vividly going there regularly on a Sunday. If mother did have a function to attend at Lady Astor's home it was agreed to allow her to take all the children to the Margaret McMillian Nursery on the Hoe. Mother could not look after the children and be expected to prepare the function, I must admit we enjoyed staying there for a day or two until mother came home, and we were well looked after.

John Jacob Astor's wife wanted my sister Diana to be trained as a nanny and work for them after leaving school but my mother said no, to this day my sister cannot understand why as she herself was keen to take the post. Diana said she could remember all the large clothing parcels coming to Elliot Terrace during the war from America for the underprivileged children. On occasion when Diana was caught in a bombing raid at Elliot Terrace she would cower under the kitchen table in the bomb proofed shelter in the basement of the house. When the raid was over Nancy ensured that her car took Diana home or the driver would drop her at the bus stop. Lady Astor contributed a tremendous amount of work, time and finance in the war years and her kindness went far beyond what was expected as she put herself out to try and improve the quality of life for so many people. One particular kindness was when my sister Diana in 1960 was about to be married, Lady Astor asked my mother to tell Diana that she could come to Elliot Terrace and collect some items which she could start up her new home. Diana was thrilled and she was given a card table, bedroom suite, couch, black and white pictures and one coloured picture of St Ives, which she still has on her wall at her home today. Lady Astor set up an Officers Club in Lockyer Street for war veterans and mother used to help out with cleaning and odd jobs.

My father died at the age of sixty-five in 1954 and Nancy, Lady Astor, sent my mother a lovely sympathy letter and I still treasure that letter today. When in 1958 the

Astors sold 35, Hill Street, the house in London, she bought a large flat at 100, Eaton Square, London, and despite all her worries and tribulations she sent my mother a card saying; "I hope all is well" How thoughtful of Lady Astor especially as she had left Plymouth many years ago. My mother died at the age of sixty in 1968 four years after the death of Lady Astor, and my Uncle John Robert Damerell died at the age of sixty-eight, for all the families it was loved ones lost and the door had closed on a page of history.

3 Elliot Terrace,
The Hoe, Plymouth.

22nd January 1954.

Dear Mrs Mapp,

I am writing to send you my sincere sympathy in your recent loss, and to let you know that if through your changed circumstances you want to earn, there will always be a job for you here.

Yours sincerely,

J.J. Astor, M.P.

88, MARSHAM COURT,
S.W.1.
VICTORIA 8181.

Feb. 9th.

Dear Mrs. Mapp.

I was so sorry to hear about your loss and I offer my deepest sympathy to you & your family.

I am sure that you made him extremely happy as you were so devoted to him & looked after him so well.

I hope that you have recovered from your ulcers.

If there is anything Mrs. Astor or I could do to help please let us know.

Yours sincerely

Ana Inés Astor.

I hope you are all well —

NANCY, VISCOUNTESS ASTOR,

with best wishes

N. Astor

100, EATON SQUARE, S.W.1.

Articles by kind permission of Mr Victor Mapp

CHAPTER TWENTY-ONE
PLYMOUTH GIRL GUIDES

Girl Guides deeds - Looking after the world - caring for others.

In 1907 some groups calling themselves 'Girl Scouts' were formed and they attended the Scout Rally at Crystal Palace in 1909 in an effort to be recognised. The Baden Powell family became involved and the first companies of the Girl Guide movement were formed in 1910 by Agnes Baden-Powell (1858-1945) sister to Lord Baden-Powell (1857-1941) and the Guides became distinctive by wearing a blue uniform. The very first royal recognition was in 1911 when Princess Louise, Duchess of Argyle became their patron. The brilliant Agnes Baden-Powell had many interests and she had knowledge of eleven languages and also took a keen interest in Astronomy and Science. Over the years the movement grew and as guiding continued to grow so did the administration work and it was evident that a headquarters' building was needed to continue the good work. In 1929 Lord Baden Powell launched the SOS appeal, for guiding purposes this meant 'Short of Stuff' and Guides all over the world were asked to give something to an appeal for a new building. The response was magnificent and in 1931 the Guide's new Headquarters was opened at 17-19 Buckingham Palace Road, London, and is the same building they occupy today.

Nancy Astor formed the first Girl Guide movement in Plymouth in the year 1917 and was instrumental in leading the Amalgamation of Girls' Organisations into the Guiding movement. In the Girl Guides' Gazette of August 1917 it is duly recorded that Division Commissioner of Plymouth was the Hon. Mrs. Astor, Cliveden, Taplow and the District Commissioner of Plympton was the Hon. Mrs. Alcock, Meadowside, Plympton. Lady Clinton, Bicton, East Budleigh was appointed County Commissioner. The December 1918 issue of the Girl Guides' Gazette confirmed the Hon. Mrs. Waldorf Astor, as resigning from being Division Commissioner for Plymouth, Devon and at the same time The Hon. Mrs. Alcock, from being District Commissioner for Plymouth, Devon also resigned. Nancy however continued to serve in Plymouth as the Devon County Vice-President until 1925. The Divisional Commissioner for Devon in 1918 was Lady Alberta Lopes of Roborough House, Roborough.

The appointments in 1917 were to change the lives of hundreds of young girls who passed through the portals of the Girl Guide movement in Plymouth. In her desire to ensure that the girls of Plymouth were given a fair deal in life, Nancy formed the first Girl Guide movement and gave countless hours of her time and her money, again her generosity on the financial side was to have a grand effect. Nancy was perturbed at the fact that several flourishing Guide Units existed in Exeter and other parts of Devon County whilst Plymouth had none. It had been noted that so much was being done for boys and so little for girls. Nancy insisted that anyone who was prepared to act as a Guider must be prepared to work and the keynote for girls who joined the Guides must be enthusiasm and also be full of the espirit de corps. They would have something to occupy their spare time instead of running about in the streets and getting into mischief. Nancy stated: " There was no town in Europe wants companies of Girl Guides more than Plymouth." (Daily Mercury May 8th 1917) The first meeting was held at Balfour Hall, Notte Street, on Monday 7th May 1917. Lady Clinton the County Commissioner and Miss Townsend the County Secretary addressed the gathering and Lady Astor became the first Divisional Commissioner for Plymouth. Further meetings were held at 3, Elliot Terrace, the Astor's home, and at the Athenaeum, Civic Guild of Help, Paradise Road School and at Bank Street. Mrs Evelyn Alcock who had organised jumble sales in Plymouth market and had amassed a good sum of money for the cause was asked to take the post as Honourable Secretary to the Guide meetings.

The movement began officially on Friday 18th May 1917 at five o'clock; members present at the ground-breaking event were, the Royal Marine Girls' Ambulance Corps, Batter Street Girls, Girls' Ambulance Brigade, Girls' Telegraph Messengers Brigade, St Luke's Nursing Brigade, St John's (Sutton) Girls' Ambulance Corps, Park Street Girls' Club, St Luke's (Stoke) Nursing Ambulance Brigade, the Young Women's Christian Association, St Dunstan's Abbey, the Primrose League, Plymouth Co-operative Guild (all areas). School representatives attending were, Cattedown Girls' School, Charles School, Charles Household of Faith, Laira School, Morice Town, Palace Court, Paradise Road, Salisbury Road, Somerset Place, St Catherine's, St George's, St James-the-less, St James-the-Great (Keyham) St Peter's, Camels Head, Oxford Street, Union Street All Girls' School and the Girls' High School, Lockyer Street. The Churches also took an active part as representatives came from the Wesleyan Church Ebrington Street, and Mount Gould Wesleyan Church. Head Teachers were invited to attend and other dignitaries came to offer their support. In attendance was the Mayoress Mrs Brown wife of Joseph Peace Brown, Lady Mary St Aubyn and Lady Bethell, wife of Knight Admiral Hon Sir Alexander Edward Bethell (1855-1932) who was at that time Commander-in-Chief Plymouth Royal Navy 1916-1918.

The very first elected Chairwoman of the local association (women today are now called Chairperson) was Mrs Palliser Hickman, wife of the Garrison Commander. The objects of the meeting were to form a local association, elect officers and generally discuss further steps to form companies. Nancy was appointed Divisional Commissioner under the County Commission. The Secretary chosen at the meeting was Mrs Evelyn Alcock, the Hon Treasurer elected was Miss Nesta Pearce, and the movement was to be non-political and non-sectarian open to all classes. It was agreed that a simple uniform and badge would show that the girls belonged to a special group and forty to fifty companies were formed in the first year. The next meeting was held at the North Road Corporation Grammar School and attendance indicated that the Guide movement was well underway. Honourable Secretary Mrs Alcock was the District Commissioner, by now one thousand girls were in training. A central fund was put into motion and donations had been received from Lord and Lady Mount Edgecumbe, Sir Henry and Lady Albertha Lopes, Admiral and Lady Bethell, Lady Ernestine Edgcumbe (1843-1925) Lady Jackson (1878-1966) Admiral Sir Arthur and Lady Hingham, General and Mrs Palliser Hickman, Mrs Evelyn Alcock, Waldorf and Nancy Astor.

By July 1917 four thousand girls were part of the Girl Guide Movement and Nancy's speech at a meeting of lady teachers and other dignitaries at the Plymouth Corporation Grammar School, was reported in the Plymouth newspaper Mercury on 3rd July 1917. Nancy had said, "I have become warmly interested in the movement, because the First World War has shown that women had not only got to do men's work, but in many cases to show them how to do it. The head of a large shipbuilding firm told me that women had done certain work not only as well as men, but had produced five times the amount. That, I think is because women went into their work with a different spirit. Men had been used to putting forth only so much in ca'canny spirit. I thought it would be a splendid thing to bring up their girls with the same sense of honour and of loyal service that was being inculcated in the boys by the Scout movement. I hope that every school will have a Guide Unit for here is a wonderful chance to do a great deal towards improving the moral tone of the town. Obedience does not mean servility; it is amazing how some people seem to be getting positively terrified of their children. The movement is one of the most important things that has happened to Plymouth in recent years."

On the 6th July 1917 more Girl Guide Units were formed and at Paradise Road School an Inspection was held, the young girls stood smartly to attention and then went through several interesting movements. Guiders and dignitaries were present and Nancy gave an interesting address emphasising the need for close study of the great quality of obedience to parents and in most of the proper things of life, as well as to cultivate a kindly considerate nature to all around, and to become careful and thrifty in their habits of life. Further meetings took place at the Mutley Young Women's Christian Association at Erme House, and the Lecture Room at 17, Lockyer Street in connection with the Primrose League, the Batter Street Club affiliated with the Girl Guide movement on the 7th July 1917. New Units were springing up all over the city.

Nancy Astor had really started something and for the girls now there would be a little bit of excitement in their lives. In May 1917 companies already established and supported by caring organisers who gave their time and money, were already proving

Photo: Evening Herald

Youth service on Plymouth Hoe. Girl Guides and Cadets. Lady Astor attended - not in photo

that it was worthwhile belonging to the movement. Captains and Lieutenants were appointed, Guides and Brownies were being formed in other areas. The 1st Plymouth Ermington Unit, the 2nd Primrose League Unit, the 3rd Mount Gould Wesleyan Unit, the 4th St Luke's Nursing and Ambulance Brigade, the 1st Devonport Nelson Unit, the 2nd Devonport Gordon Hoisell or Patriotic Girls Club Unit, the 3rd Devonport Stoke Nursing and Ambulance Brigade and the Co-operative Guilds set up Guide Units in Peverell, Ford, Devonport and Plymouth. The original Guide Uniform was a blue skirt and stockings with a jumper and neckerchief in the Guide Groups' colour. These fashions changed dramatically in the 1990's. On a Sunday in October 1917 the Plymouth Girl Guides were to have an inspection by a high-ranking royal member HRH Prince Arthur, Duke of Connaught and Strathearn (1850-1942) he was the third son of Queen Victoria. It was also hoped that Lady Baden-Powell would be present and the excitement of this occasion sped through the ranks for, at last, the Guides were considered a respected group to be recognised by members of royalty and it also meant they were now well known.

Nancy Astor's signature recorded in the minutes of that first meeting in the Guide Movement's logbook indicates the momentous historical events that were to follow. Nancy was appointed as Divisional Commissioner and continued to serve on the committee until December 1919 when she had to offer her resignation because of the commitment she had to undertake as Plymouth's first Lady Member of Parliament. Waldorf Astor had been elevated to the House of Lords and Nancy was elected to the House of Commons. The Hon Mrs Astor was immediately unanimously elected as Vice-President of the Girl Guide Association. Guiders had to work at earning qualifications with a two-year period before progressing to any higher rank; they had to show they had the capabilities to encourage young people to improve their lifestyles. Girl Guides could also earn badges when they qualified in various subjects. Proficiency Badge Tests were held and the subjects taken in the nineteen twenties varied. St John's Ambulance, Royal Drawing Society, South Kensington, astronomer, Oxford or Cambridge Senior, authoress, must have a publication, basket workers (Froebel) child nurse, norland nurse, sick nurse, cook, domestic service diploma, dancer diploma, gardener diploma, geologist, gymnast, health, housekeeper, interpreter (Oral) Oxford or Cambridge Senior, musician, Associated Board Higher Division (Froebel-Music) milliner diploma, laundress, needlewoman - full certificate.

Girlguiding girls UK in the year 2007 as they are now called, meet once a week where they follow a programme of activities. Gone are the badges for nursing, domestic service and basketwork, and in their place are badges that are very different, outdoor pursuits, holiday, sports, and water safety badges. Their activities encompass abseiling, party planning, yoga, first aid courses, global issues, raft building, climbing ropes, circus skills and survival badges. The Guides practised such things as first aid and signalling, they also went camping although they normally slept in barns, cowsheds or village halls instead of tents. At first, people didn't like the idea of young ladies taking part in 'boyish' activities. Many people complained to Lord and Lady Baden-Powell about this. However, many of the skills the Guides had learnt in 1917 became useful during World War One, the fact they were such a great help during the war helped to dispel a lot of the earlier hostility. Girls formed groups of four to eight and were called 'Patrols' and their ages are between ten years and fourteen years.

On Thinking Day held every February Girl Guides and Girl Scouts from different countries pledge to be friends and to understand each other, the first Thinking Day was held in 1927. Today there are more than ten million young women around the world taking part in World Thinking Day celebrations and it embraces one hundred and forty countries. The World Association of Girl Guides and Girl Scouts has enabled its members to develop leadership skills and self-esteem, make new friends, speak out on issues that affect them and their peers, and raise money so that Guiding can continue to empower girls and young women across the world.

Many branches of the Girls' Friendly Society had, with the sanction of the Guide Headquarters, turned themselves into Girl Guides Associations. A Girl Guide of the 1st Looe Company in simple but smart and comely navy blue serge uniform of the movement, wearing badges for proficiency in needlework, child-nursing and ambulance, came to the platform at one of the meetings. This gave the audience an insight into how smart they could look if they worked hard. The Guides went from strength to strength and the young people learned to respect others and to engage in an accepted moral lifestyle. Doing a good deed every day, all guides took that pledge with them throughout their lives. Once a Guide always a Guide, friendships were formed that lasted their lifetimes. By 1923 some Ranger Companies were formed for the older girls. One of the staunchest members of the Plymouth Guide Committee was Lady Jane Grey Clinton who gave so much of her time; she continued to serve on the committee until 1924 having spent seven years maintaining the logbook.

Guiding in the United Kingdom now is the largest voluntary organisation for girls and young women, there are approximately 600,000 members in the United Kingdom and in Plymouth the very first Guide Company Plymouth East is still going strong. Nancy attended the Girl Guides Jamboree in Central Park in the summer of 1939 to give moral support, little knowing that a few months later the country would once again be at war. The Guide movement continued into the Second World War albeit many companies were disbanded or were disrupted by children being evacuated and the loss of leaders engaged in important war work. After the war the movement gained momentum and the Guides changed their uniform style. In January 1947 the Compton District of Girl Guides in Plymouth was formed and sixty years later the young Girl Guides celebrated their 60th anniversary by wearing the various uniforms of the last seven decades and modelling them for the visiting audience. Many laughed at the old designs but the friendship was still strong as former Guides and leaders joined the celebrations.

This picture is of Mrs Fairweather, District Commissioner for Medway and was taken in 1920; the only difference would have been the colour of the cockade. Lady Astor would have worn this uniform

The Uniform of an unnamed District Commissioner circa 1915

Nancy's beloved East Division is still going strong as the Guides recently held a successful cookery competition based on a well-known television programme. Each guide company in the division held selection tests to choose pairs of guides who had to design a menu to provide a two course meal within a two hour time scale with only a budget of ten pounds. The final part of the judging was, of course, to sample the food. The guides had responded with top class entries and many sponsors helped to arrange the competition and celebrity chefs donated recipes and cookbooks. The winners were the 19th Plymouth Guides from Pennycross district and other winners of achievement were the 60th Plymouth Rainbows (junior guides) Laira and Lipson district, the 2nd Estover district Brownies and the senior Rangers from Pennycross district. How proud Nancy would have been, for all Guides, Rainbows, Brownies, and Rangers, remember your motto and your promise?

The Girl Guides motto: "Be Prepared."

The Guide Promise: I promise that I will do my best,
To love my God,
To serve the Queen and my Country,
To help other people and to keep the Guide Law.

The Guide Law:

A Guide is honest, reliable and can be trusted.
A Guide is helpful and uses her time and abilities wisely.
A Guide faces challenge and learns from her experiences.
A Guide is a good friend and a sister to all Guides.
A Guide is polite and considerate.
A Guide respects all living things and takes care of the world around her.

There are hundreds of former Girl Guides and Rangers who may have forgotten their promise and the law that was taught to them as the world has become more irreverent to everything that it held dear; time and personal problems have eroded those thoughtful ideas. Are we failing in our relationship with the younger generation? Perhaps we should all once more renew our promise and start again to lead our young people into the ways of, as Nancy Astor would say: "I thought it would be a splendid thing to bring up the girls with the same sense of honour and of loyal service…" The Trefoil Guild incorporates Guiding for Adults and they still encourage the young people and older people to participate in the Guiding Movement. Their aims and principles reflect the importance of the Trefoil Guild. Select persons could be Commissioners, a Leader, a Unit helper, a lone member, or join the Trefoil Guild. A Guider can challenge herself with the Dark Horse and Discovery Award and men too can be members. Guilds can have a minimum of six members but some Guilds have over fifty and one Guild has eighty-two. Guilds can specialise in walking, music, photography, golf and crafts. The Guild is a member of the International Scout and Guide Fellowship, also the World Association of Girl Guides and Girl Scouts. They give a helping hand at camps and large events and provide Starter Packs to new units, assist with administration work and accounts, give practical, financial and moral support to Guiding and Scouting, they also offer emergency help at meetings, run a depot or a shop and help with the traditions of the Guiding Badge; they relish opportunities and enjoy life, meet with old and new friends and make lifelong friends. Their key aim is to keep alive among members, the spirit of the Guide-Scout Promise and Law and to carry that spirit into the communities in which members live and work. Girl Guides lead the way in promoting kind acts and participating in good deeds. In September 2008 five Plymouth Girl Guides, and eleven from West Devon, participated in one of the world's highest coffee mornings in aid of Macmillan Cancer Support, it was part of the 'World's Biggest Coffee Morning' and the event which tested their courage and commitment, took place on the peak of Kala Pattar in the Himalayas, it was a demanding trek but a wonderful experience.

It is hoped that Girls Guides past, present and in the future, remember with affection the wonderful gift that Lady Astor gave to Plymouth.

3, ELLIOT TERRACE,

THE HOE,

PLYMOUTH,

May 3rd, 1917.

Dear Madam,

In order to further develop the good work done by the formation and extension of Girls' Guides, I have been requested to invite those who would probably be interested in such a useful organisation for girls, to be present at a MEETING in BALFOUR HALL, Notte Street, on MONDAY NEXT, 7th inst., 2-30 p.m., to confer upon the subject.

Lady Clinton and Miss Townsend (County Secretary) will address the gathering, and I should be glad if you would kindly invite any friends who are favourable to the movement and favour me with your presence and support.

Yours sincerely,

NANCY ASTOR.

Letter copy: by kind permission Mrs Jan Pritchard, Divisional Commissioner, Girlguiding, Plymouth

Letter from nancy Astor to invite those who would be interested in the girl guide movement written in 1917

"Mercury" 6 July 1917. *"Mercury" July 7th 19[1]*

PLYMOUTH GIRL GUIDES.

INSPECTION AT PARADISE ROAD SCHOOL.

The Girl Guide movement is making rapid development in Plymouth. Several companies of Girl Guides will be registered this week. An interesting ceremony took place at Paradise-road School, Stoke, when Mrs. Astor, as Divisional Commissioner, accompanied by Mrs. Palliser Hickman (chairwoman of the local Association) and Miss Nesta Pearce (hon. treasurer), visited the school to inspect and register the Girl Guide Company. A guard of honour, consisting of Boy Scouts connected with the school, received the official visitors. The young girls stood smartly at attention, and went through several interesting movements on parade. Various formalities were gone through by Mrs. Astor. A captain and lieutenant were appointed, Misses Gay and Cross, and badges were given to each member who had enrolled and conformed to the Guide Law. The enrolment consisted of two complete companies respectively of Girl Guides (girls over 11 years of age), and Brownies (girls from 8 to 11 years of age).

Mrs. Hickman inspected the assembly, and said it was a gratifying surprise to find so many enrolled in such a short period.

Mrs. Astor gave an interesting address, emphasising the need for close study of the great quality of obedience to parents and in most of the proper things of life, as well as to cultivate a kindly, considerate nature to all around, and to become careful and thrifty in their habits of life.

Miss Bartlett (headmistress), who has been largely instrumental in initiating the Guides at Paradise-road School, expressed the sincere thanks of the staff and scholars for the honour conferred upon them that morning by the official visit, and gave some homely advice to the enrolments, especially to the Brownies.

PLYMOUTH GIRL GUIDES.

This excellent movement is spreading throughout Plymouth, and companies of Girl Guides are springing up in many parts of the town. Despite a busy day on Thursday, Mrs. Astor, as Divisional Commissioner, inspected two new corps of Girl Guides. The Mutley Y.W.C.A. at Erme House have started an excellent body of Guides, under the direction of Misses M. C. Davis and J. Stone, and the efficiency of the enrolment reflects every credit upon the officers and others responsible. After they had paraded and gone through various movements, Mrs. Astor gave an interesting address to the girls.

Later in the evening Mrs. Astor inspected another large assembly in the Lecture Room, 17, Lockyer-street, in connection with the Primrose League, who have formed a complete company and are approaching a second contingent. The direction of the company is in the hands of Miss Boyes-Fowler, assisted by Miss Dyer, who kindly gave hints and instructions on physical drill. Excellent assistance has been given by Miss Olive Adams and Mrs. Charles Luke.

Mrs. Astor also visited the Batter-street Club as already notified in our columns. It is generally expected that this club will affiliate with the Girl Guides. When further companies are completed a central rally will be held, probably on the Hoe to be inspected by Lady Baden-Powell and probably the Duke of Connaught.

Articles by kind permission of Mrs Jan Pritchard, Divisional Commissioner, Girlguiding, Plymouth

Articles from the Daily Mercury Newspaper (Plymouth) July 1917

Copyright unknown

Lady Astor in her forties, she became
Devon County Vice-President in 1919

CHAPTER TWENTY-TWO
WOMEN FEMINISTS

'Women are paid less not only because they produce less and because their work has a lower market value, but also because women have a lower standard of life, both in physical needs and mental demands' – *Sidney Webb (1859-1947)*

In December 1919 Viscountess Astor took her seat in the House of Commons, to the outrage of Mary Stocks and her colleagues. Mary commented, "Not for this had we laboured so hard, here was an wealthy American woman known to us only by reputation as a society hostess, stepping into a safe seat vacated by her husband on his elevation to the peerage; not by reason of her own qualification but merely qua wife, we fear the worst." The fears of the women's suffrage supporters proved unfounded. Nancy emerged, in spite of her background, as an able fighter for women's rights who worked closely with some of the most radical women's suffrage campaigners. Mary Stocks first met Nancy Astor in 1920 and they became lifetime friends as both were feminists and championed the same causes. Nancy would often consult Mary Stocks on matters of feminist concerns and Mary, on having met Nancy on many occasions, softened her former opinion and admired her greatly. The Statute recognising women as full members of the University came into force in 1920. Nancy's political secretary Hilda Matheson helped in preparing Nancy's articles on state maternity services (December 1928) and the American situation for a Christmas peace number for a Journal. Nancy was invited and attended the Women's Pan American Conference in Baltimore, United States of America, in April 1922 and the English Speaking Union in Canada. The tour had been most successful as the population eagerly listened to everything she said and did; once more she was laying the foundations for unity between Britain, Canada and the United States. Whilst in the United States she visited family members and renewed old friendships.

Both Nancy Astor and Mary Stocks were keen supporters of Dame Millicent Garrett Fawcett (1847-1929) the leading suffragist with feminist's policies who had done much to fight for women's rights and to enhance equal opportunities for all. Millicent Fawcett early British Suffragist who campaigned for women's rights was also a founder member of Newnham College in Cambridge University. Its roots came from the suffrage campaigns of the 19th century and was originally the National Union of Women Suffrage Societies founded in 1897. It changed its name in 1919 to the National Union of Societies of Equal Citizenship, the year that Millicent Fawcett retired and the leadership was taken over by Eleanor Rathbone (1872-1946). The society still lives today and was renamed the Fawcett Society in honour of Dame Millicent Garrett Fawcett in 1953. Through her diplomacy, political expertise and negotiating powers, she had done more than anyone to bring about votes for women. Nancy was proud to be in league with these formidable women and followed in the footsteps of other feminists who had made their mark in the campaign for women's rights. These were women who were not afraid to challenge the all powerful, man dominated world. Nancy would read books about women feminists and she would have indeed read the deeply thought provoking book A Vindication of The Rights of Women published in 1792 by Mary Wollstonecraft (1759-1797) former nurse of the sick and a teacher who was also a founder member of women's ideals and an icon of the modern feminists.

Women's fight for the vote rallied many high profiled women to challenge the Government but also the working class woman was to have a marked effect. Nancy would have been aware of Plymouth-born activist Caroline Selina Ganley (1879-1966) who was born in East Stonehouse, Plymouth, and was the daughter of a tailor. She attended the Plymouth Church and national schools and married James William Henry Ganley a tailor's cutter. Caroline became a fierce opponent of the South African War and opposed the poor social conditions of the working-class communities in which she lived. She moved to Westminster for a time before moving to Battersea whereupon she became active in left-wing politics. She joined the Social Democratic Federation in 1906, campaigned for suffrage and was instrumental in setting up a socialist women's circle in Battersea and developing it into a branch of the Women's Labour League. She was involved in the British Committee of the International Congress; these anti-war suffragists detached themselves from the National Union of Women's Suffrage Societies to work with European women for peace. Nancy Astor, who campaigned for peace, was equally passionate and would have understood Caroline's desire to change things for the working class. After the First World War Caroline joined the Co-operative and Labour parties and in 1919 won a seat on Battersea Borough Council and through her efforts a well-equipped maternity home was opened in 1921. She became one of the first women magistrates in London and for twenty years sat on juvenile courts. She also served as a London County Councillor and was a member of the London County Education Committee. In the 1930's she sought nomination as a Co-operative Party Candidate and was elected MP for Battersea South but was defeated in the 1951 general election. In 1953 she was awarded the CBE and later became the first woman president of the London Co-operative Society. Caroline Selina Ganley died in August 1966.

Women's organisations campaigning for votes for women in Britain held frequent demonstrations proudly carrying their banners with the slogan 'The Franchise is the Keystone of our Liberty.' From their famous February 'Mud March' in 1907 the Women's Suffrage Societies, led by the veteran Labour MP Keir Hardie, gained respect from the spectators who watched that courageous march in the most atrocious weather conditions, and showed a measure of compassion for women who could face public ridicule in such adverse conditions. In 1909 Elizabeth Garratt Anderson (1836-1917) became the first Englishwoman to achieve the honour of being a doctor, and she was Britain's first woman Mayor. She served as Mayor of Aldeburgh a seaside town in Suffolk. In 1911 Dame Ethel Smyth (1858-1944) composed the March of the Women the Suffragette's battle-tune. In 1912 Ellen Cicely Wilkinson (1891-1947) known as 'Red Ellen Wilkinson' because of her shock of red hair, became a member of the National Union of Women's Suffrage Societies and in 1913 became its organiser. She was Member of Parliament for Middlesborough East, a firm pacifist who had been a student of history at Manchester University. Her interest was socialism and she was a member of the local Fabian Society and in 1920 became a founder member of the Communist Party. She committed suicide in 1947. 1912 was also the year that Sylvia Pankhurst (1882-1960) established her East London Federation of Suffragettes for working class women. Lady Astor often invited Sylvia Pankhurst to lunch or dinner at Cliveden. Sylvia was a British Suffragette, Socialist and a Communist and edited a weekly paper called The Women's Dreadnought. She was sent to prison on occasions, suffered forced feeding when on hunger strike, had advocated peace and was against Fascism. Here was another woman who was a pioneer in her own right. There were others: Highborn dames, literary and professional women, doctors, artists, and high school headmistresses, whose names will be noted in history. They led the long and hard-fought battles for equal rights. Lady Jane Maria Strachey (1840-1928) helped to gather signatures for a petition to Parliament requesting the votes for women. Lady Frances Balfour (1858-1931), prominent suffragist and woman of letters, worked with Millicent Fawcett. The Rendels (cousins to the Stracheys) Rachel (Ray) Strachey (1887-1940) Secretary of the National Union of Women's Suffrage Societies, she was also Editor of the feminist newspaper The Common Cause and later became political private Secretary to Lady Astor between the years 1929 and 1934. Rachel was to have quite an impact in Nancy's early years in Parliament and they became good friends. The future MP Eleanor Rathbone (1872-1946) who fought for improved housing and family allowances and the right to vote, became President of the National Union of Societies for Equal Citizenship when Millicent Fawcett resigned in 1919. On the death of Eleanor Rathbone in 1946 the Guardian paper said, "No Parliamentary career has been more useful and fruitful."

All these women followed in the footsteps of Bessie Rayner Parkes (1829-1925) she was a social reformer who enthused about women's rights, she and her friend Barbara Bodichon, a teacher, founded a journal called The Englishwoman's Review. In 1866 the two friends formed the first ever Women's Suffrage Committee and organised a petition and presented it to the House of Commons. Nancy had a wealth of information from the women feminists and she did everything she could to raise their issues in the House of Commons irrespective of their political beliefs. Journalist Annie Besant (1847-1933) whose doctor father died when she was five years old became a believer of the Christian Religion. A failed marriage to a clergyman led her to completely reject Christianity, and in 1874 she joined the Secular Society. She campaigned for better conditions for the young women working at the Bryant and May's match factory; she was also a member of the Fabian Society. Whilst in India, Annie joined the struggle for Indian Home Rule and was interned by the British Authorities. Annie Besant died in India in 1933. Margaret Llewelyn Davies (1861-1944) was a member of the Women's Co-operative Guild. Annie Kenney (1879-1953) a working class woman was so staunch in her belief of women's rights, that she went to prison thirteen times and was the organiser of the Women's Social and Political Union.

American ladies were soon making their mark as women feminists and they had the same ideas as their British counterparts. Nancy had been an admirer of Amelia Jenks Bloomer (1818-1894) an American reformer born in Homer, New York USA. Virtually self-educated, Amelia founded a semi-monthly periodical in 1849 called The Lily which was published in New York and was devoted to the interests of women. She was the editor and publisher, campaigning against sexual discrimination and advocating temperance and women's suffrage. Famous for her stand in favour of dress reform, she appeared at her lectures during the early 1850's wearing full trousers, gathered at the ankle under a short skirt, she was to be remembered because these garments were later called Bloomers. She married a lawyer who was a Quaker with progressive views. He edited a newspaper called the Seneca Falls County Courier and over the next few years Amelia wrote articles in favour of prohibition and women's rights. Amelia ventured into female fashion and wrote many articles at the time about tightly laced corsets, layers of petticoats and floor length dresses, she and her feminist friends suggested wearing loose bodices, ankle-length pantaloons and a dress cut to above the knee. She continued to play an active role in the campaign for women's rights for the rest of her life. Amelia died at Council Bluffs, Iowa, in December 1894.

The struggle for women's suffrage in America began in the 1820's with the writings of Frances (Fanny) Wright (1795-1852) a firm feminist and abolitionist; she favoured free secular education, liberal divorce laws and birth control. In 1840 the two founder members of the Society of Friends, Lucretia Coffin Mott (1793-1880) Quaker minister and social reformer, and Elizabeth Cady Stanton (1815-1902) social activist and leading figure of the women's rights movement, travelled to London as delegates to attend the World Anti-Slavery Convention as did the British representatives, however, they were not allowed to speak at the meeting, One can imagine their frustration. In 1848 Elizabeth and Lucretia organised the Women's rights Convention at Seneca Falls. In 1852 Susan Brownell Anthony (1820-1906) prominent, independent civil rights leader, and feminist, joined with Elizabeth Cady Stanton and Amelia Bloomer in campaigning for women's suffrage and equal pay. They promoted the causes of women's rights, temperance, marriage law reform and higher education for women. By 1866 joined by another feminist member Lucy Stone (1818-

1893) they helped to establish the American Equal Rights Association. Three years later they formed a new organisation, the National Woman Suffrage Association (NWSA). American women were campaigning throughout the states determined to obtain equality.

Meanwhile another suffrage movement was quite active in Boston U.S.A. who equally worked tirelessly for women's rights. It was soon realised that they would be more effective by uniting as one group, so in 1890 the NWSA and the American Woman Suffrage Association (AWSA) banded together to become the National American Woman Suffrage Association. (NAWSA) One particular brave feminist lady of the movement was the well-known worldwide advocate for the deaf and blind Helen Keller (1880-1968) who was herself deaf and blind. She became an author and educator; many will remember the brilliant film made of her childhood called The Miracle Worker. Patty Duke played the part of Helen Keller Anne Bancroft, portrayed the teacher, and Anne won a coveted Oscar when it received rave reviews, the film was released in 1962. On the 7th November 1893 by agreement with the constitutional amendment, all American women finally got the vote. The first to recognise the women's right to vote was the South Western State affectionally known as the Rocky Mountain in Colorado, USA. A few years later many states followed. In 1869 Wyoming had become the first American Territory to grant women the vote. Nancy Astor would have been well informed about these women as she fought for women's rights in Britain.

Margaret Wintringham (nee Longbottom) (1879-1955) member of the Liberal Party was elected to the House of Commons in 1921 and was the second woman to sit in Parliament. At last Nancy had a woman companion to speak to in Parliament where men had reigned supreme. In 1923 the Right Honourable Margaret Bonfield (1873-1953) Labour MP joined Nancy in the House of Commons and became the first woman cabinet minister, also that year Katherine Marjory Stewart-Murray, Duchess of Atholl DBE (1874-1960) Conservative representative for Perth and Kinross entered the House of Commons. She was the first woman to be elected in Scotland. After October 1924 the number of women MP's increased with Dorothy Jewson (1884-1964) Susan Lawrence (1871-1947) Mabel Philipson (1874-1960) and Vera Terrington (1889-1956). Nancy Astor was no longer alone to face the daunting task of the male dominant Parliament. They fought hard to have the Criminal Law Amendment bill accepted and the Guardianship of Infants bill, and the acceptance of Women Police. The success of these was due to the steady hard work of Nancy Astor and Margaret Wintringham.

Nancy had been embroiled with, and followed eagerly in, the steps of Eleanor Rathbone (1872-1946). Beatrice Potter Webb (1858-1943) social worker and writer with feminist sympathies, was appointed as a member of the Royal Commission on the Poor Law from 1905 to 1909. In 1909 Elizabeth Garratt Anderson was Britain's first woman mayor. Another dedicated reformer for housing and feminist rights was Octavia Hill (1838-1912) and Marie Stopes (1880-1958) made her mark as a feminist crusader who in 1921 established in London, Britain's first birth control clinic. These women were all very remarkable. Eleanor Rathbone at first was a Liverpool City Councillor, then later one of the first and most effective women Members of Parliament in women's health and women's rights. Women were to make their mark in society and local government. Dame Evelyn Adelaide Sharp (1903-1985) became the first woman to reach the upper ranks of the Civil Service. Later she was appointed to the post of Permanent Secretary in charge of a government department. In 1955 she trail blazed her way to the top of the Ministry of Housing and Local Government, eleven years later she retired. Baroness Sharp was invested in 1985 as a Knight Grand Cross Order of the British Empire (OBE) and was known as Baroness Sharp of Hornsey Greater London.

Plymouth was to experience the wrath of the suffragettes when in April 1913 they attacked Smeaton Tower on Plymouth Hoe. They painted around the base in large white letters intending it to be a greeting to coincide with the visits from the Lords of the Admiralty, including Winston Churchill. The slogan written on the seaward side read: 'To Churchill, no security till you give women votes, no matter how big the Navy!' and on the town side 'To save the state from shipwreck give women the vote.' It was clear that women were on the march and history tells us how successful they were, so ladies remember to vote when you are given the opportunity for reputations were destroyed and lives were lost to gain that privilege. Nancy Astor was a friend of the Elmhirst family of Dartington Hall, Dorothy Elmhirst who was an American had written many letters to Nancy and it was because of their friendship that Plymouth citizens were to feel the benefit during the Second World War as families were billeted at Dartington for safety after the city had been bombed. Dorothy had feminist beliefs and her interests were varied, among them being the most important was her passionate desire for peace. She was a member of the Peace Pledge Union, and was devoted to religion, politics and birth control. She had also supported the Women's Labour Union Movement and as both Nancy and Dorothy came from America they had similar ideals. Leonard and Dorothy Elmhirst founded the Dartington Hall Trust, after they purchased the Dartington Hall Estate, near Totnes, Devon, in 1925. They bought it as a home for themselves, where they would stay for most of their lives, and for the remarkable 'Dartington experiment' that they were to create.

The Champerbowes family had previously owned the estate for 300 years but due to the 19th Century depression they had fallen on bad times and the hall fell into disrepair. Dorothy Straight (nee Whitney) (1887-1968) was born in America and came from a multi millionaire family; she married Leonard Elmhirst in 1921. It was her second marriage as her first husband had died in 1918. Leonard Elmhirst (1893-1974) came from Yorkshire and he and Dorothy worked hard to establish the

Dartington Hall Trust as a successful experiment in rural regeneration partly financed by her New York heiress's fortune. The project advocated an art college, an open-air theatre, a cider press and production of beautiful crystal glass. Progressive education, arts and country crafts, were to become a welcome part of their programme and they set up various projects such as businesses involving forestry, farming, carpentry, and even included cheese making. Toward the end of their lives the Elmhirst's formed the Dartington Trust and it was most successful, now with the trust having fulfilled its duties it is privately owned and shortly the arts will be transferred to Exeter University.

In 1940 with the coalition government in control of the nation Nancy Astor along with Irene Ward, Mavis Tate and Thelma Keir initiated the formation of the Women's Power Movement. However there were political limitations and no confirmed collaboration between women moderates and the establishment. The need for women to be protected in trade unions and the labour movement, the Fabian women's group, the Co-operative guild, and the National Council of Women, sought to work together to achieve common goals. Members of Parliament launched the consultive committee on women's organisation to co-ordinate women's careers as well as providing a medium where views could be expressed. History has shown that both Dorothy Elmhirst and Nancy Astor were to have an impact on people with their human touch. During 1941-1943 Nancy took Dorothy Thompson (1894-1961) on a tour of Plymouth to show her the dreadful state the city was in from the bombing. Dorothy Thompson was an American born in New York, and was a confirmed suffragist. She became the first American Correspondent to be expelled from Nazi Germany and was a strong opponent of Hitler and his Government. On her return to the United States she wrote a newspaper column called On the Record in the New York Tribune and Nancy wanted to use her press experience to feature Plymouth's heartache appealing to the USA for help for her beloved war torn citizens. Dorothy later became a broadcaster for the NBC and an author of several books. Nancy and Dorothy had a common bond in that they both loved participation in cart wheeling.

Nancy Astor supported the National Trust and encouraged many people to give as much as they could to the trust in an effort to preserve buildings and art. Nancy secretly admired a band of eccentric women who also had a desire to preserve the countryside and buildings of architectural standing. The women were known as the Ferguson Gang and they went around the countryside making observations of England's treasures to see which needed to be rescued for the National Trust. Most of the women were well off and they would meet for picnics and outings and their exploits were a source of amusement. They were the faces behind a mysterious masked band of philanthropists who had taken to making sudden appearances at the headquarters of the National Trust (founded 1895) with sacks of money and clear instructions to direct the funds to particular causes. They would be dressed in unusual costumes. One even appeared as a highwayman. They were indeed very generous. Their passionate activities first came to light in the 1930s. They made funds available to the National Trust to enable them to purchase properties and to preserve artistic treasures. They also helped to buy a stretch of the Cornish coast to save it from potential developers. For many years no one knew who they were, however, as the generation of the secret group, who had used pseudonyms, began to die from the 1940s onward, some of their identities became known.

The leader of the Ferguson Gang who had died aged 93 had been Bill Stickers who was officially recognised in an obituary in the Times newspaper in 1996. Dr Margaret (Peggy) Steuart Pollard, aka Bill Stickers, was a brilliant Sanskrit scholar; she was fluent in Russian, a musician and a poet. She was also a Cornish Bard, historian, and a great-niece of Gladstone. She had written a book entitled Cornwall. It was published in 1947. The book also included a mention of the Ferguson Gang. Others members of the group were Red Biddy, (named for her Communist leanings) she had been a brigadier's daughter, became a doctor, saw the inside of prison, and was noted for her disinterest in soap and water. Sister Agatha, who worked as an almoner, was the gang's organiser and she once said, "We were in our twenties and it was fun. We cared about helping to save England and wanted to be involved in something of permanent value. The National Trust was the obvious recipient for our schemes as it keeps its properties for the nation forever." Kate O'Brien's chosen name was the Nark; she had crept into a National Trust office in 1934 and presented a package of money containing £500 to save a town hall. Other names were, Erb the Smasher, See Mee Run, Gerry Boham, and their spiritual head, the Right Bludy the Lord Beershop (or Bishop) of the Gladstone Islands and Mercator's Projection. Lord Beershop had been an art student at the Slade and was the gang's official artist. Only one or two men were involved with the women's group. One ally was The Artichoke, aka John Macgregor, a well-known conservation architect. He came into contact with the gang when they donated a vast sum of money to save the derelict Shalford Mill in Surrey, of which he became the tenant.

Their notoriety was widespread and they exuded an enormous sense of fun. They kept a record of their visits to the National Trust Offices in their minute book affectionately known as the Boo. They also kept the newspaper cuttings of their activities and postcards, retained photographs, and meticulously kept receipts for money given to the National Trust. It is pleasing to know that the National Trust has the majority of their records and adventures held in their precious archives. One of the National Trust projects is this year celebrating the 75th anniversary as a National Trust property because of the Ferguson Gang who saved the precious building with their financial generosity. The antics the group used to indulge in when contributing money to the National Trust encompassed mischievous stunts. The national newspaper The Telegraph, and the National Trust spring and summer edition of their 2008 magazine, gave an insight into some of their escapades. On one occasion they delivered money sewn up in the carcass of a goose; another method used was to attach

£50 notes to miniature liqueurs and on occasions they would leave a brief case packed full of money.

They purchased their masks and costumes from Harrods and the National Trust allowed them to meet in parts of their buildings to hold their clandestine meetings. Usually eight members would meet and the group would engage in the ritual of dancing around the millstone in flowing robes, and as their hands struck the millstone a battle cry emanated from their mouths. Sometimes chanting in Latin they would stay up all night to greet the four colours of dawn. A Fortnum & Mason van would arrive, and cooking smells permeated from the building. At their secret meetings high-class food would be served, pheasant, duck and lobster, and they drank champagne. The Gang were all highly educated and had connections in higher circles, but they were determined to halt the despoliation of the countryside which had become predominant with the sprawl of post First World War urban development. By the Second World War they had raised a remarkable figure of £4,500 with their own efforts and with the backing of friends.

Into the twenty-first century women are still fighting and campaigning for equal rights. Influential female leaders participate in the International Women's Day aimed at inspiring women to achieve their full potential. Today, and hopefully in the future, women will feature more predominately in the boardrooms, politics, and in high profile roles, which they could never have aspired to years ago. There are still obstacles, which prevent millions of women achieving the same status, rights and opportunity as men. Nancy Astor had fought for all these things. Many people have scorned the activities of women feminist and eccentrics and Lady Astor herself faced many critics. Yet these people in themselves were pioneers. They faced ridicule by the public to prove their worth. They had the courage of their convictions to present policies against the norm and to make their mark in the world. Critics sneered, huffed and puffed, literary minds snubbed their achievements, non-believers tittered whilst others laughed. However, whose names are remembered? The critics? The literary minds? Those who sneered? The people, who scorned, tittered and laughed? Or all the names in this chapter?

*Lady Astor; The women pioneer; having a group photograph taken in the USA in 1922.
She was on her way to Richmond, Virginia - Her public duty took up every day of her visit.*

CHAPTER TWENTY-THREE
CITY TRIBUTES

Remember this, if nothing else, there is a flame, that once lit, warms the heart in darkness, of those whose hands were warmed in light. *Anon.*

John Edward Poynder Briggs (1924-2002) Nancy Astor's Godson, author of the book 'Nancy Astor' 1980 & 1982 made this statement: 'The City has shown little sign that it is proud of the Astors' achievements or that it appreciates what they did.' Many Plymouth citizens perhaps would agree with that statement. John Briggs further pointed out in his book that an attempt was made some years ago to have Guildhall Square renamed Astor Square but the Labour party objected.

The most visible memorials to the Astors were mostly presented by themselves, including 3 Elliot Terrace, The Hoe, which was bequeathed as a residence to the City for future Lord Mayors, and to provide Civic Hospitality for visiting dignitaries, 3, Elliot Terrace, was completely refurbished in 1999. This was achieved by support from a generous donation from the Fredman Clarfelt family with grants from English Heritage and Plymouth City Council. In the year 2004 the once magnificent house was again showing the signs of wear and tear on the outside and badly in need of decoration to offset the peeling paint, as the ozone atmosphere from the sea takes it toll. In October 2007 a citizen's letter in the local Plymouth paper highlighted again the state of the outside of 3, Elliot Terrace, badly in need of repair and decoration. Angry at the shabby state of the house in a row of magnificent Victorian buildings the citizen castigated the Plymouth City Council for lack of maintaining the outside of the building.

In fairness the Plymouth City Council's Asset Management Team stated that the structural survey had been scheduled for November 2007. It had been difficult for the City Fathers to meet the date in view of civil functions being held in the former Astor home. It should not, however, have to be members of the public to constantly remind the City Council of its responsibilities in maintaining our precious heritage. Visitors who flock to Plymouth Hoe will be most surprised when they take out their cameras to photograph the once famous house. In February 2008 the planned redecoration of 3, Elliot Terrace, was once again put on hold; the Plymouth City Council were to have a structural survey of the premises as many cracks had appeared in the building which means some structural repairs may have to be undertaken before redecoration can take place. Perhaps, if regular maintenance had been applied, the building may not have got in such a state. After survey it was finally agreed that the former home of Lady Astor would be earmarked for decoration in March 2008. Citizens who have been campaigning for its restoration were pleased to see that the exterior and rear of the house coupled with the courtyard was finally decorated in April 2008.

FREEDOM OF THE CITY

In 1959 the Labour councillors had recommended that Alderman Mrs Jacquetta Marshall, who had been the first woman to serve as Lord Mayor (1950-1951) be awarded the Freedom of the City, however, the Conservatives wanted Lady Astor. At the voting, done in accordance with democratic rules for the Freedom of the City award, the votes were 36 in favour of Lady Astor and 34 votes for Mrs Jacquetta Marshall. Alderman Mrs Jacquetta Marshall O.B.E. had served on the hospital management committee for thirty years and was a former Chairman of Moorhaven hospital; she had made a great impact when serving as Lord Mayor of Plymouth and was highly respected. She was born of artisan stock; she always insisted she was an ordinary woman but there were people who thought of her as an extraordinary woman. With similar traits to Nancy in that she was blunt of speech, critical about the society, which allowed inequalities and injustice, she fought long and hard to redress the balance and gave sterling service in public life. She focused on the ordinary housewife and spent her life in trying to change living conditions in the Workhouses and Infirmaries. When it came to election time for Lord Mayor in 1950 the Council members were apprehensive at having a confirmed Socialist, however, she won them over and fulfilled her duties with honour and integrity.

The framed text of confirmation highlighting the recommendation on the 16th July 1959 for the Freedom of the City to be granted to Lady Astor, still hangs on the wall in the Astor Room in the Guildhall; all other items of Lady Astor have been removed. At a special meeting by the council when the Freedom of the City was granted, the text states: Desiring to acknowledge the eminent and distinguished services rendered to the City over many years by Nancy, Lady Astor. The Lord Mayor, Percival N. Washbourn, affixed the common seal to the declaration and J. Lloyd Jones the Town Clerk witnessed it. Why Nancy had to wait for so many years before being honoured in Plymouth has been a controversial issue amongst those who recognised her many deeds. Some critics felt that this was because she had stepped on so many self-important councillors' toes and leading councillors were not always treated politically correctly by Nancy.

The official formal occasion to award the Freedom of the City to Lady Astor took place at 3pm Thursday 16th July 1959 at the Methodist Central Hall, Plymouth; the hall was packed with dignitaries and a gathering of Nancy's friends and the event was to become transformed by Nancy's personality. Although living in London she had stayed in her former home at 3, Elliot Terrace for the special occasion. Her sons, Lord Astor, 3rd Viscount and Jakie Astor collected her from 3, Elliot Terrace at 2.45pm to take her to the Methodist Central Hall. Nancy, face flushed with pride and excited, had pieced together, with two of her trusted staff, the speech she was going to present. When Nancy was due to enter the Hall a hush settled and the congregation waited with bated breath for her entrance, the side door was opened and, preceded by the mace and accompanied by Mr Percival N.Washbourn, Lord Mayor (1959-1960) and the Bishop of Plymouth with other members, she was conducted to her seat on the platform. Lady Mayoress Mrs Washbourn presented her with a bouquet of flowers. In her speech Nancy thanked the Plymouth Council for the honour bestowed on her and further jokingly remarked that she would have liked a free bus pass, as she was a pensioner but knew that she must pay.

Nancy, at the time of the award of the Freedom of the City was an old lady of eighty, lonely, and unhappy that some former friends had drifted into obscurity; Nancy had been the inspiration to Plymothians for many years. The (1959) representatives should have cast out surely all political hatred on this occasion. To deliberately hurt someone who had been awarded a very unique gift by a City proclaiming their love and respect for all her efforts was indeed disquieting. How sad it was, that on the occasion of the presentation to Nancy, who had earned this wonderful achievement and given her all to Plymouth she was to be subjected to shocking behaviour by the non-attendance of certain Labour councillors to her function in the evening at the Duke of Cornwall hotel. Why? This was her very special day. Lady Astor was to pay a heavy price for winning the votes and without question was deeply hurt. How many will have looked into their inner self since and felt right about that cruel act? There had been disquieting factors, which could have explained this extreme discourteousness. Perhaps parliamentarians and councillors alike expected her to be a sophisticated intellectual, when she proved to be just the opposite they could not accept that trait with grace. Yes, there were many who disliked her, and it is known that many other citizens fought for the rights of the poor, however, it was Nancy who was to be recognised and courtesy to her should have been acknowledged on this occasion.

There were those, however, who did pay their respects to Nancy, acknowledging all that she had done for Plymouth and this replaced the hurt she must have felt. In the evening the City Fathers and the Councillors who did attend the function, showing their respect, gave her a wonderful dinner at the Duke of Cornwall Hotel. Two hundred and fifty people attended the evening and many of her friends were there. Nancy was in her element; she kept the audience laughing throughout the evening with her wit and sallies. For all her celebrated public speaking and well-remembered one-liners it was interesting to note that when she agreed to broadcast on Radio live in Devon she asked the presenter to hold her hand whilst she talked, a classic example that although nervous she did attempt to adjust to new and progressive ideas. At the hotel reception she wore the beautiful Cartier diamond necklace that fell almost to her waist, the long necklace was an interlocking chain which could be separated into different length pieces to form a bracelet, necklace, and earrings, which had been given to her by her beloved husband Waldorf in 1944-1945 to ease her heartache at the loss of her parliamentary career.

Nancy often said, "I am only an ordinary woman after all." What price fame? One small incident did put a spark into her life. On the day after she had been given the Freedom of the City she was on one of her walkabouts. Whilst in the vicinity of the Pannier Market a young lad from a Plymouth local school approached her and said: "Lady Astor, may I congratulate you on becoming a Freeman of Plymouth and thank you for all you have done." She was for a moment overwhelmed and tears came into her eyes, but before she could speak he was gone. It was a moment she cherished and on her return to Elliot Terrace she duly recorded it in her diary. James Mildren, a highly respected Journalist formally on the staff of the Western Morning News, chronicled a book in 1994 called '100 years of the Evening Herald' in which he highlighted important events in the paper's history. It was notable that the dates for June to October 1959 made no mention of the award of the Freedom of the City to Lady Astor, could it be that it was not considered to be of importance?

Lady Astor gave her beautiful Cartier diamonds to Plymouth City in 1959 when she was awarded the Freedom of the City, at that time their estimated value was a quarter of a million pounds, today they would be worth three times that amount. The beautiful pieces have several thousand exquisite diamonds and hundreds of sapphires in its formation and the jewels are in the shape of a May flower, the traditional flower of Virginia USA where Lady Astor was from. Nancy, in a wonderful gesture, took off the diamond necklace and placed it over the head of the then Lady Mayoress Mrs Washbourn saying, "This is a gift to be worn by you during your husband's tenure of office and by all future Lady Mayoresses of Plymouth thereafter." There were gasps of amazement and approval at the wonderful gift; such largesse by her was indeed freely bestowed.

However, there was quite a scare when she gave her diamonds to the Lady Mayoress as it was discovered that one end of the chain was missing, when Lady Astor arrived home (3, Elliot Terrace) she asked where it was and her maid Rose Harrison started an immediate search for the missing piece, Rose was adamant that she had given the whole necklace to her ladyship. A thorough search was mounted including the outside areas and the missing link was found in the gutter outside and a local jeweller called Mister Wigfull came along and refitted the missing link. So the beautiful Cartier diamonds became one of Plymouth's treasures. They are extremely valuable and can be worn by the serving Lady Mayoress. Because of the high risk in security and insurance they are usually only worn at functions six times a year. In return the Lord Mayor presented Nancy with a free ticket 'In perpetuum' on all buses in the City, indeed a gesture she fully appreciated with affection on both sides.

WHERE ARE THE ASTOR GIFTS?

Strange, too, that many of the items that were part of the Astor gifts to the City have disappeared into the unknown whilst many members of the public would love to view them. The insignia Nancy received when she was awarded the Freedom of the City and the portrait and bronze head that were to be housed in the South Room, now known as the Astor Room, were presented by Mr Michael Astor (the third son) when he visited Plymouth in April 1965 to inaugurate the Astor Room in the Guildhall. In the year 2008 the Astor Room does display a portrait of Waldorf Astor painted by Sir James Gunn R.A. but the bronze head of Lady Astor sculpted by J. Davidson in 1930, which once held pride of place in the Astor Room at the Guildhall, and the portrait of her entering Parliament with Lord Balfour and Lloyd George, which had been presented to the city by her son in April/May 1965 to inaugurate the Astor Room, is missing. Research revealed these two items are now placed in 3, Elliot Terrace, on the Hoe. Also missing is the silver casket and gavel presented to Nancy, Viscountess Astor, on the launching of HMS Plymouth on the 20th July 1959. The every day citizens do not know where they are; perhaps they are stored at Plymouth City's Museum?

Lord Astor, the third Viscount, was unable to attend the ceremony in 1965 as he had recently suffered a heart attack and had to rest as advised by his doctor. His brother Michael Astor presented the silver casket, medallion and illuminated scroll, and it was put on display with portraits of Lady Astor and Lord Astor. Other items on display in the Astor room in May 1965 were three volumes of newspaper cuttings reflecting many aspects of Plymouth's history from 1918-1959. Where are they now? They form part of a series of nearly one hundred volumes given to the city by Lady Astor in 1960. Perhaps they are lying on a shelf in the record offices gathering dust with the passing of time. The Chester Vase and Doncaster Cup, bequeathed to Plymouth by the late Viscount Waldorf Astor were also kept on view; these cups are now on view in the city's silver collection in the Council House. The third Viscount had offered a number of mementoes of his father and mother to Plymouth city council, which included a black velvet dress, which Lady Astor wore. It is not known where this dress is now, (in Plymouth Museum perhaps?) albeit it has to be noted that the dress would be ninety years old.

Also offered to the city were the portraits of her and Lord Astor and the Freedom of the City casket. The portraits, the Freedom of the City casket, and the sculpted head were placed in the South Room of the Guildhall (now the Astor Room) in tribute to the late Lord and Lady Astor, but all evidence of Nancy, except the written parchment awarding the Freedom of the City, has been removed from the Astor Room. The beautiful bronze bust is residing at 3, Elliot Terrace, as is the silver casket presented at Nancy's Freedom of the City award on the 16th July 1959. On the lid of the casket are two crests, the one on the left is Plymouth's crest, and the one on the right has an emblem, which was created by the first Viscount Astor. The Heraldic peerage flag and motto reads 'Ad Astra' and has the emblem of a falcon surmounted by an eagle, with three stars and flanked by two standing figures, an American Indian and a Fur Trapper. The framed portrait of Lady Astor entering the House of Commons with Lord Balfour and Lloyd George holds pride of place upstairs at her former home.

The decision to move the items from the Astor room to 3, Elliot Terrace, was carefully considered in the light of insufficient security, there being only one security guard on duty at the Guildhall at any one time. The Astor Room, being on the upper floor and accessible to the many visitors, was thought to be unsuitable to house the precious items and so they were removed to the Astor's former home, which now has more visitors and functions than the upper Guildhall. Judges and visiting dignitaries may stay at 3, Elliot Terrace, as also may members of the Astor family and it is here that the Lord Mayor holds his (or her) 'At Home' meetings. Tours are organised for visiting groups such as the Townswomen's Guild, the Women's Institute, visiting Americans, VIP'S and many other local groups. In April 2008 the Coldstream Guards toured and found the history of the Astors most interesting and Plymouth University hired the house for a day to interview potential candidates for the post of Vice-Chancellor. A vacancy had arisen following the untimely death of Roland Lavinsky, the former Chancellor and the post was subsequently awarded to Wendy Purcell. The hiring of 3, Elliot Terrace, provides revenue for the City.

ASTOR PLAQUES

On the North wall of the Plymouth Guildhall there is an inscribed bronze 3ft x 2ft plaque to Lord and Lady Astor placed there in May 1993, the planning committee agreed in July 1992 to have the item made at a cost of £1,000. The location of the plaque on the North wall is sited at the original entrance, which was blocked as part of post-war reconstruction. The writing inscribed on the plaque is as follows: 'Nancy Viscountess Astor born Virginia USA 1879 - died England 1964. In this building on the 28th November 1919 the election to Parliament of Lady Nancy Astor (an error perhaps by the carver, title should read Nancy, Lady Astor) was announced. She was the first woman to sit in the House of Commons and represented the Plymouth constituency of Sutton until 1945. Elected Freeman of the City of Plymouth in 1959. Formidable in politics and an indomitable champion of just cause Lady Astor's charm and wit were matched by her unflinching courage in adversity. In politics and public life they worked tirelessly for the common good of the people of Plymouth. Waldorf, second Viscount Astor born New York USA 1979, died England 1952. Waldorf Astor served as Member of Parliament for Plymouth 1910-1919. As Lord Mayor of Plymouth 1939-1944, Lord Astor presided in the council chambers near this building, which were destroyed by enemy action in 1941. In the darkest days of the war, he prepared for the reconstruction of his stricken city, and in a plan for Plymouth published 1943 was expressed the vision and hope that led to the building of the city we see today.' However, the location of the plaque is so remote from the people that only those who visit Saint Andrew's church, the Guildhall or make their way to the law courts are likely to see it.

In the courtyard of Virginia House there was a square grey plaque with gold lettering which read: Nancy and Waldorf Astor wanted Plymouth to have a centre for the advancement of voluntary social service. Virginia House Settlement is that centre. This courtyard, completed in 1996, is a celebration of the Astors' 35 years of public service in this city and was opened by David Astor on the 23rd October 1996. In the main entrance, right hand side on the wall is a round plate plaque, depicting a side profile view of Nancy Astor. CH 1879-1964 (Sculptor-Michael Rizzello OBE) Underneath this is an oblong plaque with these words: Nancy Astor founder of Virginia House Settlement in 1925 she followed her husband in representing Plymouth in the House of Commons and became the first woman member of that house. She was a member for 25 years. This plaque is presented by the two surviving of her six loving children.

On the sidewall at the Batter Street entrance of the Virginia House Settlement there is a 5ft x 3ft wooden board and inscribed on it are these words:

VIRGINIA HOUSE SETTLEMENT
FOUNDED BY THE VISCOUNT
AND VISCOUNTESS ASTOR

With the closure of Virginia House Settlement the Astor plaques on its walls may disappear forever and how will the next generation of historians and citizens know of her and remember what she did? A granite stone incorporated into the wall of the Palace Street Flats records some details of Nancy with the following inscription: City of Plymouth: This building was opened by the Viscountess Astor M.P. on the 10th day of June 1938. Alderman Solomon Stevens Lord Mayor. J.P. Councillor C.P. Holmes Chairman of the Housing Committee. Sadly the lettering is wearing away with some consonants and vowels missing, this means in time the recorded historical facts will be lost, perhaps one day funds may be found to refurbish this fine stone.

ST ANDREW'S CHURCH WINDOWS

In Saint Andrew's Church, the mother Church of Plymouth, are six stained glass windows that were designed by John Piper and made by Patrick Reyntiens. Two of these windows are dedicated to the Astors. Waldorf Astor's window known as the 'Tower Window' looks out over the city centre and is the Astor Memorial Window, the inscription written on a plaque below states: 'This window is in memory of Waldorf, 2nd Viscount Astor, Member of Parliament 1910-1919, Lord Mayor of Plymouth 1939-1944, who was granted the Freedom of the City in 1936.' Instruments of the Passion have been represented since the thirteenth century and have been more commonly used by craftsmen in the West Country than anywhere else. In the design, the ladder and the reed and spear form a St Andrew's cross in honour of the dedication of the Church. At the top of the window are shown the sun and moon in eclipse. The Central East Window, however, is roped off in the altar area, and visitors cannot approach it unless a steward is asked to remove the enclosed barrier. There is no plaque indicating what the window is, albeit there is an informative sheet on the table entering the church for all to read if so desired. It is sad indeed that here was a Lady who was a Viscountess; Member of Parliament for Sutton Division Plymouth for twenty-five years, who was generous to the extreme to Plymouth citizens, yet there is no visible recognition of her window. One could argue that she was not a Councillor, but neither was Waldorf, but they were being recognised for what they did for Plymouth. Lady Astor's window represents the four elements: air, fire, earth and water. God's purpose for the world is shown with the beginnings of life emerging from the slime, and everything is striving upwards yearning for completion.

INSCRIPTION

Rebuilding of the Tinside Swimming Pool on Plymouth Hoe in the year 2003 meant that the pavements and pedestrian access facing the foreshore were improved. An added attraction is the placing of steel bollards at intervals along the pavement edge; these bollards feature names that are linked with Plymouth's history. Inscribed on one of these bollards is the name Nancy, Lady Astor, so at last Plymouth representatives have finally recognised her without the Astor family or the Astor Estate footing the cost. In 1989 Sir John (Jakie) Astor asked Plymouth City Council to erect a permanent memorial as one was long overdue, but it was not to be. Many citizens have felt over the years that more should have been done to recognise Nancy Astor, as there were so many kind things that she did that people knew nothing about. The Astor name will live on in the beautifully refurbished Astor Hotel named after them by the people in 1960.

PRECIOUS GIFTS

In 1931 one of the most precious gifts received by Lord and Lady Astor were the two silver candlesticks and a tray made by severely disabled servicemen and inscribed with the British Legion's crest, in celebration of their silver wedding and presented to them by the then Mayor J. Clifford Tozer on behalf of the Plymouth branch of the British Legion. (Where are they now?) The Legion members adored Nancy and the party held at the Abbey Hall in 1931 is one the Astors remembered with affection. She deeply appreciated the gift from the Legion because four and a half years of her life was spent among soldiers and sailors. Twenty four thousand men passed through the hospital of one thousand beds at Cliveden, during the First World War, and it was a wonderful thing to live in a community in which everybody wanted to help everybody else. "I was a Colonel in those days," she said, amid laughter "and my rank has never been taken away, so why am I not called Colonel Astor today? It would be better for the world today if the spirit of comradeship and selflessness so apparent in the war days permeated the life of today, because on the return of that good old spirit depended the future of England."

Plymouth's celebration of the Silver Wedding of the Viscount and Viscountess Astor took place at the City Guildhall, on Friday June 12th 1931. The city council committee members organised an evening banquet to present a silver wedding gift from a grateful Plymouth. The gift was a beautiful solid silver model of the first ship to sail round the world; Sir Francis Drake's ship the Golden Hind. The ship was made by the specialist Silversmiths Page, Keen & Page. The organisers of the gift also gave an album to Lord and Lady Astor containing the names of all the subscribers. For many years the silver model of the Golden Hind was displayed at Buckland Abbey when it was under the management of the Plymouth City Council. It is thought the object is still in the care of Plymouth City Council, albeit, the ordinary citizens do not know where it is or whether it would be available for public viewing. The Navy held Nancy in high esteem and the Commander-in-Chief Admiral Sir Hubert Brand paid a very warm tribute (Western Independent Sunday June 14th 1931) at the presentation of the Astor's silver wedding gifts, saying, "I personally have a very great admiration,

Photo courtesy Miss Jean Tozer (JP Retired) Daughter of Sir Clifford & Lady Tozer

Taken in June 1931 on the occasion of Lord & Lady Astor's Silver Wedding at the Abbey Hall given by the Plymouth Branch of the British Legion.
Left to Right. Commander-in-Chief Admiral The Hon Sir Hubert Brand, Viscountess Nancy Astor, Anon, Clifford Tozer Mayor, Waldorf, Lord Astor, Mayoress Mrs J Tozer, Hon Phyllis Astor, Anon.

and, may I say, a personal affection for Lady Astor and the family. The Navy, which I represent here, I am quite sure recognises to the full the great work that Lady Astor does for the Naval personnel in this port."

Lady Astor's unique ability to speak to all classes endeared her to many barbican fishermen, coal heavers, servicemen, barbican ladies who filleted the fish catch when landed by the fishing fleet, and the barbican washer women who never failed to barrack her. Yet in a strange way they admired her and respected her whatever their class distinction. This was notable in the tributes from the roughest of men and women in Union Street, which was in those days the hub of the city at night, especially when the Fleet was in. In Union Street there used to be the only licensed picture palace St Jimmy's which had an attractive entrance with verandah portico, and a photographers' shop, a Museum and an usual name known as the Stickyback Studio Incorporated. Saturday nights at St Jimmy's was the highlight of Union Street life. The highly respected hosts of the Prince George Hotel, Stonehouse, James Doel the oldest actor in England (1778-1876) featured in the 'Plymouth Comet' (1893-1896) which included the revered figure of the beautiful Lady Astor and Henry Francis Whitfield the journalist who later wrote the book 'Plymouth and Devonport in times of War and Peace.' Sailors often brought items of interest for the Museum; four squirrels playing cards, a stuffed crocodile and even stuffed pygmies, where did the items go and where is the revered figure of Lady Astor?

Many United States forces were based in Plymouth during the war years and the officers and men of the 13th Port, US Army presented a plaque to the Astors as Lord Mayor and Lady Mayoress in appreciation of the courtesy and kindness shown to them during their stay. Perhaps the finest tribute to the Astors was the living presentation in 1952. This was when a narrative with musical interludes entitled "The Glorious Years" and relating some of the outstanding events in the lives of Lord and Lady Astor was a feature of a birthday party given to Lord and Lady Astor in the Abbey Hall Plymouth. The narrative, with musical interludes, was written and spoken by Mr Freddie P. Knox, and related some of the outstanding events in their lives. Mr Knox was Lord and Lady Astor's personal aide who arranged and organised the birthday party in honour of the celebration of their seventy-third birthdays. Lord Astor, unable to attend the party, sent his beloved wife a telegram "I join you in giving affectionate greetings to the lady who never grows old and who keeps her husband still going strong in spirit."

Plymouth Technical School of Housecraft had made beautiful birthday cakes for the occasion, one was a representation of the Palace of Westminster with the hands of Big Ben pointing to seven, and the house being in session, with a Union Flag flying from the tower. Superimposed on the building were two photographs of Lady Astor framed in white icing. One showed her, as she was when she first took her place in the house, and the other one, as she was when she left it. Many friends attended the party and it was made complete when two beautiful cakes, a personal cake for each, in the form of an open book bearing the respective dates of their election to Parliament, and to the office of Lord Mayor and Lady Mayoress of Plymouth were presented. Lord Astor's book cake had the words "Truth and Honour" and Lady Astor's had the words 'Righteousness and Love' both with 'Happy Birthday.' It was truly a magnificent tribute and there was also presented a cushion bearing Lord Astor's coat of arms and another cake bearing the city crest and the words 'Happy Birthday.' Lady Astor shook hands with all present and was presented with a bouquet of blue irises, pink carnations and sweet peas. A fanfare of trumpets signalled her arrival on the platform and everyone joined in singing 'Happy Birthday to you.'

During World War Two Lady Astor presented a standard to Lieutenant Finn, of the Royal Navy, on behalf of the Royal Naval Sick Berth Association and the standard was held in St Nicholas Chapel at the Royal Naval Hospital. On the closure of the hospital it was suggested that the standard be placed in a Royal Naval Museum, as a surviving member of the Finn family was now holding it. At that time the nearest Museum was Portsmouth and that would not have been acceptable to Plymouth's history. The Finn family graciously decided to officially hand over the Standard to the City of Plymouth. The standard has come full circle as now it has been framed and placed in the Lord Mayor's residence in 3, Elliot Terrace, Lady Astor's former home.

CITIZENS COMMENTS

In October 1951 a former social worker Mr J. J. Judge wrote a citizen's letter in the Western Morning News and pointed out the debt to the Astor family. He wanted to express his feelings and when looking over a whole generation, he remembers what Lord and Lady Astor meant to Plymouth since Waldorf Astor, known as a rather shy young man, won his Plymouth seat in the House of Commons in 1910. He said, "Did anyone think what Lord and Lady Astor would become to the town, the welfare of which would soon become a foremost and abiding duty to them? Few can know all the multitudinous ways in which this was manifested. Gifts such as the Prince Rock playing fields, the housing estate at Mount Gould, the Hall of Residence at Devonport, the Nursery School in Hoe Street, and the part they played in the institution of the Training College for Nursery School Teachers, the day nurseries, a convalescent home, and other work in children's welfare. Thousands of citizens, without party divisions, joined in presenting the beautiful silver wedding gift in May 1931, followed at a later date (1936) by the Freedom of the City to Lord Astor. Still present in our minds must be the five years of a unique and memorable Lord Mayoralty, the historic plan influenced in no small degree by Lord Astor. It is surely not necessary to say anything of the making of Parliamentary history in which Plymouth and Lady Astor joined, and women especially should know how concern for child welfare has long been woven into Lady Astor's consciousness. It is one's own consciousness that compels one, unsolicited and unprompted, to send you this letter and gives the writer the hope that another young man, courageous and not unacquainted with national and international affairs, may have a path opened to him to prove his quality, as his father so well proved his." (The young man refers to Jakie Astor)

In September 2006 a citizen wrote to the local newspapers suggesting that the new link between Millbay and Western Approach be named the 'Astor Boulevard' that would indeed be a lasting memorial to Lord and Lady Astor. In July 2007 some wonderful news greeted the citizens of Plymouth, which was reported in the City's local paper. The caption read: New University building to be named in tribute to city Member of Parliament. Fantastic news for the people who still carry Nancy Astor in their hearts for it will at last bring to the attention of the younger generation what this grand lady did for Plymouth and it will perhaps make our future generation ask the question: Who was Lady Astor, what did she do for Plymouth?

The new eleven million pound building at the Endsleigh Place development is intended to provide new accommodation for the university. The Nancy Astor Building, due for completion in September 2008 will house the Faculty of Health and Social Work, its modern design will also incorporate a café with views over Drake's Reservoir, a new gymnasium and a sports hall. It will be a splendid attempt to go green to protect our planet in that it will have its own energy centre housing a rainwater harvesting tank, boilers and hot water generation plant. The University chose the name after a consultation and with permission from the current Viscount Astor. They are to be congratulated on giving the older generation what they wanted, a fitting memorial to someone who lives on in their hearts. The Campus chiefs decided the new building would be a fitting tribute as the former Plymouth Sutton Tory MP was a champion of social issues and particularly advocated nursery education. They are proud of the choice and so will true Plymothians be proud of this magnificent recognition. The nearest Plymouth had managed to offer in statuette style of Nancy was the cardboard cut-out standing in the window of the city Museum, overlooking her beloved city. Along side her were the cardboard cut-outs of Professor Abercrombie and Forbes Watson. Now from a cardboard cut out figure in the Museum window she will be more prominent at the University in its name. (The Museum underwent a refurbishment in 2008 and when it was re-opened it was noted that the cardboard cut-outs had been completely removed.)

NEW AND REFURBISHED DEVELOPMENTS

In 2008 new homes were built at the East end of Plymouth; Cattedown is being transformed by new business premises and care homes for the elderly. One such place is the new purpose built 'Astor Court' a thirty-unit block of flats with self-contained one and two bedroom apartments of shared ownership for vulnerable adults aged fifty and over. It incorporates an extra care-housing scheme and on the ground floor a new community resource centre has been built and, in addition, four shops. It is a supported housing development by the Housing Corporation in partnership with Signpost Housing Association. With around-the-clock care staff on hand it will indeed be a pleasant place to live where residents will feel safe and comfortable and for the building to be named after the Astors is indeed a welcome reminder.

A new look Astor Park will be linked with infrastructure buildings and an open public space is to be developed during 2007, which will provide a play area, basketball court, youth shelter and paths across the park with a hardstanding to hold special events. It is hoped that the ornate iron gate entrance will not be changed and that it keeps it's unique spelling done in the olde English, (or was it a spelling mistake by the welder all those years ago who perhaps had forgotten the little phrase we were taught in school I before E except after C, when we were taught how to spell field?) The caption on the Iron Gate reads 'Plymouth Education Authority, The Astor Playing FEILD 1916' it has been there all these years and it survived the Second World War. The Cattedown residents would not want to see it changed because it is part of Plymouth's East End history, after all the spelling FEILD is a variant spelling used by William Shakespeare and Geoffery Chaucer, it was good enough for them, so why not the East End?

ASTOR DEEDS

In 1952, after the death of Viscount Astor, a newspaper report quoted: 'Although a recapitulation of the enormous amount of known good work Lord Astor did for the city would fill columns, it represents only a fractional part of his service, much of which was performed anonymously. Whatever else may be forgotten, the Virginia House Settlement, Astor Housing Trust, and Astor Playing Fields will always be memorials to him as will the Nursery School of which he and Lady Astor were pioneers.' In 2008 Virginia House Settlement, the Astor Institute, and the Astor Housing Trust no longer exist. However, the Nursery School is still going strong and the Astor Playing Field is still open, it has ensured its continuity by spending money in updating the facilities to make it available to the citizens of the East End. The little Astor Garden on the barbican is now open again after a make over for the pensioners in the Barbican area. One mystery remains with the little Astor Garden overlooking the Mayflower steps; what ever happened to the plaques that used to hang on the iron gate at the entrance? The first plaque read: 'These grounds were donated by Lady Astor for use by old age Pensioners and retired Fishermen only.' The second Plaque read: 'Open daily from 10 am to 5pm May to the end of September; keys may be had from number (here the number had been scratched out) Lambhay Street.

Nancy was instrumental in obtaining Elizabethan House on the Barbican. She became a member of a special group of citizens determined to save our heritage by salvaging old buildings and renovating them. The 'Old Plymouth Fund' was created by a temporary society who was determined to save Plymouth's historical buildings. Its leader was Mr. J.J. Judge, Honorary Treasurer, Richard Winnicott, Chairman. The group enlisted the help of Lady Astor and together they raised a sum of money to buy the property. Sir Shirley Benn supported the cause and the Astors gave £200 towards renovation. This forward thinking group supported by genuine lovers of the Barbican history is responsible for the historical gems they have saved through their compassion and care. Plymouth also has Lady Astor to thank for saving the Grade One Georgian Mansion Saltram House as she persuaded the last surviving member of the Parker family who lived at Saltram House to offer the house and its land to the National Trust; they acquired the premises in 1957 following the death of the fourth Earl of Morley. In 1964 the Morley Family heirlooms came out of the vaults and storerooms when the National Trust started selling this part of the Estate to offset the running costs and renovation of Saltram House. Antique furniture, silverware, glass, porcelain and linen were put up for auction; dealers from London and Torquay were at the auction. Names to catch the eye were Chippendale, Sheraton, Hepplewhite in furniture, Dresden, Delft, Ming, Spode and Minton in ceramics.

For the men and women, ex servicemen and widows, this was the woman they never forgot as she never forgot them. She brought hope and became a legend in their eyes, the warm smile, a reassuring pat, her generosity and showing that she really did care about people. One such letter was from a widow whose husband had died several months before and she had no pension and no income to support her. The widow appealed to Lady Astor for help. Nancy was very angry to think that this lady was left with no means of support and she told her. "Well you just leave the matter to me." Within three days the lady received her pension. The widow said, "I can never finish thanking her, and may her memory last for ever." Another citizen remembers an incident where Lady Astor accosted a lorry driver and stopped him from driving on until she spoke to him. The driver swore at Nancy for the interruption but undeterred Nancy asked him to help transport some goods for a bombed out person and he did, under duress, assist in helping the woman. Another remembers with pride the time that she was shopping in a little shop in High Street. "When I came out of the shop, whom should I see but Lady Astor with the late Duke of Kent and without ado she introduced me, what a handshake! What a thrill it gave me. But that was Lady Astor, always so friendly - apart from politics!" Mrs Stella Rose, Edgecumbe Park Road, Peverell, Chairman of Crownhill, Plymouth branch of the National Federation of Old Age Pensions Association, treasures some of the last frail writings of Lady Astor written two days before her death.

In Plymouth the only house bearing the famous Astor name is Astor House, 2 Alexandra Road, Mutley, and that building is now the office of an Accountancy firm.

The house is quite near the Mutley Conservative Club that Nancy Astor used to frequent in her electioneering years.

Lady Astor spent a small fortune in Plymouth for its welfare. In 1967 the Independent newspaper asked Plymouth citizens to write in their views on Lady Astor and the responses came from far and wide, letters flooded in from Liverpool, Oxfordshire, Glasgow and Penzance in Cornwall. Nancy, remembered as the woman whose tongue whipped men to shame; the heart that wept tears when men lost loved ones in the Plymouth blitz.

ROAD APPROVAL

In September 1992 a recommendation was lodged by the Plymouth City Council to name a small access road in the area of Mount Gould, Plymouth, after the Astors, the recommendation was approved and the road was opened with its new name on the 5th October 1992. The road was named 'Astor Drive' and is situated at what was once the Astor Institute, which later became the Venton Centre and is now the Riverview Community Centre, which cares for people with the dreadful diseases Alzheimer and dementia.

FINAL RESTING PLACE

Lady Astor's ashes are buried in the eighteenth century octagon temple at Cliveden, Buckinghamshire, with Waldorf, but for true Plymothians she lives on in our hearts. Nancy the pioneer, Nancy the giver of love and gifts to children, Nancy the friend of the poor and Nancy who fought for the rights of the common people. Would that something a bit more imaginative than a plaque on the wall to Nancy could be presented. One suggestion was perhaps a sundial on the Hoe. It would be such a tribute if we the Plymouth citizens, could install a statute of Lady Astor on the promenade at Plymouth Hoe in a dancing pose. On the bottom a brass plate could be fixed with just two words 'Our Nancy.' that would tell the world of our respect and admiration of a very special lady. Hundreds of visitors and citizens visit Plymouth Hoe and there are other statues, which are viewed and photographed by people from all over the world. A statue of Nancy Lady Astor would not go amiss in the eyes of all that would view it, for there again, she would be the first woman statute on the Promenade at Plymouth Hoe and that would have made her smile.

Deep in the hearts of all who knew her or who have benefited from her kindness this doyenne from the Astor dynasty will be a memory that will live on irrespective of her title Viscountess Nancy Astor, in the hearts and minds of Westcountry folk she will always be: 'Our Nancy.'

"OUR NANCY"
Taken when she was in her eightees at her former home Cliveden Buckinghamshire,
she would often stay at weekends as the guest of her son and daughter-in-law.

CHAPTER TWENTY-FOUR
HOUSE OF PRIDE

For a man's house is his castle and each man's home is his safest refuge.
Edward Coke 1552-1634.

Donald Alder was born in 1926 in South Wales and his mother was a Plymouth girl who married a Welsh miner. Like many children of the poor in those years, poverty and poor health was rife and young Donald's father died when he was two years old. This is what he had to say: Mother brought me back to Plymouth in 1928 and she married John Carnell in December 1931. Two more sons were born in 1932 and 1935; in those early days we lived at Ashford Road, Mutley, Plymouth. My mother worked for a time at the Margaret Macmillan nursery between the birth of my two brothers to make ends meet, and my stepfather, who was constantly unemployed, also worked there for a little time. Mum worked in the kitchen and Dad in the gardens; my brother was in the Macmillan nursery when it first opened its doors and a little later my youngest brother joined. Little was left of Mum and Dad's pay when the nursery fees were paid but they made the best of the hard times. The nursery school was one of Lady Astor favourites projects as she admired Margaret Macmillan and the school is still open today in its original site at Hoegate Street near Plymouth Hoe.

Our living accommodation was very sparse and Mum put out some feelers to see if she could be granted a house at the Astor Housing Estate, Mount Gould. To our joy we were accepted in 1937 and, issued a three-bedroomed house at 22 Mount Gould Terrace on the Astor Estate, I was now eleven years old. How proud we were and the thrill of having a bathroom and garden was wonderful. At that time the Estate consisted of Mount Gould Terrace and Mirador Place and was situated from Heathfield Road to the Astor Institute. I recall that Lady Astor took great pleasure in the estate and what was more important the people who lived there. She quite often visited the estate to see what was going on and she would knock on the doors checking the tenants and, of course, seeing that the properties were being used correctly. We were so happy in our lovely little house and the declaration of war left us worried and sad. In March 1941 during the savage bombing of Plymouth, a bomb dropped outside the house, and we had to move to number one Saint Dunstan's Terrace, Beaumont Road. We were not forgotten and Lady Astor made sure that we moved back on to the Astor estate, when it was possible, and we took up residency at 48 Mirador Place.

'Getting with it' was one of Nancy's favourite pastimes as many children at maker camp and around the estates in Plymouth will remember, for she always insisted on using the Tarzan ropes tied to trees to swing across a bank or stream, the children loved her doing that and she would be as good at it as the children were. Also, she would ask them to collect all the white butterflies, as they were damaging to the vegetables. In the war years all garden flowers and bushes had to be dug up and vegetables grown to feed the population, even public parks had to grow vegetables. Reading the papers in those days I found her a vastly different person than the articles written about her. The written word would indicate a brash and sometimes rude manner, which she showed as a Member of Parliament, but to the tenants she had the compassion and thoughts that won their respect. She was the best that a landlord could be and she was what we, the struggling poor families, needed and we loved and admired her.

I still live in Plymouth and I remember with affection how Lady Astor would round up all the children she could see and persuade them to collect litter to keep the estate clean. I witnessed, however, her wrath in 1943, when she paid one of her visits to the estate. She would leave her car at the Astor Institute and walk around. Mirador Place at the time was looking very untidy with litter everywhere; Lady Astor blew her top and, determined to do something about it, rounded up all the children on the estate; parents meanwhile came out of the houses as word got around to see what was happening. Having collected all the children she could, Lady Astor held a meeting with all present and formed the Astor Tidy Club and all the children were issued with badges marked ATC and became members of the club and were ordered to keep the place clean and tidy. It worked! Each day, children would collect all the rubbish and

Sketch: Copyright unknown

A sketch of the Astor Estate.

litter, and parents helped too on occasion, especially if their child was one of the 'keep it tidy' group, they were honour bound to follow the rules. In those days children were avid badge collectors and woe betide the parent who put the loss of the child's badge in jeopardy if the rules were not obeyed.

During the war when costs were going up the Governors asked the tenants of the Astor Housing Estate if they would voluntarily pay higher rents to save their homes. The majority would. However, the minority who refused left no option but for the estate to be sold into other hands. My lasting memory of Lady Astor was in the late nineteen forties when she began to feel the strain of all her commitments and designated the Halifax Building Society to sell off the estate. There is no doubt Lord and Lady Astor were heartbroken at the sale of the Astor Estate; they had started it as an experiment, which had failed because of the blindness of a few. Mindful, as usual, of the well being of her tenants, she directed that no tenant would be evicted and they would continue to reside in their homes for as long as they wished. She also stipulated that all tenants were given the right to buy the houses they lived in at a very reasonable price of £650. My brother was in the Merchant Navy at the time and he bought the home at Mirador Place and mum and dad lived there in comfort until 1980 when dad died. This was the compassion shown by Lady Astor to have the welfare of her tenants at heart, and I have never known any person, especially being an American, to feel such love and care for this city. She was truly a wonderful person and I wonder what she would make of it all today if she was still around, I do not think she would be able to tolerate the complacency shown today in the care of housing estates, standards have fallen by the wayside.

In 1939, just before the Second World War was declared, my stepfather and many other unemployed workmen could find little or no work and he and my mother did any work they could find. With the onset of war dad finally got a job with City Council, building Air Raid Shelters in Regent Street; it is a shame that it took a war to find so many unemployed men a decent job. Although pay was poor at least it brought some income into our family to enable us to survive. I recall that Lady Astor paid one of her visits to the estate in 1939 and, as usual, asked if we had any problems and my parents told her that lack of work was the main problem. Two weeks after her visit and my parents expressing their concern over lack of employment they received a letter from her office telling dad there was a vacancy as a labourer in His Majesty's Dockyard and dad immediately applied and was readily accepted. He remained in the employment of the Dockyard for the whole of his working life, so my family has nothing but praise and grateful thanks to the great lady. Whatever people say about Lady Astor's faults, she will always remain in our hearts, and my children and children's children have been told of our background so as they will remember in the future, her name will not be forgotten. Her love of the older generation was highlighted when the Astors bought and presented a gift of land at Lambhay, between the Hoe and the Barbican, which held a portion of the old castle quadrant for preservation as a public open space.

LADY ASTOR HOUSING TRUST.

FOUNDED BY VISCOUNT AND VISCOUNTESS ASTOR ON DECEMBER 30TH, 1924

OBJECTS

The provision of Houses for large families under conditions which secure to the Tenants as a community

(1) A share in the administration of the Estate on which they reside.

(2) An interest in the efficient maintenance of the property comprising the Estate.

(3) The use of Social, Educational and Recreative facilities.

Note.—The Deeds of the Trust provide for elected tenants becoming members of the Court of Governors of the Estate.

	TYPES OF HOUSES.		Rented per week. (Exclusion of Rates)	
			s.	d.
A3	Ground Floor. Living Room, Scullery First Floor. 3 Bedrooms	Bath, W.C. ..	8	9
A4	Ground Floor. Living Room, Scullery First Floor. 4 Bedrooms	Bath, W.C. ..	9	6
B3	Ground Floor. Parlour, Living Room, Scullery First Floor. 3 Bedrooms	Bath, W.C.	10	6
B4	Ground Floor. Parlour, Living Room, Scullery First Floor. 4 Bedrooms	Bath, W.C.	11	3

Note.—The Standard Garden area allotted to each Tenant is approximately 300 yards super ; area in excess of this may be rented by arrangement with and consent of the Governors of the Trust.

Copy from an original

Look at the Rent - those were the days!.

Duplicate.　　**Form of Agreement.**

Date July 27th 1937.

I, 　　JOHN CARNELL,
(Name)

of 　　16, Ashford Road, Plymouth,
(Present address)

having read the Regulations and Terms of Tenancy attached hereto and having received a duplicate copy thereof do hereby agree to comply with the same and to become the tenant of (A3).

28, MOUNT GOLD TERRACE, Plymouth,

at a weekly rental of eight shillings

and nine pence from the 31st day of July, 1937.

Tenant's Signature *M J Carnell*

Witness Signature *M. D. Blackard.*

Address Astor Institute, Mount Gold, Plymouth.

Agent of the Lady Astor Housing Trust.

THIS FORM OF AGREEMENT SHOULD NOT BE SIGNED UNTIL THE APPLICANT HAS BEEN ADVISED, IN WRITING, THAT HE HAS BEEN ACCEPTED AS A TENANT.

Copy from an original

The agreement that Donald's Stepfather and Mother had for their new home on the Astor Estate in 1937.

CHAPTER TWENTY-FIVE
MYTH AND TRUTH

One crowded hour of glorious life is worth an age without a name.
Thomas Osbert Mordaunt (1730-1809)

THE CLIVEDEN SET MYTH

When over-enthusiastic reporters and those regular rumourmongers plied their trade, the mud that they threw and the stigma it raised would eventually end up being glued to the Astors; frequently reports did not accurately reflect the truth. Wild press speculation subjected Nancy and Waldorf Astor to a trial by the media. Rumour mongering was the press's speciality. Throughout Nancy's life, and even after her death, the stigma levied at Nancy remained. It is now time for the real truth to be told and the myth destroyed to clear her name. Sad indeed were the false accusations levelled at Lady Astor in reference to the Cliveden Set for the truth was far different to that told to the public by communist writers, and reporters, casting aspersions and altering information on the Astors to release their reported versions to newspapers to enhance their marketing sales. The political scene and the mud throwing from bad press in the 1930s and the 1940s were indeed to have a great impact on the citizens of Great Britain and particularly the Astors. There was controversy surrounding the Astors and mumblings could be heard from those who thought they were in the know.

Amateur historians suggested that Lord and Lady Astor, as leaders of the Cliveden set, gave covert support to the Nazis in the nineteen thirties. However, this is something that was never proven. In James Fox's book The Langhorne Sisters published by Granta Books in 1999, it was pointed out that Waldorf Astor was one of the few foreign visitors to Hitler, perhaps the only one, who provoked one of his sudden fits of rage. As a member of the House of Lords and a newspaper owner, The Observer, Lord Astor had mentioned the predicament of the Jews, when he had a private meeting with Hitler. Hitler had asked why the relationship between their two countries was not better. Waldorf Astor told Hitler that it would be impossible to have good relations until he changed his policy towards the Jews. Hitler became angry, almost beside himself and had to be calmed down by his aides. This was not known generally and when Neville Chamberlain made his tragic concessions in the years before the war the Astors suffered the accusations of being pro-Hitler when in fact they were in total opposition of his political standing. The fact that Lord Astor challenged Hitler's political actions and Nancy agreed with Waldorf indicated that they were not pro-Nazi. The Cliveden Set was pure fiction.

As long as Waldorf and Nancy Astor were in the spotlight they became a target for gossip, criticism and untruth; when one is in the public eye rights of privacy are often forfeited. Both Lord and Lady Astor had been subjected to misunderstanding, a pithy statement of a truth or opinion. England was their home by choice and they would not jeopardise its national security. Lady Astor all through her career continued to cause controversy. One incident in the Daily Express April 2nd 1938 shows (supposedly) Lady Astor caught in the act as she held a meeting of her Cliveden Set at number 4 St James's Square at 12.30pm. The meeting was called for the hostess to serve a good lunch, which was totally teetotal, and her guests that day were Lord Halifax the Foreign Minister, Mr Jeffery Dawson Editor of the Times and Doctor Tom Jones ex-deputy Secretary to the Cabinet and advisor to Mr Baldwin. Lady Astor flitting around the steps of her house said, "Lot of nonsense talked about the Cliveden set, tell you what - what I am doing is lunch that's all, what's so dreadful in that?" This little group was known as very much pro Hitler, and pro Mussolini, pro Franco. Great political significance has been attached to the Cliveden Set who had been accused of these faults. Lady Astor remarked, "There, all the Cliveden gang in one!" She thought it was a huge joke. There were people in Plymouth who knew her well, knew her very well, enough to know she was not pro-Hitler. There were factions in the political field, journalism and anti-Astors who was ready to indulge in character assassination and Lady Astor was targeted frequently and things she said would often be distorted or stated out of context.

Waldorf's letter on The Cliveden Set was published in The Times newspaper in May 1938. Lord Astor in a part of his letter wrote, 'the fiction that has been written recently about an imaginary group described as the Cliveden Set, was better ignored. For years my wife and I have entertained, in the country, members of all parties, including Communists. To link our weekends with any particular clique is as absurd as is the allegation that those of us who desire to establish better relations with Germany or with Italy are pro-Fascists. Lady Astor and I are no more Fascists today than we were Communists a few years ago.'

Nancy's Cliveden Set denial letter was published in the Daily Herald newspaper also in May 1938. She indignantly denounced all Cliveden Set stories. "There is no such thing! It is a fantastic invention. It has no existence. It never did exist. One of the penalties of public life is that the line between one's private and one's public life is blurred, legends arise about public figures which have little foundation in fact. The legend, which has most distressed my husband and myself, is that associated with the so-called Cliveden Set. According to this legend, my husband and myself and our friends are somehow or other regarded as conspirators. We have had people at Cliveden because we like them. We have entertained many politicians of all countries."

Privately, 1937 and 1938 had proven most distressing years for Nancy, as in those years her beloved sister Phyllis (1880-1937) and her only surviving brother, William Henry (Buck) Langhorne of Albemarle County, Virginia, (1886-1938) had died. Neville Chamberlain (1869-1940) who was Prime Minister of Britain (1937-1940) had paid several visits to the Astor home as guest, and once confided to Lady Astor that after he became Prime Minister he intended to take most of foreign policy in his own hands, in his desire to succeed in his policies with Germany. He bypassed the Foreign Office, who took a pro French, anti German, and an anti appeasement stance, and did in fact end up conducting Britain's entire foreign policy in secrecy, even from his own Cabinet colleagues. Sir Robert Gilbert Vansittart, later 1st Baron Vansittart (1881-1957) was then permanent under-secretary at the Foreign Office (1930-1938). No gossip so rankled British Conservatives as that told about the Cliveden Set. First to name this mythical gathering as the Cliveden Set was Francis Claud Cockburn (1904-1981). He reported the infamous accusation in the newspaper. Noted as a reformist and renowned radical British journalist, he was a controversial man known for his communist sympathies. His famous cousin the novelist Evelyn Waugh must have been embarrassed.

Cockburn edited a mimeographed newssheet called The Week and later became a writer for London's Communist Daily Worker. It was well known that Cockburn disliked the Astors intensely and he would always make life difficult for them in the public eye. Many a United States and British newsman has since elaborated the original Cockburn details, spreading the story that a group of rich pro-Fascist Conservatives were meeting and regularly plotting at the Cliveden country estate of Lord and Lady Astor. It is a shame that such stigma should have been levied against the Astors who did so much to enhance good relations between nations. The truth, however, will never be accepted because the myth is set so firmly in folk consciousness as to be ineradicable. Another distressing event, which hurt Nancy deeply, was that Harold Macmillan, (1894-1986) later Lord Stockton, who in later years as Premier of Great Britain (1957-1963) was a frequent visitor to Cliveden, denied her a seat in the House of Lords during his Premiership.

JOLLY JACK TAR'S TOT OF RUM & ALLOWANCES

Mess deck rumours were widespread amongst the Naval personnel that Lady Astor had been responsible for stopping the payment to the sailors, who were known as 'the men of hard-layers' and were mostly crews serving in destroyers. It referred to the extra payment made to matelots to compensate for the discomfort of serving in small ships. She was reputed to have gone on a fact-finding trip which consisted of a day out from Harwich in a flat calm, spending most of the day in the wardroom, and subsequently announcing that she saw no sign of hardship. It was the Ministry of Defence who recommended the stoppage of this money and not Lady Astor. The worst accusation of all was that she had fought to have the issue of Jolly Jack Tar's grog, which had been a naval tradition since 1655 stopped completely, which was considered sacrilege! The daily award of an eighth of a pint of 95.5 proof spirit to every man in the fleet was finally abolished on the 31st July 1970. (Six years after Nancy's death)

This accusation was not true either; the tot was stopped much later at the instigation of a popular Naval Officer, First Sea Lord Admiral Michael Sir 'Dry Ginger' Le Fanu, (1913-1970) He was First Sea Lord from 1968 to 1970 when unfortunately he was diagnosed with a terminal illness and died that year. It was a Naval decision not influenced by the late Nancy Astor, there was no political pressure to enforce the action. It is true Lady Astor abhorred alcohol and on many occasions advocated a non-drinking way of life, however she was not responsible for the cancellation of the Navy's tot of rum. The very last tot from the store of HMS Dido was thrown over the side just off the coast of Scotland in a sealed bottle with instructions inside asking the finder to drink the Navy's health. At a mess table in Nelson's last flagship HMS Victory, the final issue was sipped with proper solemnity. The Submarine Service at HMS Dolphin, Gosport, provided a gun carriage bearing a coffin flanked by two drummers led by a piper playing a lament.

THE D-DAY DODGERS MYTH

It is generally believed that it was Nancy Astor who, during a fictional World War Two speech in Parliament, first referred to the men of the 8th Army fighting the Italian campaign as the 'D-Day Dodgers'. Her implication was that they had it easy because they were avoiding the real war in France and the future invasion. The allied soldiers in Italy were so incensed, they composed a bitingly sarcastic song to the tune of the haunting German song Lili Marlene popularised in English by Marlene Dietrich which they called The Ballad Of The D-Day Dodgers. How wrong they were, because they had been indoctrinated with false information that again Nancy was blamed for, what she really said was taken out of context. For those surviving D-Day Dodgers it is time that you knew the real truth of how that colloquialism came about: the truth about a ridiculous rumour, how it all began and what it means. Nancy remarked, "It is extraordinary that of all Members of Parliament I should have been picked out for this sort of propaganda by the enemy...." The Editor-in-Chief, British Army Newspaper Unit of the Central Mediterranean Force (CMF) finally got to the root of the alleged D-Day Dodgers infamous remark. He wrote an article to clear up the mystery for all time, it contents can be seen in the Imperial War Museum. Unfortunately it was not given the publicity to clear Nancy's name as was given to the original accusation. Had the same publicity been given, the stigma could have been permanently removed. A number of complaints had been received on this subject which reached the Service Journals and cartoonists were having a field day.

How did the D-Day Dodgers nonsense begin? In Britain nobody was serious about it, yet the origin was difficult to trace. However, as truth will out in time someone came forward with some astonishing facts.

Captain J, De Vroome, Adjutant of a Battalion of The Buffs came to the rescue with this letter, which he wrote to the Editor-in-Chief of the forces newspaper. "In early December 1944, some men of this Battalion expressed indignation as they had heard a rumour to the effect that Lady Astor said that troops in Italy were D-Day Dodgers. I enclose a copy of the letter received from Lady Astor in which she explains how the information was circulated. As I understand this rumour was prevalent throughout the Central Mediterranean Force perhaps you will be good enough to publish Lady Astor's letter." Nancy's letter was dated 19th December 1944 to which Captain J. De Vroome refers. It was signed by Nancy and came from her home in 3, Elliot Terrace, The Hoe, Plymouth. The letter started, "Dear Capt de Vroome I have just heard from your father that you and your men are indignant about my calling you D-Day Dodgers. I am not at all surprised, but you may rest assured that none of you is as indignant or hurt as I am. Oddly enough, on December 12th 1944 I received an Airgraph signed D-Day Dodgers and I thought they had nick-named their particular Company with that name, so I wrote back: Dear D-Day Dodgers: In fact I was very touched by their letter! It may interest your men to know that this rumouring about me has gone on since the beginning of the war.

First the Navy believed that I had tried to stop their hard-lying money (when I didn't even know what is was). Then the Eighth Army thought I talked about their basking in the sun while we were bombed at home. Then this was followed by another rumour that I said all men coming back from the Middle East should wear yellow armbands as a warning against Venereal Disease. In the prison camps the men believed I had said English girls wouldn't marry Englishmen because they were cowards but were marrying men from the Dominions instead! And now this one, which you have heard. Considering that my husband and I have, between us, represented a Serviceman's constituency for 35 years, it is extraordinary that of all Members of Parliament I should have been picked out for this sort of propaganda by the enemy. The only reason I can think of is that they use my name because I was the first woman in Parliament. The Airgraph had the name of 6148576 Pte. Spriggs, S., 'C' Coy, C.M.F. If you can get any message through to that Company or any Central Mediterranean Forces paper, I'd be grateful. With best wishes for a happier year in 1945. Yours sincerely (Sgd) Nancy Astor." As expected the facts were never put into the forces newspaper and Nancy had to live with that stigma for her lifetime, even after her death, such a shame that she had to endure that when she did so much for the servicemen.

Well there are the facts, the joke-in-bad-taste was never even made, but that's how rumours start.

In 1940 the Minister of Transport, Lieutenant Colonel Moore-Brabazon RFC, put forward the idea that Airgraphs be used to reduce both the bulk and weight of mail travelling between the Middle East Forces and the United Kingdom. The matter was referred to the Army Postal Service and the General Post Office, who jointly investigated the possibility of using Airgraphs. This eventually lead to a service being instituted between England and Egypt in 1941 when 70,000 Airgraphs were sent in the first batch and took three weeks to reach their destination. The use of the Airgraph was not rationed and its postage was set at three pence (3d). Although the Airgraph proved to be immediately popular its use was limited because of its size (approx; 2ins x 3ins) and lack of privacy, so when sufficient aircraft capacity became available its use declined in favour of the air letter. The Airgraph service was later extended to: Canada (1941), East Africa (1941), Burma (1942), India (1942), South Africa (1942), Australia (1943), New Zealand (1943) Ceylon (1944) and Italy (1944). The British Army Newspaper Unit of the Central Mediterranean Force (CMF) 1943-1945, issued a newspaper produced by the British Army Newspaper Unit, for the fighting men of all ranks and services in this theatre and was distributed by the Directorate of Army Welfare Services.

As the Author, while having a quiet lunch in a restaurant in August 2008 (named after Zeus the supreme God of the Greek Pantheon) I was privileged to meet Clifford Hulcuup an eighty-eight year old former serviceman, who unable to find a spare table in the restaurant asked me if I would be willing to share mine and of course I was delighted. We ordered our meals and as we chatted he told me he had served in the 43rd Wessex Division, which had fought so gallantly in the D-Day landings. I noticed he was immaculately dressed and on his blazer he wore his medals and badge with pride. During our chat I mentioned that I was writing a book about Lady Astor, his eyes immediately lit up and for a moment I thought, here comes the yarn about the D-Day Dodgers. On the contrary, he stated how thrilled he was to have met Lady Astor in 1945 at her home in Elliot Terrace. She had invited the Devon men from the 43rd Wessex Division comprising the Worcestershire Regiment and the Devon and Cornwall Light Infantry for tea at her home. They had returned home from their courageous fight in France. The veteran said how she shook hands with every one of them and it was an experience he never forgot and his passing words were these as we left the Restaurant: "Not all of us believed what was said about Lady Astor, I for one have always and will always respect her for what she did for us!"

TWO PHILANTHROPISTS ARGUE

On the local front, a Plymouth newspaper article revealed that Albert Casanova Ballard, President of the Plymouth Argyle Football Club, and owner of a well known boys' club, reacted strongly to Lady Astor's quote from her speech at a garden fete which had castigated his views on children's attitudes. Lady Astor was a tireless champion for the children, admittedly she courted criticism, but her loyalty to Plymouth was never challenged. The Primrose League was founded in 1883 similar to a lodge with regional meetings and hundreds of women joined. Ideal for a get together over a cup of tea it succeeded in helping many children and various charities and proved a very worthwhile organisation. In a speech at the Primrose League Convention in Plymouth, Nancy admonished the cinemas. She loved to watch Westerns films but she did however object strongly to the sex appeal in the films of the day. She called the sex-suggested scenes presented in some of the films, as degrading and disgusting, and added that it was not good for young children's moral upbringing. With the diminishing standards of morality in this day and age, and with the United Kingdom having the highest incidence of teenage pregnancies in the world, and children having children, what would be her views today if she saw the shocking and degenerate scenes that we see in today's films and television? Some would say we have become more extrovert in our views on sex. Have we really? Or is it an excuse to appease those who participate in unhealthy relationships debasing the moral judgement of our society? These two great philanthropists were always bickering on various subjects, each in their own way were sincere citizens, they had very strong views and both protagonists had dominating personalities.

Lady Astor opened a Country Fair at Virginia House, which was a local community centre for the poor in Plymouth. She fought hard and long for poor families living in such bad conditions and won the fight by forcing the Council to build more houses with better living standards. She set a good example by having built in Mount Gould 80 three and four-bedroom houses for poorer families with children from the Barbican area. The Astors had contributed £20,000 into a trust to provide the houses of the Astor Estate at affordable rents. When the estate was built it was said that Lady Astor had a covenant initiated stipulating that no public house was to be built on the Astor Estate. Her lifelong campaign against the evils of drink would not allow alcohol to be consumed in premises with which she had been involved. This accusation was also untrue. The factual truth is that this order was made by a property developer and builder called Mister Jinkin, a devout Methodist, and like Lady Astor a strong opponent of drink. Ten acres of land was set aside to build the houses and was formerly founded in 1926. Lady Astor interviewed a lady called Miss Land for the post of Housing Manager of the Astor Housing Estate at Mount Gould and soon families were being housed from the slum areas. How sad that the estate was sold off in 1952. A private company, Bradford Property Trust Limited, bought it, for the tenants of Mount Gould it was the end of an era.

SHABBY ACCUSATION

In December 2007 an extremist newspaper, volume 2 number 7, issued to fifty-five thousand homes in various localities around Plymouth, and reputed to be distributed in major cities in the United Kingdom and overseas, placed an article that was an insult to a Lady who is not able to defend her character. Whilst appreciating that there is freedom of speech it is a different matter when something is written that is not true, press sensationalism destroys many good moral characters with untruths. In this paper a very volatile statement was made, part of which said, 'Mrs Wallace Simpson, who the Federal Bureau of Investigation believed was passing classified information to one of her lovers, the Nazi Von Ribbentrop, with whom Nancy Astor also had an affair.' To state that Nancy Astor would have had an affair with a man she detested, and a Nazi to boot, is the lowest form of character assassination. This statement produced anger amongst genuine supporters of the late Viscountess Astor, when challenged by the Author and a former staff member of Lady Astor, the Editors avoided answering the question, which was put to them 'From which field of research did you find this evidence?' The Editors were spoken to several times, and on each occasion they promised to reveal where this evidence came from, emails were sent and not acknowledged, they promised to make contact but did not; they were evasive and continued to press home their political views but never answered our enquiries. The evidence? None was forthcoming.

We must not allow this myth to continue, as Nancy Astor would not have welcomed the sexual aspect of any affair. Deep, loving friendships yes, sex no. She adored Waldorf and her private beliefs and her religion would never compromise her morals. Lord and Lady Astor had invited Joachim von Ribbentrop (1843-1946) the Wesel born German Diplomat, to St James Square in the early 1930s for lunch, to discuss peaceful issues, and had nothing to do with the mythical Cliveden Set. Later in 1936 Lord and Lady Astor had entertained von Ribbentrop again at Sandwich when he was Ambassador to Britain (1936-1938) later he became Germany's Foreign Minister (1938-1945) His entrance did not please Nancy as when he entered the room he gave the Nazi salute shouting "Heil Hitler" and Nancy said to him: "Don't give us any of that nonsense here!" Whilst there, Ribbentrop had tried to discuss the possible outline of an Anglo-German deal with Waldorf Astor, for a revision of territories for the injustice of the Treaty of Versailles. The meeting was attended by many representatives, which also included the Astor's friend and statesman, Phillip Henry Kerr, 11th Marquess of Lothian (Lord Lothian) (1882-1940) who had devoted his life to world peace. He was appointed British Ambassador to Washington in 1939 and played a decisive part in the Anglo-American Alliance through the Destroyers-for-Bases lend lease deal. His close friendship for Nancy Astor led to their both converting to the Church of Christ Scientist together. When Phillip died in 1940 Nancy was devastated, as he had died at the height of his career.

At the lunch at which Nancy was host in 1936, she mocked Ribbentrop's mission and Ribbentrop was really rattled, it looked as though he would walk out of the guest lunch. James Fox in his book The Langhorne Sisters (Granta Books London 1999) remarked that Nancy had asked the German diplomat, "How anyone in England could be expected to take seriously a man with a little Charlie Chaplin moustache, tell him

(Hitler) that he has got to take it off!" This indelicate remark about Hitler enraged Ribbentrop so much that when he returned to Germany and reported back to Hitler, the slight put Nancy on the Nazi blacklist for immediate arrest if the Germans had successfully invaded Britain. Nancy had refused to visit Hitler and this was another slight that was recorded in the black book. Joachim von Ribbentrop was convicted at the Nuremburg trials in 1946 of war crimes and of crimes against humanity and was subsequently hanged.

Nancy Astor from 1910 to her death in 1964, although a Virginian by birth, was fiercely loyal to Plymouth and England. Do not let this false accusation of an affair with von Ribbentrop blight a woman's character, or let it deviate from the truth and the fact that she gave so much to her beloved citizens. This reported remark was another myth written by journalists seeking sensationalism.

Photo: by kind permission Charles Prynne. Copyright not known
Digital copy by Trevor Burrows Photography

A last photograph taken at Cliveden with her grandson William circa 1960 who later became Viscount Astor.

By kind permission Mr Charles Prynne. Copyright Life Magazine photographer Marie Hansen and Life correspondent Jack Bearwood USA. Digital copy: Trevor Burrows Photography

Lord and Lady Astor awaiting guests in the rich library at Mirador House, Virginia, USA. 1946.

CHAPTER TWENTY-SIX
AN ASTOR LEGACY

'Love and thanks for your devoted services to humanity'
Queen Elizabeth the Queen Mother.

Quote from a letter written by her majesty Queen Elizabeth to Lady Astor after the bombing of Plymouth 1941. *(By kind permission Buckingham Palace)*

UNIVERSITY PLACE

The year Nancy Astor died in 1964 her family gave a wonderful legacy to the young people of Plymouth for the future. The legacy was to be known as the Nancy Langhorne Astor Scholarship and it was to be awarded every three years. The money came from Nancy's own money, which she had inherited from the Langhorne family, the fund would allow for all expenses paid and the legacy was in perpetuity. The scheme operates through the auspices of a trust fund set up in memory of her and administered by the West Devon Area Education Officer. The trustees of the fund invite applications from women graduates for the scholarship at the college of William and Mary, Williamsburg, Virginia, United States of America. Graduates must have been born in England, Scotland, Wales, or Northern Ireland and be under the age of twenty-five years. They must be a resident of Plymouth and must satisfy the trustees that they or their immediate families have had their permanent homes in the city for a continuous period of eight years. They must be graduates of a University situated in England, Scotland, Wales or Northern Ireland, or have gained a degree from the Council for National Academic Awards.

The college of William and Mary USA is a multi-faceted University dedicated to intellectual inquiry, discovery and dissemination of knowledge, and is now entering its fourth century of existence, since King William 11 and Queen Mary 11 chartered it in 1693. Facilities cover a 1,200-acre campus and include academic and residential halls, a major library and museum, a student centre, a 15,000-seat stadium and extensive computer facilities. In all, the College accommodates some 5,300 undergraduates, 2,100 graduate students from 50 states within the USA and 67 foreign countries, as well as approximately 600 faculty members. Campus life is full with more than 80 per cent of students living in halls of residence, small houses and fraternity houses. All freshman normally have meals and live on campus, all dormitories have lounges, recreation areas and laundry facilities. It offers a wide range of courses in Art and Science and in Education at both Under Graduate and Post Graduate levels, and Astor scholars are normally able to arrange a programme or studies which meet their varied or more specialist interests and which, in appropriate circumstances, may lead to a Master's Degree. In later years the University grant has been allocated every three years, however, the last pupil to attend the William & Mary College was in 2003. A spokesman from the Plymouth City Council and Trustees confirmed that it was hoped the University grant would again be available in 2008.

A GRATEFUL ASTOR SCHOLAR

Miss Margaret Churchill, a former pupil of Plympton Grammar School had been awarded the Astor Scholarship for 1977/1978 and carried out post-graduate studies at the College. She was twenty-one and the only daughter of Victor and Jean Churchill who at that time lived at Lipson Road, Plymouth. Margaret was studying for her B.ed. Degree at St Mary's College, Cheltenham. In September 1977 she planned to go to America in the hope to pursue her educational studies. Already a qualified teacher she wanted to compare how their educational system operated and how it differed to the teachings in Britain. The scholarship in 1977 was valued at £2,000 and its purpose was to commemorate Nancy Astor's lifelong interest in improving educational opportunities and her many links with Plymouth. This is Margaret's story as told by her:

My father suggested that I apply for the Lady Astor scholarship to the College of William & Mary in Williamsburg, Virginia, early in 1977. I was finishing my B.Ed degree at St. Mary's College, Cheltenham, and had no firm plans on what I wanted to do after I graduated. I was interviewed by the Lord Mayor of Plymouth Mr Robert Thornton, which made me appreciate the stature of the scholarship. I was very surprised, but delighted, to win it. I could not imagine then what a profound effect this would have on my life. In preparation for going to Williamsburg I communicated with two of the previous winners of the scholarship. These were very different girls, one very studious and one much less so, who had had quite different experiences. I also entered into communication with my sponsoring Professor at the College who helped me with more practical preparations. I arrived in Williamsburg exactly thirty years ago on 25th August 1977. It is an amazing place. The College campus flows into Colonial Williamsburg which steps you back into 18th Century America. Herb Ganter of Galveston, Texas, quickly befriended me, who was the self appointed guardian of all the Lady Astor scholars. A retired Librarian, he was a fount of information about the history of the College and all things colonial.

My educational goals were to learn about the early history of America and to compare the American education system to that of the United Kingdom. I found the teaching system at the College very different. The emphasis on group projects rather than independent study really helped me to interact with a lot of students. Being the Lady Astor scholar allowed me to baby-sit for the President of the College and the

Director of Colonial Williamsburg and to meet a wide variety of fascinating people. I became very interested in the first American settlers who founded the colony at Jamestown in the early 17th Century. This led me to the Virginia Research Centre for Archaeology, whose offices were on the College campus in the original kitchen of the Wren Building. I was offered a research job there for the academic year of 1978/79 and so I was able to remain for a second year on the College campus. More important, I met Jocelin Hackathorn, a law student who became my life partner.

After I returned to the United Kingdom in the summer of 1979 I was fortunate to get a job in what has become my lifelong career, international exhibitions logistics. I was transferred to Atlanta in 1981 and have lived in the city ever since. Looking back, winning the scholarship was a life changing experience for me, as it brought me to my adopted country. It is ironic that Nancy Langhorne went to England to find her fortune and that her scholarship allowed me to come to America, to find mine. As a young woman of twenty-two, it gave me the opportunity to expand my mind and to have the kind of experiences that are life altering. I will always be grateful for all the opportunities that winning the scholarship brought to me.

FAMOUS ARTIST'S DAUGHTER

In 1992 the scholarship was awarded to Rebecca Lenkiewicz daughter of Robert Lenkiewicz (1941-2002) the celebrated contemporary Plymouth Artist. Her response was, "Thank you for a brilliant year, it really has been so very incredible. I have finished the academic year and feel that I gained such a lot from my experience here. It has been an amazing opportunity." Rebecca stayed on in America for a further year as she received a prize award for Theatrical Excellence and this funded in part her extended period.

UNIVERSITY STUDENT'S MEMORIES

As told by Andrea Symons:

In the year 2001 I started my last term at the University of Manchester. I was studying for a combined honours Bachelors degree in International Politics and Literature. Contemplating what I would do after my graduation, I felt that I would benefit from some post-graduate study abroad. Having worked for a short time in Minnesota, USA for the Young Men's Christian Association I knew that I had learnt a lot from working and living within a foreign culture, but knew that I would gain more in my career from study in another country. I started to look for scholastic grants and awards that would enable me to take this costly step. Hours were spent trawling through guidebooks, websites and information sheets at the University career library and even more were spent filling out application forms. After a couple of weeks, word must have got back to my grandparents because they mentioned a scholarship they had seen advertised in the local newspaper, the Western Evening Herald, in Plymouth.

At first, being young and feeling worldly (something I still do) I assumed that this was not the fund for me, it was a scholarship from Plymouth City Council, my home town, and any student worth their salt knows that home means hick. However, I soon began to listen harder. The scholarship had been running for many years and was actually part of a bequest made by Nancy Langhorne Astor to ensure that young female academics from Plymouth had the opportunity to study in her home state Virginia, regardless of their own personal circumstances. This seemed perfect, the first female Member of Parliament could be the person who provided me with the opportunity to further myself academically and socially and prove that being a woman was no barrier, the fund also held a rather quirky personal significance. In his younger days my grandfather had worked as an apprentice at Elliot House, Plymouth. I can remember clearly the many times my grandfather had told of Lady Astor's generosity and kindness. The story goes that working at Elliot House was a good job if ever there was one, any tradesman lucky enough to get such a job would be tipped by the lady of the house and then told to seek out the butler, who would show them off the premises. The butler would then offer another tip and show the plumber, carpenter, chimney sweep to the kitchen and be told to see cook on the way out. The cook would then provide a cup of tea and a bite to eat and a third and final tip before you even got to the back door.

Other stories followed from both my grandparents of Lady Astor's kindness, her wry sense of humour, and passion for her work. To me this sounded like a woman after my own heart and it was a chance to get involved in the programme, it seemed almost like fate. I duly applied for the scholarship, running around collecting referees and the various bits of paper needed to complete my application. It was then sent back to Plymouth from Rusholme, where I lived, and I waited with bated breath, at length I was invited to interview and the rush for train tickets, a suit and various other interview paraphernalia began. The interviews were to be held at the Lord Mayor's parlour in the heart of Plymouth. The Mayor, at the time, was councillor Dennis Camp. (Sadly this highly respected man died in March 2006). Sohail Faruqhi the head of the Education Authority, and a member of the Astor family made up the panel. Myself and five other girls were asked various questions to assess our abilities, our aims for the trip away and how we would benefit both Plymouth and our destination Williamsburg; the focus was most definitely on our role as ambassadors for our home town. At the end of the interviews we gathered together in the Parlour again for a few press shots. These moments were agonising as we all stood smiling fixedly at the photographer, secretly plotting our measured responses to the presumed failure. Sohail announced the winner of the scholarship and I found myself congratulating the girl next to me before I realised he had said my name and not one of the other girls.

Leaving the City buildings felt surreal as I floated down past the Civic Centre in the sunshine, contemplating my future stay in America. After accepting the award I decided to defer my trip for a year to give me time to earn some extra money to support myself and take a break from study before I started my degree. William and Mary University seemed a long way off, but working for the University of Plymouth, Devon, England and spending time with my boyfriend, Dan (now fiancé), soon meant that the time came for me to set off.

On August 13th I finished packing my bags and made a sad journey up to Heathrow with Dan, Mum and Sue. We made an attempt at some fun to lighten the spirits by taking a trip to Legoland, but we all knew that I was about to leave for another country and stay there for some time. Hurried goodbyes were made at Heathrow and I made my way into the departure lounge. The journey was longer than I could have anticipated, the flight from Heathrow to Washington Dulles International (the nearest international airport) took eight and a half hours, from there it takes another forty-five minutes to get into DC. I had already organised my overnight stay in DC and made myself comfortable in the hostel, next to Madam's Organ, a bar in the Adam's Morgan area of the city. The time difference meant I woke up around five o'clock in the morning so had plenty of time to marvel at the Mall, the Washington Monument and the Hirschorn Gallery before heading to Union Station and taking the train to Williamsburg, this is the only train each day and so I got in at about six thirty in the early evening, where Debbie, a local resident picked me up and helped me and my luggage to the Graduate Complex which was to be my home for the next ten months. The first thing you notice about Virginia in the summer is how humid it is. The air is damp and heavy with pollen and scent from the hundreds of flowering trees around the campus. Williamsburg is neatly divided by South Henry Street, which marks the crossing from the new town, the college, residential areas and the Colonial heritage site. The college itself is very prestigious with a reputation similar to that of Oxbridge for the quantity of work that the students produce and the quality of research from both staff and students. The campus has some very old areas and a heritage of great politicians and theorists. The second-oldest university in the United States, it is home to the architecture of John Wren and housed Thomas Jefferson as a student, just one of five United States Presidents who have studied there. The red brick buildings blend in with the red cobbles of the pathways. I would not have had this wonderful experience if it had not been for Lady Astor and her generous legacy, I shall always be grateful for the opportunity of that University Course.

JOURNALISM AWARD

Another Astor legacy is a Nancy Astor award for Journalism and in 1983 it was controversially awarded to Ireland's Erin Patria Pizzey (nee Carney). Erin was a fierce anti-feminist, she once remarked "I feel sorry for women of my generation who were tricked into believing that the so called women's movement had anything to offer women except tears." She was the Founder of the modern women's shelter movement, an International Author for USA Harper Collins and a prolific after dinner speaker. She opened the very first refuge in the world for battered women; she had angered the Feminist movement when she declared that both men and women could be violent. Her 1982 book called Prone to Violence concerning working with violent women was boycotted and censored by the feminist movement. Such was the power of the Feminist censorship that the Publisher went into receivership. The book is now available on the Internet and a hard copy is again in print.

THE ASTOR ESSAY PRIZE

Grateful thanks to the staff and research team of the Department for Children's Services, Plymouth City Council, who diligently researched this information and for their kindness in bringing its plans for the Astor Essay Prize in the future to the attention of the Plymouth citizens.

Lady Astor was a firm believer in encouraging education in the young; she would attend Schools and Colleges and make awards for good written essays. Her religious beliefs came first in her life and many times the prize given would be a Bible. One citizen remembers with enormous pride the prize given to her by Lady Astor. In the 1930's/1940's sometimes, in view of seasonal work, young people would be out of a job for a period of time, however, they could attend the Unemployment School at St Levan's Road, where they learnt shorthand and typing amongst other things. On one occasion a General Knowledge competition was held and the winner received a bible, the citizen remembers that it was a small bible and she said, "I have treasured it all my life." Other winners of the prize would perhaps receive a dictionary or a book.

The Astor Essay Prize was an original donation of £333.6s.8d, given by Lady Astor in December 1945. This was duly recorded in an extract from the minutes (number 656) of the Education Committee's meeting held on the 20th December 1945; the Plymouth City Council confirmed this on the 7th January 1946. In its resolve the council representatives agreed that the gift be accepted with grateful thanks and a scheme administered for provision of the prizes in accordance with the wishes of the donor (Lady Astor). The purpose of the monetary gift was to have it invested at 3 per cent so as to produce an annual income of £10 per annum; this would allow award prizes for pupils of Plymouth Schools on the results of an annual Essay Competition. In today's prices that seems a paltry sum but in 1945 it was a generous gift. The Director of Education in 1945 was Andrew Scotland and he and the City Treasurer ensured that this gift and its suggestion was arranged. The value of the fund in 2007 stands at £9,248,84 and is generating £286 per annum income.

The last documented prize given is in the year March 1978, which was for one guinea (old English money) it appears there have been no prizes issued since then. The full file containing the accounting statements of this fund is available for viewing at Windsor House, Derriford, Plymouth, where they now are held. The registration number of the charity is 306688 and it comes under the Charity Commission for England and Wales at Liverpool. The author, on making research enquiries, received an explanation from a designated spokesman from the department. "The representatives of the Plymouth City Council realise that an award has not been given to a pupil since 1978." The spokesperson has offered this explanation to clarify its future. "The award has not been possible to give, as the schools do not provide any volunteer personnel to administer the paper work required, and to adjudicate in the presentations of the written essays. Unfortunately, the funds to not allow expenditure on administration of the award and because of this have remained dormant since 1978. We are aware there are several trust funds that Lady Astor and other contributors have created that are not being used, as they should have been, although the interest is still being accrued. We are considering amalgamating all the small trust funds into one large fund that can be used for a more practical award in the future."

Copyright unknown

Lady Astor circa 1920-1930

Lady Astor with H. R. H. Princess Margaret Circa 1950s

CHAPTER TWENTY-SEVEN
ASTOR HOTEL

Come to Plymouth - Gateway to the South West.

The Astor Hotel, an elegant Victorian home in Elliot Street, Plymouth, Devon, has sixty-two exquisitely furnished bedrooms and superb public rooms. It offers ballroom and conference facilities in a prime location, and is situated near the beautiful Plymouth Hoe, within fifty yards of the Hoe Promenade and the splendid sea front with its breathtaking views. The Hotel was renamed after the influential Astor family the Viscountess Nancy Lady Astor (1879-1964) and Viscount Lord Waldorf Astor (1879-1952) who were synonymous with Plymouth in the 1920s, 1930's and 1940's. The Astor Hotel occupying the former even numbers twelve to twenty-two Elliot Street is situated in a very unique part of Plymouth and extends a wonderful warm welcome to overseas guests. This hotel in its present day offers excellent standards and service, and is now owned by Joseph Louei who was born in Persia (now Iran) and moved to Plymouth as a child and has worked in the hotel and catering sector for a number of years. He spent seven years undertaking management training at the Holiday Inn. Joseph's success is due to wise investment and the high standard of care and attention to the customer and their needs. He prides himself on the excellent reputation gained over the years, for attention to detail and professional service ensuring that the visitors stay at the hotel will be memorable.

The Astor Hotel was badly in need of renovation when purchased, as it had changed hands many times and had been empty for some while. It had become quite run down. However, the graceful building had registered strongly with Joseph Louei, and being an astute businessman he saw the potential. After three-and-a-half years of refurbishing at a cost of two million pounds, the facilities and appearance of the hotel are now outstanding. The Astor is regularly booked for weddings and welcomes guests from all over the world. The hotel is steeped in history and Joseph is determined to continue the precious link with the Astors. The hotel is decorated with pictures of Nancy, Lady Astor, Lord Waldorf Astor and Sir Winston Churchill. It is his intention to have more portraits displayed in the hotel and to have, as a feature, an Astor Library.

In 1785 Sir William Molesworth sold to William Clark various tracts of land, which made up the old manor of Sutton Pill, which included the Hoe Fields that extended between Millbay Road and The Hoe. The Clark family held the ownership of the land until 1820 when Colonel James Elliot of Barley House bought the Hoe Fields and in the middle of the 19th century the land and houses were developed. The old soldier Colonel Elliot died in 1859 and his name is preserved today in the naming of Elliot

Terrace and Elliot Street. The houses in Elliot Street were built between 1875-1880, and the west side of Elliot Street was called Leigham Villas, and the east side was called Hoe Villas (Odd numbers one to seven) from Citadel Road to the Hoe.

Many famous high-ranking citizens lived in the area and they had varied careers. In 1882 former citizens living in these comfortable houses were Vice-Admiral P.F. Shortland, Sir James Walker, and E.R.Jones the architect. In 1885 Leigham Villas (West Side) comprised of numbers one to ten but were later re-numbered four to twenty-two Elliot Street. Citizens of importance living in the street then were General Alfred Des Vœux and Royal Naval Captain Robert Moore. From 1893 to 1911 the houses in Elliot Street numbered sixteen, eighteen, twenty and twenty-two (formerly numbers seven, eight, nine and ten) and were mostly occupied as boarding houses. From 1893 to 1910, Mr H. R. Rogers and Mr Joshua J. Hardiman were the owners of boarding houses at numbers eighteen, twenty and twenty-two; Reverend Lewarne MA, of St Andrew's Chapel lived at number sixteen Elliot Street (formerly number seven Leigham Villas).

In 1911-1912 numbers eighteen, twenty and twenty-two Elliot Street were extended and registered as the Hoe Mansion Hotel; Mrs Hardiman, widow of Joshua Hardiman, was then the owner. The Hotel catered for Army and Naval Officers and their families. The widowed Mrs J.D. Des Vœux owned number fourteen Elliot Street (formerly number six Leigham Villas). In 1939 the hotel was extended by incorporating number sixteen as part of the Hoe Mansion Hotel and continued until 1940 when the war changed its outcome. With the dreadful bombing of 1941 the Y.M.C.A. hostel in Lockyer Street suffered a direct hit and fourteen residents were killed. On the same night the fire destroyed the Old Town Street Y.M.C.A. premises along with the divisional stores and the Scout Headquarters in Kinterbury Street. The divisional office in Buckland Terrace was destroyed and the Devonport Y.M.C.A. and the Services Y.M.C.A. were both severely damaged. The work to support the Y.M.C.A. was crippled but its importance was such that the Admiralty requisitioned the Hoe Mansion Hotel in Elliot Street and handed it over to the Y.M.C.A. It was re-opened in August 1941 and became the Young Men's Christian Association Services Club and Hostel; Mr E.C. Carter was the Secretary. A former voluntary helper at the Y.M.C.A. during the war vividly remembers meeting Lady Astor when she called in for tea and on one occasion the former helper met the Duchess of Kent when Prince Michael was a baby. At the end of the war in 1945 it reverted back to the Young Men's Christian Association only, as the services no longer required the building and by 1955 numbers fourteen and sixteen Elliot Street had been amalgamated into the Y.M.C.A.

After the war the National Council bought the block of six houses in Elliot Street and eventually a civilian hostel was set up next to the Hoe Mansions Service Men's Y.M.C.A. Dockyard extensions forced the Devonport members to vacate their home, and they too were housed in that Elliot Street block. It remained there until the new Y.M.C.A. was built at the junction of Armada Way and Cobourg Street. In 1956 Nancy Astor and the Commander-in-Chief, Plymouth Command, Admiral Sir Mark Pizey had laid the foundation stones for the new Y.M.C.A. The grand new building opened in 1959 and Hoe Mansions along with the six houses remained unoccupied for some time. Lord and Lady Astor had close links with the Astor Hotel (formerly Hoe Mansions/Y.M.C.A.) as in their lifetime they were Presidents of the old Plymouth central Y.M.C.A. Viscount Waldorf Astor became President in 1921. There were three Young Men's Christian Associations in this City, Plymouth, Devonport and the Servicemen's building on the Hoe run by the National Council. Each had real individuality. The Y.M.C.A. in Plymouth was opened in 1848 founded in the 'Year of Revolutions,' by George Williams a young London houseman who originally came from Somerset. Plymouth Congregationalist Alfred Rooker had called a meeting on the 17th January 1848 and from that meeting the Plymouth Central Y.M.C.A. was formed. They started in Frankfort Street in 1848, moved to Union Street in 1872, from there it settled in Bank Street in 1880 then in 1887 relocated on the corner of Bedford Street and Westwell Street. In 1921 it again moved to Old Town Street and by now its fame had grown. The Y.M.C.A. became a welcome place for young men and servicemen, who would stay at the Hostel to receive the home comforts and pleasures on offer. Devonport also had Y.M.C.A. facilities when the Devonport building was bought for £8,050 in 1871. Plymouth Central had a hostel in Lockyer Street, which was well supported.

During the blitz on, and after 20th March 1941, the heavy bombing had destroyed the Devonport and the Plymouth Central Y.M.C.A. The Hostel in Lockyer Street received a direct hit, which resulted in fourteen persons being killed. That same night the Lockyer Street Scout Headquarters was completely destroyed. The last man out of the burning Y.M.C.A. Central Hostel was Tom Johnstone. For a time a temporary home was found at Peverell, Plymouth, but it was not suitable for the needs of the young people and the servicemen. Another establishment obtained was the Matthews Memorial Hall in Ebrington Street. With the destruction of the Union Street Y.M.C.A making the building untenable the Admiralty, who regarded the Y.M.C.A. so highly, decided that it would take action. The Royal Navy in Plymouth had already done so much for the bombed out civilian personnel making sure they did not go hungry in those dreadful war years, and now they were taking care of the servicemen. Once more the Senior Service proved its worth. They took the decision in conjunction with the National Council, in early 1941 to requisition the Hoe Mansions Hotel and adjacent houses in Elliot Street and in August 1941 it was handed over to the National Council to continue their work. Plymouth and Devonport Y.M.C.A. then combined and moved to Hoe Mansions in Elliot Street. With derequisitioning after the war, the Y.M.C.A. acquired the block and continued their work with one house becoming a civilian hostel and another a temporary home for Plymouth Y.M.C.A.

By 1948 the site was proving too small for the activities that the Y.M.C.A wanted to give to the new generation; it needed new construction to enable functions, dances, sleeping arrangements and sport facilities and it had to meet the requirements of the many men who would pass through the threshold of the Y.M.C.A. together with National Service and Regular Enlistments involving men from all over the country and the expansion of the growing industries of the new city. The Architects designed a new building comprising one hundred bedrooms with hot and cold water in each room. (A luxury in those days) Inside would be a Chapel for which the Women's Auxiliary of the Hoe Mansions Y.M.C.A. gave £1000 as a gesture of friendship. The contractors Wakeham Brothers of Plymouth were employed to build the new premises and on Thursday October 25, 1956 the Foundation stones of the new Y.M.C.A. were laid by Nancy, Viscountess Astor, Companion of Honour, and the Commander-in-Chief, Plymouth, Admiral Sir Mark Pizey, K.B.E. C.B. D.S.O. and Bar. What could be more fitting for this ceremony than Lady Astor, whose husband and son in succession have been Presidents of the old Plymouth Central Y.M.C.A. and the Commander-in-Chief whose seat of authority at Mount Wise is so near the scene of the work of the old Devonport Y.M.C.A. and who as the senior service representative in the city honours the linking of the old Servicemen's Y.M.C.A. with its civilian brothers.

The former Hoe Mansion Hotel was for some time unoccupied and became rather derelict and in need of complete renovation. Because of its location so close to the Grand Hotel and Plymouth Hoe it would have been a tragedy if the building was lost. In May 1960 the owners of the Strathmore Hotel in Elliot Street Mr Peter (Pedros) Zessimides and brother Andrew (Andros) Zessimides with Peter's beautiful wife Georgina Zessimides, decided to buy the former neglected old Hoe Mansion Hotel/Y.M.C.A. located just opposite the Strathmore Hotel. The hotel was for sale by Woolland, Son & Manico chartered auctioneers and estate agent. It offered fifty bedrooms, two suites, proprietors flat, a passenger lift and was comfortably furnished with a conditional licence. The estimated turnover was expected to be £53,000 pounds per annum and the asking price was set at £35,000 pounds and was to be sold by private treaty. By August 1960 the Zessimides contracted Messrs Jack H. Lang (Devon) to undertake the task of complete redecoration of the Hoe Mansion Hotel in contemporary colours and the very latest wallpapers. Messrs Yeldon and Gardiner completed the electrical fittings and Hilda M. Haddon supplied the furniture. The name of the Astor Hotel was chosen by members of the public through a competition staged by Mr Peter Zessimides, who offered a prize of £25 for the best suggestion. He received over one thousand entries and found a good majority of these suggested the name Astor. He settled for it saying: "It is short, easy to remember and a popular name for an hotel, at the same time the Astor family have done much for Plymouth and I think it will be a popular choice."(See the Plymouth Independent 21st August 1960). A former receptionist who worked at the Astor Hotel in the 1960's remembers that then it had sixty-two rooms and the Zessimides set about completely restoring the

Peter Zessimides (1922-1991) and Georgina Zessimides

interior. From the outset it was deemed a high-class hotel providing a service for Masonic dinners, wedding functions and conferences.

Many famous people passed through the Astor Hotel portals including royalty in 1963 Prince Carlos of Spain, before he was crowned King, stayed at the hotel. Entertainers also visited; Cilla Black (who adored roast beef with mint sauce) The Bachelors, Gerry and the Pacemakers and the Swinging Blue Jeans. Sportsmen also graced the building in the form of Freddie Trueman, cricket Captain and the Yorkshire Cricket Team stayed at the premises, and when sailor Sir Francis Chichester arrived in Plymouth after his famous voyage, his wife stayed at the Astor and was there to greet him. In April 1999 at the Astor Hotel Chameleon was in concert featuring a choral portrait of Jerome Kern and in August the same year Carolyn Ross Quartet introduced an evening of entertainment and a Jazz singers' night.

In 1969-1970 Mervyn Pundsack was the proprietor of the Astor Hotel. In 1978 a London based hotel group invested £350,000 to again re-open the Astor Hotel on the Hoe, which had been closed for some time. Bought in March 1978 by Churchill Hotel Limited (Plymouth) under the umbrella of a London group company they immediately set about a complete reconstruction, Mr Cecil Edens, an hotelier all his life was overseeing the work. The main priority was re-roofing the building, which occupied a considerable part of the Western side of Elliot Street. The interior was upgraded with bedrooms having a private bath or shower, lavatory, television, radio and a telephone fitted. Also newly installed was plumbing, wiring, a lift, central heating, interior furnishings and new carpets, in addition an application was made for a full drinks licence and the Hotel employed thirty staff.

In 1985 the three stars Astor Hotel was sold to Mount Charlotte Hotels for one million pounds. In 1992 Andrew Swales was the General Manager of the Astor and he advertised in the Western Evening Herald inviting customers to visit the Hotel, which presented a fine cuisine with Head Chef Peter Stanton who had travelled the world and won medals at international shows. He was former Head Chef at Manadon College and the Moat House in Plymouth. At that time it was one of the ninety Mount Charlotte Thistle Hotels in key locations throughout Britain, from Brighton to Wick in Scotland. In 1989 under the management of Maurice Kelly and Chef Graham Munson the Astor specialised in wedding receptions. Designated then a three star RAC and AA approved and once again refurbished, the hotel ballroom could now cater for up to one hundred people. Dinner dances were held for the first time at the end of 1991 and continued from then on. The Plymouth Jazz Society affiliated themselves to the Astor Hotel and they held regular evenings of entertainment. In December 1993 Sammy Rimington, Europe's leading exponent of New Orleans Jazz which encompassed Jazz, Gospel and Blues entertained there.

The Astor Hotel, and the city of Plymouth in the lovely county of Devon, extends a warm welcome to all visitors. Come to this beautiful city with its stunning sea vista with the wonderful rugged Dartmoor nearby. The city offers a variety of tourist attractions.

Remember: *'Meet me at the Astor'*

**Astor Hotel 14-22 Elliot Street The Hoe, Plymouth, Devon. PL1 2PS.
Telephone (01752) 225511**

The **Astor** Hotel

 The Hoe
Plymouth

The redecorated Astor Hotel
In 1962 (Owners Zessimides family)

The beginning. Astor enthusiasts meet in June 2003 at the Astor Hotel.

Front left Joseph Louei, Managing Director of the Astor Hotel. Front right Mrs Cilla Chesworth. Behind Mr Louei to the left Vicky Norman the Author and to the left of her Mrs Joan Taskis.
Back row in red dress Mrs Doreen Braund Bideford, alongside in black? Extreme back in front of white door Mr Keith Braund President of the Braund Society Bideford. In front of fireplace seated first left Mrs Jewel Vittle (with black hair) second left Mrs Pamela Trudie Hodge third left Mrs Dorrien Peake (RIP) lady alongside with black dress Mrs Lesley Woodgate (nee Peake) to the right in pink dress Miss Thelma Jacobs, gentleman sitting with arms on table in black Mr Victor Mapp.

CHAPTER TWENTY-EIGHT
THE MEMORIAL

To stand under the stars is to show humility, to glimpse infinity, and hence eternity. *Anon.*

The Author extends sincere thanks to Mr Freddie Knox, former Personal Aide to Nancy, Lady Astor, for the copy of this tribute and to the Bishop of Plymouth, the Right Reverend John Garton, for permission for its use.

TRIBUTE TO VISCOUNTESS NANCY, LADY ASTOR, AT WESTMINSTER ABBEY MAY 1964 READ BY THE BISHOP OF PLYMOUTH THE RIGHT REVEREND NORMAN H. CLARKE. MA.LL.D. (Vicar of Saint Andrews Church Plymouth 1945-1951 and Bishop of Plymouth 1950-1962)

In the wildest flights of her imagination, in her most solemn or her most frivolous mood, she would not have dreamed that, at her passing, a congregation representative of every side of our national life would gather in this Abbey Church not so much to mourn her death, for she was full of years, as to thank God for her life.

When she made her home in England in 1906, she brought with her an inheritance of worldly wisdom, of personal charm and of social graces; but she entered into one richer still, not only in the wealth which she dispensed lavishly at least as much on others as on herself, but even more in the tradition of an English home-life rooted in deep affection. It behoves us to be reticent when we speak of the relationship of husband and wife and it has to be said that Nancy Astor would never have become the woman she was, or achieved such width of interest and concern, or accomplished as much as she did, apart from the depth of the love which she and Waldorf Astor bore for each other, a love which only became manifest to many outside the family circle in the loneliness which she experienced, and which she confessed to her friends, after his death in 1952.

That home was one of the roots of her greatness. One who shared her life in Plymouth for many years may be forgiven when he claims that the other was the experience, which she gained there. It was the experience of the rough-and-tumble of everyday life of ordinary people, the vast majority of whom were far removed from the social and political life of London. It was there that she saw at first hand the needs of the less fortunate members of the community and the working out of social theory in practice; there that she had her baptism of political campaigning as she shared in her husband's contests and learned to receive as much as she gave. No one can say what Nancy Astor would have become without that experience but it can be said with certainty that she never lost the common touch and that it fitted her to become the first woman to sit in the House of Commons. She was to represent the Sutton Division of Plymouth for twenty-five years; for five of those years, all through the war, she was also Lady Mayoress of the city. She refused to leave it during the worst of the bombing and, as much as anything else, her courage and leadership and capacity for getting things done sustained the morale of its citizens. There are some of us who think of this as "her finest hour."

It is not for one who only looked on from afar to speak of the contribution which she made to the life of the House of Commons but it is clear that she paved the way for other women, that she was impatient to the point of irreverence with pomposity in insincerity and subterfuge, that she stood apart from what she regarded as minor loyalties and courageously for what she was convinced were higher ones, that she was intolerant of delay in dealing with social evil and was always eager to give herself to causes which, however unpopular, she believed to be right. From one point of view she was unpredictable; from another there was no doubt where she stood.

Temperance, education (in particular her concern for nursery schools), housing, child welfare, the Red Cross, the opportunity for women to make their characteristic contribution to the life of the community (not only in civic and legislation affairs but also, for example, in the women police) these were only some, but perhaps the chief of her interests. It was typical of her that she tried to get to know personally those from whom she differed radically because, for her, people always mattered more than things.

So we come to the woman herself. It is impossible to do more than mention some of the characteristics of an almost shattering personality. She was often provoking but not always deliberately. She could be angry with people but she did not hate them; her hatred was reserved for evil things. She might sometimes appear unkind but she never intended to leave a wound that could not be healed by friendship. She was indifferent to what people thought about her. I shall always remember the emotion with which she spoke to me about the Freedom of Plymouth which was conferred on her in 1959 and which, I think, she appreciated at least as much as any of the honours which she received. She was rightly proud of her achievements but she was not conceited; false modesty had no part in her make-up, it is too close akin to self-pity. She was generous to a degree but not indiscriminate; she was unsparing of herself, her time and effort and money.

She had a charm and frivolity which might give the impression of superficiality but she was genuine through and through. She could walk with the humble as easily as the great and was at home in the Barbican at Plymouth as well as in a palace. She was a woman of deep feeling; she understood the needs and sorrows of others, whether in similar or very different circumstances from her own. She was able to anticipate people's feelings and in response to them revealed a side of her nature not otherwise known. Above all, she was a lover of God; for her no day was complete without its time bible-reading and prayer; it was probably the only time in the day when she was quiet, and that is significant."

The Reverend Norman Clarke once said about the war and its effect on the citizens of Plymouth these words: "Plymouth has its history and it has its future, but the coming generation cannot escape from the one which endured the war."

Lord Attlee, The Observer, 3rd May 1964

"Nancy Astor could be as bold as brass: but she was in fact a kind and compassionate woman with, especially where women were concerned, a great sense of justice. She was no respecter of persons, and would take you down a peg as soon as look at you, but not if you were getting a raw deal or down on your luck. Her most valuable work was to make it possible, often behind the scenes, for able and worthy people, welfare workers and social reformers, to get a hearing and a chance to act. She was amongst the impresarios of the Welfare State…People like Nancy Astor, quite apart from their good works are atmospheric. They make things hum."

This memorial encapsulates everything that could be said about Viscountess Nancy Astor and it is hoped that future generations will understand the significance of her life and what she did for the common good.

The Times Newspaper, 4th May 1964

In any age or country Nancy Astor would have been remarkable for outstanding vitality, personality, charm and will power. She was always a delight to the eye, small, compact, a finely drawn profile, a classic head, growing more and more exquisite with the years. She was made all of one piece, a perfect working model, always well dressed. From the first day she entered the House of Commons in neat black with touches of white at collar, in appearance she struck the exact note and set the style for feminine colleagues in years to come.

C.1948

Lady Astor in full regalia circa 1948

REFERENCES AND ACKNOWLEDGMENTS

The Author wishes to thank all those who contributed information and memorabilia.

Air Historical Branch (RAF)

Arnold L Sayers CBE Carswell Tor, Holbeton, Devon.

Barbara Hooper. Extracts from Mary Stocks (1891-1975) An Uncommonplace Life

Blaze Redgrave, Yelverton, Devon

Board of Trustees, Virginia House Settlement, Plymouth, Devon

Booklet Serving the People by Crispin Gill Plymouth Historian

Bronwen Lacey, Director for Children's Services Plymouth

Buckland Abbey Information –Courtesy of the National Trust

Buckland Monachorum Website

City of Plymouth Archives & Records, Clare Place, Plymouth, Devon

Clovelly History Society

Councillor Vivien Pengelly Leader of the Conservative Group Plymouth

Daily Mercury paper, Plymouth, Devon

David and Dina O'Connor Jones, Stratford-upon-Avon, & Plymouth, Devon

Ernest T. English General Secretary to the Guild of Social Services.

Francis Hayes, Archivist for Harrowbeer Interest Group

Frank Wintle, The Plymouth Blitz

Friends of Stoke Damerel Memories 1908-1986

Girl Guide Headquarters, 17-19 Buckingham Palace Road, London

Honourable John Rous, Clovelly, North Devon

Jack and Amelia Davey, Plymouth, Devon

James Fox, The Langhorne Sisters published by Granta Books 1999.

James Mildren, Plymouth, Devon

John Briggs Author (1924-2002)

Karen Taylor, Archivist Girl Guide Headquarters

Lady Daphne Maynard (nee Llewellyn) wife of Air Chief Marshall Sir Nigel Maynard.

Lantern Books formerly of 9, Rutger Place, Plymouth, Devon

Margaret Churchill, Reeder Circle, Atlanta, Georgia USA

Mary Osbourne, A Snapshot of Life at Harrowbeer.

Maurice Collis. Nancy Astor An Informal Biography 1960

Midweek Independent 1980

Miss Jean Tozer, (Justice of the Peace Retired) Daughter of Sir Clifford & Lady Tozer Plymouth

Miss Joan Shivey, Plymouth, Devon

Miss Joyce M. Searle, Eggbuckland, Plymouth.

Mr Adam and Mrs Carrie Southwell, Prince Hall, Dartmoor, Devon.

Mr Barry Furguson, Plymouth, Devon

Mr Bertram J. Terry, Southway, Plymouth, Devon

Mr Brian Moseley, Plymouth Local Historian

Mr Charles Irwin, Plymouth, Devon

Mr Dave Brewer, Dartmoor, Devon

Mr David Chamberlain, Plymouth, Devon

Mr David Nunn Cheriton Fitzpaine

Mr Dennys Dennis Waldorf Cowan, Plymouth, Devon

Mr Donald Alder, Plymouth, Devon

Mr Edward Clifton, Hooe, Plymouth, Devon

Mr Freddie Knox former Personal Aide to Lady Astor, Plymouth, Devon

Mr George Lomax, Heybrook Bay, Near Plymouth, Devon

Mr Gerald Wasley, Plymouth, Devon

Mr Ian Criddle, Reference Library, Local History Section

Mr Jack Hermon, Plymouth, Devon

Mr John Bennet, Plymouth, Devon

Mr John Hoskin, Fleet, Hampshire

Mr Keith McMinn, Plymouth, Devon

Mr Ken Johnson, Research Archivist (Personal)

Mr Les Hill, Macebearer Plymouth City Council (former Royal Marine Colour Sergeant)

Mr Les Palmer, Plymouth, Devon

Mr Michael Hayes, Knightstone Tearooms. Archivist (Personal Research) for Knightstone RAF Squadrons associated with and operating from RAF Harrowbeer 1941-1950.

Mr Norman Hine, Plymouth, Devon

Mr Peter Osborne, Penticton, British Columbia, Canada

Mr Rob Owens, Children's Services, Plymouth, Devon

Mr Stephen Fryer, Webmaster for the Harrowbeer Interest Group Website

Mr Steve Mallinson, Macebearer Plymouth City Council (former Royal Marine Colour Sergeant)

Mr Steven Shaw Acting Director Virginia House

Mr Thomas Charles Prynne, St Ives, Cornwall

Mr Tony Hill, Copse End, Winscombe, North Somerset

Mr Victor Hill, Plymouth, Devon

Mr Victor James Mapp, Plymouth, Devon

Mr Wally Hirons, Mannamead, Plymouth, Devon

Mrs Barbara Czarnota, Plymouth, Devon

Mrs Barbara Hogan (nee Gardner) Ernesettle, Plymouth.

Mrs Betty Britton, (nee Tribe) Plymouth, Devon

Mrs Christine Clark, (nee Asquith) Clovelly, North Devon

Mrs Dorrien Peake, (nee Pitman) Plymouth, Devon

Mrs Flo (Floss) Ponsford (nee Collins) Plymouth Devon

Mrs Georgina Zessimides Plymouth Devon

Mrs Glen Trude, (nee Gladys Crawley) Plymouth, Devon

Mrs Hermione Cowan, Plymouth, Devon

Mrs Jan Pritchard, Divisional Commissioner Girlguiding, Plymouth East

Mrs Jean Churchill, Plymouth, Devon

Mrs Jean Trevaskus, (nee Trewhela) Plymouth, Devon

Mrs Jean Willis, Vauxhall Street, Plymouth, Devon

Mrs Joan Taskis, Plymouth, Devon. Local History Enthusiast

Mrs Joy Wills, (Joy Hoskin Limited) Plymouth, Devon

Mrs Joyce Thomas (nee Tidball)

Mrs Kathleen Scarlett, Plymouth, Devon

Mrs Lilian Becker, (nee Ricketts) Crownhill, Plymouth, Devon.

Mrs Linda Downing, Buckland Monachorum, Devon

Mrs M. Sinnett, Wembury, Plymouth, Devon

Mrs Mavis Hawken, Plymstock, Plymouth, Devon

Mrs Myra Stevens (nee Harkcom) Thornbury, Plymouth, Devon

Mrs Nancy (Elizabeth) Davies Caldicot Monmouthshire

Mrs Pamela Rendall, Peverell, Plymouth, Devon

Mrs Pamela Trudie Hodge, Plymouth, Devon

Mrs Pauline Moore, (nee Hambly) Plymouth, Devon

Mrs Pauline Trenerry (nee Cowan) Plymouth, Devon

Mrs Phyllis Baggott, (nee Bartlett) Plymouth, Devon

Mrs Sandra Monaghan, Plymouth, Devon

Mrs Susan Crocker, Gunnislake, Cornwall

Mrs Sylvia Bennett, (nee Alcock) Plymouth, Devon

Nelda Bridgeman, Ohio, United States of America

New York Times Company, United States of America.

Plymouth and Plymothians by Andrew Cleuer (RIP)

Plymouth Barbican Association, South West Image Bank

Plymouth Central Library

Plymouth City Council

Plymouth Girl Guide Movement, East Division

Plymouth Guild of Social Services.

Plymouth Museum and Art Gallery

Plymouth Postcard Collectors Club & number 83 Newsletter September 2007

Plymouth Reference Library all staff

Plymouth Shotokan Karate Club & Pezz Media, UK

Research team, Children's Services, Plymouth, Devon

Right Reverend John Garton, Bishop of Plymouth, Devon

Robert Tierney, Diploma in Art. (1956) International Artist & Textile Designer Modbury Devon

Saltram House, National Trust, Plymouth

Stacey Dyer, B.A. 1st Class Single Honour Degree History, Archivist

South West Image Bank

Sunday Independent Plymouth

The Clovelly Chronicles - kind permission Honourable John Rous, Clovelly

The Daily Telegraph Newspaper

The Independent, Plymouth, Devon

The London Times Newspaper

The National Trust

Trevor Burrows Photography Limited, The Millfields, Plymouth

Weekly Independent Plymouth

Western Evening Herald, Plymouth, Devon

Western Independent, Plymouth, Devon

Western Morning News & Mercury, Plymouth, Devon

William Best Harris (RIP) book Place Names of Plymouth, Dartmoor and the Tamar Valley, Their Stories and Meanings.

William Waldorf Astor - 4th Viscount

BY JOSEPH LOUEI

This picture was taken at the Astor Hotel in one of the luxurious suites.

I am very lucky to have the best of both worlds being a British/Persian National and loving both countries. In 2001 I became the proprietor of the derelict Astor Hotel (formerly Hoe Mansions, Y.M.C.A and Hotel). For ten years I have invested every penny I earnt and I designed every room each in a different style to return the hotel to its former glory offering affordable luxury. I hope Lady Astor would be as proud of it as I am today.

The beautiful victorian building is located on picturesque Plymouth Hoe catering for weddings, business conferences and visitors from all over the world.

As a native of Persia, (now Iran) the issue of women's rights is something I have always held very dear to my heart. Great strides have been made in the country of my birth in giving women the social standing that they truly deserve. There is still a long way to go, but without the selfless dedication of a few in championing the cause of the many. we would not have even reached this point. That is why I am always inspired by women throughout history who have made great personal sacrifices to achieve the kind of rights we as men have often taken for granted.

Women I am close to continue to have a profound effect on me, both personally and professionally and my mother, sister and the mother of my children will always be the most important people in my life.

Imagine then my joy at the opportunity to publish a book about Lady Astor, the first women to enter parliament as an MP, a dedicated charity worker who did so much for the poor and underprivileged of all ages. She was a true humanitarian whose name proudly adorns the Astor hotel in Plymouth.

This book is about championing the cause of Lady Astor and great women like her, women who are perhaps the true essence of what we might refer to in modern terms as 'girl power'. I also want this fabulous book to bring about a lasting connection with Plymouth and America - the country of Lady Astor's birth.

It may surprise many to learn of my passion for America being born in Iran, but like the majority of Iranians I truly believe it is one of the great countries. I was recently asked by a student from Iran for my reaction to an Iranian politician contention that America was a country with no history. I dismissed it with disdain - America is steeped in history and embraces those of all colours and creeds. It is a fascinating country and so deserved of its status as the world super power.

But there are many stateside who still don't know what a great place Plymouth is and I hope that this book will help build even greater bridges and every American will visit Mayflower Steps - a landmark that will always connect our two great nations.

Respect for all is something my father and mother instilled into me from a very early age. My father once told me a story about an apple tree that was in our garden in Malayer. "Son" he said. "Remember the apple tree is a tree of life. When the tree bears heavy fruit, the branches bow down - this indicates that the tree, while producing the most fruit, still remembers its humble beginnings.

But I also believe that where you are is just as important as where you have come from. When I first came to Plymouth as an £80 a week kitchen porter, I saved two weeks wages and travelled to London to buy my mother Persian treats to make her feel at home when she came to visit me. How wrong could I be?..."Joseph, you are in England now and must embrace the English culture," she said. "you are breathing their air and you live in their home. You must not bite the hand that feeds; you must pay it back - with interest." That too is something I have never forgotten.

There is little doubt that is exactly how Lady Astor embraced our culture. She is credited with saving the Barbican and there isn't a family in Plymouth who has not been touched by her great generosity and the wonderful legacy she left to our great city. Much has been written about Lady Astor, but nothing captures the essence of her human kindness like this book and that is why I am so proud to be the Publisher.

I would like to thank Vicky Norman, a great and talented lady herself for her achievement in making this book happen. Finally I would like to thank Bob and his team at Latimer Trend who have worked hard to ensure the launch of this book and also everyone else who has assisted in its production. This book incites me still further to carry on my own charitable work, like Lady Astor, that is something I will always be committed to.

Sofia Hamze Louei (Joseph Louei's mother) in a victorian costume taken at Morwellham Quay (circa 1990s)

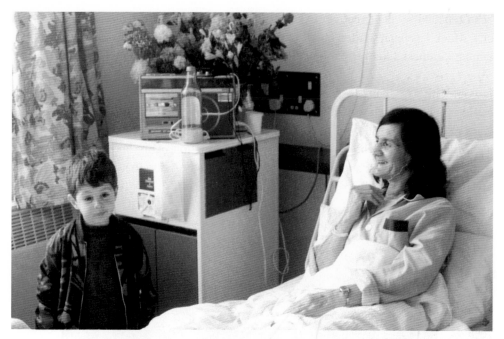

Sofia Hamze Louei in a hospital bed, Derriford Hospital, Plymouth with Joseph Louei's son Saam. Although very ill she always remarked how grateful she was for the excellent treatment she received. Unfortunately she died shortly afterwards.

Joseph pictured "with shaved head for charity" meeting Her Majesty, Empress Farah Pahlavi of Iran. "It was a great moment to meet someone who has done so much, not only for Iranian women but society as a whole, A true heroine to me."

ASTOR LADIES TABLE TENNIS TEAM BRITISH CHAMPIONS 2009

Hoping to host the European Championship 2009 in Plymouth

British Champions: (From left) Lisa Radford, Lindsey Reynolds, Liz May (Captain), and Marketa Mystova with Chairman Joseph Louei (centre).

GIRL POWER...

AN INTERNATIONAL INVITATION!

Astor Ladies Table Tennis Team is issuing an international invitation to any Ladies Team to come to Plymouth for Friendly Matches.

For further information please contact Joseph at:

joseph@astorhotel.co.uk
+44 (0) 7813 794382

www.astortabletennis.co.uk   www.josephsjournal.com

دومین نسخه را :

تقدیم به بانو شاستیه و علی جانم،

خانوادهٔ عزیز نوروزی‌زاده

شامل دو دوستانم در غربت

تقدیم می‌نمایم /

با آرزوی بهترینها

برای بهترینها

دوستتان دارم با گرمی

[illegible]